THE ESSENCE
OF RUMI'S MASNEVI

INCLUDING HIS LIFE AND WORKS

by
Prof. Dr. ERKAN TÜRKMEN

First printed May 1992
Fourth revised and corrected edition 2002
Copyright© 1992 by Erkan TÜRKMEN

Author's Tel: (0-324) 223 91 45
Fax: (0-324) 224 03 59

Composed and make-up by: Korman TÜRKMEN

Published by: Konya ve Mülhakatı
Eski Eserleri Sevenler Derneği
Konya, TURKIYE

All rights reserved
Copyright© throughout the world

No part of this book may be reproduced, stored in a retrieval system, or transmitted in any form or by any means, electronic, mechanical, photocopying, recording or otherwise, without the prior permission in writing of the publisher. Except in the case of brief quotations embodied in critical articles and reviews.

Printed by: Altunarı Ofset Ltd.
Konya, TURKIYE
Tel: (0-332) 353 69 69

ISBN 975-95630-0-2

CONTENTS

INTRODUCTION

CHAPTER I

    Political History 1
    The Social Context of Ala al-Din's Empire 4
    From Balkh to Konya 7
    Bahaeddin and his teachings 13

CHAPTER II

    Konya and Anatolia (Political History) 19
    Schools of Religion 20
    The Reign of Ghiyas al-Din Kaykhusrev II 21
    The Period of Joint Rule 22
    Rumi and the Royal family 24
    Social Context 29

CHAPTER III

    Life and works of Rumi 41
    Selah al-Din Zerkub 51
    Ziya ul-Haq Husameddin 53
    Rumi's works 58

CHAPTER IV

    The First Eighteen Verses of Rumi's Masnevi 65

CHAPTER V

    STEP I: The state of an immature man 77

CHAPTER VI

    STEP II: The awakening 141

CHAPTER VII

STEP III: The desires and quest 193

CHAPTER VIII

STEP IV: Improvement of soul through indifference
to worldly riches 219

CHAPTER IX

STEP V: Love 243

CHAPTER X

STEP VI: Devotion and Submission 273

CHAPTER XI

STEP VII: Bewilderment and need of a spiritual guide . . . 297

CHAPTER XII

STEP VIII: Observation of God in every phenomenon . . . 331

CHAPTER XIII

STEP IX: Unification 347

SELECT BIBLIOGRAPHY AND ABBREVIATIONS 367

INDEX

*If you are with everyone without me
you are with none;
If you are with me and with nobody
you are with everyone.*

(Masnevi III, 1614)

First page of Rahmattullah's commentary.

INTRODUCTION

The purpose of this book is to provide the essence of Rumi's magnum opus, *"Masnevi"* under a well organised plan which Rumi himself has indirectly given in his first eighteen verses of the work. Rumi's aim was to teach man the path of Divine Love that exalts a man from a lower stage to the highest one. It was because of this quality of the work that it became popular in India, Pakistan, Afghanistan, Central Asia and Turkey soon after Rumi's death in 1273, and later it spread all over the world.

Many commentaries have been written in Turkish, Ottoman Turkish, Urdu, Persian and English during the past centuries. In this book the chief commentaries have been brought together in a synthesis. Where the commentaries agree, they have been taken as they stand; where they disagree or are inadequate my own commentaries are supplied along with important variations. Regarding the synthesis some commentaries include irrelevant details. For example they bring in Dante, Plato and other philosophers or they go into far-fetched literary interpretations. All of this I have regarded as excessive exegesis and, therefore, have excluded from the commentaries.

Another reason for putting the essence of Rumi's Masnevi before the public is that many books about Rumi have tended to interpretations, focusing on one or more themes without a definite plan. No work has brought to light one fact that Rumi describes and discusses the principle stages of spiritual life in a random way but with a definite plan. This reorganisation of the *"Masnevi"* in accordance with the first eighteen verses has created an order that provides a spiritual sequence in nine steps that follow after the first three introductory chapters.

His Masnevi is based on moral stories, philosophical, moral and spiritual commentaries. There is no need for commentaries of the stories because they are easy to understand, but these are the philosophical ideas that require explicit explanations in the light of various commentaries. In *Tasavvuf* (Islamic mysticism) such ideas are called "the pearls" that fall from the mouth of a spiritual master and form the essence of his speech. These pearls have been inter-connected around the central themes of the spiritual stages. Each pearl is itemized and numbered so that it may represent a separate unit of the major theme that leads the reader closer to God. Each item comprises the following sections:

I- The critical edition of the original text without which no translation can be claimed to be accurate.
II- Literal translation of the text in modern English.
III- Synthesis of the best commentaries.

Consequently, this new setup gives a reader an essential skeleton of the Masnevi in a much more organised way and provides a ladder to the spiritual traveller who wants to reach a high stage of humanity.

CHAPTER I

Background to Rumi

The Khwarazm Empire

1- Political History:

The age of Rumi's father, Sultan ul-Ulama Muhammed Bahaeddin Veled (1152-1231) and Jelal al-Din Rumi (1207-1273), covers 121 years of great social and political unrest. It is not possible to understand the ideas, allusions, and parables we find in Rumi's *"Masnevi"* his magnum opus, without studying the political as well as the social structure of his days. Rumi and his father witnessed the rule of the following Turkish kings:

1- Ala al-Din Muhammed Khwarazmshah (1200-1220)
2- Ala al-Din Kayqubad I (1220-1237)
3- Ghiyas al-Din Kaykhusrev II (1237-1246)
4- Izzeddin Kaykavus II (1246-1249)
5- Izzeddin Kaykavus II + Rukneddin Qilich Arslan IV + Ala al-Din Kayqubad II (joined rule, 1249-1257)
6- Rukneddin Qilich Arslan IV (alone, 1262-1266)
7- Ghiyas al-Din Kaykhusrev III (1266-1284)

In the eleventh century some Turkish tribes after crossing the Transoxiana began to settle in the northern part of Iran. The new Muslim Turkish tribes Ghaznavids, Qarakhanids, Seljuks (the branch of Turcoman tribe called *"Kınık"*), Oghuz and the Khwarazms were the most outstanding dynasties that played a remarkable role in the intermixing of Turko-Iranian culture.

Islam spread fast in Iran during the rule of Samanids, whose religious tolerance and favour for mysticism had softened the ground for the seed of the new religion on which Mahmud of Ghazna (998-1030) was to form his great Turkish empire that extended from the north-eastern Iran into the remoter parts of India[1]. Mahmud, as a good ruler won the favour of Rumi. The loyalty of his vizier Ayyaz towards his master was compared with the loyalty of man for his creator God[2]. While the reign of the Ghaznavids remained forceful in the eastern part of Iran, the Seljuks established a powerful empire not only in Iran but also in the remote lands of Anatolia (so called

---

1 Mahmud Gaznavi, I.A, 7/173.
2 Masnevi, II vr. 1049 and Attar, The Conference of the Birds, C.N. Nott, Arkana, London (for other stories of Mahmud and Ayyaz).

"*Arz-i Rum*"). It is for this reason that Rumi is called the *Mavlana-yi Rum* (the master that belongs to Anatolia)[1].

Rumi's childhood was spent in Balkh, capital of the Khwarazm Empire. When he and his father Bahaeddin were at Balkh, the ruling king was Ala al-Din Khwarazmshah, who belonged to the dynasty first established by a Turkish slave called Anushtekin. His son Qutb al-Din Muhammed came to the throne in 1097 as "*Khwarazmshah*", the king of the Khwarazm region. Qutb al-Din was sincerely attached to the great Seljuk emperor Sanjar. When Qutb al-Din's son Atsiz came to the throne in 1127, he revolted against Sanjar and when he fell a prisoner in the hands of the Oghuz Turks in 1153, Atsiz became more powerful but when Sanjar was set free, Atsiz became obedient to him again and remained so until his death. Sanjar died in 1157 upon which Atsiz's son Arslan II. declared his freedom from the great Seljuks. Thus the Khwarazmshahs became independent rulers. Arslan II. died on 18th. March, 1172, when his son Ala al-Din Tekish was in the city Jend. His step mother the Terken Khatun put her own son Sultanshah on the throne with the help of the Karakhatai Turks. Despite this Ala al-Din Tekish returned to the capital (Gurgench) and established himself on the throne while he made his brother Sultanshah king of the minor states, Merv, Sahra, and Tus. However, when Sultanshah died in 1193, Tekish became the absolute ruler of Khorasan, the north-eastern of the Khwarazm Empire.

The Ghaznavids, another northern Turkish dynasty, were forced to leave their capital Ghazna and to refreat to India by the Ghurid army[2]. The Ghurids were unpopular among the people of Khorasan, therefore they failed to maintain authority in that area. When Tekish died, his son Ala al-Din became king. While he was being enthroned, the Ghurids took Merv, Tus and Nishapur. Once again, the Karakhatais came to rescue and forced the Ghurids to leave Andkhui, a city by the Oxus. Soon after the Ghurid king Shihab-al Din Ghuri was assassinated in India on his way to Ghazna. The Ghurid empire began to fall apart, and years later in 1201 and 1204, Ala al-Din took many towns back.

Balkh, Tirmiz, and Bukhara fell one after the other. The king of Samarqand, Osman Khan, left his previous patron Gürkhan, ruler of the Karakhatais and joined Ala al-Din, who supported him in subduing the Ghurids. Osman Khan married the Sultan's daughter at Gurgench and stayed there for some months as a groom according to the Turkish custom. His long stay began to worry his soldiers at Samarqand. Finally, when Ala al-Din returned to Samarqand without Osman, people revolted against him and asked for their king. Osman came, but now he, too, joined

---

1 For "Mavlana" means any master.
2 Merçil, p. 161.

his subjects that had complained of the cruelty of the Khwarazmian army. Ala al-Din ordered his soldiers to kill the rebels. The city was turned into a slaughter house[1], around ten thousand people were put to death. The massacre took place in 1212 when Bahaeddin and his son were in the town[2]. The scene must have left a deep impression on the mind of the young boy. Consequently, Osman was killed and Samarqand fell.

Now, Ala al-Din's empire extended in the west to the western edge of the Caspian Sea, including Azerbayjan, in the east to Samarqand, Balkh and Ghazna; and in the south to Khuzistan[3], and the capital city was Gurgench.

Against the will of his mother, Terken Khatun, Ala al-Din wanted to be the absolute ruler of the Muslim world. He refused to obey the caliph at Baghdad[4]. Soon, he became persona non grata due to his egoistic character. He began to dream of advancing as far as China, where Chengiz Khan had already entered and had taken Peking[5]. Ala al-Din did not believe in Chengiz's success, so he decided to send an envoy led by his ambassador, Bahaeddin Razi, who witnessed the Mongols massacring the Chinese.

Razi was treated well by Chengiz Khan at Peking. Chengiz had come to realise the importance of a commercial link between the two empires[6]. He sent his best wishes to the Sultan and sent his ambassadors to accompany Razi. His gifts included a huge piece of gold as big as the hump of a camel, Chinese dresses and other precious presents. Ala al-Din received the ambassadors at Transoxiana in 1218. The two emperors seemed to be determined to co-exist peacefully, the trade between their empires flourished. The first group of merchants, led by Ahmed Khojendi, Emir Huseyinoğlu and Ahmed Balchik reached China safely, and they were treated well by Chengiz, who bought all their goods. Chengiz also sent a group of 450 merchants to the Khwarazms[7]. However, the governor of Urtar, Inaljik, a close relative of Ala al-Din robbed and killed some of the Mongols. Chengiz demanded that Inaljik be punished or handed over to him[8]. The Sultan refused to do so. Upon this Chengiz invaded Urtar and killed thousands of people. Following his attack on Urtar, Chengiz began a series of massacres in Iran. The empire of the Khwarazmshahs soon came to an end.

---

1 Ibrahim, p. 189.
2 Ibid, p. 189 and the map of the empire on the last page.
3 Merçil, p. 192.
4 Ibrahim, p. 229.
5 Ibid, p. 231.
6 Ibid, p. 232.
7 Ibid, p. 235.
8 Some claim that these Mongols were spies (see IA, 274).

Rumi's father had left Balkh long before this mishap.

2- The Social Context of Ala al-Din's Empire:

The Sultan was cruel to his subjects. He was addicted to drinking and spent most of his time planning to widen his empire. No peace prevailed in the country when he began to fight with the other Turkish tribes such as Karakhatais, Qarluks, Qarakhanids, and etc. The Sultan, due to his narrow mindedness, ego and greed, failed to see his own terrible end. The historian, Ibn'ul Ethir, comments as follows:

"But if God intends evil to any people, naught can avert it, nor have they any ruler save Him. As for these Tatars, their achievements were only rendered possible by the absence of any effective obstacle; and the cause of this absence was that Muhammed Khwarazmshah had overrun the (Muslim) lands, slaying and destroying their Kings, so that he remained alone ruling over all these countries; therefore when he was defeated by the Tatars, none was left in the lands to check those or to protect these, that so God might accomplish a thing which was to be done". (Browne, 2/430).

Samarqand, Bukhara, Balkh, Merv, and Gurgench were the great cities of the Khwarazm Empire. Each city was a centre of learning like Baghdad. Balkh, the city where Rumi was born, had a mixed culture of Muslim Arabs, Sasanians, Turks, Christians and Buddhists. After the conquest of Alexander the Great, Balkh was a centre of the Graeco-Bactrians, and then of the Kushans and Hepthalites. Just before the advent of Islam it was a Buddhist centre with a famous cloister, the *"Nawbahar"*, and a centre of Zoroastrian teachings[1]. Buddhism brought the Turkish and Indian priests together. At the period of Tharids and Samanids Balkh retained its importance as a centre for learning. In the Samanid period it became a great city like Herat. The beloved hero of the Masnevi, Ibrahim Adham (A.D. 783), like Buddha, had relinquished his throne for love of God, and set an example for the Sufism that flourished later in that area "the Khorasani school". At the time of the Seljuk and Khwarazmshah empire it was surrounded by citadels. Houses were built of clay. There was a big mosque for Juma prayers called the *"Jamii Masjid"* like the one that exists in Konya at the *Ala al-Din Tepe* (mound). The city was totally destroyed by the Mongol army ever since, it has lain waste fourteen miles west of *Mazar-i Sherif.*

Bahaeddin's *"Maarif"* throws some light on the social life of Balkh:

---

[1] R.N. Fryne, Encyclopaedia of Islam, p. 1000.

"They told me that on circumcision feast day women were bare headed and had black clothes on like *Khatais* (Tatars) and were all drunk. Men and women, hand in hand, went from bazaar to bazaar. They entered a large inn. Stamping their feet, they drank Sek and women had their breasts naked while they drank sek with the men, they made love. All women came out of their houses..." (Maarif, II/p.17).

Various sects and orders were in vogue at Balkh. Sufis, scholars, and men of learning were held in high respect. Although Sunnism was the official sect, orders like Shiism, Mutaziliye (rationalism), Jabriye (fatalism) as well as Sufism of international tolerance were free to practise their beliefs[1]. There was no nationalism. All Muslims of different nations were brothers. There were other sects also such as Malikiye, Shafiya, Qadriye and Hambaliye. Rumi's father and Rumi were against Mutaziliye and Jabriya that were more influential in Balkh than in Anatolia. Seljuk and Khwarazm sultans had established Medreses that taught against Shiism, Jabriye or even Mutaziliye.

1- *Mutazile* (Islamic rationalism) is derived from the word *"itizal"* sheared or separated, because Vasil b. Ata (A.D. 748) broke with his master Hasan al-Basri (A.D. 728)[2]. The former thus became the founder of the sect. Some major points of their beliefs are:

a) They depend on intellect rather than on spiritual experience, and believe that scepticism is the first step.
b) Action and theories are both important.
c) God's attributes are beyond man's attributes. God is Necessary Existence *(Wajib ul Wujud)* and He is also the First Existence (none other can match Him).
d) Man is free to do what he wants, whether good or evil. God does not interfere with his actions.
e) One cannot see God even after death.

Rumi says this about the Mutazilites:

سـخـره حـسـن اند اهل اعـتـزال   خویش را سنی نـمایند از ضلال

هر که بیرون شد ز حس سنی ویست   اهل بینش چشم عقل خوش بیست

"The Mutazilites are the captives of their carnal senses and they pretend to be Sunnites (*Ehl-i sunna* = orthodox) due to misguidedness. He who is able to step

---
1 Cambridge History, p. 204.
2 Prof. Şerafeddin, p. 25-27.

out of the carnal senses is a real Sunnite. The man whose spiritual eyes are open has the balanced eyes of reason to guide him". (M.II/62-63)

And in the heading of (M.3, p. 86, Nicholson) he continues:

"People's intellects differ according to their original nature (though) according to the Mutazilites they are equal and the difference arises from the acquisition of knowledge".

2- *Jabriya* (predestinarianism) was established by Jehm b. Safvan (A.D. 754) who laid the following principles:

a) Everything depends upon the will of God. Man has no will. Whatsoever happens, happens because of the Divine Will.

b) All actions spring from God alone and He creates them as He creates other things.

Rumi comments:

هر که ماند از کاهلی بی شکر و صبر   او همین داند که گیرد پای جبر

هر که جبر آورد خود رنجور کرد   تا همان رنجوریش در گور کرد

"He who falls back from thanksgiving and patience because of his laziness, has no other choice but to follow the way of the predestinarian, and he who adopts this path injures himself and that very injury takes him to his grave". (M.I/1068-1069)

لفظ جبرم عشق را بی صبر کرد   وآنک عاشق نیست حبس جبر کرد

"The word "predestination" made my love impatient while for him who is not in love with God, the same word makes him prisoner of predestination". (M.I/1463)

Any order that was stilled at Baghdad by the strict views of the Caliph would find a better ground in Khorasan or Balkh. Such orders were Jehmiye, Mujismiye and Maturidi. Ebu Mansur al-Maturidi (A.D. 953) established the Maturidi branch of Sunnism. He was at Samarqand and would naturally have influenced Bahaeddin and Rumi. In Rumi's Masnevi we find the idea that good and bad can be discriminated between by means of reasoning, a principal teaching of Maturidi[1].

---

[1] Prof. Kemal Işık, Maturidi'nin Kelam Sistemi, Futuvvet Yayınları, Ankara 1980, p. 8

"*Asharia*" was introduced by Ebu'l Hasan Ali b. Ismail al-Eshari al-Basri (A.D. 975). It was born in opposition to rationalism of the Mutazilites. It began as a philosophy of religious belief but later came to regard a rational account of religion as a remote horizon, and did not renounce metaphysics altogether. Although it was against philosophy, it gradually began to include philosophical proofs and diverged from rationalism. Fahreddin Razi (A.D. 1210) was one of the chief scholars of this order. Bahaeddin opposed him bitterly and because of his philosophy called him "*mubtadi*" (heretic) (see Maarif, p. 82).

3- From Balkh to Konya:

There are two reliable sources that tell the story of Bahaeddin's journey with his family from Balkh to Konya (Iconium), the Seljuk capital of Anatolia. 1- "*Maarif*" (The Discourses of Rumi's father) 2- "*Ibtidaname*" Sultan Veled's (Rumi's son) account in verse. The traditional sources Sipahsalar and Eflaki add minor, legendary details.

Rumi's father, as we shall see in his teachings, refused to go to God under the guidance of reasoning and philosophy. He depended more on his own intuitive experiences and the mercy of God. All such Sufis were disapproved of by Fahreddin Razi and his followers including the great Sultan Ala al-Din Khwarazmshah. Therefore Bahaeddin left Balkh and began to live in Wakhsh a small town in the north east of Balkh, where he could find simpler lovers of God. This is how he sees the matter:

"It occurred to me, 'Why I am here in Wakhsh while other preachers are in big cities like Samarqand, Baghdad and Balkh; and I am left here in a corner without luxury, riches, and fame'. God inspired me, If you want to be with Me and when I am with you, then you are in no place; neither in Wakhsh nor in Baghdad, nor in Samarqand, nor with anyone. You possess no show, no superiority and no art. If you don't want to be with Me, you will always be restless, helpless, and lost. He who attains Our intimacy once, will never want to endure helplessness without our company" (Maarif, II /138). He probably stayed at Wakhsh between A.D. 1203-1210 (see Maarif p.ﻝ)

Later he adds:

"God inspired me, 'Do not seek any perfect trust of people and do not depend on them for they will destroy you...' " (Maarif I /360).

"I said to Fahreddin Razi, some other people of his faith, the Khwarazmshah and other heretics (like him), You have left thousands of peaceful hearts, vanguards of army (the saints), and spiritual wealth; and you have run to a kind of darkness and have become attached to some miracles and discourses, and you have pursued some (strange) ideas.

Whatever amount of light you may possess will not be able to eradicate your (inner) darkness; and it is because of your ego that you are subdued by it..." (Maarif I/82).

"When I woke up in the morning, it occurred to me that I wanted to tread a correct and righteous path and wanted to follow it so that I might possess a clear view of the religion (Islam) and when I stay in a place, I do not stay there for money or wealth or the rank of a judge, Vizier or Emir. If they (people) give me money or a house to live in this town, I stay, otherwise I leave. This does not fit the beliefs of Islam. A true believer has no worries for his food or for a place to live in" (Maarif, I/377).

From the above statements and the information given by Sultan Veled we can deduce what forced Bahaeddin to leave his motherland:

a) Fahreddin Razi had won the favour of the ruling king due to his logical and philosophical commentaries on the Koran. Many could not see what Rumi's father was referring to because they did not have any spiritual or intuitive insight. The Sultan began to dislike Sufis because he believed in what Fahreddin said against them.

b) God inspired Bahaeddin to leave the town as Veled says:

که جدا شو از این گروه حسود   که ز جهل اند خوار و کور و کبود

تا کنم من هلاک ایشانرا   کشم از باد و خاک ایشانرا

"Leave this jealous group because they are wretched, blind, and sad; so that I may destroy them by means of wind or dust" (Velednama, p.191).

They were "wretched" because they refused to believe in the miraculous experiences that the Sufis underwent, especially Bahaeddin, and they were easily tempted by the colourful speeches of Razi tinged with rich philosophical statements. Razi died in 1209 while Bahaeddin was still at Wakhsh. Chengiz sacked Balkh in 1220 when Bahaeddin was at Baghdad or was about to leave the city[1]. In other words, he had left Wakhsh much earlier. There is no mention of the massacre at Balkh by Bahaeddin, therefore it can be guessed that he had left the town sometime between 1215-1217[2]. These were the years when Ala al-Din was on good terms with Chengiz and there was no sign of war between the two empires. Thus the above statement of Veled can be true.

---

[1] Velednama (Persian text, p. 191).

[2] Baki gives the year 1220 which cannot be true (see p. 42).

Nothing is mentioned in Bahaeddin's *"Maarif"* about the period that covers his journey from Balkh (Wakhsh) to Konya. We have to depend on the sources Sipahsalar and Eflaki.

Bahaeddin ordered his followers and relatives to get ready for a long journey. A load that could be carried on the back of three hundred camels was provided. It contained books, food and houseware. There were forty religious men in his company. The people who stayed behind in Balkh (or Wakhsh) cried and shouted because of Bahaeddin's departure[1]. Bahaeddin marched towards Baghdad. He would not have wanted to stay any longer in the land of the Khwarazmshahs. On the way, they met the famous Persian poet Feriduddin Attar (1142-1229) at Nishapur, who upon seeing Bahaeddin and his son Rumi uttered these words, "The sea (Rumi) is going after the lake (Bahaeddin)" and gave the child his book *"Asrarnama"*[2].

At the entrance to Baghdad the guards asked the newcomers who they were. Rumi's father replied, "We are coming from God and shall go back to Him. We have come from the non-existent world and shall go there again"[3]. Upon this, the guard went to report to the Caliph, who called his beloved scholar Suhreverdi (A.D. 1145-1234), writer of the *"Awarif ul-Ma'rif"* to get information about the newcomer and his personality. People and the Caliph liked Bahaeddin's sermons and lectures. However Bahaeddin did not want to stay forever under the protection of the Caliph, who was cruel and ruthless[4]. After several years Bahaeddin went to Mecca for the *Hajj* (the Islamic pilgrimage).

At Baghdad, he must have kept the company of Suhreverdi and the Kadris (disciples of Sheykh Abdulkadir Geylani A.D. 1078-1166) who were the earliest organised Sufis, but he did not formally join them. The Caliph al-Nasir li-dinillah (A.D. 1080-1225), whom Eflaki calls cruel and ruthless, was an establisher or at least reorganiser of the political organisation *"Futuvvat"*. The aim of the organisation was to strengthen the Abbasid power over the Muslim lands cut off from the central ruling authority "Caliphate"[5].

Suhreverdi took Futuvvat to Anatolia afterwards, when Rumi's father was there. It is this movement that came to be known there as *"Ahilik"* (brotherhood). They were also Sufis, but unlike the Mevlevis, they would earn their own living by

---

[1] Eflaki (T) I/1013.
[2] This legend may not be true but the influence of Attar's "Asrarnama" is quite evident in the works of Rumi.
[3] Eflaki, I/115.
[4] Ibid, p. 11.
[5] Neşet Çağatay, Ahilik, S.Ü. Konya 1981, p. 24.

means of handicrafts, trade, and so on. They were all armed. Generally they would carry a knife with them as the Sikhs carry swords. They would fight bitterly against any infidel or non-Islamic activities. It was under this impulse that they tried to fight against the Mongol advancement in Anatolia while Rumi and his followers preferred peace and patience. Awhadeddin-i Kirmani (d. A.D. 1237)'s disciple Akhi Evren tried to spread this Sufi sect in Konya and formed a strong enmity against the followers of Rumi.

Being a peace loving man, Bahaeddin did not join Futuvvat and left Baghdad. He went to Mecca and from there to Damascus. Under the rule of the Eyyubi dynasty, Damascus enjoyed a peaceful era, especially under the brother of famous Selaheddin Eyyubi (A.D. 1193) and his son al-Mu'azzam Isa (A.D. 1227) who ruled Damascus between the years 1218-1226. It was the period of prosperity, religious culture, and magnificent buildings.

Damascus was a well organised city at the time of the Abbasids and Seljuks. They built numerous mosques, baths, medrises, hospitals, castles, bridges, and inns whose number was increased by the Eyyubids. To give an idea of the buildings, there were around one hundred baths (as stated by Ibn Jabeyr), 660 mosques, and more than 40 medrises (colleges) (as told by Ibn Sheddad)[1]. Damascus abounded in scholars and teachers of great fame. In the year 1185 there were 600 Mufti in the city[2]. Countless students and scholars would come there for education.

The head sheykh of the Sufis was called *"Sheykh ul-Sheyukh"* (the sheykh of sheykh). This holy person would be found at a *hangah* (dervish monastery) in Damascus. Probably, Tajeddin Abdullah b. Hammuya (A.D. 1171-1244) was the *Sheykh ul-Sheyukh* when Rumi's father visited the city. The Sheykh was a poet and a scholar[3].

Along with prosperity and peaceful living came the wantonness of certain Sufis who would pass beyond the religious bounds and would give themselves up to drugs, or would do strange things under the impulse of paroxysmal ecstasy[4]. In this peaceful atmosphere also arose the Qalanderiya order at Damascus which was mendicant and ignored certain strict rules of Islam.

Qalanderiya was first introduced in Damascus by Jemal al-Din Savi in the year 1213. This order believed in the following:

---

1 For other details see Ramazan, p. 304.
2 Ibid, p. 338.
3 Ibid, p. 366.
4 Ramazan, p. 454.

1- No food should be put aside for tomorrow because God is the Feeder.
2- They should travel from place to place, having no home. All places belong to God and since He is everywhere, they can also be everywhere.
3- Divine Mercy is enough for living.
4- No strict religious training should be imposed on a disciple.
5- A follower, generally speaking, was supposed to shave off his beard, moustache and head. He would also wear a special dress (see İ.A, vol.6, p.129).

This sect is widespread in India and it is likely that it was born there[1]. However, it was seen in Turkistan in the 12th century A.D. Later it went up to Damascus. The difference between Qalanderi and Malami sects is that Qalanderiya does everything openly and is therefore exposed to the public while Malamiya hides spiritual states and conceals them from others[2].

Rumi must have been influenced by these two orders for he went to Damascus three times and his great master Shams-i Tebrizi, who came from Damascus, was probably a Qalander in form and actions.

Rumi's father left Damascus and came to Erzinjan in Anatolia, and he had no bias towards Qalanderiya dervishes. The ruler of that area was Fahreddin Behramshah (A.D. 1162-1225) who was a scholar, a God-fearing man, and a conqueror. He was on good terms with the Seljuk Sultan of Anatolia.

Izzeddin Kaykavus I, married Behramshah's daughter Seljuk Khatun with great grandeur[3]. Erzinjan, under his long rule, had become a centre of trade and culture[4]. It was to this king that the famous Nizami of Ganja presented his work *"Mahzan ul-Asrar"*. Fahreddin and his wife Ismeti Khatun became devoted disciples of Bahaeddin, who, finding a favourable atmosphere, stayed there for four years[5]. Bahaeddin had to leave the town upon the death of the king and the queen in 1225. He came to Larende, now called Karaman (about a hundred km. south of Konya), where he stayed until 1228.

Today Karaman is only a small province in Turkey, but in those days it extended as far as Antalya and Mersin to the south. A great number of Christian

---

[1] Saadettin Kocatürk, Doğu Dilleri Dergisi, Dil ve Tarih Coğ. Fak., vol.II, 1971, Ankara, p. 89-121.
[2] Abdulbaki, Türk Ansiklopedisi, Kalanderiya, p. 158 and see also "Kalandarname" of Hatib-i Farsi, Süleymaniye Lib. No. 187.
[3] Ibn-i Bibi, Th. Houtsma Leiden 1902, p. 172-182.
[4] Faruk Summer, İA, 7/714.
[5] Eflaki, 1/24.

Turks also lived here, who wrote Turkish using the Greek alphabet (İA, vol. 6, p. 309). In 1210 it fell to Christians but was soon reconquered by the Seljuk Sultan Izzeddin Kaykavus in 1216. The refugee Turcomans and Khwarazms were settled in this area in order to protect the Sultanate from further attacks of the Christian invaders from Cyprus. Bahaeddin came here with these immigrants and settled in the town (İA, 6/310).

Bahaeddin's wife died at Karaman. Rumi, now a young man, married here. Today Rumi's mother's grave and its complex is called *"Mader-i Mevlana"* (Rumi's Mother), or Mevlevi tekke. Here, as usual, Bahaeddin came to the attention of Emir Musa, a ruler and commander *(subashi)* of the Sultan. Musa built a medrise for the newcomers. Bahaeddin was finally invited by Sultan Ala al-Din Kayqubad I (1220-1237) to Konya. The Sultan had heard about Bahaeddin's greatness through his commander Musa. Bahaeddin left some of his relatives at Karaman and came to Konya in 1228. He was received by the Sultan with a cordial welcome upon his arrival in Konya. The Sultan invited Bahaeddin to his palace, but he refused to go there and went to the medrise called *"Altunpa"*. Today it is totally ruined yet its site still stands behind the *Iplikçi Jami*. It was demolished in the 18th. century[1] yet a single room (cell) that was once the part of the medrise is still standing[2]. It was, as the legend says, the room of Rumi's father[3]. Upon listening to Bahaeddin's wonderful sermons at the mosque of the medrise many had become his sincere disciples, including the Sultan.

رو نهـا دند سـوی او خـالـقـان از زن و مرد و طفل و پیر و جوان

آشـكـارا كـرامـتـش دیـدند زو چه اسرارها كه بشـنـیـدند

"People, may they be women, men, children, the young or the old turned to him when they heard from him secrets and saw his miracles" (Ibtidanama, p. 191).

After two years he fell sick and passed away on 18 Rabiyulakhir, 628 H./12 January 1231 at Konya.

نار در شهر قـونـیـه افتاد از غمش سـوخت بنده و آزاد

علما سربرهـنـه و میران جمله پیش جنازه با سلطان

"Fire fell upon Konya, with grief burning slaves and free men. Scholars and officers bareheaded walked in front of the funeral in the company of the Sultan". (Ibtidanama, p. 193)

---

1 Osman Turan, Selçuklular Devri Vakfiyeleri, Belletin, sayı: 42, Ankara.
2 Ibrahim Hakkı, Konya Tarihi, Konya, 1964, p. 819.
3 Ibid, p. 823.

Bahaeddin was buried in the rose-garden of Sultan Ala al-Din Kayqubad[1]. The inscription on his grave, carved by order of the Sultan, is as follows:

"Only God is Eternal, This is the grave of our *Mevlana* (our lord) and our master. The leader of the Muhammedan Tradition, source of wisdom, reviver of the tradition, destroyer of those who go astray from the Islamic rules, guide for the world and follower of the divine path, Sultan of the learned, *Mufti* (religious magistrate) of the east and the west, *Baha* (of great value) of the nation and religion, Sheykh of Islam and the Muslims, Muhammed b. al-Huseyin b. Ahmed al-Balkhi. May God be pleased with him and his ancestors. He passed away in the morning of Friday 18th of Rabiulakhir 628 H. (12 Jan. 1230)". (Hasan Özönder, p. 3)

4- Bahaeddin and his teachings:

Rumi one day said to his son Sultan Veled, "Know this that we and our disciples will gather together under the shadow of the big Mevlana (Bahaeddin) on the resurrection day and by means of him we shall go to God" (Eflaki I/48).

Who, then, is Bahaeddin? In order to introduce him fully we give here his full name, his religion lineage, and examples from his best lectures.

His name was Muhammed Bahaeddin Veled al-Balkhi (from Balkh) son of Huseyin Khatibi (preacher), son of Ahmed Khatibi. He was born in the year H. 546/A.D. 1151 at Balkh. He was bestowed the title of *"Sultan ul-Ulama"* = (King of the learned) by Prophet Muhammed who appeared twice in the dreams of his opponents[2] and verified the title.

It is said that he was attached to the sufi Nejmeddin Kubra (1145-1226 A.D.)[3] but no mention is made of the Sheykh in Bahaeddin's Maarif. Perhaps, he had met him at Balkh or Khwarazm but it is doubtful that he ever joined his order, the Kubraviya[4]. It can be assumed that many of his ancestors were learned as they bore the title *"Khatibi"* (preachers). His grand mother belonged to the royal family of the Khwarazmshah[5].

His speeches and lectures attracted the attention of the people he visited in cities on his way to Konya. At Konya he won the favour of the great Sultan Qayqubad, who soon became his devoted disciple.

---

1 Hasan Özönder, Konya Mevlana Dergahı, Kültür Bakanlığı 1989, p. 3.
2 See Maarif, I/p. 189.
3 Nefahat ul-Uns, p. 457.
4 As stated by Berthel also IA/9, p. 164.
5 Definite relation is not known.

This is what his beloved student and disciple Burhaneddin Tirmizi says about him:

"I happened to watch 'the Guarded Tablet' *(Lavh-i Mahfuz)* on which the names of prophets and saints are written. I knew each of them. Many saints have come to this world after Muhammed but none has the rank of Mevlana Bahaeddin. I am no hypocrite, otherwise I would tell the names of all the saints that are living today" (Maarif of Tirmizi, p. 21).

Bahaeddin's sermons include[1] short Koranic verses and some Traditions of Muhammed which he explains in the light of his own spiritual experiences. Here we give examples from his lectures that throw light upon his life and his son's "Masnevi"[2]. Rumi did not put down his father's book from his hands until he met his spiritual master Shams-i Tebrizi.

From Bahaeddin's Lectures:

"When I was busy praying, I saw Allah. As people define *Huri* (the untouched female angels of Paradise) half of her body is camphor, half of saffron and hair of musk", or they say, "A certain person has a head of modesty (shyness), and the feet of righteousness"; so I see Allah full of mercy, grandeur, awe, kindness, power, precedence, and life. I see a gift of pleasures in Allah and His Epithets; and I see countless other kinds of pleasures and hope that they may be increased by Allah. He acts thus, but in accordance with the capacity of my observation. He gives me eyes in my body and out of my body; and my seeing Allah is through my senses in which He has opened some tiny eyes and has put them in front of me like a richly dressed table. Now in front of me, that is in the air in front of me, I see Allah and His attributes... (Maarif, p. 3). "All of my gifts, properties such as perception, knowledge, power, love, affection and grace, deliberation and judgement, seeing, hearing, and conscience are the eyes for Allah by means of which I observe Him" (Ibid, p. 3).

"I was looking at my thought, but I felt that the thought was not within me. It had gone somewhere else. Then I noticed that the control of my perception was not in my hands" (Maarif, p. 19).

"It was Allah who gave me awareness or unawareness and it seemed to me as if I were stuck to Him. When He went, I went; when He came, I came to myself" (Maarif, p. 20).

---

[1] See Maarif.
[2] For other details see Feruzanfer's preface to the Maarif.

"Allah inspired me, 'As long as you don't deny your selfhood and everything around you, you cannot be aware of Me'. So I said to myself: O, my soul, go from this life to the life of Allah, and whatever kind of life Allah wants you to live, be busy with that one..." (Maarif, p. 30).

"Sorrows are for the betterment of a believer. Someone asked, 'Why does Allah give troubles to His friends?' I replied: Although in appearance they look like troubles and worries and they seem to torture your body; but the heart under them smiles like roses smile under the crying Spring clouds. Since this body with its shape belongs to this world which is the place of troubles, doubtlessly, it faces troubles. On the contrary, soul belongs to the other world and, therefore, lives in the gardens of happiness" (Maarif, p. 62).

"How can a lover of Allah recall paradise or hell?" was the question. I said, "Paradise is the perfection of all powers, intellects, happiness, and pleasures of friendship and hell is the congregation of unhappiness. Thus, friendship (unity) is a part of paradise or an effect of paradise while hell lashes you towards the Friend" (Maarif, p. 64).

"Since Allah is watching you, decorate yourself like a bride because there is no better customer than Him. Anoint your eyes with the collyrium of penitence and faith, decorate your ears with the rings of consciousness; put your hands to work on pious deeds; paint your face with the powder of supplication and sincerity; put on an ankle-ring of service and improve your sense of discrimination between the bad and the good; put on the head dress of chastity and humility" (Maarif, p. 96).

"Everyone lives in accordance with the amount he can perceive Allah. If he sees more, he lives more. He who sees Allah more learns more about the realities of sciences and religions" (Maarif, p. 100).

"Even troubles are a boon from Allah, because tolerance of gaining and losing is the standard and this capability goes with you to the other world where Allah (according to your experience) grants you a better world and a better task" (Maarif, p. 102).

"When I came out of my body's covering, I drew myself out of all the states I used to undergo and went into the eternal world of Allah; and I went into His attributes. Raising myself up, I got rid of my worries and I saw Allah. He was standing behind the non-existent world and had loaded the world with all kinds of things. He was taking the things out of the non-existent world while I could watch Him..." (Maarif, p. 128).

"When I join my being with Allah, my attributes mingle with His, I see His greatness and when I see in the Being of Allah, I see all things attached to Him and thus, I realise His Magnitude" (Maarif, p. 142).

"The outer pleasures are caused by the inner pleasures and the inner pleasures are caused by Allah; and divine powers get their energies from Allah's attributes; and doubtlessly the eternal gates of the gardens (called paradise) are also attributes of Allah" (Maarif, p. 148).

"The most effective and the strongest creation of Allah is love" (Maarif, p. 152).

"Nothing created by Allah is as strong as love and nothing is stranger than love. There is no stronger life than that of a lover and it is because of this that I always remember Allah and I am always busy with Him" (Maarif, p. 152).

"Whenever I look at Allah so that He may show me miraculous things, He opens new valleys of the spiritual world to me and I see one hundred thousand herbs (spiritual manifestations) which I had never seen before... These secrets are not disclosed to all because they have curtains of negligence" (Maarif, p. 163).

"...Now listen to the music produced by some instrument so that you may be overwhelmed by pleasure given by Allah and then be driven to the holy zeal. Similarly, listen to the moanings of the painful so that you may yourself moan for the separation from Allah. They called the prophet *"Noah"* because he yearned *(noha kard)* for Allah for His love" (Maarif, p. 367).

"In order to lessen your worldly worries feel yourself a stranger in this world and whatever colours you observe or whatever pleasures you take, remember that they are all transient; and that you are only a visitor to His world" (Maarif, p. 374).

"A perfect man who deserves to be at the highest stage, lives at a high level of endeavour and in his eyes all the creatures (may they be bad or good) are born of Divine Mercy. He observes everything from the eyes of Allah; and whatever he takes, he takes from Allah. He always thanks for His dainties and welcomes whatsoever comes from Him due to His manifestation and thinks that all troubles are actually pleasures" (Maarif, p. 403).

"If one's heart is after this world, then one's head is also restless and wandering, for this earth is also wandering around restlessly" (Maarif, II/p. 96).

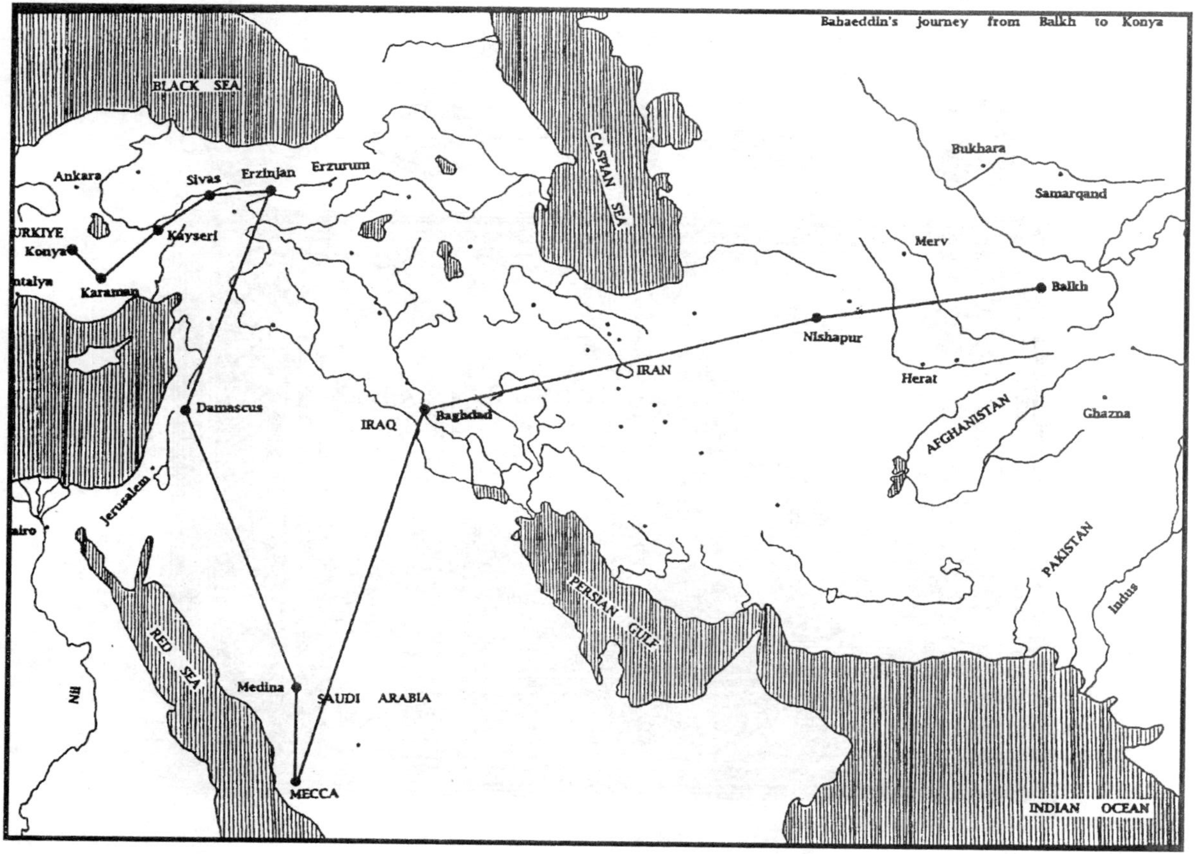
Babaeddin's journey from Balkh to Konya
BLACK SEA
CASPIAN SEA
Ankara
Sivas
Erzinjan
Erzurum
URKIYE
Konya
Kayseri
Karaman
ntalya
Bukhara
Samarqand
Merv
Balkh
Nishapur
IRAN
Herat
Ghazna
AFGHANISTAN
Damascus
IRAQ
Baghdad
Jerusalem
airo
PERSIAN GULF
PAKISTAN
Indus
RED SEA
Nil
Medina
SAUDI ARABIA
MECCA
INDIAN OCEAN

An illuminated page from the MS "G"

CHAPTER II

Konya and Anatolia

1- Political History:

The Anatolian Seljuk state came into existence in A.D. 1075 following Alp Arslan's victory at Manzikert (A.D. 1071) which defeated the Byzantines. Suleyman Shah (d. A.D. 1086), the son of Kutalmish extended the state. However, after his death the Seljuk Empire was divided into several states. A great number of *Ghuz* (Oghuz) Turks migrated from Central Asia or Iran and came to settle in Anatolia building large cities and towns[1]. This brought the Byzantine Empire face to face with the newcomers, and the Crusaders tried their best to uproot them from Anatolia. Nevertheless, the Turks were determined to settle.

Qilich Arslan (d. A.D. 1107) defeated the Crusaders and the Seljuk empire began to spread fast. A series of wars were fought between the Christians and the Turks until in A.D. 1176 when Qilich Arslan II (A.D. 1155-1192) defeated the army of Emperor Manuel. After this defeat, Christians began to accept the presence of the Turks in Anatolia[2]. The ties between the Turks and Christians improved so much that the two communities started to intermix. Qilich Arslan II himself married a Christian lady and thus set an example for his descendants. The great Sultan Kaykubad also married a Christian lady who gave birth to the Sultan Ghiyas al-Din Kaykhusrev (Sultan between A.D. 1237-1246) who like his father married the Georgian princess. This mixture bred further religious tolerance and understanding among the royal families and the ruling class.

After several years of interior political turmoil and foreign invasions came the golden era of the Seljuks under the rule of Sultan Ala al-Din Kaykubad I (ruled between A.D. 1220-1237): He built citadels around Konya, Kayseri, and Sivas to protect them from the coming Mongol invasion. He spent his winter at the beautiful Mediterranean coast at Antalya and conquered Alanya[3]. Sometimes he would go to Kayseri and Sivas but Konya remained his capital. During his reign, people lived peacefully and his commanders or officers became as rich as the Sultan himself.

The fugitive Jelal al-Din Khwarazmshah was at first on good terms with the Seljuk Sultan Ala al-Din Kaykubad, who welcomed his soldiers and allowed them to join the Turcomans of Anatolia, but when the former began to create a threat by

---

1 İbrahim, Selçuk Tarihi, preface, p. VI.
2 Yılmaz Öztuna, Türk Ansiklopedisi, Selçuklar, p. 315.
3 Merçil, 138-139.

occupying Seljuk towns the Sultan had to fight a war with him at Yassıchimen, a valley of Erzinjan, in 1230. Jelal al-Din was defeated and fled towards the east. This war helped neither side for it weakened the two Turkish armies that could have joined against the Mongols, who not only defeated Jelal al-Din, but later were able to invade Anatolia at various times[1].

After this war the Mongols discovered that the Seljuk army was weak and they came closer to the eastern borders. However, the Sultan made peace with the Mongol commander, Oktay[2]. Sultan Kaykubad was able to maintain peace and order in the country. He never stayed in one place. In order to keep an eye on the empire he moved from centre to centre[3]. If he could have lived later than 1237, Rumi would have had a better life under his patronage, for the Sultan had much respect for saintly people. He had a great love for Christ and wanted to live the life of a monk. He gave up that idea having been convinced by the famous Muslim saint Suhreverdi[4]. It was after his death that a period of unrest began. The princes began to fight for the throne. The Mongol army started to interfere with the Sultanate which finally came under their full control and the Sultans were only puppets. The marginal tribes, the Turcomans and Khwarazms had rebelled continually against the central authorities sometimes openly and sometimes in the form of religious sects or orders.

2- Schools of Religion:

Geographically, there were three major schools of ideas each of which opposed the other. In the north of Anatolia was the Tokat School, in the south east was the school of Malatya *(Melitene)*, in the centre of Anatolia was the school of Konya.

1- The School of Tokat: This school flourished under the Danishmend's patronage. This kingdom was established by Gümüş Tekin Melik Ahmed Ghazi (d. A.D. 1105)[5], a Turcoman chief[6]. He and his descendants gave importance to sciences and philosophy and for that purpose they established Medrises. An earlier book from Anatolia on astronomy belongs to this school. Its name is *"Keshfu'l Aqabe"* and was written by Ilyas b. Ahmed al-Kayseri[7] in A.D. 1101. Mystic teachings were not strong.

---

[1] Büyük İslam Tarihi, p. 8/291.
[2] Merçil, p. 145.
[3] Feruzanfer, p. 35 and Ibn-i Bibi, p. 227.
[4] Ibn-i Bibi, p. 231.
[5] Osman Turan, Selçuklular Tarihi, Dergah Yayınları, İstanbul, p. 289.
[6] Baldwin, p. 163.
[7] MSS at Süleymaniye Library No. 5426 foliae 244 b-261 a.

2- *The school of Malatya:* It was improved by the scholars that came from Iran or from the Arab lands. Sasanian influence was also strong. Most of the princes and rulers were educated in this area. The general trend was Orthodox and much importance was laid upon the teachings of the Koran and Muhammed's tradition. The Caliph had much influence on the school.

3- *The school of Konya:* Since Konya was the capital, a mixture of all kinds of schools was found here. Islamic mysticism was more dominant. Rumi, Sadrettin and Awhadeddin-i Kirmani were the most prominent sheykhs of the Sufi orders.

3- The Reign of Ghiyas al-Din Kaykhusrev II:

This Sultan came to the throne when he was only 14 years old in 1237. The Seljuk empire began to decline because his vizier Saddeddin Köpek held the reins in his hand and to be more powerful he discharged many soldiers of rank and honour. He even provoked the anger of the Khwarazmian army by killing their commander[1]. He was secretly planning to become a Sultan. His conspiracy weakened the government which gave courage to the Turcomans who rebelled under the guidance of Baba Ilyas and his follower Baba Ishak. Baba Ilyas of Khorasan gathered Turcomans under his flag.

When Baba Ilyas was killed at Amasya, his disciple Baba Ishak came on the scene. The new-muslim Turcomans followed him easily when he claimed to be their spiritual Sheykh in A.D. 1240[2]. Being a Turcoman spiritual master, he was called *"Baba"*. His revolt resisted the Seljuk army for two years and it was with the help of Frankish mercenaries that the revolt was put to an end[3]. This was the same Baba who visited Rumi and brought an ironical message of Bektashi Vali[4].

This political situation caused such a wound that the Mongol army easily proceeded up to Erzurum, a gate that opened to Iran and Turkistan in A.D. 1242. Plundering and massacring the army came to Sivas under the command of Bayju Noyan. Finally, a war at the Köse Mountain was waged to decide the fate of Anatolia. In 1243 the great Seljuk army around 80.000[5] was forced to retreat and the Sultan fled to Tokat from where he came back to Konya. After this defeat other cities in the east such as Kayseri *(Caesarea)* also fell in the hands of the Mongols

---

1 İbrahim Kafes, Selçuklu Tarihi, p. 104.
2 Not as "prophet" as mentioned by Yaşar Ocak, Babailer İsyanı, p. 104.
3 Baldwin, p. 691 and Merçil, p. 148.
4 Eflaki I/p. 381. The story may be untrue for Rumi was not a sheykh yet.
5 Büyük İslam Tarihi, 8/p. 304-305.

who burnt and plundered them brutally. A peace treaty was signed between the two and the Seljuks agreed to pay ransom to the Mongols every year. They would pay 360 thousand silver coins, 10 thousand sheep, 1000 camels and cattle[1]. The Armenians cooperated with the Mongols while the Byzantines supported the Seljuks[2].

After this treaty the central government began to sag. The bad administration of the Sultan and his addiction to heavy drinking and fondness of physical amusements led the great empire to a fatal end. Soon after his death in 1245 things became worse. The civil riots were stirred. Many Beygates announced their independence[3]. Actual ruling power went in the hands of the Mongols.

The Sultan left three sons: 1- Izzeddin Kaykavus II (11 years old) 2- Rukneddin Qilich Arslan IV (9 years old) 3- Ala al-Din Qayubad II (7 years old). Naturally, the oldest son was elevated to the throne.

4- The Period of Joint Rule:

The ruling body was composed of Shams al-Din of Isphahan (the vizier), Jelal al-Din Karatay (regent of the Sultanate), Shams al-Din Hasoğuz (chief of begates), Fahreddin Ebubekir (*Pervane* = A vizier that issues the royal commands)[4]. These men began to struggle for power. When the Mongolian Khan Güyük ascended the throne, Izzeddin was invited to join the royal ceremony. Rukneddin Qilich Arslan was sent on behalf of the Sultan in order to avoid the chaos. Shams al-Din married the widowed mother of the Sultan and gained power. Upon this the Mongol Khan Güyük appointed a new vizier Bahaeddin Terjuman who came to Konya with prince Rukneddin and killed Shams al-Din in 1249[5].

Finally, a joint Sultanate of the three brothers (A.D. 1249-1254) was established and Karatay acted as their regent. Yet the fire of revolts was not extinguished. Many statesmen went to the Mongolian Khan with rich presents in order to secure important positions already occupied by others. Actually, there were two powers the Mongols and the Seljuks, ruling the country which created political skirmishes that damaged peace. In 1254 Jelal al-Din Karatay passed away and the joint rule broke up. Ala al-Din II was poisoned at Erzurum when he was going to visit the new Khan Mongke (Mengu A.D. 1251-1260)[6]. Now, only the two brothers were left. Izzeddin II was addicted to drinking; therefore, the statesmen did not like him.

---

1 Türkiye Tarihi, p. 173.
2 Ibid, p. 174.
3 Türkiye Tarihi, p. 175.
4 Ibid, p. 176.
5 Merçil, p. 152.
6 Merçil, p. 152.

They took Qilich Arslan IV to Kayseri and declared him Sultan. There rose two powers, one at Konya, the other at Kayseri. In 1254 a war broke out between the two Sultans which ended up in favour of Izzeddin. Qilich Arslan was put in prison at the Burgulu castle. The Mongol pressure reached its peak. The Khan's commander Bayju Noyan would ask for ransom at any time of the year, twice or even thrice. The justice minister Fahreddin Ali with 100 silver coins and other presents went to Batu and asked him to fix an annual ransom and came home successfully. This act made Bayju very angry.

In 1256 once again a war was waged against Mongol army of Bayju, who was looking for a *Kishlaq* (winter resort) for his great Khan Halagu. The sultan was defeated and went to Alaiye with his family[1]. The minister for home affairs Nizammeddin Ali collected gold coins from each rich man in the palace and gave it (about four mule loads) to the angry Bayju, who upon this treatment gave up the idea of plundering Konya and satisfied himself by only demolishing the citadels of the city. Although the city was saved, new revolts of the Turcomans and Armenians ensued.

Rukneddin Qilich Arslan IV was placed on the throne at Konya by Bayju. This did not last long for he was called by Halagu Khan for his Baghdad campaign. Izzeddin went to the Byzantine emperor Theodoros Laskaris II with whose help he took the throne back in 1257. Qilich Arslan's wise vizier Muin al-Din Pervane played an outstanding role between the Mongols and the Sultan and held the power of the empire in his own hands. Izzeddin again declared war against the Mongols. Halagu Khan called the two brothers Qilich Arslan IV and Izzeddin and divided the empire between them. Izzeddin's area covered the western part of Turkey from the Byzantium up to Sivas, and Qilich Arslan's area extended from Sivas up to Erzurum. Now that everything was settled, Izzeddin went to Antalya and Kubadabad Palace (by the Beyshehir Lake) and plunged into the delights of life[2].

Muin al-Din Pervane continued to improve his relations with the Mongol Khans and his commanders. Izzeddin also sent presents to Halagu but he obtained no positive result for Pervane's anti-propaganda was stronger. Finally, in 1261 the Mongols invaded Anatolia again. This time Izzeddin asked the help of Baybars, a Turkish king in Egypt who had once defeated the Mongol army. Izzeddin received no help. In 1262 Izzeddin had to go to Istanbul for refuge where he met his old friend Mihail Paleologos[3]. Due to some political reasons Mihail put him and his family in jail. Nevertheless, he was freed and taken to Berke Khan, who gave him the two cities Soğdak and Solhad where he lived peacefully until 1279. He died near the Crimea.

---

1 Osman Turan, Türkiye Tarihi, p. 480.
2 Türkiye Tarihi, p. 179.
3 Ibid, VIII/p. 322.

When Izzeddin left Konya his brother Qilich Arslan IV sat on the throne but absolute rule was in the hands of Pervane, who became stronger and stronger with the help of the Mongols. He killed many rebels, statesmen, governors, and Turcomans. He also poisoned the Sultan in 1266 to attain full power and raised the Sultan's small son Ghiyas al-Din III to the throne[1]. This period is called "Pervane's Era" for he was the real Sultan. He appointed his relatives and dependants to important positions. He benefitted fully from the political situation and to further strengthen his power, he married the widowed Queen (the Georgian Lady).

Pervane's full name was Muin-al Din Suleyman, son of Muizzib al-Din Ali who was vizier of Sultan Kaykhusrev II. Thus belonging to an aristocratic family he rose to the topmost rank by dint of his political maneuvering. It was at the time of this vizier that Rumi passed away.

5- Rumi and the Royal family:

When all this was happening Rumi, like his father, did not participate in political activity. He watched the events on the scene of the physical world with divine eyes. Undoubtedly, he always offered his help to those who needed it; and Sultans, viziers, chieftains, and statesmen visited him for his spiritual help. He would rarely ever visit the palace as he says in his discourses:

"...that the worst of scholars is he who accepts help from Emirs (chieftains) and whose welfare and salvation is dependent on and stems from the fear of them" (Rumi's Discourses, p. 13).

During the nine years' rule of Ghiyas al-Din Kaykhusrev II, Rumi does not seem to have had close relations with the royal family. The Sultan's wife, the Georgian Lady, became Rumi's devoted follower after she married Pervane. Izzeddin Kaykavus II loved Rumi like his father. He would generally go to him to get his blessing and advice. Rumi would not pay much heed to him and would treat him like an ordinary man. One day the Sultan came to Rumi for his advice, and Rumi said this, "They have made you a shepherd, but you act like a wolf; they have made you a protector while you act like a thief, and act upon the words of Satan... upon this the Sultan began to cry and shout bareheaded, and he began to repent. Then Rumi came out and told the Sultan that God had forgiven him" (Eflaki, per. I/443).

It is understood from Rumi's letter addressed to Izzeddin that Rumi calls himself "Sultan's father" (see Baki Ist letter, and Baki's note on p. 240). This letter

---

[1] For full details about this vizier see Nejat Kaymaz, Pervane Muinüddin Süleyman, Dil Tarih ve Coğ. Yayınları No. 202, 1970.

contains thanks that Rumi wants to give to the Sultan who has favoured Nejmeddin son of Khurem, whom Rumi calls "my most dear son and emir"[1]. The following lines addressed to the Sultan are interesting: "The greatness of a lover depends upon the greatness of his beloved. The more graceful, ingenious and clean spirited is the beloved, the dearer is the lover".

There are about eight letters addressed to the Sultan[2] and we give here some interesting quotations from them[3]:

"God knows well that when we met, we cherished love and goodwill for each other. We shared each other's feelings and benedictions; we carry the same feeling even now. The vision of your face and state is still in front of my eyes. These days the separation[4] has never been in the state 'Out of sight, out of mind' ". (Letters, Tur. p. 57).

"The love (or affection) that is created by the carnal desires and selfness becomes warm and cold; like worldly climate, now winter and now summer; but the friendship beyond this worldly climate comes from God and it never becomes cold or warm" (Letters, Tur. p. 60).

"I say hello to you, because you are in my heart,
You are away from my sight, yet are in my heart,
You, though you don't show yourself, live in my heart,
Hello, to the one that is unseen yet not apart".

(Letters, p. 105, Per.)[5]

Sometimes Rumi would send the Sultan Izzeddin and his company away without seeing them, especially when he was busy with prayers to God[6].

---

1 At the top margin of the old MS of letter available here at Konya museum (no. 79) the note reads "Nama-yı Sultan Izzeddin bin Jehed-i Ibn-i Khurem", but Dr. Riyaz in his Urdu translation says that the letter is addressed to vizier Nejmeddin (Mektubat-u Khutbat-ı Rumi., p. 10 and 399).
2 They are No. 39, 57, 80, 92, 94, 95, 102 and 103.
3 The texts are long and full of literary wording.
4 For the Sultan is in Antalya.
5 Rumi calls Izzeddin as "the pride of Davud (David)" which is a reference to the Seljuk dynasty and not to the prophet David.
6 Eflaki, Tur. 3/164.

Jelal al-Din Karatay:

A vizier who acted as *Atabeg* (regent) of the ruling brothers during the years 1249-1254. Karatay was an Anatolian Greek *(Rum)* who became a pious and devoted Muslim and, therefore, he was called, "A lover of God on Earth"[1]. Rumi used to call him "Our Karatay". Karatay fought against the egoistic people who gathered round the Sultan to procure power[2]. He wanted to keep the Empire together, but when he died it shattered into pieces. Rumi's letters No. 83,126 are addressed to this pious man[3]. We come across these words to Karatay in Rumi's letters, "(You have) the attributes of angels close to God"; "The highest of the most respect worthy lords (beys)"; "The source of justice and charity". Rumi in one of his letters requests Karatay to give five hundred Dirhems as a loan to Selahuddin's relative. This shows how frank he was with Karatay (Letter, No.81, Per.).

Karatay built a great medrise (college) in A.D. 1251 which was quite often visited by Rumi. *Sema* (the Dervish dance) was held here[4]. When Karatay died he was buried here and Rumi visited the place. "...One day Rumi was passing by the medrise after Karatay's death. He stopped for a while and then said, 'Our Jelal al-Din says that he is yearning for the faces of his friends and he wishes to be comforted by my breath (prayers)'. Rumi went in accompanying his friends and sat there for some time. Some recited the Koran, others recited ghazals and verses from the Masnevi. Rumi showed great emotion and then left the place" (Eflaki, Per. 3/127).

Suleyman Muin al-Din Pervane:

He was a disciple of Rumi also and would hold sema meetings for him. In character he was just an opposite example of Rumi for he was a politician and a selfish ruler, yet he respected Rumi and would try to take his advice although quite often he could not act upon it. Again we give here some sentences that will throw light upon their relationship. There are about twenty four letters addressed to Pervane and they are generally about thanks, recommendation for some people. This is how Rumi addressed Pervane:

"The king of the worldly viziers, Ka'abe of the chieftains and great people; the order of the country; a matchless person of the present world; protector of the people; perfect in worldly wisdom and religion; an active sea for the needy and

---
1 With this title are signed his edicts (see Baki's note, Mektuplar, p. 226).
2 Kaymaz, p. 48-49.
3 The letter No. 23 is addressed to the financial minister Jelal al-Din Mestawafi and not to Karatay as said by Riyaz, p. 267.
4 It is still on food and is called "Karatay Medrise".

helpless people; a praiseworthy pearl and repairer of the columns of Islam with Islam...".

As disclosed in his letter no. 27, Rumi did not like to write letters of recommendation but he was obliged to do so upon his friends' request. In his letters Rumi advises the ruling vizier indirectly and politely. It can be deduced that Pervane despite being a clever political man loved God and dervishes. He attended lectures of Sheykh Sadreddin on Muhammed's traditions. One day Pervane asked for Rumi's advice. Rumi after some pause said to him, "I have heard that you have memorised the Koran?" Pervane answered, "Yes, I have". Rumi asked again, "You have studied the Tradition with Sheykh Sadreddin, haven't you?" Pervane said "Yes" again. Upon this Rumi went on "Since you don't act upon God's words and His prophet's traditions, how will you ever act on my words?" (Eflaki, 3/82).

Sometimes Rumi would decorate his letters with verses that alluded to some lessons that he wanted to give to Pervane:

"In this way of life there are hundreds of devils in the form of men,
So that you cannot trust all men, shaped as men". (Letters, No. 30, Per.)

Or sometimes in simple words:

"May God protect a person like you who is righteous and pious from Satan; and the waylayers that induce suspicion (about God and religion), and make one unhappy, cold-hearted, and deprived of Divine Mercy. For such religious leaders God says in the Koran, "There are indeed many among the priests and anchorites who in falsehood devour the property of men and hinder them in the path of God" (the Koran, IX /34).

Pervane's son in law, Mejededdin Atabek the financial minister[1], was also Rumi's devoted disciple. Rumi had high class and low class around him. Among ordinary people were tailors, blacksmiths, cloth dealers and so on. One day Pervane had a meeting in his palace where he said, "Rumi is a unique spiritual king. I cannot think of a master like him who has come upon earth for centuries, but his disciples are unimportant and bad people". Later when Rumi heard this, he wrote a few lines to Pervane in which he said, "If my disciples were good people, I would have been their disciple. I have accepted them as my followers to make them better in action and character" (Eflaki, Tur. 3/46).

---

1 Kaymaz, p. 106.

When Pervane began to co-operate with the Mongols, he lost Rumi's favour:

"I have spoken to Emir Pervane for this reason, that in the beginning you came forward as the shield of Muslimdom. 'I make myself a ransom', you said. 'I sacrifice my reason, deliberation, and judgment that Islam may survive and its followers multiply, so that Islam may remain secure and strong'. But inasmuch as you put your trust in your own judgment, not having God in sight and not recognising that everything proceeds from God, God therefore converted that very means and endeavour into a means bringing about the diminishment of Islam. Having made common cause with the Tatars, you are giving them assistance so as to destroy the Syrians and the Egyptians and to ruin the realm of Islam. God therefore made that very means which would have secured the survival of Islam into the means of its diminishment". (Discourses of Rumi, p. 17)

Pervane was much concerned with formal prayers and rituals while Rumi wanted him to gain esoteric qualities. This conversation between the two will make the point clearer:

"Pervane said to me, 'The fundamental things are prayers (five times ritual prayers and fasting)'. I told him: Where are the people of action and the seeker of action so that I may show them what real prayers are. Since I find no purchasers of real prayers, but purchasers only of words, I occupy myself with words only". (Discourses, Tur. 63)

The Georgian Lady and Rumi:

The wife of Sultan Qilich Arslan IV Gumach Khatun had a great respect for Rumi[1] and was his disciple, but the Georgian lady had a special devotion for him.

The Georgian Lady, Princess Tamara was the daughter of the Georgian Queen Rosudan (Rusudan A.D. 1223-1247). She had married the Sultan Ghiyas al-Din Kaykhusrev II and bore him Kaykubad II and after the death of her husband she married Pervane and became attached to Rumi's spiritual supervision.

This is the story of her attachment:

"The Georgian Lady, the Queen of the time and wife of the king, was a devotee and special disciple of Rumi's family. She would burn due to the fire of yearning for Rumi. It befell that once she had to go to Kayseri. The king hardly ever refused her requests, because she was an high-born lady and had a fair sense of judgment She could not bear the fire of separation from Rumi. In those days there lived a painter as famous as Mani[2]. He would claim that even Mani would fail in

---
[1] We learn this from Eflaki and Rumi's letter No. 45.
[2] Some other unknown painter famous those days.

competition with his paintings. He was called the Aynul Devla of Rum (Anatolia). The lady gave him presents and ordered him to draw a picture of Rumi. She told him that the picture should be as lively as possible so that she might take that with her on the journey.

Aynul Devla in the company of some officers went to Rumi and wanted to tell him about the situation, but before he could open his mouth Rumi said, "If you can draw my picture it will be a great achievement". The painter brought some paper and turned his face towards Rumi, who was standing. The painter, casting a glance at his face, began to draw Rumi's picture and looked at Rumi again, but found his face changed. Upon this he drew another picture. When he finished it, he found Rumi's face changed again. He drew twenty pictures one after another, and each time Rumi's face was different. He became astonished, broke his pen, and shouting and crying he bowed down in front of Rumi. Then Rumi uttered the following verses:

> "Alas I am so colourless and traceless,
> How can I see myself as I am?
> You tell me to reveal my secrets,
> But where is the space and where am I,
> How can my soul settle down?
> When I dwell in such a mobile spirit,
> My sea too has drowned within myself,
> Strange to say what an edgeless sea am I.

Aynul Devla came out shedding tears. People took the papers to the Georgian Lady. She took all of them and put them in her box. Whenever she desired to see Rumi's face and would try to look at those pictures, Rumi's actual face would appear in front of her, and she would feel happy" (Eflaki, 3/374).

"One day the Georgian Lady just for sake of fun asked Alameddin Kayseri 'What have you seen in Rumi that you have become so attached to him and have great love for him?' He said 'O lady of the world, may you live long; Rumi's most ordinary miracle is that a prophet is loved by a certain nation while a saint is loved by some disciples, but Rumi is loved by all nations and rulers of the world. They benefit from his secrets and praise him. Upon this answer, the lady of the world became so happy that she gave him dresses to wear and sent presents for other needy people" (Eflaki, 3/506).

When Rumi passed away, it was the Georgian Lady and Pervane who supported the construction of his tomb.

6- Social Context:

The Anatolian Seljuks ruled the country exactly with the system which their ancestors had used for Iran and even India. The system was basically a mixture of

Turko-Iranian culture tinged with Islam by means of which Arabic became dominant over Turkish, Persian, and later Urdu. Similarly, mysticism was more welcome than Islam itself by the inter-mixing nations. Hindus, Iranians, and Turks all found something in common in the mystical interpretation of the Koran and the Tradition. In Anatolia it even included Christianity. As a matter of fact, God is one Reality and religions are different kinds of interpretations of the same Fact. Water is the same, but it is the taps that differ. It is, therefore, useless to fight over the qualities of the taps when you are thirsty. Just open the tap and drink the water!

Generally speaking, the army commanders were Turks. Viziers and ministers were of Iranian origin. Religious leaders were Arabs who handed over their positions to the Iranian and Turkish scholars in the long run.

As a result of this inter-mingling three languages lived side by side: Turkish, Persian, and Arabic. Persian was the official as well as the literary language. Arabic was used for religious and scientific works. Sheykh Sadreddin wrote all of his works in Arabic. Simple soldiers and farmers would speak Turkish. That is why in Rumi's Masnevi quite often "a Turcoman" would stand for a villager or a simple person. The learned class had no concept of nationalism. They believed in the philosophy of "All Muslims, even seventy seven nations (all nations) are one and the same, and man is close to God only by the degree of his piety and perfection". However, "the unity of seventy seven nations" was not accepted by the orthodox Muslim group and for long it has been a matter of controversy among some sects.

In most cases the educated Turkish class was sieved through the Persian and Arabic culture before arriving in Anatolia. But the simple Turcomans who migrated to this land lived a nomadic life in the mountainous areas. Generally, they were unorganised, but by the time they began to settle in the marginal areas forming begataries, and they had become a challenging force against the central power. When the Mongols invaded Anatolia, these free thinking, brave Turcomans organised a separate power reinforced by the mixture of Orthodox, Islam and Shamanism. Under the thumb of dictatorship they were not allowed political freedom. Therefore, they adopted different sects of Islam for the same purpose. Akhism was one of the strongest order.

The Turcoman tribes were not poor, they had countless number of herds. Central Anatolia, where Rumi spent most of his life, was the centrifuge of the religious conflicts. Sultans, Beys, and the public were extremely rich. Beys spent money lavishly. As the ruins in Konya and around tell us, the Sultans also lived a very comfortable life. They had palaces, huge gardens, and baths. Their palaces were decorated with blue tiles, figures of eagles, lions and human figures which indicate that they were broad minded people.

The following religious groups were most prominent around Rumi:

Ibn ul-Arabi Group:

This group was centred around Sheykh Sadreddin Konevi (A.D. 1210-1274) who was born at Malatya and came to Konya in A.D. 1254[1]. When his father Ishak passed away, his mother married the famous mystic scholar Muhyiddin Ibn'ul Arabi who educated his step son carefully. He was appointed Sheykh ul-Islam at Konya. Unlike Rumi, he lived a rich life. He taught Muhammed's tradition under the light of Ibn ul-Arabi's system that was based on strange philosophical interpretations. The most outstanding difference between Rumi's and Ibn ul-Arabi's schools is that Rumi laid emphasis on love, ecstasy and intuition based on blind faith, while Ibn ul-Arabi suggests to follow the divine path with wisdom and philosophical doctrines. Besides Rumi does not enter prolonged discussions like Ibn ul-Arabi but goes directly into Divine Love with simpler language. When one reads Ibn ul-Arabi one is lead to scepticism and confusion. It is due to this fact that his step-son Sadreddin towards the end of his life ordered his disciples to sell his books on philosophy (including mysticism) and to keep only commentaries on the Koran and the Prophet's sayings[2]. Sadreddin thought that only God can conceive Himself, while human beings fail to conceive His Being. In order to practice a religion one needs intellect; and it is intellect and religion that leads to God. He further claimed that the ritual prayers were the light. Rumi invites us to go beyond the frame of the intellect with the torch of Divine Love, which is the motivation of each cause. Prayers and fasting are the alphabet of God's love.

From Eflaki we learn that Sadreddin always respected Rumi. Although they did not belong to the same sect yet their friendship was sincere. However, it is evident from Eflaki's statement that Sadreddin did not approve of Rumi's way at first[3] but after one event Sadreddin became his good friend: "Sadreddin saw in dreams many times that he was giving a massage to his feet. This really surprised him and he began to say "God forbid". The last time when he had the same dream he woke up and ordered his servant to fetch a lamp. The servant found Rumi sitting on the stairs. Sadreddin embraced him while Rumi said, "Don't worry and don't say 'God forbid'. The case is that sometimes you will give a massage to my feet and sometimes I will give one to yours"[4]. At many occasions Sadreddin favoured Rumi and invited him to the spiritual meetings and semas. Once Sadreddin praised Rumi in presence of his

---

1 Prof. Şerafeddin Gölcük, Sadreddin Konevi, Seljuk University, Selçuk Dergisi, 1989, p. 12 (Special issue on Sadreddin).
2 Mustafa Uzunpostalcı, Selçuk Dergisi, p. 41.
3 Şerafaddin, Ibid, p. 14.
4 Eflaki, 3/224.

beloved friends Fahreddin-i Iraqi, Sheref al-Din Mosli, Sheykh Seyyid-i Firgani and Nasir al-Din Konevi in the following way:

"If Juneyd-i Baghdadi and Beyazid-i Bastami had been alive now, they would have been obedient followers of this man of God (Rumi) and they would have regarded it an honour to serve him well. He is an example of the non-attachment of physical possessions suggested by Muhammed's tradition. We gain knowledge from him readily and our spiritual pleasures owe to his existence. Then he (Sadreddin) recited the following verses:

"If we have any spiritual form within us,
It is you, we neither doubt it nor deny it"[1].

Again it was Sadreddin who offered Rumi's funeral prayers and fainted when he saw angels and Muhammed joining the funeral[2].

Sadreddin wrote more than twenty four books on theology, philosophy and mysticism in Arabic[3]. Among the disciples of Sadreddin worth mentioning was Ibrahim Fahreddin-i Iraqi (A.D. 1289) who stayed at Konya with Sadreddin and after learning Ibn ul-Arabibi views went to Tokat. He was actually a follower of the famous Baha al-Din Zekeria of India whose daughter he married there. After his stay in Tokat he went to Damascus where he passed away.

"No one understood Rumi properly, he came to this world as a stranger and left as a stranger"[4], are the words he said for Rumi:

It can be assumed that fame in India of Rumi's Masnevi was first established by Fahreddin-i Iraqı.

Sadreddin's other two disciples Sheykh Davud al-Kayseri (1252-1350) who wrote commentaries on *"Fusus al-Hikem"* of Ibn ul-Arabi, and Siraj al-Din like his master did not like Rumi's way at first but later, probably through Sadreddin, became Rumi's friend. He was a respectworthy man of his time. It was he who performed the funeral prayers of Rumi when Sadreddin fainted. Siraj al-Din once visited Rumi's tomb and recited these verses:

"Alas that day when the throne of death spiked your feet,
I wish the sword in the hand of the world had stuck me too,
So that my eyes had not seen this world without you,
Now, I stand by the grave and let its dust be on my head too"[5].

---

1 Eflaki, p. 3/295.
2 Eflaki, 3/286.
3 For a complete list of works see Mustafa Can, Selçuk Dergisi (Ibid), p. 121.
4 Eflaki, p. 3/333.
5 Let me mourn for you and die.

Rumi wrote several letters to this man. The language is sincere and friendly (for instance, see No. XXXII, LXII, LXIX).

The Kubravi Group:

In this group the most active scholar at Kayseri and Sivas was Nejmeddin Daya Razi (d. A.D. 1356) who is famous for his work "*Mirsad ul-Ibad*". He was not full of passion like Rumi but kept close to the tradition of Muhammed[1]. He was a devoted disciple of Nejmeddin Kubra (d. A.D. 1145-1226) and Sheykh Mejdeddin[2]. Nejmeddin paid a visit to Rumi and Sadreddin but failed to understand the mystical activities of the two-their dervish dances and music[3] -like another Sheykh, Safiyeddin Hindi (d. A.D. 1315).

Awhadeddin-i Kirmani's group:

The biggest opponent of Rumi, as already mentioned, was Akhi Evren whose full name was Akhi Evren Sheykh Nasir al-Din Mahmud al-Khoyi. He was a disciple of Awhadeddin-i Kirmani (d. A.D. 1297) Awhadeddin and Shams-i Tebrizi were both disciples of Rukneddin Sejasi[4]. Shams did not like Awhadeddin because he was fond of beauty and would worship young boys' faces[5], claiming that he saw God's epiphany in them as Awhadeddin claims himself:

"I observe faces because they reflect spiritual beauty, this world is shape and we are all forms. One cannot see the essence but in these forms"[6].

But Rumi says just the opposite:

"If you my friends pass beyond forms, there is a paradise and rose gardens within rose gardens". (Mesnevi, III/5777)

"The love that depends on colours and shapes is not the true love, it finally ends in disgrace". (M. I/205)

Like other dervishes Awhadeddin travelled a lot. He went to Baghdad, Tebriz, and Genja respectively. He also visited Anatolia's central cities Konya (A.D. 1205), Kayseri, Sivas and Malatya.

---

1 Baki, Rumi, p. 242.
2 Dr. Emin, Mirsad ul-Ibad, Tehran, 1972, p. 35.
3 Nafahat ul-Uns, p. 435 and for Kubra see Encyclopaedia of Islam V, p. 300.
4 Menakıb-i Awhadeddin, Feruzanfer, B.T.N.K, Tehran 1969, p. 15.
5 Ibid, p. 213.
6 Commentary on Masnevi, Feruzanfer v. I, p. 31.

Some of his famous works are available at Istanbul libraries such as "*Misbah al-Arvah*" and his Rubaiyat[1].

His disciple Akhi Evren is mentioned in Eflaki's work as "*Nesreddin*", Sheykh Nesreddin or only as Nasiruddin[2]. He is the man who as a leader of Akhism joined the conspiracy against Shams-i Tebrizi which ended up with the assassination or disappearance of the latter.

Akhi Evren was a highly learned man. He wrote around 20 works[3], the most famous of which is "*Lataif-i Ghiyasiya*" in four volumes. These volumes cover philosophy, moral teachings and politics, methods of prayer and jurisprudence. During his stay in Khorasan he attended Fahreddin Razi's lectures as his student and began to show jealousy towards Rumi's family. He came to Kayseri in 1206 with Ibn ul-Arabibi group and established a leather factory there and thus became known as "*Pir-i Tabagh* = Sheykh of tanner's guild"[4]. He did so because Akhis had to engage in some sort of business to earn their living. When he came to Konya he was already a Sheykh of several sanctuaries. After a conflict with Shams at Konya he left for Kirshehir leaving his two chief representatives, Seyyid Sherafeddin and Akhi Ahmad, at Konya. He joined anti-governmental activities of the Turcomans who were also against the Mevlevis until his death in 1262 A.D.

This opposition is felt throughout in Rumi's letters, Masnevi and in Eflaki's book. Rumi in his letters requests the governing authorities to hand over some sanctuaries *(dergah and tekke)* that belonged to the Akhis to his people[5] who were poor. Those days, a sheykh lived on the income of sanctuaries and endowments. Subsequently, the more sanctuaries an order had, the stronger it was supposed to be. Eflaki's statements tell us that there was a good deal of struggle between the Mevlevis and Akhis to possess Ziya al-Din vizier's sanctuary. Akhi Ahmad and his people did not want to hand it over to Husameddin Chelebi and they took out their daggers and swords to fight while Rumi left the place silently in order to avoid violence. After this event Akhi Ahmad became a persona non grata yet his son and others later became followers of Rumi's son and Ahmad died alone. Husameddin was appointed Sheykh of the sanctuary (see Eflaki, 6/12).

---

1 Ahmed Ateş, Farsça Manzum Eserler, p. 203.
2 Mikail Bayram, Ahi Evren kimdir, Türk Kültürü Dergisi, sayı 191, Eylül, 1978 p. 658-668 (Mikail wrote his doctoral thesis on Evren).
3 As discovered by Mikail.
4 Mikail, Ibid p. 664 and the Encyclopaedia of Islam, Brill, 1986, p. 324.
5 See for example letters No. CVIII and No. LXXV in which sanctuary of Akhi Göhertaş is requested for Jemal al-Din.

The basic reason for the opposition was Akhi Ahmad's dislike of the music and the mystical dance which Rumi and his followers practised. Again Eflaki tells us that he claimed, "I have read many books (many a donkey load of books) but I found no positive statement which would allow the act". Upon this Ala al-Din, a disciple of Rumi, said, "You read them like a donkey while we read them like Christ (pure spirit) and, therefore, we understand the meaning and value of the mystical dances *(sema)* more than you do" (Eflaki, 3/187).

Ahmed Yesevi's Group:

Ahmed Yesevi is a legendary saint of the Turks of Central Asia and Anatolia. He had ninety nine thousand followers spread all over the Turkish lands[1]. He was born in a small town, Sayram *(Akshehir)*, near Chimkent of Western Turkistan. His father was also a Sheykh, known as Ibrahim, a supposed descendant of the Caliph Ali. He spent his childhood at Yesi, a big city in those days. His first master was Arslan Baba who gave the young boy his early spiritual training in the same city. From there he went to Bukhara where he became a disciple of Sheykh Yusuf-i Hemedani (A.D. 1048-1140) after whose death he was declared his successor. Ahmed finally came to Yesi and passed away there in A.D.1166. Many Turkish tribes Turcomans, Özbeks, Kazaks visit his tomb and offer prayers for a week or so. His descendants became known as *"Ata"* like Mansur Ata, Abdulmelik Ata. Actually *"ata"* is the Turkish equivalent of *"baba"* (the spiritual father).

Ahmed Yesevi's school gave importance to Muhammed's Tradition as well as to love of God. He used Turkish poetry (called *"Hikmet"* = mystical wisdom") to teach Islam and Islamic mysticism to simple Turkish folk. Bektashi Vali and Yunus Emre were his outstanding representatives in Anatolia. Many similarities can be seen between his ideas and Yunus Emre.

We give here a few lines from Yesevi:

If I say Allah repeatedly in Thy Presence,
Crying and reciting Thy names I say 'My Lord (Rab)',
And sacrifice my head in Thy way, as Thy slave,
Then will I ever be able to find Thee O my Lord? (Divan-i Hikmet, p. 143)

Your love has made me mad and known to all,
Day and night I think of Thee,
I only need Thee and that's for all,
Ever since I opened my eyes I saw Thee, only Thee,
For Thy sake I gave up all my kith and kin,

---

[1] Kemal Erarslan, Ahmed Yesevi, Divan-i Hikmet, Turizm ve Kültür Bakanlığı, 1983 Ankara p. 26.

I only need Thee and that's for all. (Divan-i Hikmet, p. 327)
The essence of love is hidden in the bottomless sea,
Yet a true lover reaches it at the cost of his life,
A vain desirer falls behind on the way to God,
Alas my friends, he sells his belief for valueless coins. (Divan-i Hikmet, p. 169)

Haji Bektashi (A.D. 1248-1337):

Legends tell us, he was directly or indirectly a disciple of Yesevi[1]. Perhaps he was Yesevi's disciple via his master Sheykh Loqman-i Perinde who gave Bektashi his early education. Bektashi was born at Nishapur of Khorasan in 1248[2]. His actual name was Mehmed and his father's name was Seyyid Sultan Ibrahim Sani[3]. Like other sheykhs he first went to Baghdad and Mecca, and then came to Anatolia's small town Sulucakarahöyük, where he is buried. He has two famous works "*Makalat* = Articles" and "*Sherh-i Bismillah* = Commentary on Bismillah".

The Bektashi order continued actively until 1925[4]. Since it was based on great tolerance and understanding, it mixed up with Shi'ism, Christianity, and pre-Islamic heretical elements. Bektashi also supported the anti-governmental movements of Baba Ishak which ended up with total failure. It is for this reason that Rumi and his followers did not approve of the order. Rumi never came face to face with Bektashi but there are two stories that we come across in Eflaki's work[5]. We give here a summary of only one of them:

"The chieftain of Kirshehir, Emir Nureddin, told Rumi about the miracles of Bektashi who gave little importance to outer appearance, rituals (five times prayers), and orthodoxy. I said to him persistently that five time prayers were important. Upon this, he told me to fetch water for ablution. I filled a jar with my own hand and brought it to him and poured it for him. I saw that the water had changed into blood which shocked me. Rumi said, "I wish he could change the blood into water because it is no art to change clean water into blood for blood is a filthy thing". After this statement Nureddin became Rumi's disciple and gave up Bektashi"[6].

There are countless poems written on Bektashi and his miracles. Here we give only one poem of Bektashi himself as an example[7]:

---

1 Fuad Köprülü, İlk Mutasavvuflar, p. 49. His legendary life can be found in many MSS of "Wilayetnama of Haji Bektash.
2 Abdulkadir Sezgin, Bektaşilik, Kültür Bakanlığı, 1990, p. 15.
3 Ibid, Sezen says the dates 1210-1271 are incorrect.
4 Encyclopaedia of Islam, vol. I, p. 1162.
5 Eflaki, 3/815 and 498.
6 Eflaki, 3/498.
7 Murat Sertoğlu, Hacı Bektaşi Veli, Şadırvan Yayın, 1966 p. 15.

"Mystical richness is neither in the robe nor in a crown,
The heat is in the fire but not in the iron-sheet,
Whatever you seek, seek within yourself,
It is not in Jerusalem, Mecca, or even in a pilgrimage,
Beware and break not anyone's heart,
And don't you disobey a true saint at all,
If you are a real man, you shall not perish be sure,
For a wolf cannot devour a lover, as he is all-protected".

Yunus Emre:

It will be unfair to finish this chapter without saying a few words about the first great Sufi poet of the Turkish language who lived between A.D. 1240-1320. He came to this world when Rumi had begun to recite his Masnevi in the Meram gardens of Konya in Persian. The aristocracy and those scholars who knew Persian were moved due to the chanting melody of Rumi's verses which gave messages of Divine Love without discrimination. What could the Turkish soldiers and simple people do? God, the most Merciful, took pity on them. He sent Yunus Emre, who gave a similar message in an easy to understand Turkish.

Recent studies[1] tell us that he was brought up in Karaman the place where Rumi's father first arrived in Anatolia. Perhaps, he came with the Khorasanian immigrants. His language is a pure Turcomanian dialect which still exists in Karaman.

His two surviving works are: his "*Divan*" (collection of his poems)[2], and *Risalat ul-Nushiye*[3]. His works show that he had good education for he uses Persian and Arabic fluently.

He was not a direct disciple of Rumi but he had love and respect for the great Saint. This is what he says about him:

1- "Ever since Mevlana, our master, has shown his favour to us,
    His magnificent eyes have been the mirror of our heart". (Timurtaş, p. 48)

2- "During our conversation with Rumi (Mevlana), we enjoyed the music,
    The Gnostic (Rumi) became enraptured in the spiritual world that only an angel can discover". (Timurtaş, p. 167 and Nushiyya, p. XIV)

---

[1] Jahid Öztelli, Yunus Emre, Karaman Turizm Derneği, Ankara 1977.
[2] The best collection is by Prof. Timurtaş, Kültür Bakanlığı Yayınları, 380, 1989, Ankara.
[3] Abdulbaki, Risalat al-Nushiyya, Eskişehir Turizm No. I, Istanbul.

When Rumi passed away, Yunus remembered him with these words:

"Fakih Ahmed, Qutb al-Din, Sultan Seyyid Nejmeddin,
Mevlana Jelal al-Din, the world's great pole *(Qutub)*: where are they all?[1].

Even a superficial glance at Yunus' "*Divan*" shows that he has much in common with Rumi. We shall bring in some of his verses to uncover Rumi's ideas in the coming chapters. However, we give some verses here to introduce the poet's feelings and his way of thinking:

"Love is our preceptor *(Imam)* while the hearts are the congregation, Face of our Beloved is a shrine *(Qıbla)* where perpetual prayers are offered".
(Ahmed Kabaklı, Yunus Emre, p. 150)

"Listen friends love is but like the sun,
The heart without love is nothing but a piece of stone". (A. Kabaklı, p. 98)

"Thy love has taken myself from me,
I need Thee, but only Thee;
In Thy love, I burn day and night,
I need Thee but only Thee;
I am neither proud of my richness nor do I belittle my poverty,
I just keep on burning in Thy love;
I need Thee, but only Thee". (Timurtaş, vr. No. 294)

"Burning, burning, I drift and tread,
Love spattered my body with blood,
I am not in my senses nor mad,
Come, see what love has done to me,

Now and then like the winds I blow,
Now and then like the roads I go,
Now and then like floods I flow,
Come see what love has done to me."[2].

---

[1] Dr. Muhiddin Jelal Duru, Mevlana ve Yunus Emre, Türk Yurdu, No. 319 1966, p. 14 (This issue is on Yunus Emre).

[2] For this poem p. 162 and for others see Talat Halman, Indiana University, Turkish Studies 2, 1981.

In some verses of Rumi and Yunus there are great similarities. For example:

1- "O, water-wheel why do you moan?"
   "I have pains, therefore I do moan,
   They found me on hills and ripped off my limbs,
   That's the reason why I have to moan"[1].

These verses of Yunus reminds us of Rumi's reed song in which the reed cries for separation from its reedland.

2- "In case you ask about my nationality or religion,
   Lovers need not any of them,
   A lover is perished so what does he know about the duties of religion?".
   (Timurtaş, p. 12)

while Rumi says:

"The nation of love is separate from all the worlds,
Lovers have different nations and religions". (M. II, vr. 1770)

Yunus suggests seven ways that lead to God: 1- To regard all nations equal. 2- Self control (killing of egoism). 3- To eliminate of all worldly pleasures. 4- Indifference to the riches of this world. The rest, he says, he will tell only to those who come to visit him[2]. Rumi, nevertheless, discloses all the stages that lead to God without hesitation, which we shall try to explain here in the following chapters. Another outstanding difference between Rumi and Yunus is that Yunus directs his attention to nature, which he thinks is the phenomenon of God, while Rumi suggests seeing or trying to find God in a saint's heart.

To sum up, Rumi being at the capital of the Seljuk Empire had good relations with the royal family, but he did not ignore the public. He served as a link between the two communities and tried to bring them together around the love of God.

After this short study, we can assume that many orders or religious sects say more or less the same thing because Reality is one and unchangeable, and it is the ego of man that leads him into opposition, separation and hatred.

---

1 Yunus Emre Divanı, Istanbul Maarif Kütüphanesi, No. 38, p. 215.
2 Baki, Risala al-Nushiyya, p. 118.

یا حضرت مولانا قدس سره

CHAPTER III

Life and works of Rumi

1- Rumi's childhood:

Rumi's actual name was Jelal al-Din Muhammed and his titles are: *Mevlana* (Ar., our master), *Khudavendigar* (Per., the Lord), *Rumi* (Per., the Anatolian). In Turkey he is known simply as *Mevlana* while in Europe as Rumi. In India, Pakistan and Iran he is famous with these titles: *Mowlana-yi Rum*, *Mowlevi-yi Manevi* (the spiritual master) and sometimes as *Mollayı* or *Monlayı Rum*. Since he was born at Balkh (or at a small town called Wakhsh near Balkh)[1] in the year A.D. 1207, an epithet "*Balkhi* =from Balkh" is added to his name. In his lyrical poetry Rumi uses the pseudonym "*Khamush* =Silent"[2]. His mother's name was Mumine Khatun while his father was known as Muhammed Baha al-Din Veled Sultan ul-Ulama (the sultan of the learned).

As already seen in the previous chapters Rumi spent most of his childhood travelling, therefore he couldn't attend a school regularly. He received his early education from his father and other scholars who accompanied them to Karaman. Rumi also met many famous scholars on the way who might as well have taught the young boy.

One of Rumi's earliest teachers was Kemal al-Din Ebu al-Kasım Omar son of Adim at Aleppo, whom he met during his stay at the Halaviyye medrise[3]. After the death of his father, Rumi was sent to Damascus by Burhaneddin Tirmizi for his further studies where he stayed for about four years. On his way to Damascus he met Kemal al-Din again in 1233. At Damascus, Rumi studied Islamic history, the Koran, the Tradition of Muhammed, the Islamic canon and Arabic.

2- Rumi's Youth and Seyyid Burhaneddin Muhaqqaq-i Tirmizi:

Rumi's father sowed the spiritual seeds in Rumi, Burhaneddin watered them, when the plant began to grow and for the flowers to bloom the sun *(Shams-i Tebrizi)* came. Later the fruit, the Masnevi, was collected by Husameddin Chelebi. After Rumi had accomplished his worldly studies, he spent some years (about 9) with Burhaneddin Tirmizi *Sirdan* (knower of the Divine secrets). Burhaneddin was one of the most devoted disciples of Bahaeddin, who appeared in the dream of his disciple and said, "Burhaneddin, what are you doing here while my son has been left

---

1 Rumi's father lived there at that time.
2 Feruzanfer, p. 4 (Tur.).
3 Previously it was a church "for details see Feruzanfer, p. 54 (Tur.)".

uneducated in Konya?"[1]. Upon this dream he left Balkh and came to Konya in A.D. 1232. When he came to the city, Rumi was in Karaman, therefore, he sent a letter to him. Rumi came to Konya. Here are verses by Rumi's son Sultan Veled about their meeting:

"Said Seyyid that the Sheykh *(Bahaeddin)* is hidden within us,
In the manner that butter is concealed within the butter-milk,
He *(Rumi)* became his disciple by soul and surrendered to him,
And like a dead body fell in his presence,
When he died in his presence, Seyyid revived him again,
He made him happy forever by taking away his pain,
He then spent nine years in his company, and being with him,
He became in speech, manners and in states like him".

(Velednama, p. 196)

Burhaneddin sent him for mundane education to Damascus and upon his return he found that Rumi still needed his help for spiritual training. They were together again for some years. Finally, Burhaneddin gave his ecstatic states (spiritual stages) to Selah al-Din and his speech (power of speaking) to Rumi[2].

The influence of Burhaneddin's teaching is seen in Rumi's Masnevi. Some outstanding examples are as follows[3]:

I- "In case you oppose to your lower self (*nafs* =carnal ego), God reconciles with you; but if you reconcile with your lower self you enter a war with God" (Burhan, Maarif, Tur. p. 80).

II- "The more you deny your lower self, the more enlightened becomes your spirit" (Ibid, p. 81).

III- "If someone performs nothing but good deeds and yet fills his stomach with food and goes to sleep, he reaches nowhere; and if someone keeps on fasting and yet he is a little negligent in performing his religious worship, he can reach some goal. However, one should get used to fasting gradually without damaging one's health" (Ibid, p. 11).

---

1 Eflaki, 2/22.
2 Ibid, 2/15.
3 For other teachings see Seyyid Burhaneddin, Maarif, Feruzanfer, Chapkhanayı Danishgah, Tehran.

IV- "The essence of worshipping God and fasting is to melt the lower self. Otherwise, physical worshipping is for the body. A saint's selfness is nothing other than the heart (nothing other than the love of God)" (Ibid, p. 19) "and the book of God is in the heart of a saint" (Ibid, p. 50).

V- "People say that particular man is rich. Let us benefit from him by means of business. They have not seen the possession of God (if they saw it, they would totally depend on Him)" (Ibid, p. 32-33).

VI- "Turn your face towards the sun so that you may become warm and bright; the sun of the heart is divine knowledge" (Ibid, p. 30).

VII- "The real knowledge is the knowledge of the other world. When you gain that knowledge, you find this knowledge part of ignorance. The knowledge of this world is for a temporary period although it may be full of pleasures. The book of God is the heart of a saint, so sit in his shadow so that you may protect yourself from the worldly sun" (Ibid, p. 23 and 41).

VIII- "When you hear the words of people, they are the words of people but not of God. When you fail to hear God's words directly, then hear them from me because in me nothing dwells other than the will of God" (p. 41-42).

IX- "In order to attain an eternal soul instead of the ordinary soul possessed by everyone, clean your inner self, for your eternal soul is not yet mature enough; and when it becomes mature enough, you feel something added to your being. The eternal soul is matured in fact, but it needs to be mature within you. It is like the window that allows the sunlight to enter, in accordance with its size or like a pitcher that contains liquids according to its capacity. Nevertheless, when you become perfect you will notice that something happens in your inner being and no evil can affect you any more" (Ibid, p. 7).

X- "It is in the Koran or the Tradition of Muhammed that you can trust in this world, although there are some commentaries written on them. Those commentaries are in reality their (scholars') own production for a created being's idea never suits the will of the Creator, just as by copying a poet you cannot be called a poet" (Ibid, p. 48).

XI- "You haven't offered genuine prayers because God says in the Koran 'Prostrate and come closer'. It is a long time that you have been walking on this path... If your prayers cannot take you to Him, then they are not truthful prayers" (Ibid, p. 50).

XII- "One day the congregation asked Burhaneddin, 'Is there an end to the path to God or not?' He replied: The way has an end but the terminus has no end for there are two kinds of journeys. One leads to God and the other is with God Himself. The journey to God has an end but the journey with God has no end:

Up to the sea foot-prints lead,
But within the sea there are no foot-prints!". (Eflaki, 2/20)

Like Yunus Emre, Burhaneddin thinks that paradise has no value without the proximity of God:

While I am with you what do I care for bad or good,
When you are with me, what value has even Paradise?

Rumi uttered the following words and verses about his teacher Burhaneddin:

Be natural and stop changing from state to state,
Go and be like Burhaneddin-i Muhaqqaq and become the Light,
When you escape from selfness, you become wholly the proof of God
Once the slave in you disappears, you are the king of kings. (M. II/1319-1320)

"They said: Seyyid Burhaneddin discourses very well, but he quotes Sanai frequently in his discourse.

The master answered: What they say is quite true: the sun is excellent but it gives light. Is that a fault? Introducing Sanai's words casts light on that discourse". (Rumi's Discourses, p. 215)

Burhaneddin also taught Rumi's son Sultan Veled and disclosed some divine secrets to him[1]. In 1240 Burhaneddin left for Kayseri and there he became imam of a mosque. Rumi would visit him from time to time. He passed away at Kayseri in A.D. 1246[2].

3- The Sunrise:

When Burhaneddin went to Kayseri, Rumi was left without a spiritual master. It was in the year 1244 that Rumi met Shams al-Din Muhammed son of Ali son of Melek Dad who brought upheaval and turmoil into the life of our great mystic. Under his guidance Rumi gained divine knowledge from heart to heart, using no books. In him Rumi discovered the light of God[3]:

---

[1] Velednama, p. 179.
[2] Abdullah Satoğlu p. 37 and Dr. Refet Yinanç p. 68 say that there are signatures of Rumi and Burhaneddin on the endowment of Hisarcik Suyu of Qaykhusrev II A.D.1246. This proves that Burhaneddin was still alive when Shams came. "Rumi went to Kayseri upon the death of his master in 1246" the words of Sultan Veled are also correct.
[3] The verse:

شمس تبریزی که نور مطلق است   آفتاب است و ز انوار حق است

Does not exist in the original MS of the Masnevi G.

شمس تبریزی تو خورشیدی چه گویم مدح تو
صد زبان دارم چو تیغ اما بو صفت الکنست

"Shams you are the sun and how can I praise you? I have a hundred tongues, sharp like swords but when I want to praise you they stutter" (Divan, p. 186).

دم مزن تا بشنوی ز آن آفتاب   آنچ نآمد در کتاب و در خطاب

"Don't speak so that you may hear from that sun what is not found in books or in discourses" (M. III/1306).

آفتاب آمد دلیل آفتاب   گرد لیلت باید از وی رو متاب

"The proof of the sun (Shams) is the sun itself, if you want the proof don't turn your face from the sun" (M. I/116).

Shams acted as the antenna of Rumi, who received the waves of divine love via him.

خامش کزین کان و ازین گنج الهی   از مکسبه و کسیه و بازار رهیدیم
هین برین کن که چو خورشید بر آمد   از حارس و از دزد و شب تاریک رهیدم

"Be silent! because of the Divine treasure and mine we have freed ourselves of earning, of pocket and market. Listen, end your talk with these words: When the sun rises we get rid of a watchman, a thief and a dark night" (Divan, p. 568).

Shams had supernatural capabilities since his childhood. Even his father failed to understand him. This is what we learn from his discourses *(Makalat)* :

"In my childhood I was in a strange state. Nobody could understand it. Even my father failed to discover what I was undergoing. He used to say to me, 'You are not mad, then what is your religious path. You did not have any discipline or spiritual training to follow this kind of way'. I answered: You and I are like a hen with its chickens. My egg was of a duck that was bred under the hen with the other chickens. Now I can jump into the (spiritual) sea for I am an aquatic bird. If you belonged to my kind, you could also swim like me" (Makalat, Tur. p. 42).

We can deduce from his discourses that he learnt Arabic during his stay in Damascus. He had studied theology and many sects and orders of Islam[1]. Later he gave up studying and devoted himself only to God and His love for he believed that knowledge with no divine concept is useless (Makalat, Tur. p. 105).

He wanted Rumi to follow the same path. He travelled from town to town in search of a true lover of God and was called "*Shams-i perinde* = a flying sun" for this reason. He was once a disciple of Sheykh Ebu Bekir Tebrizi Sillabaf (a basket knitter) who like others failed to see the reality in him (Eflaki, Per. p. 680). It was only Rumi, who could discover his inner being. Shams had met many Sheykhs and had developed a way of recognising them. He left Sheykh Ebu Bekir for the following reason: "Sheykh Ebu Bekir's intoxication came from God, but he did not possess the sobriety that comes after that intoxication" (Makalat, Tur. p. 204).

Like Rumi, Shams was also once a teacher and taught theology and the meaning of the Koran (Makalat, Tur. 2/146). He had a good knowledge of Arabic and Persian literature, which is explicit from the style of his Makalat. His remarks on Omar Khayyam shows that once he was a good scholar (see Makalat, Per. p. 207). He gave up everything for love of God.

4- Marj ul-Bahrayn (The meeting of the two seas):

There are different stories told about the meeting of the two great lovers of God, "Rumi and Shams" at Konya on 23 October 1244[2] by Eflaki, Sipahsalar and other later writers. We shall give the account of only one part of the story (the dialogue that took place between the two) which is referred to by Shams himself in his Makalat (Ibid, Tur. p. 150):

Shams: Who is greater, Muhammed or Bayazid-i Bastami (d. H. 261/A.D. 874)?

Rumi: What kind of a question is this, of course Muhammed is greater than Bayazid.

Shams: But Muhammed says, "My Lord, my heart fills with lust worldly desires many times (seventy times) a day and I fail to pray to Thee the way Thou deserves" while Bayazid says, "I am free from all defects and there is nothing left in my body under this robe except God" What do you say about this?

Rumi: Muhammed would pass many stages everyday and would ask for God's

---

[1] For other details see Makalat, (Per.) p. 87-88; 243; 303.
[2] The date has been noted down by Rumi himself on the MS of the Makalat of Shams (Fatih margin f. 122b).

forgiveness for the previous stage in which he was (he would realise his backwardness). But Bayazid got lost because of the awe of each stage he tried to cover, thinking that it was the last one.

Upon this the two lovers of God embraced each other and went to the house of Selah al-Din Zerkub and there they talked about the divine secrets for about six months. When the spiritual meeting reached its peak, Rumi was changed. He began to perform *Sema* (ecstatic dances) in the company of music. Rumi's son Veled also joined them. We learn some realities about the two spiritual friends through Veled's versified work *"Velednama"*. His statements are more sincere and to the point than that of Eflaki:

"Shams led Rumi from the stage of a lover to the stage of a Beloved of God" (Velednama, Tur. p. 249 and Per. p. 197).

"Shams said to him: Although you have already discovered the secrets of your innerself listen! I am the innerself of innerself, secret of secrets, and light of lights" (Ibid, Per. p. 197).

"The Sheykh *(Rumi)* became a student in his presence. He studied many lessons. He had finished his education but began as a beginner again. Although he was a guide, yet he became a follower. Shams invited him to a strange world, which was seen neither by an Arab nor by a Turk" (Ibid, Per. p. 198).

Rumi invited Shams to his house saying:

"This house does not deserve you, but sincerely I love you,
Whatever I possess is yours, doubtless you are the true master".
(Ibid, Per. p. 42)

Veled continues to throw light upon their relationship. He says that it was like that of Khizr and Moses. Moses was a highly learned and knowledgeable prophet but he was told by God to meet a person *(Khizr)* whose knowledge was endless for he received it from God directly (see the Koran XVIII/60-82). Rumi received this kind of knowledge from Shams. In the story narrated in the Koran, Moses accompanies Khizr on a boat. When they are in the middle of the river, Khizr scuttles it. At this Moses loses his patience and begins to ask questions "Why" and "How"? Khizr has a fair reason for doing this which Moses does not know. He tells Moses, "As for the boat it belonged to certain men in dire want: they plied on the water. I but wished to render it unserviceable, for there was after them a certain king who seized every boat by force for warlike purposes". Here actually the boat stands for carnal greed and "scuttling it" means "to struggle with the ego". The pirates represent the people of this world who due to their own greed hinder one's spiritual development[1].

---

[1] For similar deduction see Muhiddin al-Arabi, Fusus al Hikem, M.E.B. 1952, Nuri Genc Osman, p. 287.

This story also tells us that knowledge is of three kinds:

First the ordinary knowledge that we learn in schools; second the further knowledge that depends on research and makes us discover new facts and it is the knowledge that is like the doorsteps to real knowledge; and third is Divine knowledge which cannot be gained but is given by God via the universal intellect.

It is the third kind of knowledge that Shams gave to Rumi. This is why Rumi, after meeting Shams, said, "These books are now worthless for me" (Makalat, Tur. 1/60).

Rumi's disciples grew jealous when they saw that Rumi had begun to adore a simple looking man and had given up his beautiful sermons. Rumi beside his regular prayers began to perform dances in the company of music that appeared to be non Islamic. They thought that their Sheykh, son of a great muslim imam, was going astray under the guidance of a stranger (Eflaki, 3/83 and Velednama, Per. p. 43). The political group of Akhi sect also joined the conspiracy. When the opposition reached its peak, Shams left Konya and went to Damascus.

Sultan Veled gives further details:

"They (his disciples) all saw some miracles of Rumi and in him they found many (spiritual) signs, They said:

He opened our eyes and made us see, and rendered our hearts knowledgeable like that of Avicenna,
Who then is this man *(Shams)* who has taken our Sheykh from us like a stream-water that carries away a husk,
Maybe he is a wizard who has cast a spell on our Sheykh and has tied him to himself,
He *(Shams)* neither belongs to a renowned family nor do we know from where he has come." (Velednama, Per. p. 43).

But Shams did not want to leave the man who appreciated him. If he had gone to Tebriz, he would have been given a great property, riches and high ranks (Makalat, Tur. p. 264), yet his desire was to be among those who could recognise his inner world. He wanted to stay more than two years in Konya but jealousy of the people prevented him from doing so.

Unable to bear the pain of separation, Rumi abandoned his disciples totally. This was an unexpected result (Velednama, Per. p. 46). The disciples requested their Sheykh to come out of his house but he refused to do so. They began to repent of their mistake and continued to plead with Rumi for his forgiveness. Finally, the soft hearted master came out and began to deliver his sermons again.

After some time, Rumi sent his son Sultan Veled to Damascus to fetch Shams. When he found Shams there he, too, like his father, began to be charmed by his melodious talk:

"Shams began to speak and cast pearls out of his mouth. He sowed new love in my heart and soul. He, by speaking about the Koran and the Traditions of Muhammed, disclosed some secrets. He made me fly in the sky without wings and enabled me to travel around the throne God *(Arsh)*. He drew the curtains of my eyes, so that the night became like the dawn. He made me reach the sea that had no boundaries; and in that place I found peace. I, like a bird freed from a trap, felt safe from all kinds of dangers" (Velednama, Per. p. 48).

Finally, Veled and Shams came back to Konya on 8th May, 1247 (Ibid, Per. p. 48). Rumi and Shams met again and their spiritual exchanges of feelings took place as before. Rumi uttered verses after verses in praise of Shams in the following manner:

شمس دین نقل و شراب و شمس دین چنگ و رباب

شمس دین خمر و خمار و شمس دین نور و نار

نی خماری کزوی آید اند و حزن و ندم

آن خمار شمس دین کزوی فزاید افتخار

(Shams is an appetizer and wine, he is a *Chang* and a *Rubab* (rebeck)[1]. He is a drink and intoxication, he is the light and the fire. He is not the kind of intoxication that brings forth sorrow, sadness, or repentance, but he is a kind of intoxication that increases self-respect and pride) (Divan, p. 427).

شمس تبریزی بر آمد در دلم بزمی نهاد

از شراب عشق گشتست این در و دیوار مست

(Shams has appeared and has held a meeting in my heart and due to the wine of (divine) love, these walls and doors have gone mad) (Divan, p. 189).

The disciples saw in Rumi a perfect scholar, a knowledgeable man, a perfect orator, but in Shams they saw nothing. He was a simple-looking man whose ideas were weird and non-traditional. His following statements would bewilder many simple followers of Islam even today:

---

[1] Names of some musical instruments.

"The microcosm is hidden in the creation of man and the macrocosm is this the outer universe. But for prophets the outer universe is the microcosm while the inner universe is the macrocosm" (Makalat, Tur. p. 27).

"They, the lovers of God, have gone beyond this world of existence. *Sema* (the ecstatic dance with music) takes them to the other world and makes them meet God. There is a kind of *sema* (physical dance) which is forbidden, but it is a sin to say that the ecstatic dance is also forbidden" (Ibid, p. 38).

"I have nothing to do with the common people for I have not come to this world for them. I put my finger on the nerves of those who guide people to God" (Makalat, Per. p. 25).

"Now, should I be a hypocrite or speak openly? Well! Rumi is the moon and I am the sun, therefore, people can look at the moon but they cannot look at the sun directly" (Ibid, p. 81).

"One tiny mote of dirt inside the spiritual being is a hundred thousand times worse than the outer dirt" (Makalat, Tur. p. 95).

"Those people are right not to understand my words for my words come from the side of God... Let me tell you something: These people like hypocrisy; and righteousness makes them uneasy. Once I said to a certain person, 'You are the most unique and the greatest man on earth. He, holding my hand, said, 'I was yearning to see you, but I was remiss in not finding you'. The year before when I told him the reality, he became angry and my enemy. It is not unusual. In order to live happily among these people you have to be a hypocrite but if you want to tell the truth you have to go to a desert or a mountain" (Ibid, p. 61).

"These *Imams* (the Muslim priests) do not understand even the exoteric meanings of the Koran, while to understand the esoteric meaning of the Koran one needs the light of belief and not the fire of show. If they had (the true) belief they would not seek the rank of Imam for wealth" (Ibid, Per. 66).

"*Ka'abe* is in the middle of the world, all turn their faces towards it. But when you take it away, you see that they are actually prostrating themselves (worshipping) each other's souls" (Makalat, Fatih MS f. 12 b).

"Thanks to my Lord, ever since the *Ka'aba*, the house of God, has been built, God has not made an abode there, but He did dwell in the houses of our hearts; and He has never come out of there" (Ibid, f. 24 b).

5- The Sunset:

The kind of ideas given above made the orthodox Muslims and the anti-government Turcomans rebel against Shams. Rumi's younger son Ala al-Din also joined them, for unlike his brother Veled, he was not able to discover the spiritual value of Shams. His superficial education of *fıkh* and *kelam* (theology) had put a bandage on his eyes. The opposition reached its peak and a group of Akhis killed Shams as narrated by Eflaki, though Sultan Veled and Sipehsalar say that Shams disappeared once and for all. However, after this event Rumi went to Damascus twice in search of his beloved Sheykh, but he did not find him again. His restlessness and yearning increased:

> "No one gave any news about him, nobody found his trace nor any scent,
> The Sheykh and the Mufti[1] changed into a poet, he became intoxicated although he was a religious man,
> Not by the wine that is made of grapes for an illuminated body drinks only the wine of Divine Light".
>
> (Velednama, Per. 56-57)
>
> "Day and night he performed ecstatic dances,
> On earth he became like a turning wheel,
> Not a single moment he passed without dance,
> He found no peace for a moment without dance".
>
> (Ibid, p. 56-57)

Shams was killed or he disappeared in the year A.D. 1247. He left behind his discourses *(Makalat)* which were collected by his disciples and Rumi[2].

6- Selah al-Din Zerkub (the goldsmith):

Rumi became disappointed when he failed to find Shams, his radio of divine broadcast. Soon he discovered that Shams had reflected through Selah al-Din. We have no detailed information about this pious man except for a few legendary stories written about him in the works of Eflaki and Sipahsalar. Sultan Veled's statements are more reliable and we start with them:

---

[1] Mufti = Adviser in religious law, who would expound the Koran and the tradition in court.
[2] Other works such as "Merquub al-Kulub" and "Sharh-i Asma-yi Husna" do not belong to him (see Baki, p. 102).

"Even the light of the sun blushed before his face,
Whosoever saw his face became a believer,
Rumi turned his face towards him and left others.
He (Rumi) said "The sun of the religion" as we called him,
Shams has come back, why were we asleep?
He has come again in another dress and form,
So that he may show his grace and walk majestically".

(Velednama, Per. p. 64)

Rumi did not desire to be a target of people's attention as a Sheykh, a position which may lure you into vain pride. He, therefore, would use someone else as a Sheykh i.e. Shams, Selah al-Din, and Husameddin. Rumi would surrender his lower self to them and would tell others to do the same. However, people preferred to be Rumi's disciple and they refused to accept any intermediary. Some also refused to obey Selah al-Din.

Selah al-Din was a pious man and had received his spiritual training from Burhaneddin as mentioned above. His name was Selah al-Din Feridun[1] and his father was a fisherman called Yağıbasan. Selah al-Din was born in a village, Kamile, near Konya (Baki, p. 105 and Eflaki, 5/4). When Burhaneddin went to Kayseri, Selah al-Din also accompanied him. After the death of his Sheykh, he came to Konya and opened a goldsmith's shop. It was at this shop that Rumi met him but in a strange way. As told by Eflaki, one day he was passing by the shop when he heard the tinkle of the small hammer of the workmen beating gold to flatten it, Rumi began to dance. Selah al-Din also joined him saying to his apprentice, "Don't stop, keep on beating the gold even if it is damaged", This was the first sema meeting of the two friends. They were together for ten years until Selah al-Din's death in A.D. 1258 (Eflaki, 5/31).

In the Masnevi we come across these verses about Selah al-Din:

"In case you want to see divine secrets openly, Selah al-Din has shown them all, he has made eyes wide open and clear. Any eye that attains his light is able to see the (mystical) poverty" (M. II, 1321-1322).

Rumi characterises Selah al-Din with the following words in his letters No. XXIX, XLV:

"The Sheykh of Sheykhs, the Juneyd of his time, having the breath of Christ and a walking light among people...".

---

[1] From Eflaki's heading chapter no. 5.

"The king of saints (abdals), soul of Gnostics, the trust of hearts..."
and in Rumi's Discourses we find these words:

"Sheykh Selah al-Din is the very root of spiritual joy; all the seas of joy are in him" (Ibid, p. 107).

Even the scene of Selah al-Din's funeral was peculiar in the eyes of the orthodox Muslims. It was accompanied by music, singers, and ecstatic dancers. The disciples were not allowed to cry according to the will of Selah al-Din, who believed that death was only an appointment with the Beloved (Eflaki, 5/31 and Velednama Tur. p. 142).

The Sheykh said, "For my funeral:
Call the drummers, tymbal beaters and the tambourine players,
March towards my grave dancing thus,
Happy, gay and intoxicated; with hands clapping,
So that people would know that the friends of God,
Go happy and smiling towards the place of meeting".
(Velednama, p. 112).

On this occasion Rumi uttered the following verses:

"O Selah al-Din, due to separation from you, the sky and earth have begun to cry,
Our heart has drowned in blood, our intellect and soul too have begun to cry,
Since none there can fill your place on this earth, both the worlds (existent and non-existent) have begun to cry". (Divan, p. 881)

7- Ziya ul-Haq Husameddin Hasan Chelebi son of Muhammed Akhi Turk:

His title was *"Chelebi"*, probably derived from the Turkish word *"Chalab* =God", and Chelebi would mean "a man of God". He was the first Mevlevi Sheykh who bore this title and later it became a custom to call all the Sheykhs (or vicegerents of Rumi) by this name. However, the definition given by Kazim Kadri[1] is more suitable for our purpose: "a poet, an author, a learned man, a gentleman or even a lord". Husameddin was a learned man, a scholar, and a man of letters. He belonged to the Akhi order before joining Rumi. His two small treatises give the impression that he was also a poet[2]. They contain several parables and verses. Here are a few examples:

---

[1] Türk Lugatı, vol. 2, p. 426.

[2] One of his treatises was discovered by my colleague Dr. Mikail Bayram in the collection entitled *"Risalet fi Ilmul Meshayikh"* at Koyunoğlu Museum here at Konya which has been either misplaced or sold away. The above examples have been taken from the same colleague's microfilms. The other treatise *"Tavur ul- vilaya"*, which was once seen by the same scholar, has not been found.

سیمرغ کوه قاف مقام قلندری   جای قلندرست و قلندر ازو بری

"The place of a *dervish* (qalander) is the Simurgh of the Mount Kaf, yet the dervish is free from that, as well".

(Mt. *Kaf* =unity, colourlessness; *Simurgh* =a perfect man. A qalander is beyond all physical bounds).

"They said to the musk, 'You have only one defect in you and that is that you smell to all those whose company you bear'. The musk said: I do not care whose company I bear, but I do care for that what I am (and, therefore, I perform my duty of smelling)" (f. 338 a).

فلك یك نقطه از كلك كمالش   جهان یك غنچه از باغ جمالش

"The sky (universe) is only a dot of the pen of His perfection, and this world is only a bud of His garden of Beauty" (f. 332 a).

The above examples are enough to prove that Husameddin was a highly learned man and that in his later life he devoted his knowledge to the Masnevi of his master.

Rumi wrote the six volumes of the Masnevi by his encouragement and assistance, as Rumi says:

"Come along, Ziya al-Haq Husameddin, because without you nothing grows out of this saltish land (my humble being)" (M. II, 2282).

Following is the summary of how the Masnevi began to be written (for other details see Eflaki, 6/3):

"One day Husameddin said to Rumi, "Sir, if you write a work like that of Sheykh Hekim Sanai's "*Ilahinama*" and in the metre of Feriduddin Attar's "*Mantik Uttair*", it will remain as a living memory among the coming generation and will keep on soothing lovers of God and the distressed. At this request, Rumi took the first eighteen verses out of his turban and said, "Before this idea came to you the most merciful God had already inspired me to write a book of the kind".

The same incident has been referred to by Rumi in fourth volume of his Masnevi:

"O Ziya ul-Haq (the radiance of God) Husameddin you are he through whose light the Masnevi has exceeded the light of the moon. O you in whom hopes are placed, your high endeavour is drawing this work God knows to where.

You have tied the neck of the Masnevi (with a rope) and are drawing it in the direction which only you know.

Since you have been the catalyst of this work, and if this work grows in size, it will be you who have made it grow" (M. I-V vol. 4).

No sooner did the first volume of the Masnevi come to an end, Husameddin's wife passed away. Husameddin could no more assist Rumi, who patiently waited for him to return for about two years:

"This Masnevi has been delayed for some time: an interval was required in order that the blood may change into milk. Listen well! to my words. Blood does not change into sweet milk until your fortune gives birth to a new baby.

When the Light of God, Husameddin drew the reins (of his spirit) back from the zenith of Heaven,

And after he had ascended to (spiritual) realities without his life-giving spring, the buds were unburst in my heart" (M. II, I-4).

Rumi continues:

"Similarly my purpose of writing this Masnevi is you, Husameddin, the radiance of God; the whole Masnevi, with its branches and roots is yours because you have agreed to write it. Since you have planted the bough, then do water it; as you have given it freedom to grow then undo the knots" (M. VI, 754, 755, 757).

Rumi even wanted to name his Masnevi *"Husamnama"* (the book of Husam):

"It is because of the interest of a knowledgeable man like you that this book of Husam has come into circulation all over the world" (M. VI, 2).

Quite often Rumi would recite new verses all night to Husameddin who would note them down and read them back to the Master for correction (Eflaki, 6/3).

Husameddin did not hold to any definite nationality and used to say, "I slept as a Kurd at night and woke up as an Arab in the morning" (Eflaki, the heading 6/1).

The same idea is noticeable in the works of Rumi, who prefers love of God and people regardless of nationality.

Rumi trusted Husameddin in every respect. He gave all his income to him and Husam would distribute it among his family and disciples justly. After the death of Rumi, Husameddin acted as his viceregent for ten years (Eflaki, 6/25) until his own death in the year 1284.

8- Rumi's death:

When Rumi was about to finish the sixth volume of his Masnevi, he fell weak and ill. He suffered from continual fevers. One day Sheykh Sadreddin came to visit Rumi and prayed for his health. Rumi said, "After this time, may God grant you health for there has been left nothing but a thin skirt between the lover (me) and the Beloved (God)". He then recited these verses of his Masnevi:

"He said (to himself): Though his raiment was of silk and cloth of shushtars, his unscreened embrace is sweeter, I am denuded of my body, and he of (the veil of) phantasy; I am advancing successfully in the consummation of union" (Nicholson, M. VI 4618-4619 and Eflaki, 3/569).

After Sadreddin left, Rumi uttered his last ghazal, a portion of which we give here:

"Go and put your head on the pillow and set me free,
Leave me alone for I have been used to wandering at nights
(and have been lost in this kind of habit),
We are from morn till night entrapped in the waves of love,
Come, either forgive us or continue to do us injustice,
The king of beautiful faces lacks faithfulness,
O you pale-faced lover be patient and be loyal,
I have the kind of disease that has no remedy but death,
How dare then I say that please find me a cure,
Last night I saw an old man in the street of love,
Who pointed at me and said "Come to our side".
(Divan, p. 764 and Eflaki, 3/580)

Rumi passed away on 17 December 1273. The whole town of (Konya) burned with the grief of losing the fountain of spiritual water which served to quench their thirst for esoteric knowledge. This is the statement of Eflaki about the day:

"The Christians, Jews, Arabs, Turks, all nations and religious leaders as well as rulers were there to join his funeral. All went in front of the funeral holding their books in their hands according to their own customs. They were reciting verses from the Psalms, the Old Testament and the New Testament, and were crying. The Muslims could not stop them even by force. Finally, the king and master Pervane heard this. He called the religious leaders and asked them, "What involvement do you have in this event?" They answered: He, the king of religions, was our leader and guide. We learnt about Christ, Moses, and other prophets from his clear statements; and we saw in him all the characteristics of the prophets we read about in our books. You Muslims regard him as the prophet of the day, we think of him as the Moses or Christ of the day. We are a thousand times more obedient and better followers of Rumi than you are. As he (Rumi) said:

"Seventy two (many) nations heard secrets from us, we are like the *Ney* (flute) that produces hundreds of sounds from one key" (Eflaki, 3/580).

For Rumi, death was like a wedding-night *(Shab-i Arus)* when a lover meets his beloved. Rumi suggests the mourners not be sorry for his death, because love can never be buried:

"When you see my funeral, don't say 'What a separation?'
It is time for me to visit and meet the Beloved,
Since you have seen my descent, then do see my rising,
Why complain about the setting of the moon and the sun?
Which seed that went under the earth failed to grow up again?
Then why should you feel doubt about this seed (the corpse)?".
(Divan, p. 367)

Pervane, the Georgian Lady, and Alameddin Kayseri organised a fund for the building of Rumi's tomb. About 130.000 dirhams were spent for the purpose. Alameddin appointed Badreddin Tebrizi and Selimoğlu Abdulvahid for the construction of the building including the famous Green Dome *(Qubbat ul-Khazra)*. It is believed that the construction began in the Spring of A.D.1274 and was finished before the winter of the same year. The building was later expanded, restored, or reconstructed from time to time until it arrived at the present shape. Today it is a museum for those who think it so, but it is a lover's shrine *(Kaaba-yi Ushaq)* for those who come here to pay their spiritual tributes. The following lines of Rumi inscribed on his wooden sarcophagus, now placed on his father's grave, give the message that even the physical structure of his grave is full of life:

"If wheat is grown on the clay of my grave, and if you bake bread of it; your intoxication will increase, the dough and the baker will go mad and the oven will also begin to recite verses out of madness. When you pay a visit to my tomb, it will seem to be dancing for God has created me out of the wine of love and I am still the same love even if death may crush me" (For full Ghazal see Divan, Feruzan, vol. 2/p. 83).

9- Rumi's family:

Rumi married twice. At Karaman he married Gevher Khatun, the daughter of Khuaja Sharaf al-Din Samarqandi *(Lala)*. She bore him two children (perhaps twin brothers), Sultan Veled and Muhammed Ala al-Din in A.D. 1226[1]. After the death of his first wife, he married Kira Khatun, who bore two children, Emir Muzafferuddin Amil Chelebi a boy, and a daughter Melike Khatun. Emir Shams al-Din Yahya was the step son of Rumi. Some writers[2] think that Kira Khatun was a Christian because of her Greek title "*Kira* =a lady". However, this Greek word was used as a title among the Turks of Central Asia, as is "*Efendi* =a gentleman" (from the Greek root "*efendidus*" used today).

10- Rumi's works:

These include: I- The Masnevi II- The Discourses (Fihi ma fih) III- Divan-i Shams (A collection of his lyrical poems) IV- His letters V- Mejalis-i Seba (seven sessions).

I- The Masnevi:

It is Rumi's magnum opus which brought him fame, a vast versified work in six volumes. Each hemistich rhymes with the other and forms a distich or a couplet that can be called "Double Rhyme" aa, bb, cc, and so on. Each hemistich is based on a fixed prosodical metre called "*ramal*"[3] i.e.: $- \cdot - - / - \cdot - - / - \cdot -$, and in English it is equivalent to the sounds: (dum da dum dum/dum da dum dum/dum da dum). All the verses of the six volumes have the same rhyme scheme throughout, and are 51236 in number. In order to appreciate the real melody of the verses one should listen to them in Persian.

Rumi began to write his Masnevi from the year 1258 and continued to write it until he fell sick in the year 1273; and a part of the sixth volume has been left incomplete.

When the Masnevi began to spread all over the eastern world, in Iran, India (Pakistan), Afghanistan, the MSs also began to vary. Fortunately, the oldest MS of the Masnevi has been kept safely in the Mevlana Museum in Konya. It was finished and illustrated five years after the death of the author in 1278. The changes took place because of scribes' mistakes or because of snobbish scholars who did not understand the actual meaning. Some Indian dervishes even added new verses under

---

1 Since Eflaki gives the same year of their birth.
2 For instance see Vitray Meyerovitch, p. 33.
3 For details see Blochmann, Prosody of the Persians, Amsterdam, 1970, p. 38.

the flow of spiritual inspiration. Before we have a look at some important changes, it is better to divide the MSs into two major groups:

a) The Turkish Group:

This group is less damaged because quite a number of the scribes kept close to the copies written from the original ones. The first copy, which was written and corrected in the presence of the author is now lost but, as stated above, the copy available at the Museum (registered under No. 51 and marked as "G" by Nicholson) is the second copy of the first one. Its colophon is first-hand proof:

"This book has been illuminated and decorated by Mukhlis son of Abdullah from India. The Masnevi that shows the right path has been completed, thanks to God, by Muhammed b. Abdullah al-Konevi (from Konya) al-Veledi (the disciple of Sultan Veled), who being a humble slave needs God's mercy. Peace be also on Muhammed, who is the best of prophets and the created. Muhammed (the scribe) has copied this MS from the original accurate and illuminated copy that had been corrected and put in order in the presence of the Sheykh, the author, may God sanctify his secrets, during some meetings which were also attended by the vicegerent (Husameddin) and the successor (Sultan Veled). May God perpetuate their beings that are a bounty of God for the Muslims. This book was completed in the month of Rejeb (the month when God does not give heed to the bad words of His slaves) of the year 677 of Hijra.

"May God bless those who read this book, try to understand it, make use of it, or by copying it dedicate it to others' use".

It is evident from the above lines that while Husameddin read out the Masnevi to Mevlana for corrections, Sultan Veled also took some notes.

The "G" MS is a large, beautifully illuminated copy 49.7 x 73.2 cm. in size. Corrections in red ink, probably by Veled, are visible. The first foliae (five or four) of each volume have carpet designs. It is on the seventh folia that the Masnevi begins with the following lines:

بشنو این نی چون شکایت می کند   از جدائیها حکایت می کند
کز نیستان تا مرا ببریده اند   در نفیرم مرد و زن نالیده اند

The accuracy of the first line can be further proved by the line given by Eflaki in his work (Eflaki, Per. 3-4):

بشنو این نی چون **شکایت** می‌کند از جدائیها **حکایت** می‌کند

"Listen to this Nay while it complains, It tells the story of separation".

Almost all the Indian and Iranian copies give the two verses in the following manner:

بشنو از نی چون **حکایت** می‌کند از جدائیها **شکایت** می‌کند
کز نیستان تا مرا ببریده‌اند از نفیرم مرد و زن نالیده‌اند

"Listen to a (certain) nay while it tells a story; and complains about the separation".

There is another MS available at Yusuf Agha Library registered under No. 5547 and 20.50 x 30.50 in size. This MS was also copied from the two main sources, the MS of Husam and the MS of Veled. From the notes in its margin, "*Husam*" and "*Veledi*" it is clear that after the death of Rumi, Veled and Husam disagreed about several verses. The title of the scribe "*al-Veledi*" indicates that there were already two groups of disciples -those who joined Sultan Veled were called "*Veledis*" and those who joined Husameddin were called "*Husamis*". However, there was no enmity between the two groups.

The interesting point is that the scribe of the Yusuf Agha MS ("Y") had an opportunity to see the two main copies and gives the variations of both (of Husam and Veledi) and the meanings of certain words in the margin of the MS.

In this respect, "Y" is the first critical edition and commentary of the Masnevi written in the 13th. century. It was later dedicated to the use of Rumi's mother's Dergah Library at Karaman in the year A.D. 1647 by Yahya Efendi.

The scribe of "Y", for instance gives this verse in the margin and says that it belongs to the MS of Husam:

می‌نمود آن مرغ را صدگون شگفت تا که باشد کاندر آن آید بگفت

صدگون شگفت has also the form هرگون نهفت in the "G" which has been corrected as صدگونه شگفت (M. I, 258).

These three verses (after No. 1514):

چون ز عمران رسول این را شنید   روشنی در دلش آمد پدید
محو شد پیش سوال و هم جواب   گشته فارغ از خطا و از صواب
اصل را در یافت بگزشت از فروع   بهر حکمت کرد در پرسش شروع

have been copied from the Veledi MS and placed in the margin of "Y". In "G" these have been placed in the rubric by some later hand. They are missing in the critical edition of Nicholson.

Three couplets about Selah al-Din No. 1321 to 1323 of vol. II have been excluded by Husameddin but are put back by Sultan Veled in the margin of "G" (f. 123).

After our study, we have come to the following conclusion: there was an illuminated original copy of the Masnevi based upon the notes or papers *(qirtas)* of Husameddin and it was corrected in the company of the three, Rumi, Husameddin and Sultan Veled, as mentioned in the colophon of "G". Since the original papers and the first copy do not exist today, "G" is the most authentic as Nicholson and the Turkish scholar Abdulbaki agree. The presence of "Y" has given us a further opportunity to compare it with "G", to examine the variants of earlier MSs that were produced by Husam and Sultan Veled. It was, however, after Ibrahim Gulsheni (d. A.D. 1533) that some changes began to enter the Masnevi.

b) The Iranian and Indian Group:

Ibrahim Gulsheni was born at Diyarbakir and later he was sent to Azerbayjan by Omar Rushan as his representative. When Shah Ismail the Safevi proclaimed the Shi'a creed, the established religion of Persia, he left Azerbayjan and went to Cairo. He became a very popular Sheykh in the Muhammedan world. In A.D. 1528 he visited Istanbul on the invitation of Sultan Suleyman (see IA, 4/835 and Mr. Gibb II/374). He had won great favour with the Mevlevis because it was believed that Rumi, Rushani, and Gulsheni had some kind of spiritual link. Gulsheni wrote *"Ma'navi"* in verse which is the summary of Rumi's Masnevi. New copies of Rumi's Masnevi were made for Iran and India in his time. His followers changed or added new verses to the work. There are two MSs in Yusuf Agha Library that belong to Al-Vazh and Seyyid Hasan Gulsheni scribed in the years A.D. 1525 and 1618 respectively. They have undergone some changes. The first two verses are:

بشنو از نی چون حکایت می‌کند   از جدائیها شکایت می‌کند
کز نیستان تا مرا ببریده‌اند   از نفیرم مرد و زن نالیده‌اند

This is how the Iranian and Indian copies generally begin. It is impossible to give all the variations and additions in this book. A separate critical edition may be prepared later. Nevertheless, the most important verses selected for the book "The Masnevi's Essence" have been corrected in the light of the "G" and "Y" before giving their literary and literal translation. Here we shall give a few examples of the changes that present Rumi's personality in a different light:

1- شمس تبریزی که نور مطلق است   آفتاب است و ز انوار حق است

(Shams-i Tebrizi is the light of the Omnipotent, he is the sun and a part of the Divine Light).

2- یك زمانی صحبت با اولیا   بهتر از صد ساله طاعت بی ریا

(A conversation with a Saint for short while, is better than the submission (prayers) of a hundred years) (added after the 1/719).

3- صحبت صالح ترا صالح کند   صحبت طالح ترا طالح کند

(The company of a pious man makes you pious; the company of a mean person makes you mean) (after 1/727).

4- از دهانت چون بر آید حمد حق   مرغ جنت سازدش رب الفلق

(When the praise of God comes out of your mouth, God of heavens makes you a bird of paradise) (after 1/865).

5- گر زبان گوید اسرار نهان   آتش افزوزد بسوزد این جهان

(If your tongue utters the hidden secrets, fire kindles and burns this world) (after 1/1479).

6- هست دنیا جاهل و جاهل پرست   عاقل آن باشد کزین جاهل برست

(This world is ignorant and worships the ignorant. Wise is the man who escapes the ignorant) (after II/ 333, actually three verses).

7- هر که چیزی جست بیشك یافت او   چو بجید اندر طلب بشتافت او
عاقبت جوینده یابنده بود   چونکه در خدمت شتابنده بود

(He who seeks something undoubtedly finds it; but he has to run after it and strive for it seriously. In the end, a seeker is a finder, because he runs around in its service) (after 3/1449, seven verses added).

There are other verses that are well-known, yet require correction:

تو برای وصل کردن آمدی   یا برای فصل کردن آمدی

(Have you "Moses" come to this world to bring people together or to separate them?) (G).

تو برای وصل کردن آمدی   نه برای فضل کردن آمدی

(Indian text differ slightly: for instance see MM. II/ p. 173).

تو برای وصل کردن آمدی   یا خود از بهر بریدن آمدی

(Didst thou come (as a prophet) to unite, or didst thou come to sever?) (Nicholson, II/1751).

II- The Divan of Shams-i Tebrizi:

A collection of Rumi's lyrical poetry (of ghazals) and quatrains in which Rumi's main idea is love of God via Shams, Selah al-Din, and Husameddin. No definite number for the verses can be given because the MSs vary in number and form. The Divan is in a worse situation than the Masnevi because no original copy corrected by the first authorities is available. The oldest copy goes back as far as fifty years after the death of the author. About twenty per cent of the poems belong to other poets (Feruzanfer also thinks so, see Mevlana Jelal al-Din, Tur. p. 200-203). Rumi in his poems generally uses the pseudonym "*Khamush* =silent, or even" be silent "*Khamush kun*", as already mentioned in an earlier chapter. Poems with these pseudonyms may be considered by Rumi. The poems that end with Shams, Shams al-Din, Shams ul-Haq and so on should be treated with care. Needless to say if the Masnevi of which the original copies were available changed considerably in the hands of the scribes and zealous scholars, how could the Divan be saved? Many ghazals chosen as examples by some recent writers on Rumi, do not exist even in the critical edition of Feruzanfer. Dr. Afzal Iqbal's is one example. The ghazal he gives on page 110 of his book does not appear in any authentic MS:

"What is to be done, O Muslim? for I do not recognise myself,
I am neither Christian, nor Jew, nor Gabr, nor Muslim".

Unless a further critical edition of the "Divan" is made, because Feruzanfer's edition does not deal with the authenticity of the content but rather with comparison of the variants, any ghazal or rubai taken from the Divan should be carefully considered.

III- Fihi ma fih: (What is not there is here in this book)

Whatever mystic or religious problems Rumi did not disclose in details in his Masnevi are discussed in this work. Its style is after his father's work "Ma'arif" and is better organised. It was not so popular in India as his Masnevi for famous Indian scholar Shibli Nu'mani considers it a part of Rumi's letters[1]. Fihi ma fih has been translated into English by A. J. Arberry under the title "Discourses of Rumi" and into Turkish by Abdulbaki.

IV- Mektubat-i Mevlana: (The letters of Rumi)

A collection of Rumi's 150 letters of recommendation written to various governmental authorities. As literature they may have less value than the other works but historically they are important documents. The letters have been translated into Turkish by Abdulbaki and into Urdu by Dr. Muhammed Riyaz.

V- Mejalis-i Saba: (Seven Sessions)

Lectures of Rumi delivered in seven sessions. He delivered these lectures before "Fihi ma fih". A Turkish translation of this work has been made by Abdulbaki.

Other works attributed to Rumi, such as the seventh volume of the Masnevi, "Khabnama" (attributed by Eva de Vitray Meyerovitch)[2], "Tarashnama", "Ashqnama", "Risali-yi Afaaq u Enfus", "Risale-yi Akqaid" do not belong to Rumi[3].

---

[1] Shibli Nu'mani, Savanih-i Mevlana Rum, Mejalisi Taraki-yi Edeb, Club Road Lahore, p. 67.
[2] Rumi and Sufism, p. 70.
[3] For other details see Abdulbaki, Mevlana, p. 272.

CHAPTER IV

The First Eighteen Verses of Rumi's Masnevi

The first eighteen verses of Rumi's Masnevi are like an entrance to his great villa where he welcomes his guests and gives them the keys of the rooms without which the guests might get lost and falter in the corridors of his grand villa -the Masnevi. If you intend to enter the building, you should surrender humbly to the spiritual entertainment he offers at the entrance.

The first eighteen verses are the summary of the six volumes of the Masnevi. The verses begin with ب = "B" and end with م = "M", which are the first and the last letters of *"Bismillahirrahmanirrahim"* = "In the name of God, Most Gracious, Most Merciful" with which each sura of the Koran begins. It was customary among the Muslim writers to open their works with a canto in praise of God, with a eulogy to the prophet Muhammed and a panegyric on a great man and so on, but Rumi's Masnevi begins with the eighteen verses directly. Rumi wrote the verses himself. The rest of the verses he narrated to Husameddin in a tranced state.

The language of the Masnevi, including the first eighteen verses, is like the Koran based on symbolism, the units of which are metaphorical expressions, apostrophes, and personifications. It is, therefore, in many cases hard to give an accurate interpretation of Rumi's symbols without consulting various commentaries written by prominent scholars. These commentaries can be divided into the following four groups:

1- The Turkish Group:

The leading work in this group is that of Ismail Rusukhi Dede Ankaravi (d. A.D. 1631), generally known simply as Ankaravi. Many commentaries are influenced by this work, but Tahir'ul Mevlevi's (T), which is incomplete, and Abdulbaki's commentaries in the Modern Turkish are thought provoking. The basic works are:

I- Fatih ul-Abiyat, Ismail Ankaravi, Bulaq Egypt 1855 =Ankaravi.

II- Mesnevi Tercümesi ve Şerhi, Abdulbaki Gölpınarlı, Inkilap ve Aka, Istanbul 1981 =Baki.

2- The Indian Group:

From this group we have chosen the following commentaries that are based on the interpretations of particular spiritual masters or other commentaries:

I- Masnevi-yi Manevi, Muhammed Rahmatullah, Kanpur 1921 (from Persian to Persian) =Kan.

II- Masnevi-yi Mavlavi-yi Rum, Bahr'ul Ulum, Novolkishor 1877 (from Persian to Persian) =Bahr.

III- Miftah al-Ulum, Muhammad Nazir Mavlavi, Lahore (in Urdu) =Mift.

IV- Masnevi-yi Manevi, Kadi Sejjad Huseyin, Alfeysal, Lahore (the latest publication in Urdu).

3- The Iranian Group:

I- Sherh-i Masnevi Sharif, Bedi uz-Zaman Feruzanfer, Intisharat-i Danishgah-i Tehran (incomplete) =Feruzan.

II- Tefsir u Nakd u Tahlil-i Masnevi-yi Jelal al-Din Muhammad Mevlevi, Muhammad Taki Jafer, Intisharat-i Islami =Taki.

4- The European Group:

The Mathnavi of Jalalu'ddin Rumi, Reynold A. Nicholson, Luzac and Co.=Nich.

The system used here for the translation and the commentary:

The selection of the verses from the six volumes has been carried out according to a definite plan deduced from the first eighteen verses. Stories and other minor verses (that provide detail for the major idea) have been excluded. The collection of Yusuf Sinachak and Shahidi have also been consulted.

First, the text of the verse itself has been corrected, where necessary, under the guidance of the "G" and "Y" MSs (a) gives the literal meaning of the verse and (b) the literary meaning and a commentary, which is further compared with the other commentaries listed above. Since it is claimed that the Masnevi is nothing but the Koran as stated by Molla Abdurrahman Jami (A.D. 1414-1492):

« مثنوى مولوى معنوى   هست قرآن در زبان پهلوى »

(The Masnevi of the spiritual master Rumi is the Koran in the Persian language). The related verses of the Koran have been given where relevant, verses of the Bible, the Avesta, the Bhagwat Gita and so on, have also been given in support of the idea for it is the water (essence) that should be the target of a thirsty man.

Where other information is needed (c) is added to the commentary.

The First Eighteen Verses:

1- بشنو این نی چون شکایت می‌کند   از جدائیها حکایت می‌کند

a- این نی : Y + G / از نی : MM + Mift.   b- شکایت : Y + G / حکایت : MM + Mift.

a) Listen to this *Ney* (the reed-flute) that is complaining and narrating the story of separation.

b) The Ney is the body of man and the breath blown into it is the spirit (breath of God). This refers to the Koranic verse: Behold, thy Lord said to the angels, "I am about to create man, from sounding (dry) clay..." and "when I have fashioned him (man) and breathed into him My spirit fall ye down in obeisance unto him (the Koran, XV/28 and 29); and "for God has poured His love into our hearts by means of the Holy Spirit who is God's gift to us" (the Bible, Romans 4/5).

The Ney is made from the reed and is perforated. So is the body of man from clay. It also has holes -the ear, nose, mouth and so on. When the breath of God begins to feel encaged in the human body, it starts lamenting in the manner of the Ney and wants to return to its Source. This is the state in which Rumi himself was as he says, "This Ney" pointing to himself. He continues:

2- کز نیستان تا مرا ببریده‌اند   در نفیرم مرد و زن نالیده‌اند

b- از نفیرم : Y + G / در نفیرم : MM + Mift.

a) Ever since they (the people) have plucked me from the reedland, my laments have driven men and women to deep sorrow.

b) The "reed-land" here means the original place of man where he dwelt before his coming to earth. It was in the vicinity of his Beloved God (Paradise) where he was watered with His spiritual light as was the reed of the Ney once watered by a stream or a lake. Since man is deprived of the vicinity of God (see Mift. 1/24) and is separated like the piece of reed from its origin, he too laments and cries in every sort of company (of men or women). He can no more be green and fresh (attain eternal joy) unless he succeeds in obtaining spiritual water.

c) The *"Ney"* here does not necessarily mean a "perfect man" as most of the commentaries say, because being at the higher spiritual stage (being naught in God), a perfect man is already with God and he is free from any worldly worries as the Koran says: "Behold verily, with the friends of God there is no fear nor shall they grieve" (X/62-63). It can mean any man who is in love with God and has begun to feel abandonment. Moreover, it is not used here in its ordinary meaning of "*a Ney = a flute*" as Ahmed Atesh says (see his article p. 48).

It means the body of a man and God's Breath blown into it.

d) Many other mystic poets have said similar things. Here are some examples:

مینالم زار از آنکه چون نی   بی مغز شده است استخوانم

(I cry and lament like the Ney, because my bones have become empty and dry in the manner of the Ney) (Emir Khusrau Dehlevi, A.D. 1252-1325).

خرم آن روز کزین منزل ویران بروم   راحت جان طلبم وز پی جانان بروم

(What a happy day will be that day when I shall leave this deserted abode. I desire peace for my soul and shall go there where my Beloved lives) (Hafiz-ı Shirazi).

The reed-land also reminds us of the story of Adam and Eve who were expelled from Paradise (the Koran II/36-39 and the Bible, Gen. 3.22) and were deprived of the vicinity of God and direct love.

3- سینه خواهم شرحه شرحه از فراق   تا بگویم شرح درد اشتیاق

a) I want someone with chest (heart) pierced by abandonment so that I may tell him about the pain of my longing.

b) The Ney (actually Rumi or a lover of God) says that it wants to express its unbearable pains caused by the separation from the Beloved to someone who has a heart full of pain like that of its own. Those who have no feeling for love will not be able to appreciate the grief brought about by the separation.

c) For similar explanation, see Feruzanfer p. 10-11. However, other irrelevant long details of Ankaravi and Taki have been excluded.

4- هر کسی کو دور ماند از اصل خویش   باز جوید روزگار وصل خویش

a) He who falls aloof from his origin seeks an opportunity to find it again.

b) Rumi here gives a general rule that everything in the universe tends towards its origin. For instance, the physical elements of a human body desire to go back to the earth but the spirit of man wants to rejoin its Centre; and like the dry piece of reed in the shape of the Ney yearns for its reed-land. The breath blown into the Ney also wants to go back to its blower. Since the spirit is the breath of God, it wants to go back to Him. The farther the spirit falls from its Origin, the more it loses the attraction of the Centre.

5- من بهر جمیتی نالان شدم   جفت بد حالان و خوش حالان شدم

a) I am mournful in all sorts of company and am sought by the happy as well as by the unhappy.

b) The company of the Ney can be enjoyed both by the happy and the unhappy (the wretched). Here the happy are those who have attained the Divine Love and are preoccupied with it; and the unhappy are those who indulge in the temporary pleasures of the world and who are prisoners of shapes and forms. They listen to the Ney for physical entertainment but the former listen to it because they hear the voice of their Beloved.

6- هر کسی از ظن خود شد یار من   از درون من نجست اسرار من

a) Everyone becomes friends with me according to his faculty of perception and many do not seek my inner secret.

b) The "inner secret" here means the spiritual states that a Sufi experiences. Many failed to discover the states Rumi passed through, especially under the guidance of Shams, and they judged Rumi and his master just by looking at their outer appearance. Some orthodox Muslims thought that music, dance *(the Sema)*, and even poetry were non-Islamic elements.

Addressing them, Rumi says:

7- سر من از ناله ٔ من دور نیست   لیک چشم و گوش را آن نور نیست

a) My secret is not distant from my cries, but physical eyes and ears do not possess the light (to see it).

b) God says in the Koran, "Those who reject our signs (our symptoms in each phenomenon) are deaf and dumb and they are in the midst of darkness" (the Koran VI/39). "The best kind of knowledge is gained when a man may discover God by means of His signs...

The Friend is closer to me than myself,
And strange it is that I am so far from him!". (Bhagawat Gita, Per., p. 79)

Thus, the spirit of man is not concealed from the body but not all physical ears and eyes can see it. In order to see what lies behind a physical object, one needs spiritual intelligence and illumination.

Rumi adds:

8- تن ز جان و جان ز تن مستور نیست   لیك كس را دید جان دستور نیست

a) (In fact) the body from the spirit and the spirit from the body are not concealed, yet none (not many) are allowed to see it.

b) The spirit that is connected with the Divine World is not far from the human body. The spirit and the body can recognise each other, but men may not be able to discern it. Hafiz-ı Shirazi writes these lines:

میان عاشق و معشوق هیچ حایل نیست
تو خود حجاب خودی حافظ از میان برخیز

"Between the lover (man) and the Beloved there is no obstacle, but you (Hafiz) are yourself a curtain in between; so raise the curtain".

Yunus says a similar thing in a much simpler way:

"Don't ask me about myself, I no longer exist in me,
It is Someone Else who is concealed within me".

Anything too close to a man is undiscernible, as is the aqueous humour of the eye. The Koran says that God is closer to you than your jugular vein. It is, perhaps, the reason that we cannot see Him clearly although some can feel Him within themselves. The Bible also illuminates the same idea, "A person is born physically of human parents, but he is born spiritually of the Spirit" (John 3/6-7). As a matter of fact many religious books reveal the same Reality but in different words and languages tinged with the egoistic traits invented by man. Our goal should be to try to discover that Concealed One who is a part of our eternal life.

9- آتشست این بانگ نای و نیست باد   هر که این آتش ندارد نیست باد

a) The sound of Ney is fire and it is not the ordinary wind but he who does not have this fire may he become non-existent.

b) For many people the wind blown into the Ney and its sound are ordinary phenomena, while for a lover of God it is the fire that burns in the core of his heart. The person who has no feelings of love might as well die, because without the divine love, life is meaningless. As the heat of physical body is essential for life so is the love of God for the spirit.

c) Some commentators think that "may he become non-existent" is an imprecation (Nich. 1/10; Ahmed Atesh, p. 49) but actually it is the goodwill of Rumi for those whose hearts have not yet begun to beat for the love of God because "the physical death" in mysticism means the lessening of the carnal desires of the earthly body. Rumi explains this fact further in his Discourses, as follows:

"A city in which you find everything that you desire, handsome people, pleasures, all that the natural man craves for, ornaments of every kind, you find not one intelligent man there. Would that it had been the very opposite of this!

That city is the human being. If there be in him a hundred thousand accomplishments but not that essential element (the loving heart) better it were that that city were in ruins" (the Discourses, p. 195).

10- آتش عشقست کاندر نی افتاد   جوشش عشقست کاندر می افتاد

a) It is the fire of Divine love that has entered the Ney, it is the yearning for love that has brought the wine into action.

b) Fermentation of wine, the vibration of the musical instruments or even the motivation of the living beings is due to the hidden attraction of the Divine Love. The lovers of God are all in search of their Origin and when they hear the sound of the Ney their fire of love increases too (Mift, p. 29).

c) Like the word "*Ney*", wine is also a well known metaphor in the Sufi language. It means "the esoteric joy or a paroxysm of ecstasy"[1]. If wine is taken in this sense then it would mean that zeal of a Sufi is because of his spiritual drunkenness and due to his physical pleasure.

---

1 See Ferheng , p. 281; Ferheng-i Zeban-i Farsi , p. 638.

11- نی حریف هر که از یاری برید   پرده‌هااش پرده‌های ما درید

a) The Ney is friends with anyone who has been deserted, and its musical divisions have torn off veils too.

b) It is not possible to hide the moaning of the Ney when it is played. Similarly, a lover of God *(Sufi)* cannot hide his feelings of love. Thus the notes of the Ney *(perde)* tear off the curtains *(perdes)* of a lover. The Persian word *"perde"* in the above verse has been used rhetorically in the double meanings (Homonym).

12- همچو نی زهری و تریاقی کی دید   همچو نی دمساز و مشتاقی کی دید

a) Who has seen an antidote as well as a poison like the Ney; who has seen a sympathising and longing lover like the Ney?

b) The Ney is a poison to those who fail to pass from sensory phenomena to intelligible noumena under the light of intuitive guidance, and who remain the prisoners of the outer forms. For those whose spiritual eyes have been opened, the Ney is like an antidote which consoles them when they burn with the fire of love. "The Ney is poison" also refers to orthodox Muslims who give more importance to physical rituals than to inner enlightening.

c) Mift's explanation is also worth considering: "The Ney has a poisonous effect upon those who become aware of the spiritual world for they begin to give up their worldly desires and it is also an antidote for them because they begin to feel God's presence close by" (Ibid, 1/31). Taki. seems to agree to the above commentary (see 1/18). However, in the light of the historical events of Rumi's time our definition (b) would be more logical.

13- نی حدیث راه پر خون می کند   قصه‌های عشق مجنون می کند

a) The Ney speaks about the bloody and dangerous path and tells stories of Majnun (who sacrificed himself for his beloved Leyli).

b) The path of Divine Love is not a bed of roses for in this path one has to sacrifice all his selfish, carnal desires, egoistic intelligence, and passions. One's heart should be filled with nothing else but the love of God.

14- محرم این هوش جز بیهوش نیست   مر زبان را مشتری جز گوش نیست

a) None other but he who has abandoned his worldly senses can comprehend the secret of my heart (or the story of the Ney); and it is the ear that is the customer (receiver) of the tongue.

b) In order to understand the spiritual state of a lover of God (or the Ney) one has to move out of the bounds of this physical intellect and attain the intuition and spiritual illumination with the heat of Divine Love and devotion. In order to receive the celestial message one has to possess spiritual ears.

15- در غم ما روزها بیگاه شد   روزها با سوزها همراه شد

16- روزها گر رفت گو رو باك نیست   تو بمان ای آنکه چون تو پاك نیست

a) In sorrow our days have lost sense of time and they have become fellow travelers with our griefs. If the days have passed away, tell them to keep on going there is nothing to worry about; but O you the purest one (the love of God) stay with us.

b) The love of God makes a lover oblivious of time; and along with this he forgets his worries. The time, fame and wealth of this world are transient but love is eternal and in its presence, the fear of death and the cruelty of time have no value. It is the enduring love that converts all worries into real happiness, so be with such a love. As Sadi Shirazi says:

آب حیات منست خاك سر كوی دوست
گر دو جهان خرمیست ما و غم روی دوست

(The dust of my friend's street-edge is life-giving water to me,
May there be happiness in the two worlds; yet my friend's face and we,
that is all which is dear to me).

c) The "pure one" does not mean God Himself as indicated by Nicholson with the capital letter "Thou" (Nich. 1/5) nor is it a reference to Husameddin but "*Ma* =we" refers to all lovers.

17- هر که جز ماهی ز آبش سیر شد   هر که بی روزیست روزش دیر شد

a) Everyone except a fish is sated with water and he who is not provided with his daily bread (earning) fails to pass days in comfort.

b) "Fish" is again a symbol. It means a lover of God whose desire for spiritual water is endless because he is in the Sea of Mercy and Love. Like a fish the more he drinks of the reviving water of God's love, the more he desires it. But the man who has never been in such a Sea, he is like a person without wages or a job for he cannot buy spiritual food for himself. The currency of this world is of no use in the love-land of God.

c) Some explanations given regarding this verse by Mift. are insipid (as said by Feruzanfer of other commentaries) but the following sentences may be of some interest: "Fish" means those who are not satisfied with the religious books and want more. Their aim is the Face of God, and no spiritual attainment is sufficient for them. Some orthodox Muslims are satisfied with what they read in books on religion. They are prisoners of their own tiny wisdom.

Nevertheless, in the Islamic mysticism "fish" means "A perfect Gnostic who is submerged in the sea of divine knowledge" (see Ferheng-i Zeban-i Farsi, p. 938).

A famous Urdu poet, Akbar Allahabadi uttered the following verse about this subject:

فلسفی کو بحث کے اندر خدا ملتا نہیں   ڈور کو سلجھا رہا ہے اور سرا ملتا نہیں

"A philosopher (including a theologian) does not find God by means of discussion, he is trying to undo the rope yet cannot find the other end of it".

پس سخن کوتاه باید و السلام   18- در نیابد حال پخته هیچ خام

a) Since a raw (immature) man is unable to perceive the state of a ripe (mature) man, it is better to cut a long story short and bid him farewell.

b) "An immature man" means a person who is preoccupied with sensory pleasures and is detained from journeying further on the path of love, while "a ripe man" is a person who has gone further towards Truth. Immature man also refers to a fanatic Muslim who does not understand the story of the *Ney (Rumi)* and who would scorn the musical companies of *Sema* and the recitation of the Masnevi. To such people Rumi suggests that we should say "farewell" only. In Urdu there is a proverb, "To play the *Ney (Biin)* in front of a buffalo" or the English "To cast pearls before swine" is what is meant here.

It is evident that in the first eighteen verses Rumi has tried to give us eighteen steps that lead to salvation or unification with God. In order to facilitate the divisions of the following chapters, these steps have been reduced to nine[1]. This will enable us to simplify partially the "peculiar" looseness in the association of ideas of the Masnevi (as put by Jan Rypka, p. 241). Rumi brought in parables and tales that may or may not relate to the theme of his Masnevi to attract the attention of his reader. These parables have been excluded from this book to save time. Moreover, they do not need explanation. Their exclusion from the text may result in a certain monotony, although the verses selected here cover extracts from them, too.

The Steps:

1- The state of an immature man (a materialistic man).
2- The awakening (searching for daily bread or spiritual food).
3- The desire and quest (feeling of separation from the Origin like that of the Ney).
4- Indifference to worldly riches (Majnun's submission).
5- Divine Love (the blood stained path of love).
6- Devotion and sacrifice.
7- Bewilderment (tearing of veils).
8- Observation of God in every phenomenon.
9- Unification.

---

[1] For full steps see Erkan Türkmen, On the First Eighteen Verses of Rumi's Masnevi, Islam and the Modern Age, 9.1983.

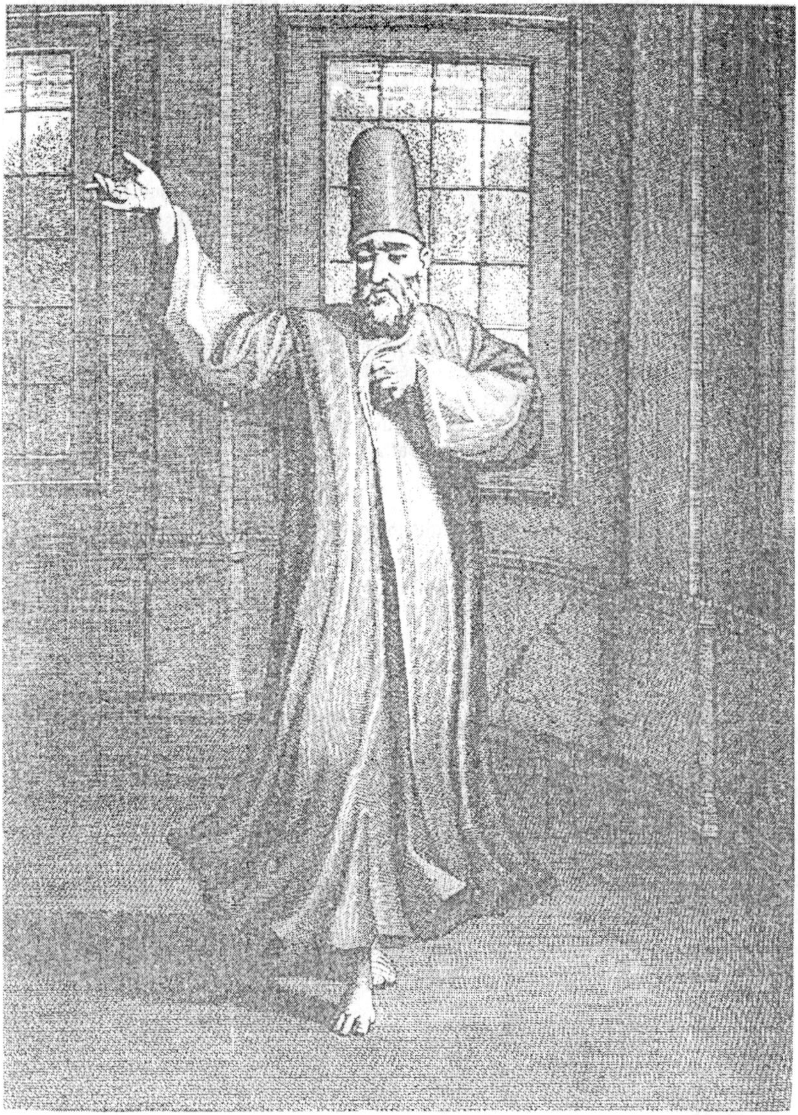

CHAPTER V

Step I: The state of an immature man

1- How long will you be slave of silver and gold?:

بند بگسل باش آزاد ای پسر   چند باشی بند سیم و بند زر
گر بریزی بحر را در کوزه   چند گنجد قسمت یك روزه
کوزه چشم حریصان پر نشد   تا صدف قانع نشد پر درنشد
(I / 19-20-21)

a) O son, break all the ties and be free, for how long will you be captive of gold and silver? If you try to pour the sea into a pitcher, the pitcher will take only the need of a day. The pitcher of greedy people's eyes is never filled, but an oyster is not satiated unless it is filled with a pearl.

b) "Gold and silver" means the collecting of wealth. If you are preoccupied with collecting worldly riches, you get lost in it and forget to reach God. It is like falling in love with the traffic signs and ignoring the path which leads you to the actual goal. Your body is like a pitcher and if you dip it in the sea of the riches of this world, it can only take what it can hold. There is no end to the desires of a greedy person. You should try to be satisfied with what God has given you so that, like an oyster, you may also become filled with a pearl (the purity of soul).

c) Oyster: It was believed that an oyster could swallow a rain drop and change it into a pearl by settling at the bottom of the sea (Tahir, 1/77).

2- A man is responsible for his own deeds:

گرچه دیوار افکند سایه دراز   باز گردد سوی او و آن سایه باز
این جهان کوهست و فعل ما ندا   سوی ما آید نداها را صدا
(I / 214-215)

a) Although a wall casts a long shadow, the shadow goes back to the wall (ultimately). This world is like a mountain and our acts are like the sounds that echo back to us.

b) This world is the farm of the invisible world, "What you sow so shall you reap". God says in the Koran, "Then shall anyone who has done an atom's weight of good see it, and anyone who has done an atom's weight of evil shall see it" (XCIX/ 7-8).

3- Physically men may look the same, but spiritually they are different:

همسری با انبیا بر داشتند   اولیا را همچو خود پنداشتند

گفته اینک ما بشر ایشان بشر   ما و ایشان بسته خوابیم و خور

هر دو گون زنبور خوردند از محل   لیک شد ز آن نیش و زین دیگر عسل

هر دو نی خوردند از یک آب خور   این یکی خالی و آن دیگر شکر

(I / 265-266-268-270)

a) They, the non-believers, claimed equality with the prophets and thought saints like themselves. They said, "We are human beings and they are also. They sleep and eat like us". But they did not think that the wasp and the bee both eat from the same source yet one produces only a sting (poison) while the other produces honey. Similarly, both the reeds sip water from the same place; one is hollow and the other (sugar cane) contains sugar.

b) From time to time God sent prophets to earth. Many refused to believe them and their words. At the time of Muhammed non-believers said, "What sort of apostle is this who eats and walks through the streets. Why has an angel not been sent down to him to give admonition with him?" (XXV/7). They failed to understand the difference between an ordinary man and a prophet.

4- There are two kinds of ladder -the ladder of this world and the ladder of the other world:

حس دنیا نردبان این جهان   حس دینی نردبان آسمان

صحت این حس بجویید از طبیب   صحت آن حس بخواهید از حبیب

صحت این حس ز معموری تن   صحت آن حس ز ویرانی بدن

(I / 303-304-305)

a) The worldly senses are the ladder for this world, the religious (spiritual) senses are the ladder for Heaven. Seek the health of the carnal senses from a doctor, but seek the health of the celestial senses from the Beloved. The health of the carnal senses depends on the flourishing of the physical body while the health of the celestial senses depends on the destruction of the physical body.

b) As one can improve the carnal senses, one can also improve the spiritual senses. By means of science and intellect one can reach the highest stage of comfort but it is via spiritual training that one can attain eternal happiness.

5- Anger is part of animal desire:

خشم و شهوت مرد را احول کند   ز استقامت روح را مبدل کند
چون غرض آمد هنر پوشیده شد   صد حجاب از دل بسوی دیده شد
(I / 333-334)

a) Anger and lust make a man squint-eyed and force the spirit to go astray from its right path. When self-interest comes (overcomes), virtue disappears and a hundred veils from the heart rise to the eyes.

b) Two things destroy a man -rage and carnal desires for wealth and sex. When one grows greedy and selfish, one loses a spiritual sight and love for God and His people.

6- This world is full of snares:

صد هزاران دام و دانه ست ای خدا   ما چو مرغان حریص بی نوا
دم بدم ما بسته دام نویم   هر یکی گر باز و سیمرغی شویم
می رهانی هر دمی ما را و باز   سوی دامی میرویم ای بی نیاز
(I / 374-375-376)

a) Oh my God, there are a hundred thousand (many) traps and snares and we are like greedy helpless birds. Although we may look strong like a hawk or the Simurg, every time we are entrapped by some sort of snare. You, Oh God, Who are without want, free us from the trap but we always go to a new one.

b) This world is full of materialistic charms that attract us in the manner of a bait which draws a fish towards it. It is only by help of God that we can free ourselves or protect ourselves from these charms. The love of God which helps us to sacrifice our greedy desires, jealousies and rage (aggressiveness) can protect us from the worldly charms (see also Bhagawat Gita, chapter 12) because in this world we are being tested; as the Koran says, "That which is on earth We have made but as a glittering show for the earth, in order that We may test them (the people) as to which of them are best in conduct" (XVIII/7) and "Your riches and your children may be but a trial..." (LXIV/15).

7- Our ego (or selfness) is a destructive mouse:

ما در این انبار گندم می کنیم   گندم جمع آمده گم می کنیم
موش تا انبار ما حفره زدست   وز فنش انبار ما ویران شدست
اول ای جان دفع شر موش کن   و آنگهان در جمع گندم جوش کن
378 a انبار G : انبان. Mift.   (I / 378-379-380)

a) Each time we collect wheat (corn) in this barn, we lose it. A mouse has made a hole to our barn, and by his tricks he is destroying our store. First of all, my friend, get rid of this mouse and set your heart on collecting the corn.

b) We aim to perform good deeds but it is our selfness that spoils all which we do, like a mouse in a barn. So we must first of all curb the ego.

c) All the Indian MSs have the word "*Anban* =a bag" instead of the word "*Anbar* =a barn".

8- Materialistic wakefulness is a deep sleep to the other world:

هر که بیدار است او در خواب تر   هست بیداریش از خوابش بتر
چون بحق بیدار نبود جان ما   هست بیداری چو در بندان ما
                                    (I / 409-410)

a) He who is awake (to this world) is the more asleep (to the spiritual world); his wakefulness is worse than his sleep. When our soul is not awake to God, our wakefulness is like being awake in a prison.

b) The more a man indulges in the riches of this world and seems to be active to this end, he is away from wakefulness to the spiritual world. Thus his wisdom and alertness is actually a deep sleep.

c) The word "*derbandan* =prisons" and Nich. gives "closing our doors (to Divine influences)" which sounds incorrect.

9- Even inanimate objects obey the command of God:

خاك سرها را نکرده آشکار   تا نشـان حق نیـآرد نـو بـهار
این خبرها و ین امانت و ین سداد   آن جوادی که جمـادی بداد
عاقلان را کرده قهر او ضریر   مر جمـادی را کند فـضـلش خبیـر
(I / 511-512-513)

511 b نکرده : M+G نسازد : Mift. - 511 a نیآرد : N+G نیابد : Mift.

a) Until the spring brings a mandate from God, the soil does not expose its secrets. God is Bounteous Who gives this information, righteousness and security to the inanimate. While his grace makes the inanimate knowledgeable, His wrath makes the wise men blind.

b) Even inanimate objects are aware of God's commands and mandates; and they obey them sincerely without objection. But some people, though they have intelligence, fail to be aware of His being and commands.

c) "*Nishan*" here means a mandate "Tahir., Mift. and Baki. all agree to this meaning. Nich. translates this as a "a token of God".

10- The heart-broken win the favour of God:

جز شکسته می نگیرید فضل شاه   فهم و خاطر تیز کردن نیست راه
موج آبی محو و سکرست و فناست   موج خاکی وهم و فهم و فکر ماست
تا از ین مستی از آن جامی تو کور   تا در ین سکری از آن سکری تو دور
(I / 532-575-576)

576 b کور N + G نفور Mift.

a) The divine path is not to sharpen intelligence and strengthen hearts because the King's Mercy falls on the heart-broken. Our imaginations, conceptions and thoughts are earthly waves; but the waves of water (spiritual activities) are self-effacement, intoxication and annihilation. As long as you are intoxicated by this mortal world, you are far away from the mystical drunkenness; and while you are intoxicated with this you are blind to that cup (the spiritual drink).

b) By being clever and smart you cannot win Divine Favour (Mercy) but it is possible to win God's Favour by being humble and heart-broken. The earthly waves (mortal pleasures) are our mere thoughts, vain ideas and conceptions; but the spiritual activities bring about the following stages: 1- Obliterate the lower self 2- Divine intoxication 3- Annihilation (of selfness in God). If you are fond of this world, you are drunk in this world and the worldly intoxication will prevent you from seeing the cup of the real (spiritual) drink.

11- Control the loving senses of forms in order to see the Truth:

صورت سركش گدازان كن بـرنـج   تا ببینی زیر او وحدت چو گنج
ور تـو نگدازی عنایتهای او   خود گدازد ای دلم مولای او
منبسط بودیم و یك جوهر همه   بی سر و بی پا بودیم آن سر همه
یك گهر بودیم همچون آفتاب   بی گره بودیم و صافی همچو آب
چون بصورت آمد آن نور سره   شد عدد چون سایه هائی کنگره
                                  (I / 683-684-686-687-688)

a) By means of sorrows and tribulation melt the rebellious shapes so that you may see under them the hidden treasures of Unity. If you fail to do so (ultimately) His Mercy (to whom my heart is a slave) will melt them. We before creation were one substance, shining like the sun, and we were faultless and clean like water. When that pure light changed into forms there rose up numbers like the shadows of the battlements (fallen on the earth).

b) Before creation all souls were one. When they were fashioned into forms (bodies) they became divided into many shapes like shadow cast by the battlements, although the source (the sun) is the same. In order to rejoin the Essence we must become pure and clean as we used to be before creation. It is after that that we should ask for the help of God. As the Koran says, "And those who strive in Our (Cause) We will certainly guide them to Our paths. For verily God is with those who do right" (XXIX/69).

12- Worldly tricks are of no use:

مکرها در کسب دنیا بار دست   مکرها در ترك دنیا واردست
این جهان زندان و ما زندانیان   حفره کن زندان و خود را وارهان
چیست دنیا از خدا غافل بدن   نی قماش و نقره و میزان و زن
983 b میزان N + G : فرزندان Kan. (I / 980-982-983)

a) Tricks for gaining this world are worthless but for abandoning this world are licit. This world is a prison and we are prisoners. Make a hole in the prison and set yourself free. After all, what is the world? It does not mean cloth, silver, houseware, a weighing scale (business) or a wife. Is it being unaware of God?

b) The tricks played in this world for reputation, wealth and fame are of no avail. They are like the waves of the sea that rise and fall. On the contrary, the playing of tricks to abandon this world is the right thing to do.

c) "Abandoning the world" does not mean here to quit it totally but it means to lessen carnal greed and to give more attention to God. It is suggested in the Koran to plead to God in this way: "Our Lord give us good in this world and in the Hereafter" (II/201) (also see Mift. II/35). It is, therefore, the duty of a believer to live a modest life here without being greedy. One has to balance it well as Rumi says:

آب در کشتی هلاك کشتی است   آب اندر زیر کشتی پشتی است
(I / 985)

"Water in the boat ruins it, while under the boat, supports it".

13- A Sufi does not drown in the sea of worldly beauty:

کوزه سربسته اندر آب زفت   از دل پر باد فوق آب رفت
باد درویش چو در باطن بود   بر سر آب جهان ساکن بود
(I / 987-988)

a) An empty head-tied jar floats over the rough water. Similarly, when a Sufi *(dervish)* has the air of Sufism inside his heart, he floats above the water of this world.

b) When a Sufi has nothing else but love or knowledge of God in his heart he dwells over the materialistic sea without being immersed into it.

14- It is the inner shape of a human being that counts:

گر بصورت آدمی انسان بدی   احمد و بوجهل خود یکسان بدی
(I / 1019)

a) If all human being were man in shape, Abu Jehil and Ahmed (Muhammed) would be just the same.

b) Abu Jehil (the father of the ignorant) is a title given to Abu'l Hakam Amr b. Hisham b. al-Mugira who being contemporary with Prophet Muhammed, opposed the prophet bitterly and planned to kill him many times (İA, 4/15). Thus if all men were equal in accordance with their appearance, Muhammed and Abu Jehil would also be equal in the eyes of God.

15- Sell these donkey's ears:

گوش خر بفروش و دیگر گوش خر   کین سخن را در نیابد گوش خر
(I / 1027)

a) Sell the donkey's ears (these worldly ears) and buy another ear, because the worldly ears cannot receive secret words about God.

b) The "donkey's ears" means the ear of a man who has no spiritual senses (as mentioned in the eighteen verses above). Mift. says that it means the ear of a man, who has a black heart and takes no lesson from anything. As the Koran says, "They have ears but they listen not" (I/54).

16- The source of Divine Light is not the sun and the stars:

این برون از آفتاب و از سها   و اندرون از عکس انوار علی
باز نور نور دل نور خداست   کو ز نور عقل و حس پاک و جداست
پس نهانیها بضد پیدا شود   چونک حق را نیست ضد پنهان بود
Kan. سماست b - علاست a 1125   (I / 1125-1127-1131)

a) The outer light comes from the sun and the star *(Suha)* while the inner light is a reflection of Divine Light. The light that enlightens the heart is the Light of God, Which is separate from and purer than the light of the intellect and carnal senses. Certainly, the hidden things are manifested by their opposites. Since God has no opposite, He is hidden (from our conception).

b) We observe things by means of the light of the sun, a tiny star *(Suha)* or a lamp. Similarly, if we want to observe the objects that belong to the other world, we must try to possess the inner light that is obtained by means of Divine Love and spiritual discipline. "God is the Light of the heavens and the earth" (the Koran, XXIV/35). If this is true, then there must be a way to discover the light. It can be discovered by means of cleaning our hearts and it is by this light that we can see God's world which has no opposite. Since our carnal senses are bound to know things by their opposites then how can we see God without the Divine Light? As the Koran says, "No vision can grasp Him, but His grasp is over all that can be seen: He is above all comprehension, yet is acquainted with all things" (VI/103).

17- Our real name is known only by God:

اسم هر چیزی بر ما ظاهرش   اسم هر چیزی بر خالق سرش
صورتی بود این منی اندر عدم   پیش حق موجود نه بیش و نه کم
حاصل آن آمد حقیقت نام ما   پیش حضرت کآن بود انجام ما
ای خنک آنکو نکو کاری گرفت   زور را بگذاشت او زاری گرفت
(I / 1239-1243-1244-1257)

a) For us the name of everything is its outer appearance but with the Creator the name of everything is its inner reality. While it was in the nonexistent world the semen had a definite (no less no more) shape in the Presence of God. Consequently, our real name, with God, is in accordance with our end. How nice it is for the man who has chosen to be pious and has adapted lamentation instead of cruelty.

b) It is God who gives life to the clot in the fertilized ovum. He then changes the clot into man, in other words from animality into a human whose essence is pre-planned in the non-existent world. This is what the Koran says, "Then We placed him (man) as (a drop of) sperm in a place of rest, firmly fixed. Then We made the sperm into a clot of congealed blood; then from that clot We made a (foetus) lump, then We made out of that lump bones and clothed the bones with flesh; then We developed out of it another creature. So blessed be God, the Best Creator!" (XXIII/13-14). Man's physical structure is preplanned by the DNA and the RNA (the genetic code) of the parents but spiritual structure is the breath of God which takes man from animal life to human life.

18- Troubles come your way to make you stronger:

این قضا صد بار اگر راهت زند   بر فراز چرخ خرگاهت زند
از کرم دان این می ترساندت   تا بملک ایمنی بنشاندت
(I / 1260-1261)

a) If Divine destiny robs you a hundred times yet it pitches a tent for you in the high heavens. It is because of His Mercy that He frightens you with troubles and then places you in the kingdom of security.

b) Troubles of this life are like the traffic signs that lead you to the path and then train you so that you may earn the place to be given Hereafter. In this respect, it is the Mercy of God Who is training you for a higher stage.

19- Since the macrocosm is restless how can the microcosm be at peace?:

آتـشی کو باد دارد در بروت   هم یکی بادی برو خواند یـموت
چرخ سرگردان که اندر جستجوست   حال او چون حال فرزندان اوست
خود ای جزوی ز کلها مختلط   فهم می کن حالت هر منبسط
چونکه کلیات را رنجست و درد   جزو ایشان چون نباشد روی زرد

Mift. تـمرت : N+G یـموت b 1285   (I / 1285-1287-1289-1290)

a) The fire that has stretched out its moustache (has puffed up with pride) is extinguished by a gust of the same wind that had puffed it up. The universe is whirling in searching and in seeking and its state is like its children (the atoms of substances) that are also restless. O part made up of wholes, recognise the state of each simple (unmixed) body. Since the wholes suffer from griefs and pains, how should their parts not be pale faced (sick and subject to decay).

b) A man who is proud of his fame and wealth is destroyed by the same possessions. If the whole universe is in search of the Reality, then how can an atom (or the part of the whole) be at peace? However, if you lessen your selfness you may lessen the effect of the physical environment by transferring your attention from your materialistic being to the spiritual body.

c) The verse explained by Taki after No.1293 does not exist in the G or any other old MS. (see Taki I/574).

20- You are liable to fall in the ditch you dig for others:

ای که تو از ظلم چاهی می کنی   از برای خویش دامی می کنی
گرد خود چون کرم پیله بر متن   بهر خود چه می‌کنی اندازه کن

(I / 1311-1312)

a) O you who are busy digging a well for others from cruelty, you are, actually, setting a trap for yourself. Don't weave (a cocoon) round yourself like the silkworm. Just think for a while what are you digging for yourself!

b) If you are trying to push others into the well of cruelty, you are actually pushing yourself into it. In case you are weaving silk (jealousy and cunning plans) around yourself don't forget that you will die for it as the silkworm is killed for the silk.

21- First take the log from your own eye, and then take the speck out of your brother's eye:

در خود آن بد را نمی بینی عیان　　　　ورنه دشمن بودی خود را بجان
چون بقعر خوی خود اندر رسی　　　　پس بدانی کز تو بود آن ناکسی
پیش چشمت داشتی شیشه کبود　　　　زآن سبب عالم کبودت می نمود
گرنه کوری این کبودی دان ز خویش　　　خویش را بد گو مگر کس را تو بیش
(I / 1322-1324-1329-1330)

a) You do not clearly see the evil in you, otherwise you would hate yourself wholeheartedly. When you reach the bottom of the abyss of your own nature, you will realise that it was your fault. You have held a blue glass before your eyes and because of that the world looks blue to you. If you are not blind then feel that the blueness is because of you. Therefore, speak ill of yourself and not of others.

b) The spectacles of your ego can hide your selfness and you try to find faults in others. After you discover your own self, you see the reality.

As Yunus Emre says, "Knowledge is to know yourself, if you can't know yourself then of what good is knowledge?".

22- Extinguish your fire of lust with the water of Divine Light:

اندك اندك آب را بر آتش بزن　　　　تا شود نار تو نور ای بوالحزن
ای تو شیری در ته این چاه فرد　　　　نفس چون خرگوش خونت ریخت وخورد
نفس خر گوشت بصحرا در چرا　　　　تو بقعر این چه چون و چرا
1333 a نور را بر نار زن .T آب ... بزن G　　　　(I / 1333-1351-1352)

a) Slowly pour water on your fire so that your fire may change into light, O man full of sorrow. You are like a lion at the bottom of a lonely well and your ego is like a hare that has shed the blood of the lion. The hare is grazing happily in the desert and you are at the bottom of the well of "How?" and "Why?".

b) In these lines the "Hare" stands for "the ego of a man". The "lion" is the holy spirit while "the well" is the body in which the spirit is kept prisoner. "Fire" means the sexual desires of man.

Extinguish your lustful desires so that divine light may rule over your abyss of darkness. Your spirit can be strong like a lion but it has been captive by a hare (the ego) which is grazing happily in the desert (the world). Your logic of "How?" and "Why?" hinders the way to freedom.

c) Miftah. says you cannot free yourself from the well then go and find a saint to free you from there (Ibid, 2/163).

23- Our lower selfness (Nafs) is our biggest enemy:

ای شهان کشتیم ما خصم برون   ماند خصمی زو بتر در اندرون

کشتن این کار عقل و هوش نیست   شیر باطن سخره خرگوش نیست

دوزخست این نفس و دوزخ اژدهاست   کو بدریاها نگردد کم و کاست

چونک جزو دوزخست این نفس ما   طبع کل دارند جمله جزوها

(I / 1373-1374-1375-1382)

a) O kings, we have killed our outer enemies but the inner enemy, which is worse than the outer one, is still living. It is not possible to kill it by means of our carnal senses and intelligence because the inner lion cannot be subdued by the hare. This carnal selfness is Hell, and Hell is a dragon, the fire of which cannot be extinguished by many oceans for our selfness is part of Hell and a part has the same nature as the whole.

b) These verses refer to the sayings of Muhammed, "We now turn from the small war to the greater war (of ego)". The small war is carried out on the battlefield but the greater war is the war waged by man with himself and his own cunning carnal senses (see Mift. 2/178). Rumi continues, O kings, the great warriors, you have killed your outer enemies but what about the inner enemy? Your fire of greed is like the fire of Hell so look for the water of Divine Light to put out this fire and pray to God for His help as Zulaiha did in the Koran: "Nor do I absolve my own self (of blame), the (human) soul is certainly prone to evil. Unless my Lord gives His Mercy, but surely My Lord is Often-Forgiving the Most Merciful" (XII/53).

c) In these verses the word "lion" is used in an entirely different meaning than in the vr.1357. Here it means "the strong ego of man" which cannot be killed by the powerless hare (carnal intelligence).

24- Be straight like an arrow:

راست شو چون تیر و واره از کمان   کز کمان هر راست بجهد بیگمان
سهل شیری دان که صفها بشکند   شیر آنست که خود را بشکند
(I / 1385-1389)

a) Be straight like an arrow and free yourself from the bow because, without doubt, every straight arrow can dart from the bow (to its target). One who breaks the lines of enemies is an ordinary lion, but he who breaks himself (his ego) is the real lion.

b) If you want to reach the real goal (the Divine Vicinity) then be straight and have a good character. To fight in the battlefield bravely is easier than to fight with one's own selfness. A straight arrow goes farther and faster towards the goal. Similarly, a soul that is not crooked goes to God without much hindrance.

25- Do not poke cotton into your spiritual ears:

گر نخواهی در تردد هوش جان   کم فشار این پنبه اندر گوش جان
تا کنی فهم آن معماهاش را   تا کنی ادراک رمز و فاش را
گوش جان و چشم جان جز این حس است   گوش عقل و گوش ظن زین مفلس است
(I / 1459-1460-1462)

a) If you don't want your intellect to be in a state of perplexity, then do not poke cotton into your ears so that you may understand His riddles and what is open and what is secret. The spiritual eyes and ears are different from these sensual ears and eyes and the latter fail to understand what the former perceive.

b) As said before, the sensual ears and eyes are not able to discern what the spiritual world offers. If you desire to discover the spiritual world to possess those feelings then work for them because nothing is granted in this world, and even more so in the other world, without labour.

26- Man is stuck in this cage of life because of his ignorance:

مرغ کو اندر قفص زندانی است   می نجوید رستن از نادانی است
روحهایی کز قفصها رسته اند   انبیای رهبر شایسته اند
(I / 1541-1542)

a) The bird that is imprisoned in a cage and does not try to attain freedom is really ignorant. The souls that have escaped from their cages are prophets and are worthy leaders.

b) The soul that has much indulged in physical pleasures is like a bird that has become happy with the cage it is captive in and is ignorant of the eternal happiness that lies beyond his captivity.

27- The body of a greedy man is like a camel:

خار دان آنرا که خرما دیده‌ٔ   زآنکه بس نان کور و بس نادیده‌ٔ

اشتر آمد این وجود خارخوار   مصطفی زادی برین اشتر سوار

اشترا تنگ گلی بر پشت تست   کز نسیمش در تو صد گلزار رست

(I / 1964-1966-1967)

a) Whatever you have seen as a date, regard it as a thorn for your greed is without gratitude. This body is like a camel and mounted on this camel is the son of Mustafa (Muhammed). O camel, on your back there is a basket of flowers the scent of which makes many (hundreds of) rose gardens grow in you.

b) Your selfish ego makes materialistic things charming to you, although the same things seem bad (like thorns) to the spiritual eyes (Mift. 3/25). Your soul (the child of Muhammed) is riding your camel (the body) which is fond of thorns, although there are wonderful flowers at the back of the camel that send you the scent of gnostic information and good tidings (see T. 3-4/978).

c) "The children of Muhammed" means the believers who are enlightened by the light of the divine messages given by the prophet Muhammed.

28- The spiritual world is non-dimensional:

زیر و بالا پیش و پس وصف تن است   بی جهت آن ذات جان روشن است

بر گشا از نور پاک شه نظر   تا نپنداری تو چون کوته نظر

که همینی در غم و شادی و بس   ای عدم کو مر عدم را پیش و پس

(I / 2008-2009-2010)

a) "Below" and "above", "before" and "behind" are the attributes of this physical body; the essence of the bright spirit is non-dimensional. Open your spiritual eyes with the light of the King (God) so that you do not continue to think narrow-mindedly. If you keep on thinking in this way (narrow-mindedly and sceptically), you cannot get rid of (worldly) sorrow and happiness. O non-existence! where are "before" or "behind" in the non-existent world?

b) Unless you try to leave the sphere of these worldly bounds slowly, you cannot attain real happiness for you are tied by the shapes and carnal senses of this mortal world. The more you lessen your worldly desires, the happier you become.

c) Some verses of Mift. (3/42) are not found in the "G".

29- A flower is a sign of the Beloved's cheek:

دستها بر کرده اند از خاکدان	این درختانند همچون خاکیان
و آنك گوشتش عبارت میکنند	سوی خلقان صد اشارت میکنند
از ضمیر خاك می گویند راز	بازبان سبز و با دست دراز
زنده شان کرد از بهار و داد برگ	در زمستانشان اگر چه داد مرگ
آن گل از اسرار گل گویا بود	هر گلی کاندر درون بویا بود
(I / 2014-2015-2016-2019-2022)	

a) These trees are like the buried dead, they lift their hands from the earth. They (trees and plants) are making a hundred signs to people and they are speaking to him who has spiritual ears. With their green tongues and long hands (fingers) they reveal secrets from the heart of the soil. Although God puts them to death in winter, He gives them life again by means of Spring and gives them leaves again.

b) Many believe that there is no life after death, although there are countless signs of God in Nature that prove that there is life after death. For example, a seed is analogous to the dead body and the spiritual revival. When a seed is sown in the soil, God revives it and it begins to change into a plant and then into a tree. In winter the tree-leaves fall but they begin to grow again with the arrival of spring. A new life begins -flowers smell with different scents although they are the product of the same soil as, Hafiz says:

"Every newly blossomed flower reminds me of the cheek of my Beloved;
But where is the ear that can hear and where is the eye that can see?"

Similarly, a man dies physically but he is reborn spiritually. God says in the Koran, "It is Who brings the living from the dead and brings the dead from the living and Who gives life to the earth after it is dead and thus shall ye be brought out (from the dead)" (XXX/19). He who has his spiritual eyes open can see these facts clearly.

30- If the other world was revealed to everyone, no one would stay in this world a while:

مثنوی در حجم گر بودی چو چرخ   در نگنجیدی درو زین نیم برخ
کآن زمین و آسمان بس فراخ   کرد از تنگی دلم را شاخ شاخ
این جهان و راهش ار پیدا بدی   کم کسی یک لحظه آنجا بدی
(I / 2098-2099-2101)

a) If the Masnevi was as wide as the universe, not half a description of the other world could be contained. The width of the spiritual universe would certainly have pierced my heart due to its narrowness. If the path to that world were visible, no one would stay here even for a single moment.

b) In these verses Rumi wants to express the vastness of the other world, which has no limits. This being the case, it is not possible to put information about that world into words or to define it with the language of man. This world is narrow and tight to the spirit of a man, like a foot in a tight shoe.

31- The language of the heart is the real language:

آن ندایی کاصل هر بانگ و نواست   خود ندا آنست واین باقی صداست
ترک و کرد و پارسی گو و عرب   فهم کرده آن ندا بی گوش و لب
خود چه جای ترک و تاجیکست و زنگ   فهم کردست آن ندا را چوب و سنگ
(I / 2107-2108-2109)

a) The voice that is the origin of every sound and cry is the actual voice, the rest is the echo of it. A man may he be a Turk, Kurd, Persian speaker or an Arab, can understand that sound without ears and lips. Without mentioning a Turk, Tajik or a negro even stones and wood can understand it (the language of heart).

b) Rumi is speaking of the same sound of Reality that he heard in the moaning of the reed flute. The sound of one's heart is the Divine Language and it needs no physical ear to hear it. It does not discriminate between races. Even stones are able to understand the Divine command and obey it. Why, then, should man remain inactive and dull?

32- Treasures are found in ruins:

آنچه تو گنجـش توهم می کنی   ز آن توهم گنج را گم می کنی
چون عمارت دان تو وهم و رایها   گنج نبود در عمارت جایها
در عمارت هستی و جنگی بود   نیست را از هست ها ننگی بود
نی که هست از نیستی فریاد کرد   بلک نیست آن هست را واداد کرد
تو مگو که من گریزانم ز نیست   بلک او از تو گریزانست بیست

(I / 2475-2476-2477-2478-2479)

a) What you think to be the treasure, through vain thought you lose the (real) treasure. Ideas and opinions are like populated areas and treasure is not found in such a place. In the populated areas there is a struggle for existence (ego) while the non-existent is shy of existence. It is not the case that existence begged for help against non-existence to escape but it is the non-existent that repelled the existent. Don't say, "I am running away from the non-existent", for it is non-existence that is running from you, stop and think!

b) If you think that this world is the real treasure, you may lose the real treasure of that world. Treasure is not found in populated areas. It is found in barren places (where no greed exists). In this materialistic world there is a struggle for fame and wealth which those who are in the non-existent world reject. So, don't say that you are running from the non-existent; it is the non-existent world that is avoiding you because of your greed and self-conceit.

33- The sense of having faults and doubts leads you to the right path:

اشتباهی و گمانی در درون   رحمت حقست بهر رهنمون

(I / 2504)

a) Your inner sense of having faults and doubts is actually the gifts of God for they help you in finding the path.

b) Your worries about the mistakes that you make and your sceptical ideas, like the fence beside the road, lead you to the right path. Without them life would be simple and insipid (Taki, 2/227).

34- There are no worries or trials for saints or lovers of God:

گر ولی زهری خورد نوشی شود   ور خورد طالب سیه هوشی شود

بیم سر یا بیم سر یا بیم دین   امتحانی نیست ما را مثل این

(I / 2603-2608)

a) If a saint drinks poison, it changes into a normal drink. But if a disciple drinks it, his mind gets darkened. Fear of losing one's head, fear of revealing secrets or of losing-there are no such trials for us (the saints).

b) If a perfect man or a lover of God drinks poison, it changes into an antidote (as Rumi himself proved, see Eflaki, 3/40). This verse also means that a saint even if he is rich, he is free from the materialistic fetters and spends his money for the betterment of God's creatures while a disciple who is still a novice can be attracted by the charm of wealth and fame.

35- Lovers give gifts to one another through love:

گر بیان معنوی کافی شدی   خلق عالم عاطل و باطل بدی

گر محبت فکرت و معنیستی   صورت روزه و نمازت نیستی

هدیه هائی دوستان با یک دیگر   نیست اندر دوستی الا صور

(I / 2624-2625-2626)

a) If spiritual explanation were sufficient, the creation of this world would have been meaningless and without wisdom (Mift, 3/223). If love depended only on thought and inner acts, there would be no use of formal fasting and five time prayers *(namaz)*. The exchanging of presents among friends is a sign of real friendship.

b) If the other world had been manifest, there would have been no use of creating this world and the corporeal struggles to gain nirvana would have also been absurd. In Rumi's mysticism (or even in the Islamic mysticism) the denying of selfhood is different from the kind enjoined by Buddhism. In the Islamic Mysticism you have to give up your greedy self and attain a new personality that spends more time with God and His created beings. After killing your lower self, you see everything with the Eyes of God that have no bounds. You achieve the Universal insight and understanding, as Muhammed Iqbal puts it:

کافر کی یہ پہچان کہ آفاق میں گم ہے

مومن کی یہ پہچان کہ گم اس میں ہیں آفاق

"The sign of an infidel is that he is confined by the horizons; while the sign of a true believer is that the horizons are confined by him".

We shall further discuss this theme in the course of our commentaries on Rumi's verses.

In order to show our sympathy or love for others we exchange presents. If we want to thank God what kind of present can we give Him? He is above need. You can thank Him by means of prayers and fasting. Rumi gives a beautiful insight into prostrating before God in the following lines from his Divan:

بر یاد لبت لال نگین می بوسم   آنم چو بدست نیست این می بوسم
دستم چو بر آسمان تو می نرسد   میارم سجده و زمین می بوسم

"In the memory of Thy Lips, the red diamond of my ring I kiss;
Since I cannot reach Thy Lips, I kiss this,
As I have no access to Your sky (Your Height),
I prostrate myself and this earth I kiss".

36- If your abode is briny water do you know of sweet water?:

ای که اندر چشمه شورست جات   تو چه دانی شط جیحون و فرات
ای تو نارسته ازین فانی رباط   تو چه دانی محو و سکر و انبساط
(I / 2725-2726)

a) O you who have your abode in briny water, how can you know the beauty of the waters of the Shatt, the Jeyhun and the Euphrates? O you who have not been able to get out of this temporary abode, what can you know about self-extinction, mystical intoxication and spiritual expansion?

b) If a person has no knowledge of the other world, he is satisfied with what he has in this material world (the briny water). A fish that has never seen the expanse of the sea and has lived in an aquarium, cannot realise what real freedom is. Spiritual expansion is the stage after the spiritual depression *(qabz)*. The expansion is attained when God's light rules over the darkness of lower self. Dimensional walls disappear and an endless expansion takes place (for other details see Tahir, 3-4/ p. 1294).

37- You would certainly break your jar (of selfhood) if you discovered the sweet waters of the spiritual sea:

گر زدجله با خبر بودی چو ما   او نبردی آن سبو را جا بجا
بلک از دجله اگر واقف بدی   آن سبو را بر سر سنگی زدی
کل عالم را سبودان ای پسر   کو بود از علم و خوبی تا بسر
آنک دیدندش همیشه بی خودند   بی خودانه بر سبو سنگی زدند
(I / 2851-2852-2860-2865)

a) If he had known the river Tigris, like we do, he would not have carried the jar from place to place. He would have dashed the jar against a stone, if he knew that there was a river Tigris. So, regard the whole universe as a jar filled with knowledge and beauty up to the brim. Those who have seen it (the Great Tigris) are always out of themselves and they dash their jars (of selfhood) against stones like an intoxicated man.

b) "The jar" refers to the jar of a simple villager who took rain water to the Caliph of the time not knowing that there were rivers and the great Tigris there. Now, Rumi says that a man who has not seen the world Hereafter will think that this world is wonderful and is full of wisdom and beauty.

38- Some people like darkness and are happy with it:

چون ندارد روی همچون آفتاب   او نخواهد جز شبی همچون نقاب
و آنکه سر تا پا گلست و سوسنست   پس بهار او را دو چشم روشنست
خار بی معنی خزان خواهد خزان   تا زند پهلوی خود با گلستان
پس خزان او را بهارست و حیات   یک نماید سنگ و یاقوت زکات
(I / 2919-2921-2922-2924)

a) Since his face is not shining like the sun, he wants nothing else but the veiling darkness of the night. However if one is like roses and lilies from top to toe, spring is a pair of bright eyes. The unspiritual thorn desires for autumn and autumn only, so that it may contend in rivalry with a rose garden. For the thorn autumn is spring and life; and for it (the thorn) the stone and ruby are alike.

b) God-loving men will have faces bright with Divine Light on the day of resurrection and the presence of God will make them happier; while the infidels being fond of darkness, will not be content in that light. There is a verse in the Koran which is referred to here: "On the Day (of resurrection) when some faces will be (lit up with) white and some faces will be (in the gloom) of black..." (III/106).

39- Don't feed your dog (selfhood) until it is full:

چون در معنی زنی بازت کنند   پر فکرت زن که شهبازت کنند
نان گلست و گوشت کمتر خور ازین   تا نمانی همچو گل اندر زمین
چون شدی تو سیر مرداری شدی   بی خبر بی پا چو دیواری شدی
زآنکه سگ چون سیر شد سرکش شود   کی سوی صید و شکار خوش رود
(I / 2870-2872-2874-2877)

a) When you knock at the door of the spiritual world, they open it. Beat your wings of ideas so that they can make a king falcon out of you. Bread and meat are, in fact, clay so eat less of them, in order that you may not remain like clay in the earth. When you eat your fill, you become like a corpse and thus you become as unaware and unconscious as a wall. Because when a dog has eaten its fill, being a rebel it does not run properly after its prey.

b) If you want to fly higher like a falcon (a lover of God), do not give up thinking about God and His world. If you want to fly towards Him faster, then eat a little for too much eating makes the falcon lazy.

40- A blossom is a mere form while the fruit is the essence:

میوه معنی و شکوفه صورتش   آن شکوفه مژده میوه نعمتش
چون شکوفه ریخت میوه شد پدید   چونک آن گم شد این اندر مزید
تا که نان نشکست قوت کی دهد   ناشکسته خوشه های کی می دهد
(I / 2930-2931-2932)

a) The fruit is the essence while the blossom is a mere form; the blossom is the good news and the fruit is the reward for it. When the blossom is shed, the fruit appears. When the former disappears, the latter begins to grow. Unless you break the bread, it does not give energy to the body. Similarly, uncrushed grapes do not turn into wine.

b) This simply means that in order to get the essence we must tolerate the shattering of the physical body. To this end, we should fast (or eat a little) and sleep a little.

41- Worldly wealth is a Divine test:

مال دنیا شد تبسمهای حق   کرد ما را مست و مغرور و خلق
فقر و رنجوری به است ای سند   کآن تبسم دام خود را بر کند
(I / 3040-3041)

a) Worldly riches are the tricks (smiles) of God, which make us drunk, proud and worn-out. O noble man, poverty and sickness are better for you so that they remove the lure of the trick.

b) The glamour of mundane wealth can make man blind and can keep him busy until he dies. If God gives wealth and health to the infidel and to the evil hearted, it does not mean that He loves them. It is to trick them further with things that will come to a fatal end. This is the greatest punishment. They will be sorry to lose what they collected in their lives. This is what the Koran says: "Let not the unbelievers think that Our respite to them is good for themselves; We grant them respite that they may grow in their iniquity but they will have a shameful punishment" (III/178). They deserve this punishment because they ignore needy people and try all kinds of tricks to satisfy their excessive greed.

42- Others' death is a reminder of your own potential fate:

عاقل آن باشد که گیرد عبرت از   مرگ یاران در بلای محترز
عاقل از سر بنهد این هستی و باد   چون شنید انجام فرعونان وعاد
(I / 3114-3122)

a) A wise man is a person who learn a lesson from the death of friends who die through a sudden calamity (which he could avoid). The wise man surrenders his personality and pride (to God) when he listens to the story of Pharaoh and Ad.

b) The death of others should teach those who deny God like the Pharaoh and the people of Ad. The people of Ad defied their prophet Hud, upon which they were destroyed in a great flood. The story of Ad belongs to Arabian tradition and they are believed to be Noah's generation who were settled in Southern Arabia (their name is mentioned many times in the Koran, see for example VII/65-72'). Pharoah, the King of Egypt's story is told in both the Koran and in the Old-Testament. He symbolises those who are proud of their worldly power and reputation, and deny God's Presence. These are stories which provide a good lesson to a reader, if he is wise enough to take it.

43- Surrender your "I" and "We" to God:

چون بمردم از حواس بوالبشر / حق مرا شد سمع و ادراك و بصر
چونك من از من نیستم این دم زهوست / پیش این دم هر که دم زد کافر اوست
جمله ما و من بپیش او نهید / ملك ملك اوست ملك او را دهید
آنك او بی نقش ساده سینه شد / نقشهای غیب را آیینه شد
(I / 3125-3126-3138-3146)

a) When I am dead to senses of man, God has become my hearing, perception and sight. Since it is not me, and my breath is His breath, then anyone who claims to be something in my presence is an infidel. Put all the "We" and "I" in front of Him, for everything belongs to Him, thus give your ownership of "We" and "I" to Him. He who has become clear-hearted and has no (worldly) impressions on the heart, is the mirror of the reflections of the Unseen.

b) These are the words of the prophet Noah to his people who did not believe him. In Rumi's eyes prophets and saints are the representatives of God and as they have set their egos aside in the path of God, they have God with them. They speak and act on behalf of His Will.

44- What present can you take to God?:

بر در یاران تهی دست آمدن / هست بی گندم سوی طاحون شدن
اندکی جنبشی بکن همچون جنین / تا ببخشندت حواس نور بین
اندکی صرفه بکن از خواب و خور / ارمغان بهر ملاقاتش ببر
شو قلیل النوم مما یهجعون / باش در اسحار از یستغفرون
(I / 3171-3180-3178-3179)   ای فتی ... در آسیا   a 3171 بردر ... شدن N + G
(in the Margin of G.) (G) اندك a 3180

a) Going to the doors of friends empty handed (without presents) is like going to a mill without wheat. Move about a bit like the embryo so that they may bestow on you the senses that allow you to see the divine light. Sacrifice a part of your sleep and food and take it as a present to God. Form the habit of sleeping a little at night and join those who pray for forgiveness early in the morning.

b) It is a custom to take a present to your friends when you pay visits to their houses. What can we take to our spiritual friends who are waiting for us in the Hereafter? What present can a man take to those who are in need of nothing from this world? Rumi suggests that you can take the bit of sleep and food that you sacrifice for God. Sleep sacrificed for the morning prayers and food that you saved for the needy or the food you did not eat to keep awake. The verse is a reference to this Koranic verse: "They (the righteous) were in the habit of sleeping but little by night, and in the hours of early dawn they were found praying for forgiveness" (LI/17 and 18). "An infidel is fond of stomach while a believer is fond of the spiritual world" is the saying of Muhammed (see Mift. 4/84).

c) "Move about a bit like the embryo" means give up laziness and try as much as possible, though you may not able to walk like a grown-up man (a matured man=a perfect man).

"They" or "the friends" here mean -as Rumi, often names them as *"Merkeziyan"* ="the holy spirits of the Centre" - are the spirits who have won God's favour and are in His vicinity. They perform duties given to them by God.

45- Philosophers are slaves of partial insight:

گو برو سر را بر این دیوار زن   فلسفی منکر شود در فکر و ظن
در جهان او فلسفی پنها نیست   هر کرا در دل شك و پیچا نیست
(I / 3278-3285)

a) A philosopher becomes an infidel due to his vain thoughts and opinions. Tell him to go and dash his head against the wall. He who has any doubts and bends in his heart is secretly a philosopher in this world.

b) Rumi does not belittle scientists and scholars but he wants them to widen their horizon of thought. He also wants them to acquire spiritual knowledge which is acquired via prophets or the living saints or by means of divine inspirations. Prophets or saints may be unlettered, but they are enlightened by the unclouded sun (see Chittick, p. 35). The knowledge of scientists or philosophers depends on their egoistic intellect which lures them just as toys lure a child. In this sense, philosophers and scientists are imprisoned in the time capsule of their birth and death. However, if they go further in knowledge and discover the Universal Insight, which is the ocean of divine wisdom, they can attain unlimited knowledge.

46- All that glitters is not gold:

بر دکان هر زر نما خندان شدست   ز آنک سنگ امتحان پنهان شدست
پرده ای ستار از ما بر مگیر   باش اندر امتحان ما مجیر
                                    (I / 3292-3293)

a) In the shop (of a goldsmith), each gilded (counterfeit) coin smiles because the touchstone is out of sight. O Veiler of our sins! don't lift up our veils and be a Protector of us during our test.

b) A hypocrite can cheat people by presenting himself as a pious man but sooner or later God removes his veils either in this world or in the world Hereafter (Ankaravi, I/601). After this explanation, Rumi prays to God, "You are a Veiler (Sitar) so, please, veil our sins here and at the Day of Judgement".

47- A rebellious partial insight is obliged to surrender to the Universal Insight:

جمله حیوان را پی انسان بکش   جمله انسان را بکش از بهر هش
هش چه باشد عقل کل هوشمند   هوش جزوی هش بود اما نژند
جمله حیوانات وحشی ز آدمی   باشد از حیوان انسی در کمی
خون آنها خلق را باشد سبیل   چون نشد اعمال انسان را قبیل
لا جرم کفار را شد خون مباح   همچو وحشی پیش نشاب و رماح
                                    (I / 3309-3310-3311-3312-3318)

a) Kill all animals (insects and other creatures) for the sake of human beings and kill all human beings for the sake of the Universal Insight. What is intellect (reason)? It is the total insight of a wise man but it is restless and low in quality. All the wild beasts that refrain from man are lower in rank than pets (that surrender to the will of man). Since wild beasts have not been capable of human actions, shedding their blood is lawful. Consequently, shedding the blood of the infidel is also permitted like that of wild beasts by means of arrows and lances (Nich. and Baki).

b) For the safety of man, dangerous insects like scorpions, snakes, germs, and wild animals etc. are killed. Pets are spared because they obey man. Similarly, if protection of the Universal Insight or purpose is required the disobedient (infidel) can be sacrificed to maintain the balance of the universe and its essence. In regard to the essence, this physical universe and its forms are like a tiny husk (see vr. No. I/3339). They can be obliterated if they do not obey the Divine Purpose.

48- The state of a vain religious man:

آتشی در وی ز دوزخ شد پدید   خویش بین چون از کسی جر می بدید
ننگرد در خویش نفس گبر را   حمیت دین خواند او و آن کبر را
(I / 3347-3348)   b 3348 گبر را G + کبریا N

a) When a vain man happens to see others' faults, the fire of hell appears in him (due to anger). He calls this pride "A defence of the religion" and yet fails to see his own faithless lower self.

b) A vain man becomes angry and begins to burn like fire of hell when he sees others' sins. He is mistaken if he thinks that to find faults in others is to protect his religion. In fact, he fails to see his own faithless lower self (MM, p. 346). The real defence of the religion is entirely different. It makes the whole world green and pleasant (see M. vr. 3349).

49- The sensual desires of ordinary people are like the toys of children:

نیست بالغ جز رهیده از هوا   خلق اطفال اند جز مست خدا
جمله بی معنی و بی مغز و مهان   جنگ خلقان همچو جنگ کودکان
همچو نی دان مرکب کودك هلا   وهم و فکر و حس و ادراك شما
(I / 3430-3435-3445)

a) Ordinary people are like children except those who are intoxicated with God and none is mature except that who is free from his sensual desires. The wars of peoples are like the children's fights, all of them meaningless, nonsense and contemptible. Accept that your thoughts, senses and ideas are like the piece of the Ney (or a stick) on which children ride (thinking it a horse).

b) Ordinary people being deprived of spiritual eyes think that whatever is around them on earth is real; and they keep busy with these things like children with their toys. Their wars on earth waged for reputation and wealth are like children's fighting for their toys.

50- Rebirth of the spiritual baby:

تن چو مادر طفل جان را حامله   مرگ درد زادنست و زلزله
جمله جانهای گذشته منتظر   تا چگونه زاید آن جان بطر
(I / 3514-3515)

a) The physical body, like a mother, is pregnant with the spiritual child; and death is the pain of birth. All the spirits that have passed to the other world wait for the spirit to see how the proud baby will be born.

b) The spirit in the body is like a baby in the womb. When the baby is born in the other world it is given a new name according to its capability. If the spirit is pure, the holy spirits waits for the newcomer, exactly the way parents waited for it in this world and they give the baby a new name.

51- What can extinguish your fire of selfhood?:

بعد از آن این نار نار شهوتست   کاندرو اصل گناه و زلتست
نار بیرونی بآبی بفسرد   نار شهوت تا بدوزخ می برد
چه کشد این نار را نور خدا   نور ابراهیم را ساز اوستا
چونکه هیزم باز گیری نار مرد   زآنکه تقوی آب سوی نار برد
(I / 3697-3698-3701-3705)

a) After this, there is a fire of lust in which is the root of sin and the substance of baseness. The external fire can be quenched by water, but the fire of lust takes you to Hell (for it is part of Hell by nature). Then what can kill the fire of lust? It is only the Light of God that can kill it, therefore, make the light of Abraham your teacher for when you take out the wood, the fire dies away. Fear of God carries "fire extinguishing water" to the fire.

b) There is no water that can quench the fire of greed except the Light of God that saved Abraham from the fire he was thrown in by the king Nimrud. When Abraham refused to worship idols, and he smashed the idols made by his father, Nimrud, the ruler of Mesopotamia, ordered his soldiers to throw Abraham into a big fire. It was at this time that the help of God came. He changed the fire into a bed of roses (called "*Gulzar-i İbrahim*"). These verses in the Koran refer to the incident: Abraham said, "Do ye then worship, besides God, things that can neither be of any good to you nor do you harm? Fie upon you, and upon the things that ye worship besides God, have you no sense?" They said, "Burn him and protect your gods, if ye do anything at all". We said, "O Fire be thou cool and protect Abraham" (XXI/66-69).

Many people worship worldly forms and beauty like the subjects of Nimrud and they need the love of God to save them from the darkness of the materialistic veils of forms.

52- It is only by means of God's help that we can be saved from the lure of lust:

باد خشــم و باد شهـوت باد آز   برد او را که نبود اهل نماز
بنـده شهـوت ندارد خود خلاص   جز بفضــل ایزد و انعــم خاص
در چهی انداخت او خود را که من   در خور قعرش نمی یابم رسن
(I / 3796-3817-3818)   Nich different: Y+G   در چهی ... یا بم رسن   a 3818

a) The wind of anger, the wind of lust and the wind of greed will take over him who offers no regular prayers. A slave of lust cannot set himself free except by means of God's mercy and His favour. A man full of lust has thrown himself into the depths of the well (of worldly) desires and I cannot find any rope long enough to rescue him from there.

b) When the animal spirit dominates over a man, he can get free of it by means of regular prayers and fasting that have the effect of acid on it or attract the Mercy of God to him by shedding tears of repentance, as Rumi suggests in other verses.

53- The lions of God seek spiritual freedom:

ما چو مصنوعیم و صانع نیستیم   جز زبون و جز که قانع نیستیم
غیر تو هر چه خوشست و ناخوشست   آدمی سوزست و عین آتشست
شیر دنیــا جوید اشکاری و برگ   شیر مولی جوید آزادی و مرگ
(I / 3917-3921-3965)

a) Since we are the created being and not the Creator, we should be humble and content. Anything other than you, be it good or bad, is man-burning and is actual fire. The lion of this world seeks prey and provision, the lion of God seeks freedom and the death of carnal lust.

b) Since we are not the Creator of this world and depend on God's mercy it is best for us to surrender to the will of God, Who is the Creator. You cannot know what is good and what is bad for your future with certainty and what you think will be good may be a burning fire. Pray to God for His help Who can enable you to feel what is good for you.

54- First deserve then desire:

او چو می خواند مرا من بنگرم / لایق جذبم ویا بد پیکرم
گر لطیفی زشت را در پی کند / تسخری باشد که او بروی کند
چاره آن باشد که خود را بنگرم / ورنه او خندد مرا من کی خرم
« طبیات الطیبین » بر وی بخوان / خوب خوبی را کند جزب این بدان
80 a طبیات از بهر که ... .Mift (II / 90-91-78-80)

a) Since He (the Beloved) is calling me, let me see whether I deserve His attraction or am ugly? For if a charming person invites (pays heed to) an ugly one, this (act) can become an object of fun (and a matter of embarrassment for the ugly one). So the remedy for this is that I see myself in the mirror first and then give a response to His call, otherwise He will laugh at me and I will fail to gain His love. Go and read this verse from the Koran, "the good women are for the good men" and remember that the beautiful attracts the beautiful.

b) In order to deserve the love of God, we must first of all make ourselves spiritually beautiful like a woman who does her make up to attract a man. Our make up is the piety of heart and the purity of soul. The mirror is the saintly man.

c) The full Koranic verse referred to here is, "Women impure are for men impure, and men impure for women impure; and good women of purity are for good men of purity..." (XXIV/26).

55- Cogito ergo sum:

ای برادر تو همآن اندیشه' / ما بقی تو استخوان و ریشه'
گر گلست اندیشه تو گلشنی / ور بود خاری تو هیمه گلخنی
(II / 277-278)

a) O brother, you are only thought, the rest of you is flesh and bone. If your ideas are flowers, you are a garden of flowers; if your ideas are thorns, then you are fuel for the stove (of baths).

b) As long as a man can think properly and discriminate between the good and the bad, he is a rational animal. But if he cannot think and fails to see any difference between the good and the bad, he is still at the level of animality. If you cultivate negative feelings towards others, you deserve the fire of hell as thorns burn well.

56- It is the heart that is blind to Divine Knowledge but not these physical eyes:

پس کلام پاک در دلهای کور   می نباید میرود تا اصل نور
گر چه حکمت را بتکرار آوری   چون تو نا اهلی شود از تو بری
ور نخوانی و ببیند سوز تو   علم باشد مرغ دست آموز تو
(II / 316-318-321)

a) The holy words (of God) do not affect blind hearts, and when they are not wanted they go back to their Source (the origin of the light). Although you learn the wisdom of this world by heart (by repeating it), yet it leaves you if you are not able to use it. And if you do not memorise (read) it yet you have an attraction to knowledge, it becomes like a docile bird in your hand.

b) Some people who are preoccupied with the transient charms of this world refuse to recognise what God's words offer them. The windows of their hearts are so tightly closed that they let no divine light or fresh wind in. Divine words are like the sunlight which, if it finds no receiver goes back to its Source. To understand and digest the words of God, one needs a sensitive heart with spiritual ears. Only such a heart can absorb the Divine Light.

c) "Heart" here means "The ultimate centre of man's essence or the nucleus of the eternal body" or "the secret treasure of God". It has four veils: 1- the heart that receives inspiration 2- the core that has the light of the belief 3- the essence that discerns God's Beauty 4- the nucleus where Love of God dwells (for a similar explanation see Dr. Seyyid Jafer's Dictionary, p. 212).

57- Weeping clouds make the plants greener:

هین سگ نفس ترا زنده مخواه   کو عدو جان تست از دیر گاه
خاک بر سر استخوانی را که آن   مانع این سگ بود از صید جان
دیده آبر دیگران نوحه گری   مدتی بنشین و بر خود می گری
ز ابر گریان شاخ سبز و تر شود   زآنک شمع از گریه روشن تر شود
a 479 دیده N + G : کرده MM   (II / 474-475-479-480)

a) Beware! Don't desire your dog-like selfhood alive (alert) for it has been your bitter enemy for ages. Pour dust on the head of these bones (let them perish) if they hinder the killing of the dog (selfhood). You have shed tears for others, weep for yourself for a while, because it is due to the crying clouds that the boughs and trees become green and the candle burns brighter with tears.

b) Don't let your lower self's desires rule over your spiritual ascension and in the presence of God be humble, as the Bible says, "Be clothed with humility" (Peter, 5/5) shed tears of penitence so that God may forgive you. God's desire is higher than our desire: "From now, then, you must live the rest of your earthly life controlled by God's will and not by human desires" (The Bible, Peter 4/2). The word "Islam" means to surrender to God totally. Here is one example of how this word is used in the Koran: Behold! his (Abraham's) Lord said to him "Bow (thy will to Me)" He said, "I bow (my will) to the Lord and Cherisher of the Universe" (II/131).

58- A believer says, "God" with the core of his heart:

کافر و مؤمن خدا گویند لیك   در میان هر دو فرقی هست لیك
آن گدا گوید خدا از بهر نان   متقی گوید خدا از عین جان
(II / 497-498)

a) A true believer and an infidel both say "God" but there is a big difference between the two; the beggar (infidel) says "God" for the sake of bread while the true believer says "God" in his very soul.

b) An infidel utters the word "God" insincerely, for a materialistic purpose, while a believer has no such aim. He loves God without the greed of the lower self, like Majnun.

59- If hypocrites said "God" from the core of their hearts they would melt away:

سالها گوید خدا آن نان خواه   همچو خر مصحف کشد از بهر کاه
گر بدل در تافتی گفت لبش   ذره ذره گشته بودی قالبش
(II / 500-501)

a) For years that bread seeker (hypocrite) says God and carries the Koran (or the Pentateuch) like a donkey that carries a load for the sake of straw (food). If the words uttered by his lips had shone in his heart, his body (being) would have shattered.

b) Those religious people who carry their books and do not become enlightened by what the books say are like donkeys that carry loads and know nothing of the load. Many religious books express the same thing (reality) but the readers do not understand their essence. As the Koran says, "The similarity of those who were charged with the (obligations of the) Mosaic Law, but who subsequently failed in those (obligations) is that of a donkey which carries huge tomes (but understands them not)..." (LXII/5). If such hypocritical people were to understand what the books said spiritually, their bodies would fall to pieces (or be destroyed) by the Light of God (for the last sentence see MM, II/60).

60- Satan's mask is painted with worldly pleasures and charms:

هر که سردت کرد میدان کو دروست   دیو پنهان گشته اندر زیر پوست

گه خیال فرجه و گاهی دکان   گه خیال علم و گاهی خان و مان

آدمی در حبس دنیا ز آن بود   تا بود کافلاس او ثابت بود

کون پر چاره ست و هیچت چاره نی   تا که نگشاید خدایت روز نی

کارگاه صنع حق چون نیستیست   پس برون کارگه بی قیمتیست

(II / 639-641-653-682-690)

a) He who tries to make you less active in divine affairs is a devil hidden by skin. He will cheat you now and then with thoughts of recreation (amusement), the shop (business), knowledge or the household. Man is in the prison of the world, so that his insolvency may be proved. Although this world is full of remedies, yet you do not see them unless God opens a window for you. Since God's workshop is non-existence, anything that falls out of it is worthless so, "Be content with God".

b) Satan keeps a man busy with something or other in this world in order to deprive him of Divine Love and Beauty. Satan does not come to cheat you directly, but by means of your friends, especially by means of those who are fond of this world and its riches. Once you surrender yourself to God, He opens many windows of remedies on you; and then you are able to know what is good for you and what is bad. You are willing to lose the worldly opportunities for the better alternatives that God has planned for you in the non-existent world.

61- Greed is like raw fruit that can hurt your digestive system:

معنی آن باشد که بستاند ترا   بی نیاز از نقش گرداند ترا

طمع خامست آن مخور خام ای پسر   خام خوردن علت آرد در بشر

کار بختست آن و آن هم نادرست   کسب باید کرد تا تن قادرست

(II / 720-732-734)

a) Spiritual reality is that which overwhelms you and sets you free from captivity to forms. Greed is raw, don't eat that my son, because eating raw things brings sickness to man. Finding (a treasure) occurs by chance and that is rare, so, toil as long as your body is able to do so.

b) Spiritual discipline of self-control and the physical discipline of prayers and fasting should free you from the walls and barriers of earthly shapes. Some people may have this quality by birth like Christ, but you can also acquire it by endeavour.

62- More words on ego:

هین بکش او را که بهر آن دنی   هر دمی قصد عزیزی می کنی

ازوی این دنیای خوش برتست تنگ   از پی او و حق و با خلق جنگ

نفس کشتی باز رستی ز اعتذار   کس ترا دشمن نماند در دیار

(II / 783-784-785)

a) Beware! kill the one (your selfhood) that brings you meanness and makes you injure your beloved friends. Due to lower self, this fair world is distressful to you and you are at war with God and His creatures. If you deny your lower self, you are freed from apologising people (that torture you) and you have no enemy on earth.

b) The lower self (ego) is the root of all evil. A saint or a godly man is loved because he is a giver but not a taker. Nobody grudges him for he is without greed. The moment your lower self becomes active, the troubles start. Others who want what you want begin to fight with you, but if you don't claim anything in this world you are more at peace and God meets your needs. The following verse of M. Iqbal is significant:

خودی کو کر بلند اتنا کہ ہر تقدیر سے پہلے

خدا بندے سے خود پو چھے بتا تیری رضا کیا ہے

(Raise your being to the extent that while writing your fate God may ask for your opinion).

63- The real food of man is the Light of God:

هست بر مؤمن شهیدی زندگی   بر منافق مردنست و زندگی

چون کسی کو از مرض گل داشت دوست   گر چه پندارد که آن خود قوت اوست

قوت اصلی بشر نور خداست   قوت حیوانی مرو را ناسزاست

از پی طاق و طرم خواری کشند   بر امید عز در خواری خوشند

چون نمی آیند اینجا کی منم   کاندرین عز آفتاب روشنم

(II / 1076-1080-1083-1104-1106)

a) For a true lover martyrdom is life while for the hypocrite it is death and destruction. It is like a person who gets used to eating clay because of sickness and thinks that it is his food. As the real food of man is the Divine Light, animal food does not suit him. People, because of pomp and show, tolerate disgrace and in the hope of their own honour they are happy to be insulted. Why don't they come to the place where I am, to the place where I shine clearly like the Sun with spiritual glory?

b) For the lovers of God death is only a change from this life to the other. In the Koran God says: And say not of those who are slain in the way of God, "They are dead". Nay they are living, though ye perceive not (II/154). When the sensual desires of people rule their spiritual desires, they do not think of the life after death. They are sick like those who become addicted to eating clay and think that, that is the best food for them. They become so fond of this world that in the hope of reputation (or rank), they tolerate all sorts of humiliation and ignore the real everlasting glory.

c) The last verse refers to the state where no worldly disgrace exists and the rays of the spiritual sun fall directly. Nazir says that Rumi does not praise himself or his state, but he, sincerely, invites others to the state where he experiences real happiness (Mift. 2-2/114).

64- The earth is not a suitable place for the lovers of God:

من نخواهم بود اینجا می روم   سوی شاهنشاه راجع می شوم
خویشتن مکشید ای جغدان که من   نه مقیمم می روم سوی وطن
این خراب آباد در چشم شماست   ورنه ما را ساعد شه باز جاست
(II / 1139-1140-1141)

a) "I don't want to stay here" (says the falcon). "So I shall return to the King of Kings. Don't kill yourselves (with agitation), O owls, because I am going to my homeland. This barren land is like a populated city in your eyes, yet for me the forearm of the King (God) is a suitable place for dwelling".

b) "Falcon" here represents a lover of God whose actual home is in the vicinity of God. "Owls" are worldly people who are happy with physical forms and worldly pleasures. In Rumi's story a falcon happens to fall among owls that are happy with the parched barren land. In the eyes of the owls the barren land is like a paradise while the falcon who knows a better place (the vicinity of God) wants to return there as soon as possible.

Physically, the falcon is with the owls but spiritually he is with his real Master (God) whose fore-arm is the peaceful abode for him. Therefore, the falcon has no home in the barren land and he tells the owls not to worry about him for he needs nothing from their land (see Mift. 2-3/126-7 and MM 113).

65- God has provided the rope of His mercy for this well:

لب ببند و کف پر زر بر گشا   بخل تن بگذار پیش آور سخا
ترک شهوتها و لذتها سخاست   هر که در شهوت فرو شد بر نخاست
یوسف حسنی و این عالم چو چاه   وین رسن صبرست بر امر اله
حمدلله کین رسن آویختند   فضل و رحمت را بهم آمیختند

(II / 1271-1272-1276-1278)

a) Close your lips and open your palms full of gold, stop being a miser with your body and bring forth your generosity. It is generosity to give up sensual lust and worldly pleasures. No one who is drowned in lust can rise up again. However, you are in beauty like Joseph, this world is like a well and the rope is your patience with the command of God. Thanks to God they have hung the rope (in the well) of grace and mercy.

b) In order to get out of this well (the world), be generous and speak less (about your generosity). To be generous also means to give up your lust. If you want the rope of God's Mercy and Grace that saved Joseph from the well, then adapt generosity and patience.

c) An allusion is made to the story of Joseph, son of the patriarch Jacob and his jealous brothers, who to get rid of their youngest brother threw him down a well. Joseph was later freed by a caravan of travellers and was taken to Egypt (for the full story see Koran XII and the Bible Gen.37).

66- The temporary and the permanent light:

برق آفل باشد و بس بی وفا   آفل از باقی ندانی بی صفا
برق را چو یخطف الابصار دان   نور باقی را همه انصار دان
عاقبت بین است عقل از خاصیت   نفس باشد کو نبیند عاقبت

b 1545 انصار N + G : ابصار MM   (II / 1542-1545-1548)

a) Lightning is transient and very faithless, you cannot differentiate between the temporary and permanent light unless you have a clean mind. Think of the lightning as something that takes away sight; regard the eternal light as the helpful one. Insight (intellect), due to its nature, is able to see far but it is the lower self that does not see the coming result.

b) The charm and beauty of this world is transient. If you have a pure sight you can also feel it. However, your lower self does not let you see this fact. Your carnal sense is like the lightning that makes you see things temporarily but the Divine Light is eternal. So, do not trust worldly beauty and try to see everything through the eyes of God. The second verse refers to this Koranic verse: "The lightning all but snatches away their (non-believers') sight; every time the light (helps) them, they walk therein, and when the darkness grows on them they stand still" (II/20).

67- The sensory eyes are deceptive:

ديده حس دشمن عقلست و كيش	خاك زن در ديده حس بين خويش
بت پرستش گفت و ضد ماش خواند	ديده حس را خدا اعماش خواند
هفت بحر آن قطره را باشد اسير	قطره كز بحر وحدت شد سفير
پيش خاكش سر نهد افلاك او	گر كف خاكى شود چالاك او
او ز عين درد انگيزد دوا	حاكمست و يفعل الله ما يشا

(II / 1607-1608-1612-1613-1619)

a) Put dust (pay no attention) on the selfish sensory eyes because they are enemies of insight and belief. God has called (the sensual eye) idolater and enemy in the Koran. Any drop that has become a messenger (envoy) of the Sea of unity, seven seas become captive to that single drop. If a handful of earth becomes active because of the duties imposed by Him, before that handful of earth the heavens will prostrate (in reverence). He is the Ruler, "He does what He wills", out of pain He produces the remedy.

b) The physical eyes and brain are selfish and don't let you think of anything else but the demands of the body. Such eyes and hearts are of no use, "They (the infidels) have hearts with which they understand not; they have eyes with which they don't see" (VII/179). In case God chooses someone, may he be a handful of earth or a tiny drop of the Sea of Unity like the prophets or saints, the whole universe bows to them out of respect. It is the Will of God, "Thou givest power to whom Thou pleasest and Thou strippest off power from whom Thou pleasest" (III/26). This does not mean that God will not give you enlightenment but that you must labour for His Mercy and Love.

68- God does not love those who sink:

این زمیـن از حلـم حـق دارد اثر   تا نجاسـت بـرد و گلهـا داد بر

تا بپوشـد او پلیدیهـای ما   در عوض بر رویـد از وی غنچها

هر گیـا را کـش بود میـل علا   در مزیـدست و حیـات و در نما

میـل روحت چون سـوی بالا بود   در تزایـد مرجعـت آنجـا بود

ور نگونسـاری سرت سـوی زمین   آفلـی حـق لایـحب الآفلـین

(II / 1803-1804-1812-1814-1815)

a) This earth has the mark of Divine Mercy, for it absorbs the filth (manure) and gives out flowers. Similarly, if God takes our evil deeds buds grow out of them. Any herb that has a tendency to grow upwards has more life and liveliness in growing. When the tendency of your spirit is upwards too, it tries to go faster to that lofty world. But if you are upside down with your head towards the earth, you sink and doubtlessly God does not like those who sink.

b) The earth is merciful because of God's command. It accepts dead bodies, filth and all kinds of dirt and gives out sweet smelling flowers instead. If the earth did not absorb them, we all would be sick. God also absorbs our sins and can change them into flowers, but struggle is essential. It should be directed upwards (like a seed) not downwards to the earth (to sensual greed). "God does not love those who set" is the sentence taken from the Koran, "I love not those that set" (the Koran, VI/76) is uttered by Abraham about the moon and the sun which he thought were God.

69- You have given up Christ and are in the service of a donkey:

جـز بشـب جلـوه نباشـد ماه را   جـز بدرد دل مجو دلخـواه را

تـرک عیسی کـرده خـر پـرورده   لا جرم چـون خر بـرون پـرده

رحم بـر عیسی کـن و بر خر مکـن   طبـع را بر عقل خود سـرور مکن

سـالها خـر بنـده بـودی بـس بود   زآنـک خـر بنـده ز خر واپـس بود

زآنـک از عاقـل جفایـی گـر رود   از وفـای جاهلان آن بـه بود

(II / 1849-1850-1853-1855-1876)

113

a) The moon shines with splendour only at night, without having heart-ache. Don't be in search of a beloved. You have given up Christ to feed the donkey, without doubt, you are like a donkey outside a tent. Have pity on Christ and not on the donkey; don't allow your carnal nature to dominate over your insight. For years you have been in the service of a donkey but a donkey's slave is behind (lower than) a donkey. And if an unkind act comes from a wise man, it is better than the loyalty of an ignorant man.

b) These verses are full of symbols. "The moon=the divine light", "the night=when the heart is full of pain", "Christ=the spirit", "Donkey=the physical body" (T. 7-8/590), "the tent=the protection of God".

If you want to attract the Mercy of your Beloved, then have a painful heart for He likes to cure sick hearts. You have ignored your spirit (Christ) and have begun to look after his donkey (the body). Since a slave of a donkey is lower (in rank) than a donkey itself, you have made yourself lower than a donkey. A wise enemy (intellect) as a friend is better than the ignorant (your body).

70- A man is known by the company he keeps:

گر خفاشی را ز خورشیدی خوریست   آن دلیل آمد که آن خورشید نیست
نفرت خفاشکان باشد دلیل   که منم خورشید تابان جلیل
کی پرد مرغی مگر با جنس خود   صحبت ناجنس گورست و لحد
بلبلان را جای می زیبد چمن   مر جعل را در چین خوشتر وطن

(II / 2084-2085-2102-2116)

a) If a bat begins to receive spiritual food from the sun, it is the proof that the sun is no longer a sun; and if the bats hate the sun, it proves that the sun is the real shining sun. A bird flies only with its own kind, the intimacy of the uncongenial is death (grave and tomb). For nightingales the most suitable place is the garden and for the beetle the best place is the dung-hill.

b) Those who are lost in greed for wealth cannot make friends with a holy man, shining like the sun. The sunlight (a spiritual message) will make them uneasy. If crows and nightingales are put together in the same cage, the crows will claim that the melodious voices of the nightingales are hideous; and the crows will even try to kill them for "Birds of a feather flock together", to such birds (people) it is better to bid "Farewell".

71- Oppose your lower self:

آنچ گوید نفس تو کاینجا بدست   مشنوش چون کار او ضد آمدست
مشورت با نفس خویش اندر فعال   هرچ گوید عکس آن باشد کمال
گر نماز و روزه می فرمایدت   نفس مکارست مکری زایدت
(II / 2266-2275-2274)

a) Don't listen to your lower self because it is bad and its deeds are upside-down. When you consult your lower self about any task, the best cause is the opposite of what it says. Even if your lower self recommends prayers and fasting to you, (beware) lower self is cunning, it may plot against you.

b) Lower self is like a snake in your body. As long as you feed it with milk, it is content with you. The moment you let it get hungry and want to take it out of your body, it rebels and begins to attack you. Being part of Satan, it plots against you. If your lower self advises you to offer regular prayers and fasting, it may mean that it wants you to show others that you are a pious man. So be careful with what your deceptive lower self says to you.

72- How does Divine curse affect a man?:

لعنت این باشد که کژبینش کند   حاسد و خودبین و پر کینش کند
تا نداند که هر آنکه کرد بد   عاقبت باز آید و بروی زند
ز آنک او گر هیچ بیند خویش را   مهلک و ناسور بیند ریش را
درد خیزد زین چنین دیدن درون   درد او را از حجاب آرد برون
(II / 2513-2514-2516-2517)

a) The Divine curse makes one see falsely and makes one jealous, vain, and full of malice. Such a person does not know what he has done until the evil comes back and strikes him. If he could discover that his lower self is nothing, he would find that his wound (disease) of being vain is unrecoverable. Pain will arise within him when he begins to feel so, and that pain will bring him out of the veils.

b) He who is cursed by God fails to see within himself and cannot remove the mask of his lower self. He is destroyed by his own malice and pride like the King of Egypt (Pharaoh) who opposed Moses. It is by means of humility that one can discover his own conceit and can eliminate the malice he cherishes for others. As the Bible says, "God resists the proud, but shows favour to the humble" (l Peter 5/5). According to the Koran, "Before thee We sent apostles to many nations and We afflicted the nations with suffering and adversity that they might learn humility" (VI/42).

73- Sometimes the lower self tricks you with the words "God is Merciful":

هیچ نکشد نفس را جز ظل پیر   دامن آن نفس کش را سخت گیر

کسب دین عشقست و جذب اندرون   قابلیت نور حق دان ای حرون

کسب فانی خواهدت این نفس خس   چند کسب خس کنی بگذار بس

آنچ می گوید درین اندیشه ام   آن هم از دستان آن نفس است هم

وآنچ میگوید غفورست و رحیم   نیست آن جز حیله نفس لئیم

(II / 2528-2601-2602-3086-3087)

a) Nothing else but the shadow of a saint can kill your lower self, so hold his skirt tight for he is a good killer of lower self. Procurement of religion is love and inner rapture and it is capability of the Divine Light, O you the obstinate one! your mean lower self is after mortal affairs, how long will you deal with the mean affairs, give them up. Someone who says "I am thinking to deny my lower self" is still captive to the lower self, and he who says, "God is Merciful and Kind" is also being cheated by lower self.

b) You can say very sincerely that you will control your selfish ego but it is not easy. Therefore, you need a saint to help you because your carnal desires will continue to trick you. In many cases you may think that God is Forgiving and Merciful and that He will forgive your sins. This idea is also put into your heart by your ego, which is in the command of Satan. Without doubt, God is Forgiving but there is a limit to that because He is Just at the same time: "We shall set up scales of justice for the day of judgment, so that not a single soul will be dealt with unjustly" (the Koran, XXI/47) and "God did not save angels who sinned" (the Bible, 2 Pet./4). God is unlikely to place those who sacrifice their lower self for the love of God in the same scale with those who depend on God's Mercy without deserving it.

74- Don't trust the courtesy of the faithless:

لطف کآید بی دل و جان در زبان   همچو سبزه ٔ تون بود ای دوستان

سوی لطف بی وفایان هین مرو   کآن پل ویران بود نیکو شنو

2842 b هین - G - خود Nich.   (II / 2840-2842)

a) The courtesy that rises up to the tongue without (rising from) the soul and heart is like the plants on the ash-heap, O my friends. Don't show bias towards the courtesy of the faithless, beware! because their courtesy is like an abandoned bridge, listen to me carefully.

b) The kindness and favours of the faithless (hypocrites) are like an abandoned bridge that may collapse if you step on it, or like plants grown on an ash-heap that can be toppled at any time by a gust of wind. The Koran also warns, "They have made their oaths a screen (for their deeds) thus they obstruct men from the Path of God; truly evil are their deeds" (LXIII/2). Rumi adds this verse:

گر بکاری کوشش اهل مجاز   تو بتو گنده بود همچون پیاز

"If you try to discover the deeds of the hypocritical (Muslims or other believers), you will find each of their deeds stinking like the layers of an onion" (II, 2900).

75- Saints are the sons of God:

اولیا اطفال حقند ای پسر   غایبی و حاضری بس با خبر
از برای امتحان خوار و یتیم   لیک اندر سر منم یار و ندیم
(III / 79-82)

a) O son, the saints are children of God. He (God) knows whatever happens to them in their presence or absence. They look deserted (orphaned) and disgraced outwardly but inwardly I (God) am their Friend and Intimate.

b) Saints (or Sheykhs) are the sons of God but not in the physical sense. They are protected by God continuously. Whenever they have troubles, God comes to help them as a mother comes to a crying baby. As God says in the Koran, "Behold verily on the friends of God there is no fear, nor shall they grieve" (X/62; this verse is repeated many times in the Koran). God hides them under His protection, although they may look poor and abandoned physically.

76- A materialistic man scrutinizes everything with the impulse of greed:

مو بمو بیند ز صرفه حرص و انس   رقص بی مقصود دارد همچو خرس
رقص آنجا کن که خود را بشکنی   پنبه را از ریش شهوت بر کنی
(III / 94-95)

a) A sensual man scrutinizes everything hair by hair because of greed and want; and he dances like a bear (meaninglessly); dance at the spot where you break up your ego into pieces and where you rip off the cotton from the sore of your lust.

b) Many materialistic scholars and philosophers undertake their studies for reputation and do not see whose signs they come across during their research. They are short sighted, and when they discover something new, they begin to dance with joy like a bear. Could they lift the curtain of their selfhood from their eyes, they would discover God's epiphany.

77- Grief is better than the empire of this world:

بوی کبر و بوی حرص و بوی آز   در سخن گفتن بیآید چون پیاز
درد آمد بهتر از ملك جهان   تا بخوانی مر خدا را در نهان
جان بده از بهر این جام ای پسر   بی جهاد و صبر کی باشد ظفر

(III / 166-203-211)

a) The smell of pride, the smell of greed and the smell of lust is felt like the smell of onion (from one's mouth). Grief is better than the empire of this world, so that you call to God in secret. Because of this cup (divine knowledge) sacrifice your worldly life for how can one be victorious without war and patience.

b) If someone's speech is full of vanity, greed, and lusty desires, these elements can be smelt. It is better to be a humble person and cry to God in secret than to be proud of your transient wealth. The price of divine knowledge is your lower self, so give it up.

78- The faithful give heed to divine warnings:

چون تو وردی ترك كردی درروش   بر تو قبضی آید از رنج و تبش
پیش از آن کین قبض زنجیری شود   این که دل گیریست پاگیری شود
رنج معقولت شود محسوس و فاش   تا نگیری این اشارت را بلاش
بی وفائی چون سگان را عار بود   بی وفائی چون روا داری نمود

(III / 349-351-352-322)

a) When you break the continuity of your regular prayers, you feel the stress of unhappiness and heat (because of repentance). Act before this stress changes into chains and the warnings of the heart become a fetter gripping the foot. Spiritual stress (contraction) will be revealed to the senses (after death) so take these warnings seriously. Even for dogs unfaithfulness is a disgrace, how dare you show unfaithfulness to God, your Lord?

b) When you stop your regular prayers to God or the *zikr* and do something bad, God sends your heart a warning (in the form of stress); and if you pay no further attention to the warnings, they change into chains and fetters for the spiritual body. Your disobedience is not recognised by your spiritual senses until you die. Then there is no remedy. Dogs are faithful to their masters. How can you as a human being be disloyal to God?

79- Don't lose the whole treasure for the sake of a piece of gold:

هرچ از یارت جدا اندازد آن   مشنو آنرا کآن زیان دارد زیان

گر بود آن سود صد در صد مگیر   بهر زر مسکل ز گنجورای فقیر

(III / 419-420)

a) Whatsoever takes you away from your Friend don't listen to that because that brings a loss, a real loss. May it be a hundred percent profitable deed, O Sufi, don't leave the treasure for the sake of a piece of gold.

b) There are many profitable things on the earth, at least they seem to be so. But if they hinder your friendship with God, Who is the possessor of all treasures then why burn a blanket for a tiny flea!

80- Be submissive like the earth:

گر شود ذرات عالم حیله پیچ   با قضای آسمان هیچند هیچ

هرچ آید ز آسمان سوی زمین   نی مفر دارد نه چاره نی کمین

او شده تسلیم او ایوب وار   کی اسیرم هرچ میخواهی بیار

ای که جزو این زمینی سرمکش   چونک بینی حکم یزدان در مکش

بین که اندر خاک تخمی کاشتم   گرد خاکی و منش افراشتم

حمله دیگر تو خاکی پیشه گیر   تا کنم بر جمله میرانت امیر

اصل نعمتها ز گردون تا بخاک   زیر آمد شد غذای جان پاک

از تواضع چون ز گردون شد بزیر   گشت جزو آدمی حی دلیر

جمله اجزا در تحرک در سکون   ناطقان کانا الیه راجعون

(III / 447-449-452-453-455-456-460-461-464)

a) If all the atoms of the world (universe) begin to conspire and start making plans, their tricks are of no use in the presence of the celestial ordinance. Whatever comes from Heaven to earth, it (earth) has no remedy, no refuge, or means to refuse what comes down. The earth has surrendered to the Divine Ordinance like the prophet Jacob and says, "I am Thy captive, bring on me whatever Ye want". You too who are part of this earth, don't rebel when you receive God's ordinance. Do notice! I sowed you in the clay and while you were only dust I exalted you. Move on once again and be the nature of earth (humble) so that I may make you a ruler over rulers (spiritually). The essence of the gifts which ascend from Heaven to earth, changes into food for our pure soul. Since it (the essence) comes down to earth due to humility, it becomes part of the human being, lively and brave. All elements, whether at rest or in action, speak and say, "We have come from God and to Him shall we return".

b) Every atom of the universe is submissive to the divine ordinance and none can rebel. Then why should man rebel against divine fate? The earth is submissive to God and grows whatever is sown. Similarly, the seed of man (the spirit) in the clay of man's body can change into a plant, if his body remains submissive. All the minerals that came to earth from other planets are in the service of man. The essence (soul) also came from the other world and became a part and parcel of the human being. All this happens because every particle obeys God and knows that it will go back to Him. Man is no exception, as God says in the Koran, "From earth did We create you, and into it shall We return you and from it shall We bring you out once again" (XX/55); "To God we belong and to Him is our return" (II/56); and "To Him belongs the dominion of the heavens and the earth; in the end it is to Him that ye shall be brought back" (XXXIX/44). The universe is going in a certain direction and man cannot stop it.

81- War teaches peace:

خشـمهای خلق بهر آتشیـست   دام راحت دایماً بی راحتیـست
بهر یاری مار جوید آدمی   غم خورد بهر حریف بی غمی
(III / 990-994)

a 990 خشمهای N + G : جنگهای MM
b 990 بهر یاری N + G : بهربازی MM

a) The anger (wars) of mankind is for the sake of peace and restlessness is always a trap of relaxation (peace). For the sake of friendship, man seeks a snake; and worries for the one who does not care for you.

b) Man wages war and takes troubles to learn the value of peace. If a man does not face the difficulties of war, how can he realise the value of peace? A snake catcher or a snake charmer makes friends with a snake to earn his living while the snake does not care a straw for him (see also Baki, III/64). In other words there is no peace or earning a living without danger. The body of man is also like a snake. You feed it but it does not care for you and rebels when you need it. Consequently, it is the spiritual body that is eternal and deserves your attention.

82- Everyone is created for some kind of job:

میل آنرا در دلش انداختند   هر کسی را بهر کاری ساختند

خار و خس بی آب و بادی کی رود   دست و پا بی میل جنبان کی شود

پر دولت بر گشا همچون هما   گر ببینی میل خود سوی سما

نوحه می کن هیچ منشین از حنین   ور ببینی میل خود سوی زمین

(III / 1618-1619-1620-1621)

a) Everyone is created for some job or business and the tendency to that very job is also placed in his heart. Otherwise how could hands and feet move without the tendency? And how can husks and thorns (dry herbs) float over water without the help of wind (and water)? Now, if you find that your tendency is towards Heaven stretch your wings of victory like the Huma, but if you find that your tendency is towards the earth (this world), then continue to cry and moan.

b) Everyone on earth has some kind of business to carry out. If a dervish receives the fresh wind of the north (of God), he no longer needs people's breath or their speeches. His business is to be busy with Divine Love. Others do what God puts in their hearts. However, if your heart inclines towards this mortal world, then pray to God for He may change your duty; but if you are created for good deeds, then try your best in that position.

c) The word "*Shamul*" has been translated in different ways: "Inclusion of the Divine Mercy" (Mift.); "Riches and dainties" (Baki.); "Love wine" (T.); "North wind" (Nich.). Perhaps the best translation is "the fresh north wind that increases the fermentation of wine" (see Anand., vol. 4, p. 2675). Here it means "the holy wind that increased the intoxication of the dervish". "*Huma*" = the lammergeier (great bearded vulture). According to popular belief, the falling of its shadow on someone was a sign that he would become a king (Nich. foot note, III/p. 91).

83- Life and rebirth:

چون جنین را در شکم حق جان دهد / جذب اجزا در مزاج او نهد
از خورش او جذب اجزا می کند / تار و پود جسم خود را می تند
جزب اجزا روح را تعلیم کرد / چون نداند جذب اجزا شاه فرد
جامع این ذرها خورشید بود / بی غذا اجزات را داند ربود
(III / 1756-1757-1759-1760)

a) When God gives life (spirit) to the embryo in the womb, He places genetic heredity in it so that it may absorb the elements. By means of food, it absorbs the elements and weaves the warp and woof of its body. The Only King Who taught the spirit to absorb those elements, doesn't He then know how to gather the elements together again and create man from them? (Baki, III/p. 125). The collector of those elements was the Sun which is able to gather them together again without nutrition.

b) When God gives life to the embryo He provides a genetic programme by means of which the embryo absorbs the essential elements via food. God, Who taught the same to the spirit, thereby gives it a new body. God is like the Sun, Whose radiation is the source of life. Rumi gives another illustration of the same idea (see M. vr. No.1761): "At night, you go to sleep forgetting everything, and when you wake up your memory and ideas come back again. Now, if God wanted, you could forget everything forever. In this respect you are helpless. Similarly, in your life after death, God can transfer your memory and ideas of this world to the other world". This is what the Koran says: "We have decreed death to be your common lot, and We are not to be frustrated from changing your forms and creating you (again) in forms that ye know not" (LVI/60-61).

84- Rumi disapproves of homosexuality:

شهوت و حرص نران پیشی بود / وآن حیزان ننگ و بد کیشی بود
حرص مردان از ره پیشی بود / در مخنث حرص سوی پس رود
آن یکی حرص از کمال مردیست / وآن دگر حرص افتضاح و سردیست
(III / 1956-1957-1958)

a) The lust and greed of the man is in his front while that of the homosexual (effeminate) is shame and irreligion. The greed of a true man is in his front side, the greed of the effeminate goes backward. The one greed belongs to the completeness of manliness, while the other greed is opprobrium and disgust.

b) Rumi disapproves of homosexuality because it is against the Divine Order. Woman is created for man and man is created for woman. The lust of a Sufi by dint of spiritual training changes into desires for the love of God, but the lusty desire of the evil-minded changes into effeminacy (Mift. 3-1/338).

85- Spiritual filth can be cleaned by tears:

این نجاسه ظاهر از آبی رود   آن نجاسه باطن افزون میشود

جز بآب چشم نتوان شستن آن   چون نجاسات بواطن شد عیان

(III / 2092-2093)

a) This outer dirt can be cleaned with water, but the inner dirt keeps on increasing; it can be cleansed only by water of the eyes (tears) when it becomes manifest.

b) If someone can discover his inner dirt (sin), he can clean it by crying to God. The water used for ablution can only clean the outer dirt. The smell of the outer dirt can be felt only from twenty yards while the smell of inner dirt of an infidel is felt even from Heaven (see vr. 2096). If you want to clean the rust of your interior mirror, then shed tears of repentance over your sins.

86- A worldly man possesses nothing yet he is afraid of thieves:

مرد دنیا مفلس است و ترسناک   هیچ او را نیست از دزدانش باك

او برهنه آمد و عریان رود   وز غم دزدش جگر خون میشود

وقت مرگش که بود صد نوحه پیش   خنده آید جانش را زین ترس خویش

صد هزاران فضل داند از علوم   جان خود را می نداند آن ظلوم

داند او خاصیت هر جوهری   در بیان جوهر خود چون خری

آن اصول دین بدانستی تو لیك   بنگر اندر اصل خود گرهست نیك

(III / 2632-2633-2634-2648-2649-2655)

a) The worldly man is penniless and timid. He has nothing in his own possession yet he is afraid of a thief (see T. and Baki.). Although he comes to this world and goes from this wofull of pain because of this. When at his death many shed tears and lament, he begins to laugh at his own fear. Although he (the worldly man) knows a hundred thousand (many) uses of knowledge yet he, the cruel knows nothing about himself (his soul). He knows the properties of every substance but as defining his own essence he is as ignorant as a donkey. He has learnt the fundamentals of religion, but he has not learnt whether he himself is pious or not.

b) A worldly (materialistic) man comes into this world naked like all others but when he dies, he has nothing in his hand spiritually and returns empty handed to the other world. In this respect, he is penniless in the eyes of a saint or a lover of God. If a scientist has not used his knowledge for knowing God and His signs, he is still as ignorant as a donkey. Yunus Emre adds this: "Learning means to learn about yourself, and if you don't know yourself then what kind of learning is this?" A theologian (philosopher) is also proud of his knowledge about God's religion. He knows something about God but he does not know God. A worldly man when he dies discovers that he was afraid of thieves (other greedy people) for nothing, because whatever he possessed was, in fact, not property but only a deception. It is then that he realises his folly (for the last sentence see Koner p. 365).

87- It is better to embark on the journey to the other world by taking some precautions:

یا بحال اولینان بنگرید یا سوی آخر بحزمی در پرید

حزم چه بود در دو تدبیر احتیاط از دو آن گیری که دورست از خباط

حزم آن باشد که برگیری تو آب تارهی از ترس و باشی بر صواب

گر بود در راه آب این را بریز ور نباشد وای بر مرد ستیز

(III / 2841-2842-2845-2846)

a) Either think of the people who lived in the past, or think of the present situation and fly towards the aim prudently. What is prudence? It means to decide between two alternatives and you should select the one that is far from danger (T. 9-10/740). It is prudent to take water with you so that you may be free from fear (of thirst) and be on the right path, and if you find fresh water on the way, spill the one you had taken with you; and if there be none on the way, alas for the obstinate!

b) There are two ways of obeying God. Either learn from the lives of people who lived in the past, as the Koran says, "Say, travel through the earth and see what was the end of those before you, most of them worshipped others besides God" (XXX/42), or to learn from the life of people in the present who go astray from God and meet a bad end. You had better choose the wiser cause. The way of God is to take precautions against worldly tricks and traps. Take with you the water (your piety) if you want to pass through the desert (this world), so that you have no fear of thirst; and if you find the fresh water (the divine light and Mercy of God) on the way then you may throw away your own water. But wretched is the man who finds no water on the way and has been negligent in bringing none with him.

88- A godless man adheres to this world like an embryo to the womb of its mother:

چون جنین کش میکشد بیرون کرم میگریزد او سپس سوی شکم
که اگر بیرون فتم زین شهر و کام ای عجب بینم بدیده این مقام
(III / 3964-3966)

a) (The worldly man) is like the embryo that is drawn out by Mercy of God, but runs back towards the belly (womb) of its mother thinking that if it leaves that abode it may not be able to see that home (place) again (Mift, 3-4/255 and T.II-12/1034).

b) Death for a faithless materialistic man can be painful for he has no idea about the life Hereafter. He wants to stay in this world which he thinks is the only abode, like a baby which thinks that its mother's womb is the only place suitable for life.

89- The heart of an infidel:

گبر ترسان دل بود کو از گمان می زید در شک ز حال آنجهان
می رود در ره نداند منزلی گام ترسان می نهد اعمی دلی
پس مشو همراه این اشتر دلان زآنک وقت ضیق و بیمند آفلان
نفس و شیطان هر دو یک تن بوده اند در دو صورت خویش را بنموده اند
(III / 4027-4028-4032-4053)

a) The non-believer has a timid heart because he is doubtful about the state of the other world. He walks on the path yet he does not know of the terminus. Since his heart is blind, he treads timidly. Do not join those camel-hearted, for at the time of hunger and danger they sink. The carnal senses and the devil are the same, although they seem to have two different shapes.

b) An atheist is like a blind man who feels in the darkness and whose scepticism and partial insight makes him stumble around on the earth. He is camel hearted (full of suspicion) and can rebel at a crucial moment, so do not trust him.

90- Evil deeds bring evil results:

زآنکه تخمست و برویاند خداش   چونک بد کردی بترس آمن مباش

آیدت زآن بد پشیمان و حیا   چند گاهی او بپوشاند که تا

باز گیرد از پی اظهار عدل   بارها پوشد پی اظهار فضل

آن مبشر گردد این منذر شود   تا که این هر دو صفت ظاهر شود

(IV / 165-166-170-171)

a) When you have done evil (to some one) don't feel safe because evil is seed and God will make it grow. Sometimes, God hides your sins so that you may feel ashamed and repent them. Many times He hides your evils out of His Mercy, but He gets hold of a sinner for the sake of justice, so that both His attributes may become manifest, "Giver of good tidings" and "the Warner".

b) God is both Merciful and Just at the same time. He forgives some people out of His clemency. He can punish others because He is just. If you commit an evil act against another, it will harm you. This is what the Koran says: "In the long run evil in the extreme will be the end of those who do evil..." (XXX /10).

91- Not all deserve the Mercy of God:

چونک در بازار عطاران رسید   آن یکی افتاد بیهوش و خمید

بوی مشک آرد برو رنجی پدید   آنک در تون زاد و پاکی را ندید

در خور و لایق نباشد ای ثقات   مر خبیثان را نسازد طیبات

(IV / 257-256-282)

a) When a certain man (a tanner) went to a perfumer's market, he fell down, fainted, and bent double. He, who is born in the stove and hasn't seen cleanness, to him the smell of musk will be unbearable and nasty. You trusty one, soft words have no effect upon the wicked and they don't suit them.

b) The man who is brought up in bad company does not have the sense to reform his character and he will not listen to advice, because your sweet words about God will make him restless as the scent of musk does to a tanner who is used to the stink of leather. About such people Muhammed Iqbal says:

"Maybe it is possible to cut the core of a diamond with a rose-petal, but soft and modest words have no effect on an ignorant person". To such people it is better to say only "Goodbye". As the Koran says, "And the servants of God Most Gracious are those who walk on the earth in humility, and when the ignorant addresses them they say, "Peace" (XXV/63).

92- Every atom is part of the Divine Army:

جمله ذرات زمین و آسمان   لشکر حقند گاه امتحان
چونک جان جان هر چیزی ویست   دشمنی با جان جان آسان کیست
جزو جزوت لشکر او در وفاق   مر ترا اکنون مطیعند از نفاق
(IV / 783-797-793)

a) All the atoms of the earth and sky (Heaven) are the army of God at the time of trial. Since the Soul of Soul is God, it is not easy to be the enemy of that Soul of Souls. Each particle of your elements is part of His army and is at His beck and call. However, they look obedient to you because they pretend to be so.

b) Every atom is obedient to God, including man's body and its elements. As God says in the Koran, "His are all things in the Heaven and on the earth" and "To God belong the forces (army) of the heavens and the earth" (XLVII/4). In case anyone resists God's command, He tests them and His army begins to act. New diseases appear and catastrophes take place in order to remind men of God's being.

93- **This world is the idol-temple of lust and wealth:**

احمد و بوجهل در بتخانه رفت   زین شدن تا آن شدن فرقیست زفت
این در آید سر نهند او را بتان   آن در آید سر نهد چون امتان
اینجهان شهوتی بتخانه ایست   انبیا و کافران را لانه ایست
لیک شهوت بنده پاکان بود   زر نسوزد زآنک نقد کان بود
(IV / 816-817-818-819)

a) Ahmed (the prophet Muhammed) and Abu Jehil both went to the idol-temple but there is a great difference between Muhammed's going and Abu Jehil's going there. When Muhammed went there, idols bowed to him and when Abu Jehil went there he bowed to the idols (being their worshipper). This world, too, is the idol-temple of lust and is the abode of the infidel and the prophets, but lust is the slave of the pious men (prophets and saints) for gold does not burn away (lose its value) by being in the mine (with dust, stones, and minerals).

b) In the idol-temple the infidel (Abu Jehil) worships the idols, while the same idols worship the lovers of God for they are part of God themselves. This world is also like a huge temple where some infidels worship wealth and gold. But wealth and gold worship a prophet or a man of God.

94- What you sow, so shall you reap:

محسنان مردند و احسانها بماند   ای خنک آنرا که این مرکب براند
ظالمان مردند و ماند آن ظلمها   وای جانی کو کند مکر و دها
(IV / 1201-1202)

a) The beneficent die but their good deeds remain. Lucky is the man who rides this horse (of beneficence). The cruel die and their cruelty remains and alas for the soul that practises deceit and fraud.

b) Good deeds have everlasting good memories while cruelty (injustice) has the opposite effect. Deceit and fraud in the end receive punishment (Konevi, IV, p. 251). Since God is the creator of man, He knows all the tricks man can play: "And (the unbelievers) plotted and planned (their tricks) and God too planned and the best of planners is God (He knows their intricate plans)" (the Koran, III/54) and "God loves those who are kind (beneficent)" (V/14).

95- Your greedy lower self is like a crow that takes you to the graveyard:

عقل تو دستور و مغلوب هواست   در وجودت رهزن راه خداست
عقل جزوی عقل استخراج نیست   جز پذیرای فن و محتاج نیست
عقل جزوی را وزیر خود مگیر   عقل کل را ساز ای سلطان وزیر
هین مدو اندر پی نفس چو زاغ   کو بگورستان برد نه سوی باغ
گاو گر واقف ز قصابان بدی   کی پی ایشان بدآن دکان شدی
(IV / 1246-1295-1258-1312-1327)

a) Your carnal intellect is like a vizier and is obedient to your carnal desires. In your body it is like a bandit who hinders your way to God. Partial insight is unable to make any deduction. It depends on what science tells you. Don't let your partial insight be your vizier, make the universal insight your vizier or Sultan. Don't run after your lower self which is like a crow that takes you towards the graveyard and not towards the garden. If a cow knew what a butcher is, she would not follow him to his shop.

b) If you follow only your own intellect, and disregard the spiritual warning of a saint or a prophet, you will be led to a graveyard (a bad end) because your ego is selfish like a crow. The sensual intellect depends on worldly knowledge which is also a product of ego. There is no harm in using worldly knowledge as long as it does not hinder your path to God, for "A crow is a wise bird but it lives on dirt".

96- The lower self never keeps its promise and is deceptive:

هر دو اندر بی وفائی یك دلند	این جهان و اهل او بی حاصلند
گرچه رو آرد بتو آن رو قفاست	زاده دنیا چو دنیا بی وفاست
تا ابد در عهد و پیمان مستمر	اهل آن عالم چو آن عالم زبر
او دنی و قبله گاه او دنیست	نفس بی عهدست زآن روكشتنیست
(IV / 1649-1650-1651-1654)	

a) This world and its followers are all good-for-nothing, both suit each other in the matter of faithlessness. The world-born (worldling) is faithless like the world, though his face is towards you; actually, it is not his face but his back. But the one that belongs to the other world is strong (in character) like the other world and keeps his promise and words forever. Selfness never keeps its promise and, therefore, deserves death. It is mean and its aims are also mean.

b) The people who worship this world are the children of this world and they depend on it. As this world is transient and deceptive so are her children. But those who believe in God and the eternal Hereafter are not deceptive and keep their promises.

97- Death is the touchstone of our deeds:

سنگ مرگ آمد نمکها را محك	هر کسی را دعوی حسن و نمك
در صفآ ای قلب و اکنون لاف زن	چون محك پنهان شدست از مرد و زن
زر خالص را چه نقصانست گاز	مرگ تن هدیه ست بر اصحاب راز
(IV / 1674-1677-1681)	

a) Everyone claims beauty and charm (saltness). It is death which is the touchstone of such claims. Since the touchstone (death) has hidden itself from men and women (people), O counterfeit coin, come in the line with the genuine ones and then boast! The death of the body is a gift to the people who know the secret; (after all) what damage can scissors do to gold?

b) There is no remedy for death, as the Koran says: "The death from which ye flee will truly overtake ye; then ye will be sent back to the Knower of things, secret and open, and He will tell ye (the truth) the things ye did" (IXII/8). Those who deny God and His love will learn upon death the reality. Many try to present themselves as good people but death serves as a touchstone and tells which is the real coin and which is the false one. Some can keep on cheating outwardly like the gilded iron rod, but when death comes it reveals the inner reality of the rod.

98- Your immediate enemy is your carnal soul:

و اندرون خوش گشته با نفس گران تو هم از بیرون بدی با دیگران
وز برون تهمت بهر کس مینهی خود عدوت اوست قندش میدهی
(IV / 1918-1919)

a) You, too, are outwardly bad with others and have become friendly with your inner enemy (the lower self). As a matter of fact, the real enmity is that you feed your inner lower self with sugar and outwardly you accuse others.

b) There is a Turkish proverb: "An acidulous vinegar damages its own jar". Similarly, a hypocritical man damages himself little by little. One should first fight with the egoistic lower self the real enemy and then blame others, for "Charity begins at home".

99- Man imprisons himself because of his own greed:

در متاع فانیی چون فانی اند خلق را بنگر که چون ظلمانی اند
وآنگهی مفتاح زندانش بدست این عجب که جان بزندان اندرست
مرده از جان زنده اندر مخرقه از تکبر جمله اندر تفرقه
کز گزافه دل نمی جوید پناه نور پنهانست و جست و جو گواه
(IV / 2032-2034-2033-2037)

a) See the people (human kind) they are in the darkness and along with mortal wealth they perish. The most amazing point is that such people, although they have the key of the prison, yet they are in prison! Due to their own pride they are scattered, they are dead spiritually but are (pretending to be) alive with obstinacy. The light of God is hidden but the search is its proof because the heart does not look for shelter in vain.

b) Many people get lost in the riches of this world and are so charmed by them that they imprison themselves in the walls of forms, although the key of freedom is in their own hand. The lock is their own pride, and it is the pride that has divided them into social and religious groups. The heart is like a sensitive detector, it looks for divine light, but the ego covers it with heavy clouds.

100- Why wine is forbidden in Islam?:

نه همه جا بی خودی شر میکند   بی ادب را می چنان تر میکند
گر بود عاقل نکوفر می شود   ور بود بد خوی بتر می شود
لیک اغلب چون بدند و ناپسند   بر همه می را محرم کرده اند
حکم اغلب راست چون غالب بدند   تیغ را از دست ره زن بستدند
(IV / 2156-2157-2158-2159)

a) Intoxication does not cause mischief on every occasion (time) but wine makes an unmannered person more mischievous. If the wine drinker is intelligent, his intelligence increases, but if he is ill-mannered, his negative character becomes more forceful. Since many people are bad and ill-mannered, wine has been forbidden to all. Cases are decided by the general rules; since the majority is evil, the sword is taken from the hands of the bandit.

b) Wine can make some people more intelligent and well-mannered but it provokes a great number of people to commit crime and sin. God has forbidden it without exception and, therefore, has tried to take the sword from the hands of the cruel. Even if wine is good, let us sacrifice it for sake of those who forget themselves when they drink.

c) The verse « بی خودی...گردد مدام » (Selfness becomes well-mannered through wine and the well-mannered become evil for ever because of wine) does not exist in the "G" or even in "Nich." It has been added later (for this verse see MM, III-IV/209).

These are some Koranic verses about wine: They ask thee concerning wine and gambling, say to them, "In them is great sin and some profit for men, but the sin is greater than the profit" (II/219), and "Satan's plan is to excite enmity and hatred among you with intoxication and gambling; and hinder you from the remembrance of God, and from prayers. Will ye not then abstain?" (V/93).

101- Give your temporary kingdom to God so that He may give you the permanent one:

نردبان خلق این ما و منیست   عاقبت زین نردبان افتاد نیست
هر که بالاتر رود ابله ترست   کاستخوان او بتر خواهد شکست
ده خداوندی عاریت بحق   تا خداوندیت بخشد متفق
(IV / 2763-2764-2778)

a) The egoism and selfhood of the ladder from which one falls in the end and he who goes higher is more foolish because his bones will be more badly broken. Give your rented kingdom to God so that He may give you the kingdom that is liked by everyone.

b) Ordinary people are crazy for fame, reputation and wealth. But it is a ladder from which they slip and fall in the end. The higher they climb, the further they fall. Ranks, fame and wealth are attractive but to lose them is painful. Sacrifice them to please God so that He may grant you eternal pleasure.

102- Unbelievers depend on what they see physically:

حجت منکر همین آمد که من   غیر این ظاهر نمی بینم وطن
هیچ نندیشد که هر جا ظاهریست   آن ز حکمتهای پنهان مخبریست
فایده هر ظاهری خود باطن است   همچو نفع اندر دواها کامن است
(IV / 2878-2879-2880)

a) The sign of an unbeliever is that he says, "I see no country (abode) other than this (phenomenal world)". He does not think that where there is something manifest, there is also hidden wisdom (behind). The benefit of each manifest object is in its hidden (esoteric) part, like the medicine in a herb.

b) Unbelievers seek outer proof while they forget that they must try to probe into the esoteric reality that will give them the proof of the other world and God. Take for example an onion or a leaf. Before the invention of the electromicroscope they were viewed as simple objects but later they revealed new worlds. Similarly, man's spiritual world will also be discovered one day. The lovers of God know this world and the world to come by means of Divine Knowledge. Rumi throws further light on the subject when he says:

"No painter paints a picture regardless of any object or benefit behind it. No jar maker makes a jar without thinking of water or any other liquid. All outer forms are for unseen objects, and even the unseen ones are for the further unseen ones, layers after layers and their benefits are also in accordance with their numbers" (IV/vr. 2881-2884-2887-2888).

103- What kind of selfhood is preferable?:

این منی و هستیِ اول بود   که برو دیده کژ و احول بود

آن منی و هستبت باشد حلال   که درو بینی صفات ذوالجلال

دانك هر شهوت چو خمرست و چو بنگ   پرده هوشست و عاقل زوست دنگ

بی مجاعت نیست تن جنبش کنان   آهن سردیست میکوبی بدان

(IV / 3562-3573-3612-3623)

a) This is your lower self and your prime being as long as it (the prime being) is there, you see everything twisted and oblique. Only that kind of self is allowed (or is legal) in which you see only the attributes of God. Know that sensual desires are like wine and *beng* which unveils the intelligence of a wise man, who is thus stupefied. Without hunger nobody will come into action; to train a well-fed body is like hammering a cold piece of iron.

b) Rumi is referring to the kind of self that expresses the attributes of God, which in Islam are 99 in number (101 in the Avesta). If we want to be with God or be His friend, we should try to possess some of His attributes (see step 9 here for other details). To do this we must first of all try to keep our stomach empty because a full stomach can keep us lazy and lusty. Beng or bheng: dried hemp leaves.

104- Kill the four birds:

سر ببر این چار مرغ زنده را   سرمدی کن خلق نا پاینده را

بط حرصست و خروس آن شهوتست   جاه چون طاوس و زاغ امنیتست

(V / 42-44)

a) Cut off the heads of these four lively birds and make (your) mortal being immortal. The duck is greed, the cock is lust, rank (reputation) is the peacock, and crow is the lower self (of a materialistic man).

b) The duck is the symbol of a greedy person because it keeps eating all day and pecks its beak in the mud and dirt. The cock has sex in its mind even when it pecks at dirt, and, therefore, is a symbol of lusty desires. The peacock very much wants to show its beautiful feathers, and represents a self-important person who likes fame. The crow likes to eat and enjoys its life, hence it symbolises the greedy lower self of a person. Consequently, by killing these birds man can be at peace (see also Koner, p. 620). In the Koran, God asks Abraham to tame four birds (see II/260). The peacock and the duck are also mentioned in "The Conference of the Birds" by Feriduddin Attar, which Rumi must have read carefully. In that book the two birds are content with this world and do not want to go in search of the mystical Simurgh bird.

105- Men seek different aims because the real Aim has been concealed from them:

چون ملک از لوح محفوظ آن خرد   هر صباحی درس هر روزه برد
بر عدم تحریرها ببین بی بنان   واز سوادش حیرت سوداییان
هر کسی شد بر خیالی ریش گاو   گشته در سودای گنجی کنج کاو
وآن دگر بهر ترهب در کنشت   وآن یکی اندر حریصی سوی کشت
قبله جان را چو پنهان کرده اند   هر کسی رو جانبی آورده اند

b 320 کنج کاو N + G : گنج گاو MM   (V / 317-319-320-323-329)

a) Like the angels our insight reads its lesson from the preserved-tablet (a spiritual tablet on which everything is noted by God) every morning. See those words written without fingers on non-existence and they (the written words and their blackness) drive blind lovers (true lovers) mad. Everyone has become crazy over some idea (fantasy) and has begun to dig some corner from love of a treasure. While one goes to church to become a monk, the other goes to the farm for hope of grain. Since they have hidden the centre of prostration *(Qibla)* everyone prostrates in a different direction.

b) Confusion in this world is due to the fact that God has hidden His Beauty and put forth physical forms as a curtain. People love these forms because they cannot see God clearly. Had His Beauty been exposed to all people, they would not have run after any other goal but God. God says in the Koran, "All that they do is noted in their books of deeds, every matter, small and great, is on record" (LIV/52-53 and Ankaravi, V, p. 91). As there are two kinds of insights: partial insight *(akl-i juz)* and universal insight *(akl-i kul)*, similarly there are two destinies: 1- partial destiny *(kadr-i juz)* and 2- universal destiny *(kadr-i kul)*. The latter is written on the preserved-tablet *(lawh-i mahfuz)* and the former belongs to an individual who can control it. Universal insight forces a man to perform his duties in accordance with the written fate for which he has been sent to this world, but partial insight, being mundane in nature, forces man to serve his physical body only. Little by little man can surrender his lower self to universal destiny and gain the state of saintliness. It is like connecting your personal computer to the main frame. The lovers of God are able to read the preserved-tablet and are surprised when they notice that people do something else other than that they were predestined for.

106- Your righteous deeds are the only faithful friends of yours:

در زمانه مر ترا سه همرهند   آن یکی وافی و این دو غدرمند

آن یکی یاران ودیگر رخت و مال   وآن سوم وافیست آن حسن الغِعال

مال نآید با تو بیرون از قصور   یار آید لیك آید تا بگور

فعل تو وافیست زو کن ملتحد   که در آید با تو در قعر لحد

اولش علمست آن گاهی عمل   تا دهد بر بعد مهلت یا اجل

(V / 1045-1046-1047-1050-1057)

a) In this world you have three friends (fellow travellers), only one of them is faithful and the others are treacherous. Your only faithful friend is your righteousness (good deeds) while your friends and wealth are disloyal. Your property or wealth does not leave your palaces with you, but your faithful friend accompanies you to the grave. First gain knowledge then act accordingly so that you may receive its fruit after some time or after death.

b) We have three friends in this world: 1- Friends whom we trust 2- Wealth 3- Good deeds. Wealth is left behind, friends come to the grave only, but good deeds go with you to the other world. As the Koran says, "But those who have faith and work righteousness, they are Companion of the garden (paradise), there they shall abide forever" (II/82). In order to discriminate between the right and the wrong, we need religious or divine knowledge. Almost all religious books suggest the same righteous deeds. For example, the Koran suggests the following deeds: "But it is righteousness to believe in God and in the last day, and the angels, and the books and the messengers (all the prophets); to spend your wealth willingly for your kin, for orphans, for the needy, for the wayfarer, for those who ask, and for the ransom of slaves; to be steadfast in prayer, and practise regular charity; to fulfill the contracts (promises) that you have made; and to be firm and patient, in pain or suffering and adversity and throughout all periods of panic. Such are the people of truth, the God fearing" (II/I77). Some other good deeds in Islam are: 1- To tell the truth 2- To fast 3- To be just 4- Not to steal anything 5- To avoid alcohol and fornication and 6- To avoid jealousy and malice. After this basic physical training one should try to possess attributes of God, His love, and the spiritual perfection that suits a lover of God.

107- Christ in the form of a man was homogeneous with the angels:

هست تن چون ریسمان بر پای جان / می کشاند بر زمینش ز آسمان

موش تن زآن ریسمان بازش کشد / چند تلخی زین کشش جای میچشد

عقل را افغان ز نفس پر عیوب / همچو بینیئ بدی بر روی خوب

فرق زشت و نغز از عقل آورید / نی ز چشمی کز سیه گفت و سپید

نیست جنسیت بصورت لی و لك / عیسی آمد در بشر جنس ملك

(VI / 2735-2737-2951-2967-2973)

a) The body is like a string tied on the foot of the soul that draws it down to earth from Heaven. The mouse of the body pulls it back and the soul feels great bitterness because of this pulling. Intelligence (reason) complains about the defective carnal body, like the bad nose on a beautiful face. Try to find the difference between black and white not by means of the eye that tells you "This is black and this is white" but by means of reason. Homogeneity does not depend on shape or forms; Christ came among people in the form of a man while inwardly he was homogeneous with the angels.

b) Rumi again warns us to be careful of trusting physical eyes. They are liable to deceive us. Whatever they show us can be of different kind. In shape Christ looked like a man but spiritually he was homogeneous with the angels. As the Bible says, "Outward appearance is not important" (see James 2). If one lacks spiritual insight, one can at least use intellect instead of the deceptive physical eye, to decide others' character because it is only God who knows what people possess esoterically. It is useless to depend on physical objects because they themselves depend on others (see also vr. VI/3747). There is a Turkish proverb that applies here: "Don't lean against the wall, it shall fall down, don't trust a man, he will die; trust only God, Who will never die". All actions are referred to God. When our senses become impervious to good and we begin to worship only forms and materialistic charms, God being Kind increases the charm of this world which can deprive men of Reality. As the Koran says, "Deaf, dumb and blind they will not return (to the right path)" (II/18); at such stage we should cry to God for His Mercy. As the Bible tells us, "World's friend is God's enemy" (James 4/4).

108- It is better to accept the guidance of your parents than to fall into the hands of the evil:

گور با رهبر به از تنها یقین / زآن یکی ننگست و صد ننگست ازین

می گریزی از جفاهای پدر / در میان لوطیان و شور و شر

هر ضریری کز مسیحی سرکشد / او جهودانه بماند از رشد

(VI / 4108-4110-4115)

a) Certainly it is better for a blind man to follow a guide because with a guide he may have one humiliation, but without him he may have a hundred more. You may run away from the unkindness of your father (or parents) but you fall into the hands of scoundrels, the mischievous, and the troublesome. The blind man who turns away his face from Jesus (in rebellion) will be left, like the Jews, without guidance.

b) Many young people disobey their parents and fall into the hands of mischievous people. It is better for a blind man to follow a guide even if it brings a humiliation than not to follow any. Similarly, it is better for the young to tolerate their parents, although they may find it humiliating to follow their advice. If they leave their parents, they will be left without guidance as the Jews were left without the guidance of Christ. The Bible also says, "Respect your father and mother" (Ephesians 6/2 and Dent 5/16), and the Koran says, "To parents, whether one or both of them attain old age in thy life, say not to them a word of contempt" (XVII/23).

109- All we eat is earth, in different colours and shapes:

لیک خاکی را که آن رنگین شدست	این دهان خود خاك خواری آمدست
خاك رنگینست و نقشین ای پسر	این کباب واین شراب واین شکر
رنگ لحمش داد واین هم خاك کوست	چونك خوردی و شد آنها لحم و پوست
جمله یك رنگ اند اندر گور خوش	هندو و قفچاق و رومی و حبش
جمله رو پوشست و مکرو مستعار	تا بدانی کآن همه رنگ و نگار
غیر آن بر بسته دان همچون جرس	رنگ باقی صبغة الله است و بس

(VI / 4705-4706-4707-4709-4710-4711)

a) This mouth has always been an eater of earth, but earth in different colours. This roasted meat, wine, and sugar are all merely coloured and painted earth, O son. When you eat them, you change into the skin and flesh which shall change into earth again (after death) and into the dust of a street (Baki and Mift. have deleted the last words). May he be an Indian, a *Kifchaq* (Turk), an Anatolian or an Abyssinian, they all have the same colour in the grave. So you may know that all those colours and pictures are nothing but illusions, disguises, and temporary shapes. The eternal colour is the Colour of God, the rest of the colours are like a tied up bell.

b) Whatever we eat and drink, may it be fruits, roasted meat, or wine is actually earth in different colours. They are all coloured to deceive you and hang around your neck like the bells hung on the neck of animals. Not being part of your real essence, they are deposited back to the earth for they are part of the earth. They are shaped in various colours, like the prismatic of the sun's rays, but in fact they are minerals, salts, metals and so on. There is only one colour that rules over all other physical colours and that is the Colour of God.

110- Jealousy is dangerous:

چون همی سوزند عامه از حسد / در نعیم فانئ مال و جسد
از حسد خویشان خود را میکند / پادشاهان بین که لشکر می کشند
از حسد دو ضره خود را می خورند / این زنانی کز همه مشفق ترند
از حسد تا در کدامین منزل اند / تا که مردانی که خود سنگین دل اند
(V / 1201-1202-1208-1209)

a) It is because of the pleasures of their physical bodies and mortal riches that the people (the common public) burn in the fire of jealousy. Notice that Kings wage wars and kill their own kins out of jealousy. Women, who are kinder than all other creatures, when they happen to be fellow-wives fight with each other because of jealousy. If this is the case with women then what degree of jealousy will stone-hearted men possess?

b) Because of the carnal self people envy each other while a lover of God looks at them with the sympathy of a mother who let her babies play with their toys until they go to sleep or feel hungry. It is the love of God that burns jealousy, the fruit of ego, to ashes. This is what the Koran and the Bible say about jealousy: "Or do they envy mankind for what God hath given them of His bounty..." (the Koran, IV/54); "When the Jews saw the crowds they were filled with jealousy" (the Bible, Acts., 13/45). It was jealousy that deprived Jews of the eternal life. Rumi recommends that we change jealousy to love.

111- Does the light of the moon get dirty?:

گر زند آن نور بر هر نیک و بد / نورمه آلودگی گردد ابد
همچو نور عقل و جان سوی اله / او ز جمله پاک وا گردد بماه
(V / 1258-1259)

a) Does the moonlight ever get dirty though it falls on bad as well as good things? It (moonlight) returns to the moon cleaner than before, as the light of intelligence and soul goes back to God.

b) If the soul of a saint comes to this world it cannot get dirty. It goes back to God cleaner than before, like the soul of Christ. The sun's rays or the moon's light do not get dirty by falling on any filthy surface, similarly a pious man's soul does not get dirty by being here in this world; it goes back to God without being dirty.

112- The heavy food of this world hampers the spiritual food:

وا رهی زین روزی ریزه کثیف   در فتی در لوت در قوت شریف
گر خوری کم گرسنه مانی چو زاغ   ور خوری پر گیرد آروغت دماغ
باش در روزه شکیبا و مصر   دم بدم قوت خدا را منتظر
(V / 1743-1746-1749)

a) If you rid yourself of these gross scraps of food, you can obtain the high spiritual food instead (Mift., p. 335). If you eat less, you remain hungry like a greedy crow; and if you eat your fill the gasses of your stomach will hinder your (proper) thinking. So be patient and persistent in fasting, and wait for Divine food every moment.

b) Worldly food needs balance. If you eat much, your brain functions will slow; and if you eat very little, your hunger will keep you greedy like a crow. So, the solution is to fast patiently until you begin to receive divine food. This is what Rumi's masters Burhaneddin and Shams did.

113- All your good ideas that you nourish in your mind will manifest on the day of resurrection:

هست ما را خواب و بیداری ما   بر نشان مرگ و محشر دو گوا
در مهندس بین خیال خانه   در دلش چون در زمینی دانه
آن خیال از اندرون آید برون   چون زمین که زآید از تخم درون
هر خیالی کو کند در دل وطن   روز محشر صورتی خواهد شدن
(V / 1787-1791-1792-1793)

a) Our sleep and awakening are two witnesses (proofs) of death and resurrection. Notice that a civil engineer has an idea of a house in his mind, it is like a seed under the earth in his heart. That idea comes out from inside as the seed gives forth a plant. (In the same way) any idea that begins to live in our heart will take a certain shape on the day of resurrection.

b) All that we plan in this world and act on, as we programme a computer disc, will bring us a new life in the world Hereafter. We sleep at night and wake up in the morning but our ideas and feelings, all recorded, take shape. In the same way, in life after death we will be aware of our celestial body and we will be able to see what the seeds that we sowed here produce there. "Many that sleep in the dust of the earth will awake" (the Bible, Daniel 12/2); "Man says, 'What, when I am dead, shall I then be raised up alive?' But does not man call to mind that we created him before out of nothing" (the Koran, XIX/66-67).

114- Every atom of the Hereafter is alive:

آن جهان چون ذره ذره زنده اند / نکته دانند و سخن گوینده اند

در جهان مرده شان آرام نیست / کین علف جز لایق انعام نیست

دختران را لعبت مرده دهند / که زلعب زندگان بی آگهند

کافران قانع بنقش انبیا / که نگاریده ست اندر دیرها

چشم ظاهر ضابط حلیه بشر / چشم سر حیران مازاغ البصر

این که در وقتست باشد تا اجل / وآن دگر یار ابد قرن ازل

روزه داران را بود آن نان و خوان / خرمگس را چه ابا چه دیگ دان

(V / 3591-3592-3597-3599-3604-3607-3634)

a) Every atom of that (spiritual) world is alive and is able to speak and criticise. In this world their (the prophets and saints') physical bodies have no peace (comfort) because this world (fodder) is fit only for cattle. People give lifeless dolls to young girls, for they are unaware of the games of the alive. The infidels are satisfied with the pictures of prophets that are painted on the walls of temples. The outer eyes discern the figures, the spiritual eyes are bewildered because, "His sight never swerved nor did it go wrong". Those who are bound by time live only until death but those who belong to the spiritual world live forever. Nice dishes are served to those who fast, for the horse-fly what difference is there between the soup or the dish.

b) Every atom of the other world is full of life, unlike this world. For those who have seen or felt the other world, this world is boring and insipid, but for the ignorant (infidels) this world is full of charm. Some are satisfied only with the picture of the prophets and they do not seek the Beauty of God, just as dolls are attractive to young girls who do not know the real games of this world yet. The spiritual eyes never "swerve" as the Koran says, "His (the prophet's) sight never swerved nor did it go wrong" (LIII/17). A reward is for those who can be patient like those who fast, but not for those who are satisfied with this world's deceptive forms and accept this world as their only home.

c) The above verses are a summary of this chapter and they refer to the following Koranic verses:

"What is life of this world but amusement and play. But verily the home in the Hereafter -that is life indeed, if they (the people) but knew" (XXIX/64).

CHAPTER VI

Step II: The awakening

In this section Rumi reveals the awakening state of a man who has lessened his carnal desires and is able to see out of the window of physical imprisonment. In other words, he is ready to begin a journey towards his Creator (God) through righteousness, learning and patience. At this stage a struggle between his lower self (heedlessness) and spiritual awakening is strong. He has begun to feel that spiritual food is better than worldly food and that his spiritual earnings (the "daily bread") free him gradually from this world of dust and clay.

115- The ill mannered is deprived of Divine Mercy:

از خدا جوییم توفیق ادب   بی ادب محروم شد از لطف رب

بی ادب تنها نه خود را داشت بد   بلک آتش در همه آفاق زد

هر چه بر تو آید از ظلمات و غم   آن ز بی باکی و گستاخیست هم

از ادب پر نور گشتست این فلک   وز ادب معصوم و پاک آمد ملک

78 b محروم شد از لطف G : محروم ماند از فضل Mift.   (I / 78-79-89-91)

a) From God we shall seek for His grace so that He may give us fine manners, because the ill-mannered is deprived of God's mercy. The ill-mannered does not only harm himself but he also sets fire in the universe (skies). Whatever grief and gloom befall you is due to your disrespect and impudence. Because of refined manners this sky has been filled with light and because of refined manners the angels are clean and innocent.

b) The word *"Edeb"* has no English equivalent, although in the Mevleviya sect it has a significant importance. It can, however be defined as: "fine manners, respect to elders and avoidance of whatever God has forbidden". It also includes respect for the traditions and customs of a group of people (for the last sentence see Baki, I/p. 41). When a man chooses to be fine-mannered, he refrains from evil deeds (Tahir I/p. 113). He is afraid to insult others because, "A self respecting man respects others." He hesitates to commit sins or to tell lies for the sake of later embarrassment. It was for this reason that the Anatolian Mevlevi gave much importance to *"edeb"*; and even today we find tablets inscribed *"Edeb Yahu"* ="Behave yourself". They (the Mevlevi) would speak to others in a low mild voice out of reverence and they would try their best not to break others' hearts. *Edeb* is the outcome of patience; and it is patience that God likes: "Be patient and persevering for God is with those who patiently persevere" (the Koran, 5 VIII/46).

116- Perseverance and patience have a better reward:

بهر آنست این ریاضت وین جفا   تا بر آرد کوره از نقره جفا

بهر آنست امتحان نیک و بد   تا بجوشد بر سر آرد زر زبد

(I / 232-233)

a) The purpose of suffering and religious hardships (in this world) is like the furnace which extracts the dross from silver. The good and bad may be tested and the gold may melt and let its scum rise to the top.

b) The hardships of regular prayers and fasting are for our own good, because they purify our being by taking the scum (evil feelings) out of our body. As the Koran says, "But (all this was) that God might test what is in your breasts and purge what is in your hearts. For God knoweth well the secrets of your hearts" (III/154), and "Thus doth God show forth truth and vanity. For the scum disappears like froth cast out; while that which is for the good of mankind remains on the earth" (XIII/17).

117- Troubles are for mercy:

بچه می لرزد از آن نیش حجام   مادر مشفق در آن غم شاد کام

نیم جان بستاند و صد جان دهد   آنک در وهمت نیاید آن دهد

244 a حجام G : احتجام Mift.   (I / 244-245)

a) The child trembles at the barber's under the spiky tools while the kind hearted mother is happy although the child is unhappy. He (God) takes half lives and gives a hundred lives instead and what He gives in return you fail to perceive.

b) A child is afraid of being at the barber's while his mother is happy because she knows that her child will be nice looking after the haircut. Similarly, man on earth is restless because of worldly troubles (as is the child under the barber's scissors) but God is happy because He knows that a man will come back to Him in much better condition. Thus the troubles of this world which train a man to be better are actually due to the mercy of God and, therefore, we should not rebel against them.

118- All worries and troubles awaken in us the love of God:

من کریمم نان نمایم بنده را   تا بگریاند طمع آن زنده را

بینی طفلی بمالد مادری   تا شود بیدار واجوید خوری

چون بگریانم بجوشد رحمتم   آن خروشنده بنوشد نعمتم

(II / 361-362-373)

a) I am Kind, and show bread to my obedient servant so that he may cry for it in need. A mother rubs the nose of her baby to wake it and make the baby look for food and when I make man cry, my mercy is aroused and the weeping person receives my bounties.

b) In order to keep people busy on earth, God has granted them the need of food, so that they may struggle for it. When people are unhappy and they cry to God, He becomes kinder to them like a mother and provides them with what they want. A Turkish proverb in support of this idea: "No milk for those babies who don't cry".

119- Crying arouses the Mercy of God:

چون خدا خواهد که مان یاری کند   میـل مـا را جانب زاری کند
ای خنك چشمی که آن گریان اوست   ای همایون دل که آن بریان اوست
هر کجا آب روان سبـزه بـود   هر کجا اشکی دوان رحمت شود
اشك خواهی رحم کن بر اشك بار   رحم خواهی بر ضعیفان رحم آر
(I / 817-818-820-822)

a) When God wants to help us, He turns our inclination towards lamenting (and repentance). How fortunate is the eye that cries for Him and how auspicious is the heart that burns for Him. Wherever there is running water, there is greenery; wherever there are running tears, there the Mercy of God is. If you want such tears then take pity on those who shed tears; if you desire mercy, take mercy on others.

b) God likes the humble and those who repent their sins. If you feel that God is not merciful enough to you, then take mercy on others so that His Mercy may increase. However, to be a good man is in our hands but to be a perfect man is reliant on divine help and mercy. Tears shed with sincerity wipe away the darkness of our hearts (for this sentence see Mift. p. 311).

120- Pray to God if you are in trouble:

چونکه غم بینی تو استغفار کن   غم بامر خالق آمد کار کن
چون بخواهد عین غم شادی شود   عین بند پای آزادی شود
(I / 836-837)

a) When you face troubles, ask pardon of God; troubles and worries come your way through the command of the Creator, so do act, because if God wants He can change your sorrows into happiness or can change your captivity into freedom.

b) God has full control of our fates. "Thou enduest with honour whom Thou pleasest and Thou bringest low whom Thou pleasest; in Thy hand is all Good" (the Koran, III/26). So if we are tested by God with worries and unhappiness, we should try to attract God's mercy by crying and shedding tears.

121- Those spiritual causes bring these worldly causes into action:

این سبب را آن سبب عامل کند   باز گاهی بی بر و عاطل کند
این سبب را محرم آمد عقلها   وآن سببها راست محرم انبیا
(I / 845-846)

a) These causes are affected by the spiritual causes, sometimes the spiritual causes render the causes of this world fruitless. Ordinary (partial) insight can perceive the causes of this world but the spiritual causes are known only by the prophets.

b) Since partial insight is bound to this world it can understand the mundane causes; but Divine Wisdom can comprehend the causes of this world as well as those of the other world. Scientists may think that the whirling of the planets is due to the galaxies, but a godly man (prophet) knows that they rotate through God's command (Mift. I/p. 316).

122- He who seeks wisdom becomes a source of wisdom himself:

خاتم ملک سلیمانست علم   جمله عالم صورت و جانست علم
منبع حکمت شود حکمت طلب   فارغ آید او ز تحصیل و سبب
چون معلم بود عقلش ز ابتدا   بعد ازین شد عقل شاگردی ورا
a 1065 ز ابتدا : G , مرد را : N.   (I / 1030-1063-1065)

a) Knowledge is the seal of the kingdom of Solomon, the whole world is form and its essence is knowledge. He who seeks wisdom becomes a source of wisdom himself; and he becomes free from learning and causes. While his Divine Wisdom was his teacher from the very beginning, his (partial) insight remains as his student.

b) The essence of every phenomenon is a kind of knowledge. As the spirit is essential for a body, so is knowledge (for this sentence see Mift. 2/55). A person who is guided by God Himself (like the prophet Solomon), does not need to study because his knowledge comes via Divine Wisdom; and his partial insight becomes the student of the former. However, those who did not have the universal intellect by birth can attain it by means of divine knowledge especially under the guidance of a spiritual guide, as Rumi says elsewhere:

"The beauty of a Friend becomes the teacher for His lovers; for them the Beloved's face is a note book, lessons and learning" (M, III/3847).

123- Your hidden enemy:

آدمی با حذر عاقل کسیست	آدمی را دشمن پنهان بسیست
می زند بر دل بهر دم کوبشان	خلق پنهان زشتشان و خوبشان
از هزاران کس بود نی یک کسه	خار خار وحیها و وسوسه
تا ببینیشان و مشکل حل شود	باش تا حسهای تو مبدل شود
(I / 1034-1035-1038-1039)	

a) There are numerous hidden enemies of man. A cautious man is a wise one. There are hidden creatures, evil and good, they strike blows at hearts at every opportunity. The pricks of inner ideas and temptations are caused by many (thousands) and not by one. Be patient until your feelings change and you see the reality and solve the problems.

b) The hidden powers that tempt a man may be the diabolic hidden powers, or selfness (as explained by Mift. p. 56-57). Today germs, microbes and viruses can be added to these dangerous forces. In addition to these forces there are evil ideas and satanic temptations that a wise man has to be careful of. Praying to God regularly, or *zikr* (remembrance) of God is a protection against such elements as Mift. suggests. We come across these verses in the Koran, "No authority has Satan over those who believe and put their trust in their Lord" (XVI/99). Rumi suggests in the case of such problems to wait until your temptation calms down and you begin to see the reality.

124- God is always after a new grandeur:

در هوا کی پاید آید تا خدا	فکر ما تیریست از هو در هوا
بی خبر از نو شدن اندر بقا	هر نفس نو می شود دنیا و ما
مستمری می نماید در جسد	عمر همچون جوی نو نو می رسد
(I / 1143-1144-1145)	

a) Our ideas are like the arrows shot by God. How can an arrow stay in the air (without motion) it goes back to Him. Every moment the world is being renewed but we are unaware of the changes for its form looks unchanged. Your life in your body keeps on freshening like a stream of water, although it looks static in form.

b) It is now scientifically proved that the entire universe is in action including its tiniest units, the atom, electron and proton. The body while growing up changes its cells; similarly life also changes, physically as well as spiritually. It is interesting to see this line in the Koran, "Everyday in (new) Splendour doth He shine" (LV/29). Splendour here means that He is after new inventions and acts every moment. Then why should man, His viceroy on the earth, sit idle? Today, we also know that some stars are born while others die away. The action of God is endless. It was this concept of action that made Rumi whirl in harmony with the planets and atoms.

125- Ignorance is a prison:

گر بجهل آییم آن زندان اوست   ور بعلم آییم آن ایوان اوست
ور بخواب آییم مستان وییم   ور به بیداری بدستان وییم
(I / 1510-1511)

a) If we fall into ignorance, it is His prison and if we gain knowledge, we are in His palace. If we go to sleep, we are intoxicated for Him and if we are wakeful we are in His Hands (control).

b) Ignorance is like a prison and knowing God is the real knowing, for when you know Him your sleep and your wakefulness are equal.

c) Mift. gives "we tell tales about him" instead of "in the Hands of Him" (see Mift., 2/216).

126- The illegal morsel gives birth to evil:

گر تو این انبان ز نان خالی کنی   پر ز گوهرهای اجلالی کنی
علم و حکمت زاید از لقمه حلال   عشق و رقت آید از لقمه حلال
چون ز لقمه تو حسد بینی و دام   جهل و غفلت زاید آنرا دان حرام
لقمه تخمست و برش اندیشها   لقمه بحر و گوهرش اندیشها
(I / 1639-1644-1645-1647)

a) If you empty this bag (your stomach) of bread, it will be filled with glorious jewels instead. From the legal morsel are born knowledge, love and tenderness. If you see that jealousy, deception, ignorance and negligence are born from a morsel, know that it was unlawful. The morsel is a seed and thoughts are its fruit, the morsel is the sea and thoughts are its pearls.

b) Rumi suggests to eat less, because if your stomach is full you cannot unveil the divine secrets. It was customary among the sheykhs to keep their disciples hungry for some days in order to train them against the greedy lower self. Another thing should be avoided is the illegal morsel. This means that he who wants to follow God's path *(Suluk)* must not eat anything bought by illegal money for he will lose piety. Mift. says that the illegal morsel will cause your limbs and body to rebel against you (see Mift. 2/262).

127- Don't open yourself to the jealousy of people:

دانه باشی مرغکانت بر چنند   غنچه باشی کودکانت بر کنند
دانه پنهان کن بکلی دام شو   غنچه پنهان کن گیاه بام شو
یعنی ای مطرب شده با عام و خاص   مرده شو چون من که تا یابی خلاص
در پناه لطف حق باید گریخت   کو هزاران لطف بر ارواح ریخت
(I / 1833-1835-1832-1839)

a) If you are like a grain, birds will peck you up; and if you are like a bud, children will pluck you off. Hide the grain and be just a snare, hide the buds and be the grass on the roof (a valueless thing). Be dead like me so that you may get freedom, and don't be like the musician who sings for everyone. Run towards the shelter of God's grace because He has poured on man's spirits grace and kindness a thousandfold.

b) If you, like a grain, open yourself to people and become famous, they will peck at you like birds. If you have some rare qualities, hide them until they grow into a tree for birds cannot harm the whole tree, but they can take away the seeds. Bees and flies gather around the flowers smelling full of nectar, so don't be too showy so that you are saved, until you become bright like the sun.

128- Without the divine mercy and the favour of the elect ones we are nothing:

این همه گفتیم لیک اندر بسیج   بی عنایات خدا هیچیم هیچ
بی عنایات حق و خاصان حق   گر ملک باشد سیاهستش ورق
(I / 1878-1879)

a) We have uttered all these things (verses) under our strong will (without break) (see T., 3-4/p. 941) but we are nothing without the Mercy of God or His lovers, even an angel's page of destiny is black.

b) Rumi declares that whatever he has uttered was by the spiritual assistance of God. Without His help Rumi would be able to say nothing of the divine secrets because without God's or His lover's favour, he could do nothing.

129- Better to be a slave than a proud sultan:

تن قفص شکلست تن شد خارجان   در فریب داخلان و خارجان
لطف و سالوس جهان خوش لقمه ایست   کمترش خور کآن پر آتش لقمه ایست
او چو بیند خلق را سرمست خویش   از تکبر می رود از دست خویش
تو مگو آن مدح را من کی خورم   از طمع می گوید او پی می برم
مادحت گر هجو گوید بر ملا   روزها سوزد دلت زان سوزها
تا توانی بنده شو سلطان مباش   زخمکش چون گوی شو چوگان مباش
(I / 1849-1855-1853-1857-1858-1868)

a) The body is like a cage and has become a thorn to the soul because of the tricks of the inner and the outer ones. The world's kindness and hypocrisy is a sweet morsel, eat less of it, for it is a morsel full of fire. When he (the famous person) sees the people intoxicated because of him, due to pride he goes out of himself. He might say, "I don't care for praises", but I think he says so out of pride. Well, if a praiser criticises him, his heart burns for days on account of that injury. It is better to be a slave than to be a king. Bear pains (blows) like a ball and don't strike like a bat.

b) Soul is like a bird in the cage of your body. It cannot escape from those who praise you hypocritically for your physical attainments and your inner worries and anxieties. So you are placed between the devil and the deep sea. The only way to get rid of this situation is to forget about your rank and fame and surrender to the will of God humbly. Rumi says further, "When your beauty fades away and loses its charm, your praisers will feel fed up of you" (M. I/1871) for when the wine is finished in a jar, the glasses around it also fall afar.

130- Man's knowledge is a drop:

قطره دانش که بخشیدی زبیش   متصل گردان بدریاهای خویش
قطره علمست اندر جان من   وا رهانش از هوا وز خاک تن
پیش از آن کین خاکها خسفش کند   پیش از آن کین بادها نسفش کند
(I / 1882-1883-1884)

a) A drop of knowledge that You have bestowed upon me, please put it back in Your sea. There is a drop of knowledge in my soul, set it free from the air (show) and from the clay of my body before the wind dries it up and sweeps it away.

b) These verses are one of the golden verses of Rumi. Here Rumi pleads to God to transfer his partial insight (worth only a drop) to God's sea of knowledge (Divine Wisdom) so that Rumi may also become the sea like God. He further requests God to transmit his knowledge to the soul so that it may become eternal; it otherwise, will perish in this world due to its physical confinement.

131- If you are not Joseph then be Jacob:

از عدمها سوی هستی هر زمان   هست یارب کاروان در کاروان
خاصه هر شب جمله افکار و عقول   نیست گردد غرق در بحر نغول
باز وقت صبح آن الـلهیـان   بر زنند از بحر سر چون ماهیان
این سخنهـایی که از عقل کلست   بوی آن گلزار و سرو و سنبلست
تو که یوسف نیستی یعقوب باش   همچو او با گریه و آشوب باش
(I / 1889-1890-1891-1899-1904)

a) There are caravans after caravans that pass from non-existence to existence every moment. In particular every night all ideas and insights become lost in the sea of sleep. Yet in the morning again, those Divine ones lift up their heads from the sea like fishes. These words that come from Divine Insight are the scent of that garden of cypresses and hyacinths. If you are not Joseph, then be Jacob cry and pine like him.

b) At night when we go to sleep our ideas and thoughts disappear, but at the time of dawn they all come back. Similarly, from the non-existent world inspirations after inspirations come to us (to the men of God). If you are not handsome (spiritually) like the prophet Joseph then be like his father Jacob who shed tears to God, pining and praying.

132- Seek the universal wisdom:

مر ترا عقلیست جزوی در نهان   کامل العقلی بجو اندر جهان
جزو تو از کل او کلی شود   عقل کل بر نفس چون غلی شود
گفتهای اولیا نرم و درشت   تن مپوشان زآنک دینت راست پشت
بر دل عاقل هزاران غم بود   گر ز باغ دل خلالی کم بود
(I / 2052-2053-2055-2059)

149

a) You have a partial insight concealed within you. Look for a person in this world who has a perfect insight. Your partial insight becomes universal with his insight, and the universal wisdom acts like a fetter on your lower self. Words of a saint be they soft or harsh should not be rejected by you because they strengthen your belief. If a single straw is lost from a wise man's garden of the heart, it gives him a thousand pains.

b) A real saint (sheykh) is connected to be universal insight and if we also went to be connected to it we should follow a saint humbly. Once you are connected to the universal wisdom your lower self will surrender by and by; and you also become like a saint. If a wise man loses anything of this world, he does not care much but if he loses a straw of the spiritual world his heart pines.

133- Not all hearts are capable of receiving God's message:

می‌رسد از غیب چون آب روان   در وجود آدمی جان و روان
امر حق را در نیابد هر دلی   امر حق را باز جو از واصلی
(I / 2222-2229)

a) The spirit and soul come to the human body from the other world like running water. Seek the Command (Message) of God for not every heart can receive His Command.

b) The essence of man is connected to the other world and he receives messages (inspirations) from here but some hearts fail to do so because their lower self rules their spirituality. In his Discourses Rumi says, "All knowledge has its origin beyond, transferring from the other world without letters and sounds into the world of letters and sounds" (the Discourses, p. 164). Open your heart like a large concave antenna to the messages that God sends us day and night.

134- Prefer the far-sighted eyes:

چشم آخُر بین غرورست و خطاست   چشم آخر بین تواند دید راست
لیک زهر اندر شکر مضمر بود   ای بسا شیرین که چون شکر بود
وآن دگر چون برلب و دندان زدش   آنک زیرک تر ببو بشناسدش

b 2583 آخر G: اول. Mift. – a 2585 ببود N: بشود T   (I / 2583-2584-2585)

a) The eye that is able to see the end can also see the right thing but the eye that can see only a stable (this world) is mistaken and is vain. Many things that seem to be sugar-sweet have actually poison in them. He who is wiser knows poison by smell and another knows it only when he feels it with his tongue.

b) A person who has developed his spiritual senses is able to foresee a consequence, yet he whose eyes are fixed on the minor things of this world is proud of his mortal possessions. Many objects, sweet as they may be, are deceptive and poisonous but many eat them regardless of their harm except those who are far-sighted (specially those who have universal insight).

135- Only through Divine Light one can see what is good and what is bad:

آن مرایی در صیام و در صلاست   تا گمان آید که او مست و لاست
یارب آن تمییز ده مارا بخواست   تا شناسیم آن نشان کژ ز راست
حس را تمییز دانی چون شود   آنک حس ینظر بنور الله بود
(I / 2631-2633-2634)

a) That hypocrite is busy praying and fasting so that he may make others think that he is drunk with saintliness. O God give us, according to Your Own Will, the sense of discrimination which enables us to judge bad and good signs. Do you know when the senses are able to discriminate (between the good and the bad)? They do so when they see things with Divine Light.

b) Man can easily be cheated by an impostor or a false saint who is a representative of Satan on earth. We should pray to God to give us the ability to discriminate between "good" and "evil" so that we may recognise a false saint (sheykh).

136- Patience is rewarded:

گر تو اشکالی بکلی و حرج   صبر کن الصبر مفتاح الفرج
صبر شیرین از خیال خوش شدست   کآن خیالات فرج پیش آمدست
آن فرج آید ز ایمان در ضمیر   ضعف ایمان نا امیدی و زحیر
(I / 2908 - II / 598-599)

a) If you face a lot of trouble and stress then be patient for "patience is the key to relief". Patience becomes sweet through a nice fancy, when the idea of getting free from the trouble occurs. The idea of being free is a product of faith (in God); if your faith is weak, hopelessness and torment are born.

b) If a man has a strong faith in God, he can be patient but if his belief is weak, he is liable to disappointment and distress. "Be patient in your troubles, and pray at all times" says the Bible (Rom. 12/12). On patience Rumi has these verses also:

"Please yourself by your bravery and make your reason teach you patience that may become your guide. When your guide of patience becomes a wing for you, your spirit will reach as high a stage as the Divine Throne" (M. VI/3977-3978), and here see items No. 116, 117, and 120.

137- The outer eyes are the shadow of the spiritual eyes:

چشم ظاهر سایه آن چشم دان   هر چه آن بیند بگردد این بد آن
تو مکانی اصل تو در لامکان   این دکان بر بند و بگشا آن دکان
(II / 611-612)

a) The outer eyes are the shadow of the real (spiritual) eyes. Whatever the latter observes, the former turns towards that. You are here in the mortal world while your real being is in the non-existent world, so close this shop and open the other one.

b) Here Rumi wants to say clearly that "This world is the shadow of the other, invisible world" as most Sufis believed. They believed also in the "*Ayan-i sabita* =the world of fixed prototype" (for other details see Gibb, I/p. 55). When you develop your spiritual senses, you begin to feel the other world and the eye of your heart begins to see many secrets (like the eyes of Jacob or of any other prophet). When you know that this world is the shadow of the spiritual world, then labour for that world (MM, 2/p. 69). Since that world is the anti-materialistic world, you can see it only by means of your spiritual senses, so improve them. This is what Rumi suggests in his Mejalis-i Sab'a :

"In search of God blow like a wind, drink the poison of His troubles like sweet syrup... for he who has a house by the sea-shore receives many waves and he who claims to be a lover has to bear many pains.

Unless you throw everything into the fire (fire of love),
Nothing can go right and higher" (Mejalis-i Sab'a, p. 52).

138- If gold and silver had not been hidden, they would not have been valuable:

گور خانه راز تو چون دل شود   آن مرادت زودتر حاصل شود
دانه ها چون در زمین پنهان شود   سر آن سر سبزی بستان شود
زر و نقره گر نبودندی نهان   پرورش کی یافتندی زیر کان
(I / 175-177-178)

a) When your heart becomes the grave of your secrets, then your will becomes true (faster than ever). When seeds are hidden in the earth, their secret turns into the greenness of a garden. If gold and silver were not concealed under the earth they would not be grown (developed) in the mines.

b) Rumi emphasises the importance of keeping secrets until they become true, especially divine secrets. If we see a spiritual event, we should keep it secret. Let seeds change into plants for if birds discover the seeds, they will peck them up easily; but when seeds grow into plants only a tiny part can be pecked by the birds (the jealous people).

139- Knowledge in the service of lower self is burdensome while in the service of the spiritual goal it is fruitful:

علمهای اهل تن احمالشان   علمهای اهل دل حمالشان

علم چون بر تن زند باری شود   علم چون بردل زند یاری شود

پاك كن خود را ز خود هین یكسری   گر ز نام و حرف خواهی بگذری

تا ببینی ذات پاك صاف خود   خویشرا صافی كن از اوصاف خود

بی كتاب و بی معید و اوستا   بینی اندر دل علوم انبیا

(I / 3446-3447-3458-3460-3461)

a) The knowledge of lovers of God raises them up, while the knowledge of worldlings is burden to them. Knowledge when applied to the heart is friend, but when applied to the physical body it is a burden. If you want to pass beyond names and letters (titles) then clean yourself of your lower self from top to toe. Clean yourself of (worldly) attributes so that you may see the pure essence of yourself; and you may observe within your heart, without books, teachers, and preceptors, the knowledge of the prophets.

b) Knowledge when used for attaining sensual desires for example, wealth, fame and ranks is a burden on the human body. When it is used for spiritual purposes, for discovering God's signs and His greatness, for the betterment of His creatures, and for discovering eternal happiness, it is useful and exalting. Discover yourself by means of knowledge and see how powerless you are in the Presence of God. Do away with the heavy and thick curtains of your lower self so that you may reach your pure essence, which is able to receive the real knowledge (divine knowledge).

140- Your clean heart is the mirror of your deeds:

آینه تو جست بیرون از غلاف   آینه و میزان کجا گوید خلاف
آینه و میزان کجا بندد نفس   بهر آزار و حیای هیچ کس
(I / 3545-3546)

a) Your mirror has jumped (come) out of its case, mirror and scale do not hesitate to tell the truth. They are not bound by their ego and can tell the truth without being afraid of hurting or shaming anyone.

b) "The mirror has come out of its case" means that you have now recognised your faults or sins clearly as your heart has become clean like a mirror. If your heart is cleansed you can not only judge your own character but also that of others. If your own heart is like a mirror it can reflect your faults without hypocrisy.

141- A believer's heart is the mirror of another believer:

عقل با عقل دگر دوتا شود   نور افزون گشت و ره پیدا شود
نفس با نفس دگر خندان شود   ظلمت افزون گشت ره پنهان شود
چون ز تنهایی تو نومیدی شوی   زیر سایه یار خرشیدی شوی
رو بجو یار خدایی را تو زود   چون چنان کردی خدا یار تو بود
چونک مؤمن آینه مومن بود   روی او ز آلودگی ایمن بود
(II / 26-27-22-23-30)

a) If the intellect of a believer joins the intellect of another (believer), it becomes double and light increases while the path becomes more illuminated. The lower self is happy with another lower self, and darkness increases, and the way becomes hidden (lost). When you feel disappointed out of loneliness, go and stand in the shadow of your friend to become a shining sun. Go and seek a friend of God without delay, and when you do so God becomes your Friend, because a believer is the mirror of a believer and his (the friend's) face is safe from dust and dirt.

b) If we fail to clean the mirror of our heart, then we must try to find a lover of God whose heart is clean, in which we can see our real face. As a mirror of a believer's heart is the mirror of another believer (as said by Muhammed), so is the heart of a non-believer the mirror of another non-believer; and both are content with each other.

142- The waves of Sea of Knowledge:

شد حواس و نطق با پایان ما   محو علم و دانش سلطان ما
حس‌ها و عقل‌هاشان در درون   موج در موج لدینا محضرون
(I / 3671-3672)

a) Our senses and finite words have drowned in the knowledge and Wisdom of our King (God). Their (the saint's) inner feelings and wisdom are like wave on wave, and they are "Brought up before Us".

b) Here Rumi confesses that his drop of knowledge has joined the Sea and he, like other saints, has become attached to God directly. "Brought up before Us" is part of this Koranic verse, "It will be no more than a single blast, when they will be brought up before Us" (XXXVI/53).

143- The Sufi and a scholar:

دفتر صوفی سواد و حرف نیست   جز دل اسپید همچون برف نیست
زاد دانشمند آثار قلم   زاد صوفی چیست آثار قدم
همچو صیادی سوی اشکار شد   گام آهو دید بر آثار شد
چند گاهش گام آهو در خورست   بعد از آن خود ناف آهو رهبرست
رفتن یک منزلی بر بوی ناف   بهتر از صد منزل گام و طواف
(II / 159-160-161-162-164)

a) The book of a Sufi is without ink and a letter. He has a heart as white as snow (very clean). A scholar's (a learned man's) provisions are the impressions of his pen while a Sufi's provisions are the foot prints of a saint. Like a hunter he follows his prey, he sees the foot prints of a deer and follows them. For some time, the foot-prints are his guide but afterwards the smell of the deer's navel (musk-gland) becomes his guide. To travel a distance tracing the smell of the musk is better than walking and roaming in a hundred (many) places.

b) The source (or the travelling-provision) of a Sufi's divine knowledge is the foot-prints of his master (a Sheykh) while the source of a scholar's knowledge are written words and books. The Sufi, after chasing his master, begins to possess divine light himself and begins to receive spiritual messages (the musk) directly. A journey with divine light inside is better than a hundred tours to holy places.

c) "the Deer"=a Saint; "scent of musk"=divine light or inspiration (see Bahr ul-Ulum), or even the sweet smell of God via His lovers.

144- God can be contained in the heart of a believer:

گفت پیغمبر که حق فرموده است   من نگنجم هیچ در بالا و پست

در زمین و آسمان عرش نیز   من نگنجم این یقین دان ای عزیز

در دل مؤمن بگنجم ای عجب   گر مرا جویی در آن دلها طلب

(I / 2653-2654-2655)

a) The prophet (Muhammed) said that God says, "I cannot be contained either upwards or downwards, I cannot be contained by the earth or by the sky or even by the whole universe, yet it is strange to say that I can be contained in the heart of a believer, so if you seek Me, seek Me in his heart".

b) God is not confined by the dimensional world. For Him up or down has no meaning. Man, especially His lover, carries an atom of His Essence that in time commands his lower self and his body.

145- Possess spiritual sight in order to see diamonds instead of pebbles:

این همه عالم طلب گار خوشند   وز خوش تزویر اندر آتشند

تا بود کز دیدگان هفت رنگ   دیده پیدا کند صبر و درنگ

رنگها بینی بجز این رنگها   گوهران بینی بجای سنگها

کارگه چون جای باش عاملست   آنک بیرون است از وی غافلست

پس در آ در کارگه یعنی عدم   تا ببینی صنع و صانع را بهم

(II / 743-756-757-761-762)

a) The whole world is desirous of happiness and due to false happiness they are on fire. It may happen that your eyes that observe seven colours may produce a new spiritual eye by means of patience and perseverance; and you may begin to see other colours than these, and pearls instead of stones. Since the workshop is the place where the Artist works, anyone who falls away from it (the Divine Workshop) is unaware of Him. Thus come to it, the workshop of non-existence so that you may see the work and the Worker together.

b) These sensory eyes are created to see only the seven colours but if you want to see colours other than them, then open your spiritual eye so that you are able to see the Workshop of God and His creation of spiritual colours in the world of non-existence.

c) Mift. gives "Your eyes that have seven curtains" instead of "your eyes that observe seven colours" which does not suit vr. No. 757 (see Mift. II-I/274).

146- A rabbit was offended with a mountain and the mountain did not know it:

گازری گر خشم گیرد ز آفتاب   ماهئی گر خشم می گیرد ز آب
تو یکی بنگر کرا دارد زیان   عاقبت که بود سیاه اختر از آن
خود حسد نقصان و عیبی دیگرست   بلک از جمله کمیها بترست
(II / 800-801-805)

a) If a linen washer becomes angry with the sun or a fish becomes angry with the water, look carefully, who is the real loser; or who has a black star (is wretched)? Actually, malice (grudge) is itself a fault and defect and it is indeed worse than all inferiorities.

b) Infidels can torture or injure the men of God but what can they do to them? What harm is there if a washer-man is angry with the sun? The Turkish proverb, "A rabbit got offended with a mountain and the mountain did not know it", fits here for God is Protector of the believers and who can hurt God?

147- The target of the burning fire is iron and steel:

هست آن آهن فقیر سخت کش   زیر پتک و آتش است او سرخ و خوش
پس فقیر آنست کوبی واسطه است   شعلها را با وجودش رابطه است
پس دل عالم ویست ایرا که تن   می رسد از واسطه این دل بفن
پس نظرگاه شعاع آن آهنست   پس نظرگاه خدا دل نی تن است
(II / 830-835-836-838)

a) The iron is the dervish who bears hardship and is red-faced and happy in spite of the hammer and the fire (of hardships). So, dervish is he who has no intermediary and the flame of fire is connected to his body (rather directly). Thus he is the heart of the world, for it is the heart by means of which this world attains to art. Therefore, the iron is the target of the flames of Divine Sight - not the heart but the body.

b) God imposes hardships on the body of the dervish but not on his heart. The dervish is like a piece of steel ready to receive the hammer of hardship for the sake of Divine Love. As Muhammed Iqbal says:

"A dervish is the reckoner of the stars, the moon, and the sun; he is not a mount but a rider of the days" *(Zarb-i Kelim)*.

Why should a dervish be concerned about his physical torment, for flames are required to give a form to glass.

148- If your worshipping God does not train your spirit, then it is like killing a shadow of a goat:

چونك لایبقی زمانین انتفی   این عرض‌های نماز و روزه را

لیک از جوهر برند امراض را   نقل نتوان کرد مر اعراض را

چون ز پرهیزی که زایل شد مرض   تا مبدل گشت جوهر زین عرض

دخل آن اعراض را بنما مرم   پس مگو که من عملها کرده‌ام

سایه بز را پی قربان مکش   این صفت کردن عرض باشد خمش

(II / 946-947-948-956-957)

a) These physical acts of prayers and fasting are momentary because they cannot exist for two moments, you cannot transfer them to the other world but they can cure the diseases of your substance. The substance also becomes healthy (by getting free of defects) as sickness is avoided by dint of abstinence. So don't claim, "I have performed all deeds". Show me the result of those acts (performances); don't run away from my advice. Be silent! this attribution of qualities is only accidental and don't slaughter the shadow of a goat instead of the goat itself.

b) If the accidental physical prayers and fasting cannot train and affect your spiritual being (essence), they are useless, like running a knife across the throat of a goat's shadow.

149- Trust in God and do the right:

چشم او بر کشتهای اولست   کار عارف راست کو نه احولست

عاقبت بر روید آن کشته اله   گر بروید ور بریزد صد گیاه

این دوم فانیست و آن اول درست   کشت نو کارید بر کشت نخست

چون اسیر دوستی ای دوستدار   هر چه کاری از برای او بکار

هرچه آن نه کار حق هیچست هیچ   گرد نفس دزد و کار او مپیچ

(II / 1052-1057-1058-1061-1062-1063)

a) The business (work) that belongs to a gnostic (knower of God) is straightforward because he is not a squinter and his eyes are fixed on the things first sown. Though a hundred herbs grow and fade away, yet the things sown by God will grow in the end. He (the clever man) has sown new seeds upon the previous ones, but the former are transient while the later are enduring. Only the crop which is raised by God is fruitful, and whatever is sowed by God grows first. Whatever you sow, sow for Him because you are a captive of that Beloved. Don't obey your thievish carnal selfhood for whatever is not done for God is bound to die.

b) A saint's eyes are able to see that God has predestined for a person, because his sight is straight (he has no squint eyes or mistaken conception, see Mift. II-I/94). In the long run, it is universal destiny that dominates over partial destiny. This does not mean that we should do nothing, but on the contrary try to sow the seed (purpose) for which God has created us, so that our acts may suit the First Cause.

150- Beware the jungle of your body:

پیشه آمد وجود آدمی بر حذر شو زین وجود ارز آن دمی
در وجود ما هزاران گرگ و خوک صالح و ناصالح و خوب و خشوک
سیرتی کآن در وجودت غالبست هم بر آن تصویر حشرت واجبست
(II / 1416-1417-1419)

a) Man's body is like the jungle, be aware of this body if you belong to that (Divine) Breath. In our body there are many wolves and hogs, pious and impious, fair and unfair. The resurrection will be realised according to whichever of these attributes (picture) rules our body.

b) God has ninety-nine attributes comprehensible to man. Our sensual body has many animal attributes that God does not have. Some of us are like wolves, while others are like greedy ducks or like an innocent pigeon. Our body has all kinds of animals within it. We should try to get rid of the animal soul in order to journey towards God. If we fail to give up the animal attributes, we will be resurrected in the form of the animal that dominated our sensual body.

151- Not all hearts deserve God's Mercy:

هر دلی را سجده هم دستور نیست   مزد رحمت قسم هر مزدور نیست

هین بپشت آن مکن جرم و گناه   که کنم توبه در آیم در پناه

می بباید تاب و آبی توبه را   شرط شد برق و سحابی توبه را

تا نباشد برق دل و ابر دو چشم   کی نشیند آتش تهدید و خشم

(II / 1651-1652-1653-1655)

a) Not every heart has permission to prostrate (surrender) itself to God, and not every labourer has the right to receive the wages of Divine Mercy. Beware! don't commit sins and crimes in the hope that "I will be forgiven by God, if I repent my sins". For repentance there needs to be a glowing inner feeling and (a flood of) tears, lightning and rain clouds are essential for repentance. Unless one has the lightning of the heart and the clouds of two weeping eyes, the fire of anger and threats does not lessen.

b) Not every heart has the ability to attract Divine Mercy. Without doubt, God is Merciful but He is at the same time Just and will come to help His lovers who are tortured by the infidel and a tyrant like the Pharaoh.

c) In relation to the above lines, it is necessary to say a few words on the following quatrain which has been dedicated to Rumi:

باز آ باز آ هر آنچه هستی باز آ   گر کافر و گبر و بت پرستی باز آ

درگاه ما درگاه نومیدی نیست   صد بار گر توبه شکستی باز آ

(Come again and come again, whatever you are come again,
If you are an infidel, pagan, or an idolater, come again,
Our gate (God's threshold) is not of hopelessness,
If you have broken your vows a hundred times, come again).

In the above lines the Persian idiom "*Baz a*" has been used literally, i.e. "*Baz amadan*" = literally means "to come again" and literarily it means to "give up". Here it has been used in its literary meaning, as in:

میان ابروت ای عشق این زمان گرهست   که نیست لایق آن روی خوب از آن باز آ

"Time O my love, is like a knot (wen) between your eyebrows, therefore it does not suit your beautiful face, give it (the face) up or leave it" (Rumi, the Divan, p. 152).

Here (in the verse) the idiom "give it up" cannot be replaced with "come again". This Persian idiom has also entered Urdu and Turkish, preserving its literal meaning "*Baz ana*" (Ur.) =to give up or quit; "*Vaz gelmek*" (Tur.) =to give up. The above idiom cannot be translated as "Come again, come again..." Whoever the writer of the above quatrain was meant to refer to this Koranic verse: "Say, O my servants who have transgressed against their souls, despair not of the Mercy of God; for God forgives all sins, for He is Oft-Forgiving, Most Merciful" (XXXIX/53).

152- Don't believe or trust the friendship of a fool:

دوستی ابله بتر از دشمنیست   او بهر حیله که دانی راند نیست
عهد او سست است و ویران و ضعیف   گفت او رفت و وفای او نحیف
گر خورد سوگند هم باور مکن   بشکند سوگند مرد کژ سخن
(II / 2015-2131-2132)

a) The friendship of a stupid man is worse than that of an enemy. The best will be to get rid of him by means of some trick. His promises are weak, empty and infirm; his words may appear great but his loyalty is feeble. If he swears, still don't trust him because a man who speaks falsely is liable to break his oath.

b) It is a famous proverb in almost all languages that it is better to be friends with a wise enemy than with a fool. A foolish friend, since he has no stability in his character, cannot be reliable. Rumi further explains the point in his verses No. 2570-2595 M/III: Jesus, son of Mary, was fleeing to a mountain as if he was running from a lion that might shed his blood. A certain man followed him and said to him, "Be all well with you, there is nobody chasing you. Why do you fly like a bird? From whom are you running in this direction, O merciful and respectworthy one? There is no lion, no enemy, no fear or danger behind you". Jesus said, "Be away, I am running from a fool, don't get in my way". You need to escape from the fool just as Jesus did, because the company of the foolish results in a great deal of bloodshed.

153- Worldly knowledge is transient:

آدمی داند که خانه حادثست   عنکبوتی نه که در وی عابثست
کرم کاندر چوب زاید سست حال   کی بداند چوب را وقت نهال
ور بداند کرم از ماهیتش   عقل باشد کرم باشد صورتش
گرچه عقلت سوی بالا می پرد   مرغ تقلیدت بپستی می چرد
علم تقلیدی و بال جان ماست   عاریه ست و ما نشسته کآن ماست
چون پی دانه نه بهر روشنیست   همچو طالب علم دنیای نیست
(II / 2320-2322-2323-2326-2327-2430)

a) Man knows that a house is made but a spider (settled in a house) is not aware of this fact. The worm that is born miserably in a piece of dry wood cannot know the form of the wood when it was a (green) twig and if it does know the state of the twig, then this is intellect but in the form of the worm. It is true that intellect takes (draws) you upwards while the physical bird (your body) forces you to feed yourself from the low. The false knowledge of this world is temporary though we think it belongs to us (for ever) and therefore it endangers our life. Since worldly knowledge is for sustenance and fame and not for (spiritual) enlightenment, he who learns this kind of knowledge is as mean as the world itself.

b) A person whose spiritual senses are awakened knows clearly that the real knowledge is that which is enlightened by Divine Knowledge. Worldly knowledge is like a torch, the battery of which will soon be discharged while real knowledge comes from an endless source. We are on our planet like a miserable worm in a piece of wood, which was once green like the branches of a tree in spring. Similarly, we keep on living on earth without knowing much about the universe, because we possess partial insight. But those who have Divine Knowledge, not only know the purpose of the universe but also the real invisible world. Those who are proud of their bookish knowledge are mistaken, because this kind of knowledge is produced by self-seeking men.

c) The word *"dunya"* has double meaning "the world" and "the low or mean place". In the above verse "the mean world" is meant, not "the religious knowledge" as given by Nich. p. 374, vol. 2 vr. 2430.

154- Greed kills knowledge:

جهل را بی علتی عالم کند   علم را علت کژ و ظالم کند

تا تو رشوت نستدی بیننده   چون طمع کردی ضریر و بنده

(II / 2752- 2753)

a) Lack of self-interest (selfishness) makes an ignorant man wise, but the presence of greed makes knowledge go astray and cruel. As long as you are not bribed, you are observant, but if you retain self-interest, you can turn blind and slave of your ego.

b) By giving up greed and lower self one can become divinely knowledgeable, and one's heart capable of perceiving divine secrets.

c) "to be bribed" here means to be lured by the lower self or material charms. The word *"illet"* is defined as "the disease of selfishness" by the Turkish and Urdu commentaries while Nich. defines it as "prejudice".

155- Everything is made known to man by its opposites:

همچنانك هر كسی در معرفت	میكند موصوف غیبی را صفت
فلسفی از نوع دیگر كرده شرح	باحثی مر گفت او را كرده جرح
این حقیقت دان نه حق اند این همه	نی بكلی گمرهانند این رمه
گر نبودی در جهان نقدی روان	قلبها را خرج كردن كی توان
تا نباشد راست كی باشد دروغ	آن دروغ از راست میگیرد فروغ
پس مگو جمله خیالست و ضلال	بی حقیقت نیست در عالم خیال
آنك گوید جمله حقند احمقیست	و آنك گوید جمله باطل او شقیست

(II / 2923-2924-2927-2929-2930-2934-2942)

a) Just as everyone in the matter of Divine Knowledge (gnosis) describes the Unseen differently, a philosopher, too gives various kinds of explanations. A scholistic theologian tries to deny the philosopher's statements. Not all of them are right, be sure, nor are they all astray. If there were no lies, there would be no truth. Falsehood gets its power from the truth. Do not say then that all this (the world) is false and imaginary. There is no idea without its reality. He who says "All is true" is foolish and he who says "All is false" is damned.

b) There is a Persian proverb, "*Herkes ba kader-i akli ust* = Everyone is in proportion to his intellect". People try to judge God in accordance with the capacity of their wisdom and that wisdom is not enough to comprehend God. It is said in the Koran, "On the day that God will raise them all up again and show them the truth (and meaning) of their conduct" (LVIII/6), the Reality will be revealed. Man can conceive things only by their opposites. God is above these confines of good and bad. Rumi further clarifies this matter in his Discourses: "So all things, though appearing opposite in relation to their opposites, in relation to the wise man are all performing the same work and are not opposed. Show me the evil thing in this world wherein no good is contained and the good thing wherein no evil is contained! For instance, a man was intent on murder, then busied himself with fornication, so that he shed no blood. Inasmuch as it was fornication, it was evil; but inasmuch as it prevented murder, it was good. So evil and good are one and indivisible. That is the substance of our quarrel with the Magians. They say there are Gods, one the creator of good and one the creator of evil. Now show me good without evil, that I may acknowledge that there is God of evil and God of good! This is impossible, for good does not exist apart from evil. Since good and evil are not two and there is no separation between them, therefore it is impossible that there should be two creators." (Discourses, p. 221).

No idea is without a reality behind it (T. 7-8/p. 883). But if one claims that everything is true one is mistaken.

c) In MM. we come across this translation: "all religions are true", due to an error in the text (see p. 278 vr. 2933), *"damha"* being written as *"dinha"*.

156- This world is the sea, the body is the fish, and your spirit is like the prophet Jonah:

هر که دید آن بحر را آن ماهیست   هر که دید الله را اللهیست

یونس محجوب از نور صبوح   این جهان دریاست و تن ماهی و روح

گوش تو تسبیحشان آخر شنید   ماهیان را گر نمی بینی پدید

صبر کن کآنست تسبیح درست   صبر کردن جان تسبیحات تست

خاصه صبر از بهر آن نقش چگل   تو چه دانی ذوق صبر ای شیشه دل

(II / 3139-3140-3144-3145-3149)

a) He who has seen God belongs to God and he who has seen the Sea is the fish. This world is like a sea and the body is like a fish while the spirit is like the prophet Jonah, who was hidden from the morning light. He who celebrates the praise of God (as Jonah did) is freed from the belly of the fish, otherwise he dies, being digested in the body of the fish. The fishes (holy spirits) are falling upon you (Mift. 2-4/p. 89); or striking you (MM.2/p. 296), open your eyes so that you may see them. If you don't see the fishes clearly at least your ears can hear their reciting the praises of God (glorification of God). The essence of your giving glory to God is your patience, so be patient because that is your real glorification. What do you know, O you the glass hearted (soft hearted), of the pleasure of patience? Especially the kind of pleasure that is required for the beauty of (town) Chigil.

b) Rumi relates the story of Jonah. Jonah was raised to warn the Assyrian capital Nineveh. When his first warning was ignored by the people of the town, he asked for the wrath of God. But they repented and God forgave them temporarily. However, Jonah was angry with the people and left the town without completing his mission. He took a boat but the sailors threw him into the sea (see the Bible, Jonah 4/1). At God's command a fish swallowed Jonah, and he was forced to remain for several days (according to the Bible three days) in the fish. There he cried to God and confessed his weakness and repeatedly uttered these words to God, "There is no God but Thee; glory to Thee, I was indeed wrong" (the Koran, XXI/87) and "In my distress, O Lord, I called to you, and you answered me from deep in the world of the dead; I cried for help, and you heard me... But I will sing praises to you... Salvation comes from the Lord" (for the full prayer see the Bible, Jonah 4/2).

The "fish" which devoured Jonah represents the physical body while "the sea" represents this world, and the spirit encaged in the body is Jonah. Now, Jonah (spirit) must shed tears of repentance for salvation and pray to God for His forgiveness. Rumi tells us that there are many other fishes (the holy spirits) that are ready to help us and to take us out of this dark sea (the world) if we pay attention to them. They keep touching us with affection but generally we do not respond to their love. Their praises to God can be heard, if our spiritual ears are open. Again, Rumi advises us to keep on praying patiently until that Beauty is known to us.

c) Chigil was a town in central Asia famous for its beautiful women. Here it means the land of God's Eternal Beauty.

157- Once any of the carnal senses observes non-existence, all other senses follow it:

چون یکی حس در روش بگشاد بند   مابقی حسها همه مبدل شوند
چون یکی حس غیر محسوسات دید   گشت غیبی بر همه حسها پدید
حسها با حس تو گویند راز   بی زبان و بی حقیقت بی مجاز
پس فلک قشرست و نور روح مغز   این پدیدست آن خفی زین رو ملغز
(II / 3240-3241-3246-3252)

b 3246 بی حقیقت و بی زبان G : بی زبان و بی حقیقت N

a) When one sense in the course of its progress loses its (physical) ties, the rest of the senses also change (and begin to set themselves free from the physical ties). When one begins to perceive any of the divine secrets (Koner. p. 254) the secrets of the world unseen are also disclosed to all other carnal senses. Your one carnal sense tells the other carnal senses secrets without a tongue, a reality or a curtain. Thus the universe is the husk and light of the spirit is its essence (the kernel). The former is manifest while the latter is hidden, don't deny this fact.

b) While following the divine path, if one of the carnal senses comes to realise the godly realities, all the others begin to follow it. Thus all the other doors of imprisonment for the physical body are opened. In other words, these worldly senses change into spiritual senses. It is after this change that we begin to observe the Essence of the universe (the macrocosm) and our body (the microcosm).

158- The physical body, spirit, wisdom and inner ideas:

جسم ظاهر روح مخفی آمدست   جسم هچون آستین جان همچو دست
باز عقل از روح مخفی تر بود   حس سوی روح زوتر ره بود
روح وحی از عقل پنهان تر بود   زآنک او غیبست او زآن سر بود
(II / 3253-3254-3258)

a) The physical body is manifest while the spirit is hidden. The body is like a sleeve and the spirit is like a hand (arm). Again the intellect is more hidden than the spirit. The senses perceive the spirit faster than they perceive the intelligence. The essence of (divine) inspiration is more concealed because it belongs to the unseen world and comes from the far world.

b) It is easier for the physical body to perceive the spirit than to perceive intelligence, and it is much more difficult for the physical body to perceive the source of inspiration because it comes from the Divine World. Ordinary insight is like the intellect of a mouse, enough for his daily need, but it is Divine Wisdom that opens new gates to God. Ask for such an intellect for God gives in proportion to whatever is asked, as Rumi says:

"Because without need God does not give anything to any one, so increase your demand (for Divine Wisdom) in order that the Sea of Mercy may surge up in loving kindness" (M. II/ 3274-3290).

159- The body is the river-bed while the spirit is the water flowing in it:

لفظ چون وکرست و معنی طایرست   جسم جوی و روح آب سایرست
او روانست و تو گویی واقف است   او دوانست و تو گویی عاکف است
قشرها بر روی این آب روان   از ثمار باغ غیبی شد دوان
(II / 3292-3293-3297)

a) The word is like the nest and meaning (essence)is the bird, the body is like the river-bed and the spirit is the water flowing in it. The water is flowing but you think that it is still. The skins (peels) that come floating over the water come from the fruit of the gardens of the invisible world.

b) As the meaning of a word is like a bird that goes and comes to its nest, so the spirit is like the water flowing in the physical body. Along with water peels of fruit (tokens) from the other world come continuously. Now, a wise man notices what kind of fruits there are in the world of non-existence.

160- Physically, we may be animals but spiritually we belong to the world of the angels:

مادر تو بط آن دریا بدست   دایه ات خاکی بد و خشکی پرست
دایه را بگذار بر خشک و بران   اندر آ در بحر معنی چون بطان
تو ز کرمنا بنی آدم شهی   هم بخشکی هم بدریا پا نهی
تو بتن حیوان بجانی از ملك   تا روی هم بر زمین هم بر فلك
ما همه مرغ آبیانیم ای غلام   بحر میداند زبان ما تمام

(II / 3767-3770-3773-3776-3779)

a) Your mother is a duck of that Spiritual Sea, your nurse is that of the earth devoted to dry land. Leave your nurse on the earth and come to the Sea of spiritual reality like the ducks. You are a king because God says, "We have ennobled the sons of Adam". You can place your feet on the land and in the sea. Physically you are an animal but spiritually you belong to the angels so that you can walk on the earth and in the sky. O son, we are ducks and the Sea knows our language perfectly.

b) Rumi uses "duck" in the sense of the spirit, and "nurse" in the sense of the world. Since spirit is able to swim in the Divine Sea, why should we be afraid of the Sea and why should we ignore our ability to swim? "We have honoured the sons of Adam, provided them with transport on land and sea" (the Koran, XVII/70).

161- Uncertainty and scepticism are the doors of your prison:

این تردد حبس و زندانی بود   کی بنگذارد که جان سویی رود
این بدین سو آن بدآن سو می کشد   هر یکی گویا منم راه رشد
این تردد عقبه راه حقست   ای خنک آنرا که پایش مطلقست
گام آهو را بگیر و رو معاف   تا رسی از گام آهو تا بناف

(III / 488-489-490-492)

a) Hesitation (uncertainty) becomes a prison for it does not let the soul go anywhere. One impulse of hesitation draws you towards earth (the materialistic life), the other impulse draws you towards the spiritual life, and each of them claims to be right. These impulses of hesitation are a barrier on the way to God, lucky is the man whose steps are firm. Follow the steps of the deer (the saint) and advance safely, and you may reach the musk (essence) of the deer by following its steps.

b) Scepticism and hesitation are barriers on the path of God. A true believer has no hesitation in believing in God and His signs. If you experience hesitation in believing in God, follow a saint's way until you reach the Scent of God.

162- Knowledge is double winged while opinions and suspicions are single winged:

علم را دو پر گمان را یک پرست   ناقص آمد ظن پر پرواز ابترست

مرغ یک پر زود افتد سر نگون   باز بر پرد دو گامی یا فزون

چون ز ظن وارست علمش رو نمود   شد دو پر آن مرغ یک پر پر گشود

گر همه عالم بگویندش تویی   بر ره یزدان و دین مستوی

ور همه گویند او را گمرهی   کوه پنداری و تو برگ کهی

(III / 1510-1511-1513-1516-1518)

a) Knowledge has two wings while opinion has only one. Opinion hinders flight. A single winged bird soon falls down and flies again but only a few steps. When one is freed from opinions, one gains real knowledge. It is then that a single winged bird becomes double winged. If all the world says to him, "You are on God's path and you follow the right religion" or "You are astray, you think yourself a mountain though you are a blade of straw (something valueless)" it makes no difference to him.

b) A person who knows God through knowledge, especially by means of divine knowledge and not by opinion or personal judgement, has a strong belief. He does not care what people say about him. Praise or depreciation is all the same to him, because he is like a two winged bird that knows how to go back to its nest.

c) Here knowledge does not only mean divine knowledge but also the scientific knowledge that leads to God in the long run.

163- Patience is the best remedy:

صبر را با حق قرین کرد ای فلان   آخر « و العصر » را آگه بخوان

صد هزاران کیمیا حق آفرید   کیمیایی همچو صبر آدم ندید

(III / 1853-1854)

a) God has joined patience with the Truth, O reader, read the last lines of the (Koranic) verse "al-Asr" carefully where God (the Truth) is mentioned side by with patience. God has created countless elixirs (remedies) but none is so effective as patience.

b) God says in the sura of "al-Asr", "Verily man is the loser, except those that have faith and do righteous deeds and join in the mutual teaching of Truth, and of patience and constancy" (C III, 2-3). Thus patience is as important as knowing "Truth" (*Haqq* =God).

164- The physical body is the captive of time and space but the spirit has no such bounds:

آن دراز و کوته اوصاف تنست   رفتن ارواح دیگر رفتنست
تو سفر کردی ز نطفه تا بعقل   نی بگامی بود نی منزل نه نقل
سیر جان بی چون بود در دور و دیر   جسم ما از جان بیاموزید سیر
جمله تلوینها ز ساعت خاستست   رست از تلوین که از ساعت برست

(III / 1978-1979-1980-2074)

a) "Long" and "short" are attributes of the body, the development of the spirit is quite another thing. You have journeyed from the sperm-seed to reason, without taking steps, without a goal, and without going from place to place. The journey of the spirit is outside time and space (see Mift. 3-1/340) and our body learns the way through the spirit. All colours (physical forms) are born of hours (time), he who is freed from (the concept of) colours is freed from time.

b) In the spiritual world there is no concept of time or space. Man journeys from a seed (sperm) to the stage of reason without walking or changing place; so is spiritual development which one cannot see clearly. It is a journey of the heart (or essence), and if the heart is intoxicated with the wine of divine love, no obstacles of time or space such as physical forms (colours) can bother us.

165- Gratitude is above opulence and bounty:

شکر نعمت خوشتر از نعمت بود   شکر باره کی سوی نعمت رود
نعمت آرد غفلت و شکر انتباه   صید نعمت کن بدام شکر شاه

(III / 2895-2897)

a) Gratitude for riches (bounties) is sweeter than riches. He who loves gratitude, how can he run after riches, because riches bring about negligence while gratitude brings alertness. By means of God's snare of gratitude hunt riches.

b) These verses allude to the following Koranic verses: "If ye are grateful, I will add more (favours) unto ye, but if ye show ingratitude, truly My punishment is terrible indeed" (XIV/7). The point is that gratitude keeps a man obedient to God while wealth may make a man forget God.

166- Unprofitable knowledge:

ای بسا عالم ز دانش بی نصیب   حافظ علمست آنکس نی حبیب

جاریه پیش نحاسی سر سریست   در کف او از برای مشتریست

b 3038 حبیب N + G : حسیب Mift.   (III / 3038-3041)

a) Many a learned man does not profit from his own knowledge, he memorises the knowledge (but does not digest it). He is not a lover of God (see T. 9-10/ p. 793). A slave girl is useless to the slave girl dealer, because she is in his hands for a customer.

b) Some learned men commit knowledge to memory and do not bother to digest it spiritually or use it for seeking God. Knowledge for them is a medium for earning money or fame.

167- God created the universe to help:

حق تعالی گر سموات آفرید   از برای دفع حاجات آفرید

هر کجا دردی دوا آنجا رود   هر کجا فقری نوا آنجا رود

عبرت و بیداری از یزدان طلب   نه از کتاب و از مقال و حرف و لب

(III / 3209-3210-3271)

a) If God Most High has created the heavens, He has done so to meet needs (of people). Where there is pain, the medicine goes; where there is poverty, food goes. Ask for spiritual wakefulness and a lesson from God, and not from books, speeches, words or lips.

b) As in the previous verses Rumi lays much emphasis on divine knowledge, communicated directly from heart to heart by the mercy of God. Therefore, it is better to ask God for this kind of knowledge. "God has created the heavens to meet needs of people" has a double meaning, physical as well as spiritual. In the physical sense it means "the skies" and refers to the planets that assist mankind in providing future. Spiritually, it may mean the centre where the angels and holy spirits dwell and from where they are sent to us to help. The Koran says, "Who gives you sustenance from the heavens (or skies) and the earth? Say, it is God..." (XXXIV/24). Then let us benefit by asking God for help.

168- If you burn hearts, you will be burnt by Hell:

چون ز خشم آتش تو در دلها زدی   مایه نار جهنم آمدی

چون ز دستت زخم بر مظلوم رست   آن درختی گشت از و زقوم رست

خشم تو تخم سعیر دوزخست   هین بکش این دوزخت را کین فخ است

کشتن این نار نبود جز بنور   نورک اطفا نارنا نحن الشکور

(III / 3472-3471-3480-3481)

a) Since you have burnt the hearts of people with the fire of your rage, you have become the source of Hell-fire. When your hands wound a victim of injustice (an innocent person) they become a tree in Hell and grow *Zaqqum* (poison) for you. Your anger is the seed of Hell-fire, be careful, kill this fire because it is a trap. You cannot extinguish this fire except with the Divine Light and the people in Hell will say, "Your light (the Divine light) has extinguished our fire and, therefore, we are thankful to you".

b) Rage belongs to Hell and, therefore, it does not exist in the heart of a lover of God. If you torture a helpless and innocent person, his moans will change into poison in Hell. The last words in the verse are the words of Muhammed. It is also a reference to this Koranic verse, "One day shalt thou see the believing men and the believing women -how their light runs forward in front of them" (LVII/12).

169- Death is not the end of life:

از جمادی مردم و نامی شدم   وز نما مردم بحیوان بر زدم

مردم از حیوانی و آدم شدم   پس چه ترسم که ز مردن کم شدم

حمله دیگر بمیرم از بشر   تا بر آرم از ملایک پر و سر

بار دیگر از ملک قربان شوم   آنچ اندر وهم ناید آن شوم

(III / 3901-3902-3903-3905)

a) I died from the mineral (inorganic state) and became a growing thing (plant) and I died from the vegetative state and attained to animality. I died to the vegetative state, too, and became a man, now why should I be afraid of death since I have never lost anything by dying. Through the next attempt I shall die to man so that I may raise my head (rise up to the angelic state) and grow my wings like that of angels (have their attributes). Once again, I shall be sacrificed and die to the angelic state and be that which is beyond conception.

b) These verses describe the evolution of the spirit and the commentators have different views about them. However, most of the commentators agree to the following: 1- Man undergoes these stages: I- Inorganic (mineral state), II- Vegetative life, III- Animality, IV- Man, V- Angel. 2- Cycle of the physical life: minerals help the growth of vegetables, vegetables help the growth of animals, animals help the growth of man, and so on. Since Rumi's Masnevi, as already said, depends on the Koran and the Tradition of Muhammed, the Hindu ideology of *Tanasukh* (transmigration of souls) or the Darwinian Theory have no place. Besides, like any other Muslim, Rumi believes in the creation of Adam. The following verses of the Masnevi throw further light on this subject:

"When bread is on the table it is *"Jamad"* (minerals) but when it is in the body of a man it becomes a happy soul" (M. I/1474).

"When minerals make their way to plants, life grows from the tree of its fortune" (M. VI/126).

It is more likely that latter explanation of the Cycle of Physical Life is what Rumi meant (also see Ankaravi III/p. 652, Schimmel, Triumphal Sun, p. 326-328).

170- It is the Mercy of God not His Wrath that trains your physical body:

رحمتش سابق بدست از قهر ز آن   تا ز رحمت گردد اهل امتحان
رحمتش بر قهر از آن سابق شدست   تا که سرمایه وجود آید بدست
باز لطف آید برای عذر او   که بکردی غسل و بر جستی زجو
ای نخود می جوش اندر ابتلا   تا نه هستی و نه خود ماند ترا
(III / 4166-4167-4170-4178)

a) The Mercy of God is beyond His wrath and it is because of this that He may test people (Baki, III/p. 287); His Mercy is beyond His rage so that the essence of existence (literally the "the capital of being") may be obtained (by Him). After His wrath comes His Mercy (as an excuse) saying, "Now you have taken a bath and have come out of the river" O boiling chickpea! (a person under test) continue boiling so that neither your existence nor your self-being (ego) remains.

b) If worries come to you, they are not due to God's Wrath, but due to His Mercy. When a lady boils chickpeas, she boils them to give taste and flavour to them but not to torture them with fire (see vr. 4163). Chickpeas, not knowing the fact, try to jump out of the pot because they can't tolerate the heat (see Schimmel, Triumphal Sun, p. 322) Similarly, God tests His lovers in order to train them to get ready to leave their earthly bodies easily and to enable them to transfer their knowledge to the eternal body. It is like training an astronaut who is to be sent to a better planet.

171- A believer's lower self is like a porcupine, the more you torture it the stronger it becomes:

در حقیقت هر عدو داروی تست / کیمیا و نافع و دلجوی تست
که از او اندر گریزی در خلا / استعانت جویی از لطف خدا
در حقیقت دوستانت دشمنند / که ز حضرت دور و مشغولت کنند
نفس مؤمن اشغری آمد یقین / کو بزخم رنج زفتست و سمین
زین سبب بر انبیا رنج و شکست / از همه خلق جهان افزون ترست
که بلای دوست تطهیر شماست / علم او بالای تدبیر شماست

(IV / 94-95-96-99-100-107)

a) In fact each foe is your medicine. He is an elixir, useful and the winner of your heart, because you flee from him towards solitude and ask for the grace of God. In reality your friends are your enemies in the sense that they make you busy with other things than God. Surely, the lower self of a believer is like a porcupine that becomes stouter and fatter because of the stick that beats and inflicts pains. It is for this reason that the prophets had to suffer pain and torment more than all the people of the world. The affliction sent by your Friend is for your purification and His (your Friend's) knowledge is beyond your plans (plots).

b) Those friends who lead you astray from God are not good friends. Enemies are better in this respect, because they push you back towards God. If you are preoccupied with your belongings in this world, like a baby with its toys, He has to take away the toys, one by one, to divert your attention to the realities. God wants to make you stronger for the eternal journey. A porcupine becomes more experienced in protecting itself from blows and so does the lover of God by means of worldly worries and afflictions. As Muhammed Iqbal says in one of his verses:

تندی باد مخالف سے نہ گھبرا اے عقاب
یہ تو اڑتی ہے تجھے اونچا اڑانے کے لئے

"O flying hawk, don't be afraid of heavy gusts of wind for they blow to lift you higher".

172- Piety is a bath while the riches of this world are like bath-stoves:

شهوت دنیا مثال گلخنست	که از و حمام تقوی روشنست
اغنیا ماننده سرگین کشان	بهر آتش کردن گرمابه بان
اندر ایشان حرص بنهاده خدا	تا بود گرمابه گرم و با نوا
ترک این تون گوی و در گرمابه ران	ترک تون را عین آن گرمابه دان
240 a G اغنیا : Y توانگران	(IV / 238-240-241-242)

a) The lust of this world is like the bath-stove and due to it the bath of piety is burning (bright). The rich are like the dung carriers for the bath. In them God has placed cupidity (and desire for riches) so that the bath should be kept burning and hot. Leave the stove and step into the bath, beware abandonment of the stove is the very essence of the bath.

b) The riches and charms of this visible world are like the fuel for the real wealthy (the pious people) who are spiritually rich. Those who are lost in earning more and more to be rich are like the fuel carriers for the stove who are smothered in dirt and do not enter the baths where they could clean themselves.

c) The Y. gives "*Tawangaran* =the rich and powerful" instead of "*Aghniya* =the rich".

173- Two observant eyes are worth many parents:

پس دو چشم روشن ای صاحب نظر	مر ترا صد مادرست و صد پدر
خاصه چشم دل که آن هفتاد توست	وین دو چشم حس خوشه چین اوست
338 b دین دو : N + G پیش MM	(IV / 337-338)

a) O man of vision, two enlightened eyes are like a hundred mothers and a hundred fathers. Especially spiritual eyes are seventy times more valuable and these two physical eyes are in need of them (or are fed by them).

b) If one has no spiritual (inner) eyes, one's manifest physical eyes are of no use. Once one's spiritual eyes are opened, they are more helpful than parents who protect their children from worldly dangers.

174- God also loves the earth because His lovers are produced from it:

عشقها داریم با این خاك ما   زآنك افتادست در قعده رضا
صد هزاران عاشق و معشوق ازو   در فغان و در نفیر و جست و جو
این فضیلت خاك را زآن رو دهیم   كه نواله پیش بی برگان نهیم
زآنكه دارد خاك شكل اغبری   وز درون دارد صفات انوری
هر كه با خود بهر حق باشد بجنگ   تا شود معنیش خصم بو و رنگ
(IV / 1002-1004-1006-1007-1021)

a) We love this earth because it has bowed to Our Will. Many (thousands of) lovers and beloveds because of this (the earth) cry, lament, yearn and are seeking Us. We grant this superiority to the earth just as we put morsels of food in front of the destitute. The earth may look dull and full of dust but inwardly it contains many shiny objects (qualities). He who is at war with himself (or his ego) for the sake of God, his essence becomes the enemy of scent and colour (forms).

b) God loves even the earth because by being obedient to His command, it produces many lovers of God who cry and lament in search of Him. As the earth has won the favour of God by being obedient to Him, the physical body that is made from dust and clay like the earth can also win His favour by means of obedience and love.

175- A bad workman quarrels with his tools:

بد گهر را علم و فن آموختن   دادن تیغی بدست راه زن
مال و منصب ناكسی كآرد بدست   طالب رسوایی خویش او شدست
یا كند بخل و عطاها كم دهد   یا سخا آرد بنا موضع نهد
احمقان سرور شدستند و ز بیم   عاقلان سرها كشیده در گلیم
(IV / 1436-1444-1445-1452)

a) To teach knowledge and science (skill) to an evil-natured man is like putting a sword in the hand of a brigand. If a worthless man possess wealth and office (rank), he has asked for disgrace. He (the worthless man) either becomes a miser and gives no gifts or he becomes generous and spends all his money on useless things (Baki). The fools have become rulers, while the wise have drawn their heads into their cloaks.

b) There are people who have a mean character by birth. To teach them art and knowledge and to appoint them to important positions or high ranks is not only dangerous for others but also for themselves and society. They use knowledge and rank to serve their evil feelings and fraud. Where fools and people full of lust become rulers, the wise hide themselves away (Koner, p. 499).

176- Physical blindness does not matter, it is the spiritual blindness that counts:

کوری کوران ز رحمت دور نیست   کوری حرص است کآن معذور نیست

ماهیا آخر نگر منگر بشست   بد گلویی چشم آخر بینت بست

اعور آن باشد که حالی دید و بس   چون بهایم بی خبر از باز پس

ای دل از کین و کراهت پاک شو   وآنگهان الحمد خوان چالاک شو

وآنگهان گفته خدا که ننگرم   من بظاهر من بباطن ناظرم

(IV / 1706-1708-1710-1736-1738)

b 1710 باز پس : N + G پیش و پس Mift.

a) The blindness of the (physically) blind is not far from Divine Mercy, but it is the blindness caused by greed that is inexcusable. O fish see the result not the hook (bait). Your bad appetite has covered your far-seeing eyes. A one-eyed man is he who sees only this moment, and like a beast is unaware of what comes after. O heart! be cleaned of hatred (enmity) and malice and chant "Glory to God", and be active (in remembering God). Moreover, God has said, "I do not look at your outer forms, I look at your interior being".

b) It is not physical blindness, but esoteric blindness that matters, for God does not look at the outer form; He looks at the spiritual essence. In order to gain the spiritual improvement, give up your malice and jealousy. Don't jump at temporary opportunities like fish that bite the baits, but take your time and try to foresee the results. Notice that the mother of all evil deeds is greed and lust.

177- A Sufi's food is Divine Light:

شاد آن صوفی که رزقش کم شود   آن شبه ش در گردد و او یم شود

زآن جرای روح چون نقصان شود   جانش از نقصان آن لرزان شود

مایده عقلست نی نان و شوی   نور عقلست ای پسر جانرا غذی

نیست غیر نور آدم را خورش   از جز آن جان نیابد پرورش

چون خوری یکبار از ماکول نور   خاک ریزی بر سر نان و تنور

(IV / 1860-1862-1954-1955-1959)

a) Lucky is the Sufi who eats less, whose black coral changes into a pearl, and who becomes a sea. When he eats spiritual food less, he begins to tremble (with fear). Intelligence is the table not bread or roasted meat. The food of life is intelligence, O my son (not the bread). Man has no other food than Divine Light. It is this element that nourishes the spirit. Once you eat of Divine Light, you throw away (pour ashes on) the bread of the oven.

b) A Sufi whose heart is filled with nothing but love of God, gives more importance to spiritual food than to the food of this world.

178- A candle burns only until dawn:

نقل آمد عقل او آواره شد   صبح آمد شمع او بیچاره شد

عقل سایه حق بود حق آفتاب   سایه را با آفتاب او چه تاب

2109 a نقل Y + G : عقل Mift.   (IV / 2109-2111)

a) Savouries came and his intellect became uncontrollable; morning came, his candle became weak (helpless). Intellect is the shadow of God while God is the Sun, how can a shadow shine in front of that Sun?

b) "*Nuql* =savoury tidbits that accompany drinks". Here it means the Divine Phenomenon which makes a Sufi (or lover of God) drunk and lose his partial insight, for when the sunlight comes the candle is put out.

179- Those who are bound by causes are short sighted:

گاو در بغداد آید ناگهان   بگذرد او و زین سران تا آن سران

از همه عیش و خوشیها و مزه   او نبیند جز که قشر خربزه

مدتی حس را بشو ز آب عیان   این چنین دان جامه شوی صوفیان

چون شدی تو پاک پرده بر کند   جان پاکان خویش را بر تو میزند

(IV / 2377-2378-2385-2386)

a) Suddenly a cow appears in the city of Baghdad and passes from one end to the other; and out of all pleasures, joys, and delights, she chooses nothing but the skins of melons. Wash your senses for a time with pure (clairvoyant) water, know this is the way the Sufis wash their clothes. When you thus become clean, they undo the veil and connect their pious souls with yours (or you begin to see their light).

b) As long as one is limited to the carnal sphere of perception one fails to see what lies beyond it. A cow, being an animal sees only what her hungry stomach makes her see. So it is with a materialistic person who is controlled by his lower self. He cannot see or even feel the spiritual world unless he is able to wash his carnal senses in pure divine water. It is after this purification that the help of the angels or saints comes to him. Each physical sense: seeing, smelling, tasting, and feeling has different functions, and the organs perform them without knowing the functions of the other senses, while a saint's senses are greatly expanded and he becomes an eye from top to toe (see Koner, p. 550). Rumi also says these words:

"O my son don't think that the aqueous substance (fat) of an eye is the source of vision, otherwise how could one see pictures (forms) in dreams?" (IV/2403). Similarly, your soul can see without eyes.

180- The door of repentance is always open:

توبه را از جانب مغرب دری   باز باشد تا قیامت بر وری
هست جنت را ز رحمت هشت در   یك در توبه ست زآن هشت ای پسر
هین غنیمت دار در بازست زود   رخت آنجا كش بكوری حسود
(IV / 2504-2506-2508)

a) There is a door of repentance from the west to Paradise which is open to mankind until the last day. Paradise has by Mercy of God eight doors and one of them is for repentance. Consider it an opportunity. Hurry up, take your luggage there in spite of (Devil's) jealousy.

b) The door of paradise is always open to those who repent their sins, as the Koran says, "And who despairs of the Mercy of his God, but such as go astray" (XV/56) and "O my servants who have transgressed against their souls despair not of the mercy of God, for God forgives all sins, for He is Oft-forgiving Most Merciful" (XXXIX/53). So, hurry up and take your things (sins) to the door of Divine Forgiveness with the key of repentance.

c) Almost all the commentaries give the following eight names of the gates of Paradise according to the Islamic belief: 1- Gate of repentance (tawba), 2- Gate of charity *(zekat)*, 3- Gate of prayers, 4- Gate of fasters, 5- Gate of pilgrimage *(hajj)*, 6- Gate of warriors or martyrs, 7- Gate of the pious 8- Gate of those who behave well to their kith and kin (see T. 13-14/656). For the names of the Paradises see Gibb 1/p. 36.

181- Man can learn the Divine Secrets in proportion to the illumination of his heart:

غیب را بیند بقدر صیقلی   هر کســی اندازه روشــن دلی
نیز این توفیق صیقل زآن عطاست   گر تو گویی کآن صفا فضل خداست
لیـس الانسـان الا ما سعی   قدر همت باشد آن جهد و دعا
(IV / 2909-2911-2912)

a) Everyone sees the Divine Secret in proportion to the illumination of his heart. If you say that spiritual purity is the grace of God then the illumination of the heart is His gift. Those prayers and labours are in proportion to your courage, because God says (in the Koran), "Man can have nothing but what he strives for" (LIII/39).

b) Without doubt discerning the Divine Secrets is dependent on the Mercy of God, but it does not mean that one should give up hope. Man should always strive for the love of God and His Mercy. Your destiny is not a barrier to your efforts and submission (see Mift. IV/p. 193).

182- The spirit is like butter while the body is like buttermilk:

روحهای تیره گلناك هست   در خلایق روحهای پاك هست
در یکی درست و در دیگر شبه   این صدفها نیست دریك مرتبه
همچنانك اظهار گندمها ز کاه   واجبست اظهار این نیك و تباه
همچو طعم روغن اندر طعم دوغ   جوهر صدقت خفی شد در دروغ
تا که دوغ آن روغن از دل بازداد   جنبشی بایست اندر اجتهاد
(IV / 3025-3026-3027-3030-3046)

b 3030 همچو طعم ... دوغ : N + G همچنان روغن اندر متن دوغ Koner + Y

a) There are pure spirits as well as dark and muddy ones. Oysters are not all equal in value, one has a pearl in it and the other has only a bead. All the creatures of this world have been brought into creation because God wanted to manifest the hidden treasures of His providence (Divine Wisdom) to mankind. It is compulsory to show (the difference between) good and evil, just as it is necessary to discriminate between the wheat and its husk. Your true essence has been concealed in your falsehood (the clayish body) as the taste of butter is hidden in the taste of buttermilk. A great shaking is required in order to get that butter out of the core of the buttermilk.

b) Rumi gives a beautiful analogy between butter and buttermilk; soul and the human body. In order to obtain butter from buttermilk we have to shake it. Similarly, in order to get the pure essence (spirit) out of the body, we have to shake it (struggle by fasting, praying, and performing good deeds). God created bad and good to show His full Divine Craft, it is now the duty of His lover to find God in the good.

183- Those who have no spiritual feelings think that the Masnevi is nothing but a collection of stories:

یا تو پنداری که حرف مثنوی   چون بخوانی رایگانش بشنوی
اندر آید لیک چون افسانها   پوست بنماید نه مغز دانها
شاه نامه یا کلیله پیش تو   همچنان باشد که قرآن از عتو
فرق آنگه باشد از حق و مجاز   که کند کحل عنایت چشم باز
(IV / 3459-3461-3463-3464)

a) Do you think that when you read the Masnevi you understand it without paying much attention? It may seem to you that it is a collection of stories for it shows you only its skin and not its kernel (its essence). Due to your obstinacy the Koran is also as simple for you as the *Shahnama* (of Firdawsi) or the *Kalila and Dimna* (the fables of Bidpai). The difference between truth and falsehood is visible only when the collyrium of (Divine) Mercy opens your spiritual eyes.

b) To read and appreciate the Masnevi of Rumi one has to possess open spiritual eyes and understanding. This is equally true with the Koran. It is useless to hold a mirror in front of a blind person.

184- Rumi's advice to those who speak to non-believers:

آب اگر در روغن جوشان کنی   دیگدان و دیگ را ویران کنی
نرم گو لیکن مگو غیر صواب   وسوسه مفروض درین الخطاب
(IV / 3816-3817)

a) If you pour water on the boiling oil, you will spoil the pan and the stove. Speak softly and don't speak anything else but the facts. For being soft do not say evil or sceptical things.

b) If you speak to a person who does not think like you (especially in religious matters), don't force him to think like you, because it is like pouring water on the boiling oil which can spoil the pan as well as the kitchen. Speak to a non-believer softly yet do not depart from the truth to show him that you are a nice person.

185- God does not like hypocrisy and insanity:

هم گواهی دادنست از اعتقاد	این نماز و روزه و حج و جهاد
هم گواهی دادنست از سر خود	این زکات و هدیه و ترک حسد
شد گواه آنك هستم با تو خوش	هدیها و ارمغان و پیش کش
نه ز رحم و جود بل بهر شکار	هست صیاد ار کند دانه نثار
ذره عقلت به از صوم و نماز	بس نکو گفت آن رسول خوش جواز
این دو در تکمیل آن شد منقرض	ز آنك عقلت جوهرست این دو عرض

(V / 183-184-186-192-454-455)

a) These (five time) ritual prayers, fasting, pilgrimage, and holy wars are all proof of inner belief. This giving of alms, presents, and the abandonment of envy are all proof of inner feelings. Gifts, presents, and offerings are examples of the affirmation, "I am pleased with you". If these are done for show and to cheat people, these illustrations are not accepted by the Justice of God. If a bird catcher casts grain, he does not do it for the sake of mercy or generosity, but for the sake of hunting the bird. How nicely the prophet (Muhammed), who always willed good things for others, uttered these words, "One drop of your intelligence is better than your fasting and offering prayers because your intelligence is the essence while these two (fasting and praying) are accidental or transient (and a mad man and a child are not obliged to offer prayers).

b) Prayers or fasting are worldly gifts to God but if they are offered for show, they are like the tricking of birds by a hunter. God cannot be tricked. If intelligence (wisdom) were not valued in Islam, prayers and fasting would be imposed even on a mad man and a child. So, when you pray to God, pray to Him intelligently and not hypocritically. In Islam intelligence has a great importance. God in the Koran invites men to thinking, research and knowledge: "Men who celebrate the praises of God, standing, sitting, and lying on their sides (in every position) and contemplate (wonders of) creation in the heavens and the earth (and they say) 'Our Lord Thou hast created nothing in vain' (are those who love God)" (III/191) and "There are signs (of God in everything) for those who understand (XIII/4). How can one appreciate God's created beings without a sharp intelligence and scientific research?

186- The eternal reward:

این نشان زر نماند بر محک   زر بماند نیک نام و بی زشک
این صلات و این جهاد و این صیام   هم نماند جان بماند نیک نام
چون ملک تسبیح حق را کن غذا   تا رهی همچون ملایک از اذا
گر جهان باغی پراز نعمت شود   قسم موش و مار هم خاکی بود
(V / 249-250-298-301)

a) This mark of gold does not remain on the touchstone, but, certainly, gold itself remains and keeps its good name. Similarly, your prayers, fasting, and wars for God do not remain either. They all disappear but your spirit remains with a good name (nice attributes). Like the angels, remember God and make it your food and be free from vexation like the angels. Even if the world becomes an orchard full of fruit yet snakes and mice (and other animals of their kind) prefer the dirt of the earth.

b) Prayers and other deeds performed for God do not survive after death but the spirit endures being purified by these deeds. If you feel that your spirit has not been cleaned enough then keep on praying to God and be free of anxiety like the angels. The spiritual world may offer a better life than that of this world, but a materialistic man, like snakes and other animals, prefers to live in the darkness of the earth.

187- It is better to discover yourself first:

حد اعیان و عرض دانسته گیر   حد خود را دان که نبود زین گزیر
چون بدانی حد خود زین حد گریز   تا ببی حد در رسی ای خاک بیز
عمر در محمول و در موضوع رفت   بی بصیرت عمر در مسموع رفت
هر دلیلی بی نتیجه و بی اثر   باطل آمد در نتیجه خود نگر
(V / 564-565-566-567)

a) You may learn the definition of all objects (substances) of this world as well as of the other world but the best thing is to learn the definition of your own self that is inevitable. When you come to know your own limit avoid this (world of limits) so that you may reach the One Who has no definition, O you who are busy sifting dust (dealing with useless matters), your life has passed in discussing logical questions such as "What is the subject?" and "What is the predicate?" and so on; you keep on wasting your life in listening to these kinds of discussions. Every proof that has no effect or result is meaningless (see Baki, p. 60); think of your own result!

b) Instead of wasting our lives on meaningless discussions we should try to find ways to purify our souls by discovering ourselves. We should know our shortcomings and evil feelings to mend our character. Vain imaginations or suspicions are the production of our lower self; and must, therefore, be avoided as suggested in other verses.

188- Show pity to three groups of men:

گفت پیغمبر که با این سه گروه   رحم آرید ار ز سنگید و ز کوه
آنك او بعد از رئیسی خوار شد   و آن توانگر هم که بی دینار شد
و آن سوم آن عالمی کاندر جهان   مبتلی گردد میان ابلهان
ز آنك از عزت بخواری آمدن   همچو قطع عضو باشد از بدن
(V / 825-826-827-828)

a) The prophet Muhammed said, "Take pity on these three classes of men even if you have a heart like stone. Take pity on him who has become helpless (rankless) after being a chief (boss), on him who has become penniless after having been rich, and on a learned man who has been forced to live among the foolish. This is because to come down from a high rank to a low one is like losing a limb.

b) These verses narrating the tradition of Muhammed are self-explanatory. However, a few words may be added from the commentary of Koner (see p. 649): "When a rich man or a man of rank falls, all the hypocritical and selfish people whom he trusted leave him. A learned man is unlucky if he happens to be among the ignorant for they don't listen to him because he speaks the truth". There is a Turkish proverb, "A man who tells the truth is expelled from the seven villages".

189- Beauty, power, virtue, and knowledge all come from God:

آن جمال و قدرت و فضل و هنر   ز آفتاب حسن کرد این سوسفر
باز میگردند چون استارها   نور آن خورشید زین دیوارها
آنك کرد او در رخ خوبانت دنگ   نور خورشیدست از شیشه سه رنگ
شیشه های رنگ رنگ آن نور را   می نمایند این چنین رنگین بما
چون نماند شیشهای رنگ رنگ   نور بی رنگت کند آنگاه دنگ
خوی کن بی شیشه دیدن نور را   تا چو شیشه بشکند نبود عمی
قانعی با دانش آموخته   در چراغ غیر چشم افروخته
او چراغ خویش بر باید که تا   تو بدانی مستعیری نی فتا
گر تو کردی شکر و سعی مجتهد   غم مخور که صد چنان بازت دهد
(V / 985-986-988-989-990-991-992-993-994)

a) Beauty, power, virtue, and knowledge have come to this side (of the world) from the Sun of Comeliness and go back to the Sun like the stars or like the sun light from these walls. The beauty that makes you mad is from the light of the same Sun that comes to you through three-coloured glass. That light comes to us in colours because of coloured glass (Baki., p. 100). But when the coloured glasses are removed, the colourless light (of God) amazes you. Form the habit of seeing that light without the glass, so that if the glass is broken, you may not go blind. You are satisfied with your self-gained knowledge and have enlightened your eyes with other's (borrowed) lamps. He (God) takes that borrowed lamp from you so that you may discover that it was not yours. Nevertheless, don't worry, He will give you many lamps (of knowledge) again if you thank Him and toil for the lamps.

b) The beauty of this world, comes from the Beauty of God (or light of God), but indirectly, through three coloured glass (the primary colours- red, yellow and blue are referred to). After death the Real Beauty becomes more manifest and worldly beauty disappears like stars at night. It is better to get used to the Real Beauty before death so that we may not get dazzled when we are exposed to God's Light. If we remain trapped in worldly colours, we are no better than a blind man. Therefore, enlighten your inner being to the degree that it may not be dazzled in the presence of Divine Beauty.

190- Seek the Mercy of God but not His instrument:

احمقانه از سنان رحمت مجو   زآن شهی جو کآن بود در دست او

چون قضا آید طبیب ابله شود   و آن دوا در نفع هم گمره شود

(V / 1682-1707)

a) Don't ask for mercy from the spear (instrument) foolishly, but ask mercy from the King in Whose Hand the spear is. When death comes the doctor becomes puzzled and the medicine that is useful normally becomes useless.

b) Rumi wants to say that if you want to ask for mercy or favour ask it of God, not of His created beings (His instrument), because God's Mercy rules His wrath. What can a doctor (the instrument of God) do? He also needs a doctor when death comes, so ask only the help of God.

c) "the Wrath" is probably a better word than "cruelty" (used by Nich. p. 101) because God is never cruel according to Islamic belief.

191- If you eat husk and barley you are slaughtered like goats:

هر که کاه و جو خورد قربان شود   هر که نور حق خورد قرآن شود
علم اندر نور چون فرغرده شد   پس ز علمت نور یابد قوم لد
آسمان شو ابر شو باران ببار   ناودان بارش کند نبود بکار
معده را بگذار و سوی دل خرام   تا که بی پرده ز حق آید سلام
                                    (V / 2478-2488-2490-2514)

a) He who eats husk and barley (like goats) deserves to be slaughtered (for sacrifice), and he who lives on the Light of God becomes the Koran. When your knowledge is amalgamated with the Divine Light, the most obstinate nations will begin to receive the light from your knowledge (see MM. p. 254). Be the sky, be the clouds and pour rain. The spouts rain, too, but their rain is of no use. Leave your stomach aside and walk towards your heart, in order that there comes to you a direct "Hello" from God.

b) Goats and sheep are slaughtered because they eat husk and barley. Similarly, a worldly man lives on trivial things unlike a lover of God whose food is Divine Light. When Divine Light is mixed with knowledge, the Koran is born (you begin to receive Divine Knowledge). If your knowledge is mundane, it is like the rain water of the spout that flows away without being useful for farms. But if your knowledge is mixed with Divine Knowledge, it is fruitful for others.

192- A poisonous snake is better than a bad friend:

حق ذات پاک الله الصمد   که بود به مار بد از یار بد
مار بد جانی ستاند از سلیم   یار بد آرد سوی نار مقیم
از قرین بی قول و گفت و گوی او   خود بدزدد دل نهان از خوی او
دیده عقلت بدو بیرون جهد   طعن اوت اندر کف طاعون نهد
b 2635 مقیم G : جحیم Mift.   (V / 2634-2635-2636-2639)

a) I swear by the truth of God Who is "*Samad*" (the Eternal and Absolute) that a bad friend is worse than a snake. A bad snake takes the life of a person whom it bites but a bad friend leads him to an everlasting fire. The heart steals the characteristics of a (bad) friend secretly, even if he does not speak to you. The eyes of your intelligence become blind and his reproaching will lead you into the hands of pestilence (hell).

b) A bad friend is more dangerous than a snake because a snake can only torture your body but a bad friend does not only torture your body but also your spirit. A bad friend can silently influence your heart.

c) The verse... مار بد زخم ... یار بد بر جان seen in the Indian text is not found in the "G".

193- God is your only friend in bad days:

عاشق آن عاشقان غیب باش   عاشقان پنج روزه کم تراش
وقت صحت جمله یارند و حریف   وقت درد و غم بجز حق کوالیف
(V / 3203-3206)

a) Love the lovers of the Unseen and do not love friends of this temporary (five days') world. When you are healthy (and strong), they are all friends but at the time of pain and worries who can be a better friend than God?

b) Spiritual friends who love God and His lovers are friends indeed. Worldly friends are transient and deceptive like all other things but God is Everlasting.

194- Lucky is the man who can discover his inner self:

ای برون از وهم و قال و قیل من   خاک بر فرق من و تمثیل من
بنده نشکیبد ز تصویر خوشت   هر دمت گوید که جانم مفرشت
ما بدانستیم ما این تن نه‌ایم   از ورای تن بیزدان می زییم
ای خنک آنرا که ذات خود شناخت   اندر امن سرمدی قصری بساخت
a 3340 ما ... ما این G : چون ... ما کن MM   (V / 3318-3319-3340-3341)

a) O You (My Lord) Who are beyond my speech and thought, dust be on my head and my metaphors (I bring to reveal Your Being). Man (Your slave) cannot bear the idea of Your Beauty although he may say everytime "May my life be a floor (carpet) under Your feet (be sacrificed for You)". We have come to know that we are not only this body but are living with God beyond this body. How lucky is the man who has come to know himself and thus has built a palace in the security of the Everlasting.

b) Rumi wrote six volumes to explain God and the path that leads to Him by means of rich phrases, idioms, similes, and metaphors and yet he could not explain God properly because His Beauty is beyond speech and comprehension. All words uttered by man to praise God are simple, for God can be praised only by our feelings. In this respect, the man who discovers his inner being and prays to God with the language of that inner being is truly lucky.

195- There is a secret "You (Thou)" within yourself:

هست اندر سود تو در بیسوی	این توی ظاهر که پنداری توئی
من غلام مرد خودبینی چنین	توی تو در دیگری آمد دفین
که در آخر واقف بیرون شوست	او توست اما نه این تو آن توست
(VI / -3776-3774)	

a) This apparent "you" which you think is "you" is bound by dimensions while your (real) "you" is in the non-dimensional world. Your "youness" is buried in another "youness" and I am a slave of a man who can (feel) his "real self". The prophet (saint or angelic soul) is you, not this you but the other "you" that is aware of getting out of this "bodily you" in the long run.

b) The "me" referred to here by Rumi is the part of that which is experienced by prophets and saints. That "me" has a direct connection with God and those who can discover that "me" or "inner self" are the luckiest people on the earth.

c) ... این توی ظاهر has been added to the text of the "Y" by a later hand. The other two verses found in MM (p. 361) ... بر صوف ... بگزار ز دوی are not found in "N", "Y" or even in "G".

196- Worldly titles and rank are the source of worries, pains, and destruction:

در نهانش مرگ و درد و جان دهی	نام میری و وزیری و شهی
چون جنازه نه که بر گردن برند	بنده باش و بر زمین رو چون سمند
چون سوار مرده آرندش بگور	جمله را حمال خود خواهد کفور
(VI / 323-324-325)	Mift. + Jafer مرگ و در اله نیست : G ... درنهانش b 323
	Mift. قبور اهل ... مردوم بار : G بگور ... چون b 325

187

a) The names (titles) "*Prince*", "*Vizierate*", and "*Kingship*" have a hidden meaning: "death, pain, and loss of life". Be a slave of God and walk on earth like a horse, but not like a coffin that is carried on the shoulders of people. The ungrateful person wishes all people to be his porters until they carry him to the grave.

b) A true dervish never pays attention to worldly fame and reputation because they lead an individual to a bad end. A man who is fond of fame likes to be carried on the shoulders of people until the same people carry his coffin on their shoulders to the graveyard. It is better to be like a horse that spends its life in humble service in order to pass through the riches of this world quickly. The prophets (Christ, Muhammed) can be taken as examples of people who paid little attention to the riches of this world but instead gave more importance to the poor and the destitute.

197- Hurry makes no curry:

پایه پایه بر توان رفتن ببام در تانی گوید ای عجول خام
کار نآید قلیه دیوانه جوش دیگ را تدریج و استادانه جوش
(VI / 1211-1212)

a) He (the saint) says, "O you immature one, who are in a hurry, you can climb up to the roof step by step. Boil your pot slowly because a pot boiled in a mad haste is of no use".

b) In the spiritual path hurry is no good. It takes time to train one's lower self. Even God created the universe gradually while He could have created it in a moment. Try to improve your spiritual being slowly and steadily.

198- Don't be afraid of death but be afraid of your body:

آن خیالت لاشی و تو لاشیی از وجودی ترس کاکنون درویی
هیچ نی مر هیچ نی را ره زدست لاشیی بر لاشیی عاشق شدست
گشت نا معقول تو بر تو عیان چون برون شد این خیالات از میان
(VI / 1447-1448-1449)

a) Be afraid of the body in which you are still (living), it is your illusion and it is nothing. You are nothing and are in love with nothing (your body). Nothing has thus waylaid nothingness (Baki 492 and so on, your idea of nothingness has robbed you Mift. p. 339). When these vain ideas leave you, then you will begin to see openly what your intelligence has failed to see.

b) Being captive to this mortal world, we have been deceived by our carnal senses. This is the situation to be afraid of, not death. We see what we were a prisoner of when our Divine Wisdom begins to flow.

199- Your own story of life is worse than other stories:

ای فسانه گشته و محو از وجود   چند افسانه بخواهی آزمود
ای فرو رفته بگور جهل و شك   چند جویی لاغ و دستان فلك
(VI / 1709-1711)

a) O you who have become a story of your own after being decayed by your body, how long will you continue to listen to stories about others? O you, who have gone down into the deceptive stories of time (universe).

b) This world is like an old lady that keeps cheating you with her interesting stories and transient charms. While you are busy listening to her stories, the story of your own life is coming to a tragic end. Think of your own goal and wake up, for this world will spare none (for similar meaning see Mift. 6-2 p. 21).

200- No piece of knowledge can be attained without God's permission:

گر بیابان پر شود زر و نقود   بی رضاء حق جوی نتوان ربود
ور بخوانی صد صحف بی سکته   بی قدر یادت نماند نکته
تا بدانی کآسمانها، سمی   هست عکس مدرکات آدمی
(VI / 1930-1931-1935)

a) Although a desert may be filled with gold and money yet not a single bit (barley) of it can be taken without the Will of God. Similarly, if you read a hundred pages without a break and God does not give you permission, you cannot commit a single point to your memory from those pages. Finally, you come to know that all that you see in the heaven is nothing but reflection of man's conception.

b) Unless God desires it, no spiritual knowledge can be gained. The microcosm is the reflection of the macrocosm. Man can find within himself all that there exists in the macrocosm (see Ankaravi, p. 473). Whatever is in the universe is the creation of Divine Wisdom and partial insight is bound by it.

201- A moustache or beard is no sign of sagacity:

در شرابی که نگنجد تار مو   باد سبلت کی بگنجد و آب رو
خواجه را از ریش و سبلت و ارهان   در ده ای ساقی یکی رطلی گران
(VI / 2021-2022)

a) How can the wine that does not contain a single hair contain the show of moustache and fame (the water of the face)? O cup bearer, hand over a heavy goblet (of spiritual) wine to the lord (a rich master) and free him from the moustache and the beard.

b) The spiritual wine offered by a saint (the cup bearer) has no room for show and ceremony, so let him offer a large cup to a wealthy master who is proud of his beard and moustache (worldly riches and reputation). When he becomes drunk from Divine Wine, he will give up show and change into a simple sincere lover of God.

202- God is Oft-Forgiving:

عرش لرزد از انین المذنبین   چون بر آرند از پشیمانی حنین
دستشان گیرد ببالا میکشد   آنچنان لرزد که مادر برولد
(VI / 3625-3626)

a) When through repentance they (people) begin to moan, God's throne begins to tremble from their outcries. It (God's throne) trembles like the mother trembles at her baby and holds the baby's hand and draws it up.

b) Where sinners begin to cry over their sins and feel repentance, God's Mercy begins to stir and He forgives them as a mother forgives her children. Much importance is given to repentance in Islam and Christianity: "Repentance toward God and faith toward our Lord Jesus Christ" (the Bible, Acts XX/21), and "If any of you did evil in ignorance, and thereafter repented and amended (his conduct), lo He is Oft-Forgiving, Most Merciful" (the Koran, VI/54), and "He is the One that accepts repentance from His servants and forgives sins, and He knows all that you do" (the Koran, XLII/25).

203- God guides those whom He pleases:

کژ روی را محصد احسان کند   گمرهی را منهج ایمان کند
تا نباشد هیچ خاین بی رجا   تا نباشد هیچ محسن بی وجا
در گنه خلعت نهد آن مغفرت   نیست مخفی در نماز آن مکرمت
(VI / 4342-4343-4345)   b 4342 محصد G : مقصد MM

a) (If God wills) He changes a loser's way into a right way that leads to a true faith, and He by means of His Grace diverts a wrong path into a path that leads to the harvest (of His Mercy). He does this to the end that no righteous man may be without fear and no traitor (a sinner) may be without hope. Divine bounty is not hidden in ritual prayers (only) but Divine Forgiveness bestows a robe of honour even in the case of sins.

b) These verses refer to the following Koranic verses: "Now God leaves straying those whom He pleases, and guides whom He pleases (to a righteous path) and He is Exalted in power, full of wisdom" (XIV/4). Rumi here adds some further reasons for God not fully pleasing true believers. If God bestows all that pleases a believer, the believer will forget his goal and will be spoilt like a child who gives up his studies because of his family's wealth. God is not bound by any restrictions, He can forgive a sinner if He wants to. This is a matter between God and His slave (lover).

204- The celestial mill gives you nothing if you have no wheat:

همچو مرغ خاك كآید در بحار   زآن چه یابد جز هلاك و جز خسار

آسیای چرخ بر بی گندمان   مو سپیدی بخشد و ضعف میان

لیك با با گندمان این آسیا   ملك بخش آمد دهد كار و كیا

اول استعداد جنت بایدت   تا ز جنت زندگانی زایدت

(VI / 4430-4432-4433-4434)

a) If a land bird happens to be in the sea (sea waters) what can it gain there except death and loss? The celestial mill (universe) gives nothing but whiteness of hair and weakness in the loins. But if you have wheat with you this mill will give you an empire and a sovereign. You should first try to deserve Paradise so that it may give you a new life.

b) If one goes to a flour-mill without wheat what shall he gain? Nothing but the whiteness of his beard and hair (because of the flour). Similarly if you have no good deeds to take with you to the other world, you will gain nothing but pain in the heart, and if you have developed your spiritual being, you will gain honour and Divine Love.

205- Don't dwell in the box:

تا ز صندوق بدنمان وا خرند	ای خدا بگمار قومی رحمند
که بداند کو بصندوق اندرست	از هزاران یك کسی خوش منظرست
از قفص اندر قفص دارد گذر	دایما محبوس عقلش در صور
این سخن با جن وانس آمد زهو	در نبی ان استطعتم فانفذوا
او سمایی نیست صندوقی بود	گر ز صندوقی بصندوقی رود
کو نباشد بی فغان و بی هراس	آنك داند این نشانش آن شناس

(VI / 4503-4505-4511-4513-4515-4518)

a) My Lord send us a merciful nation so that they may buy us (free us) from our boxes of bodies. Out of thousands only one will be far-sighted if he discovers that he is in a box (this body). (Some people's) reason is a captive of forms for ever and they pass from one box to another box. It is said in the Koran (by God) to men and Jinns, "If it be, ye can pass beyond". If your soul passes from box to box, you do not belong to Heaven but to the box. He who knows this point well, does not cry and has no fear of death.

b) Rumi prays to God and says, "My Lord, send us the people (like prophets and saints, see verse No. 4504) who may free us from this worldly imprisonment and show us a better place". Some people are fond of this mortal world to the extent that they want to move from box to box (from one body to another) and not bother to get out of the dark tunnel of the physical life. For those souls that are stuck in this world God says in the Koran, "O ye the assembly of Jinns and men if it be, ye can pass beyond the zones of the heavens and the earth, pass ye, not without power shall ye be able to pass" (LV/33). Spirit is able to pass many stages or layers towards God, yet effort and God's help are required.

CHAPTER VII

Step III: The desires and quest

The theme of this chapter concerns a man who has been able to control his lower self to some extent and has begun to realise that the spiritual sea does exist, and that he is only a drop of that sea; and he has to reach that sea ultimately by toiling and persevering. Rumi's lines in his *"Mejalis-i Saba"* provide a summary of this chapter:

"Blow like a wind in search of Him, eat the poison of troubles like sugar and drink that solution like honey syrup, tell the heart that it should say 'farewell' to health, and tell the body to say 'goodbye' to its sound constitution because he who builds a house by the sea side is liable to receive countless sea waves. He who claims to be a lover has to drink the poison of worries and pain" (Mejalis, Per., p. 60).

206- Every night souls are set free from their cages:

گر هزاران دام باشد در قدم   چون تو با مایی نباشد هیچ غم
هر شبی از دام تن ارواح را   می رهانی می کنی الواح را
می رهند ارواح هر شب زین قفص   فارغان از حکم و گفتار و قصص
شب ز زندان بی خبر زندانیان   شب ز دولت بی خبر سلطانیان
نی غم و اندیشه سود و زیان   نی خیال این فلان و آن فلان
حال عارف این بود بی خواب هم   گفت ایزد هم رقود زین مرم

(I / 387-388-389-390-391-392)

a) Even if there are thousands of traps on the path since You are with us we have nothing to worry about. Every night You set our souls free from our body-snares along with their tablets of memories. Every night souls are released from their cages (bodies) and they are no more the captive of speeches, stories, or orders. At night (even) prisoners are not aware of their imprisonment and Sultans are unconscious of their powers. They neither worry about profit nor about loss. They neither worry about this man nor about that man. Saints have a similar state without sleeping. As God says in the Koran, "You will think them awake although they are asleep", do not deny this.

b) Once you win the favour of God, His guidance will lead you out of all kinds of traps, as at night we lose our memories, good or bad, and we wake up with them all back. Saints or lovers of God enjoy a similar state without sleeping because their hearts are busy with God. Physically they are asleep but spiritually they are wide awake, like the companions of the cave who slept for centuries. This is a summary of the legend:

"*Ashab ul-Kahf*" (the Companion of the Cave) are mentioned in Christian as well as in Islamic literature. In the reign of an Anatolian Roman Emperor (Decius A.D. 249-251) who persecuted the Christians, seven Christian youths of Ephesus and their dog left the town (Ephesus) and hid themselves in a cave (perhaps a cave near Ephesus or Tarsus). They fell asleep and remained there for centuries (about 309 years see Baki, his commentary I-II/94). When the wall that closed the cave was demolished, they woke up. They thought that they had gone to sleep only for a while. When one of them came out to buy food (bread) his money and dress drew the attention of the people who took him to the king of that time (Theodosius II, A.D. 408-450). By then the Christian religion had become the state religion. The man went back to the cave, which closed again (see Abdullah Yusuf's notes, the Holy Koran p. 730, for references see IA./4/371).

207- This world has little value in the Eyes of God:

صد چو عالم در نظر پیدا کند   چون که چشمت را بخود بینا کند
گر جهان پیشت بزرگ و بی بنیست   پیش قدرت ذره می دان که نیست
524 a بی بنیست G : بی تنی است. Mift.   (I / 523-524)

a) If God makes you see from His Eyes, He creates hundreds of worlds in front of your eyes. Although this world seems to you large and endless, it is nothing but a tiny atom in the Eyes of Almighty.

b) If your esoteric eyes open, you will be able to see countless worlds. As Muhammed Iqbal says: "ستاروں سے آگے جہاں اور بھی ہیں" = "There are other worlds beyond these stars!". The eyes of a Sufi (lover of God) have a wider boundary than that of a worldling, as Iqbal continues:

پرواز ہے دونوں کی ایک فضا میں
کرگس کا جہاں اور ہے شاہین کا جہاں اور

"They both have the same mode of flight in space,
Yet a vulture's world is different from the world of a hawk".

In the Eyes of God the heart of a lover is like a tiny lamp in the darkness of existence while this large universe has little value for Him.

208- A person is unhappy if he is aloof from his Essence:

وز زهد صافی بدم در جوی تو / از کید فارغ بدم یا روی تو

وز وجود نقد خود ببریدنست / این دریغاها خیال دیدنست

(I / 1710-1711)

a) The view of Your Face kept me free from the worldly body (and worries) and in Your stream (of light) I was cleansed of foam (griefs). These cries of "*Alas*" are caused by the idea of seeing You and by the feeling of separation from my own Essence.

b) These worldly worries for a lover of God are a summons to the real home. His moaning is due to separation from God.

209- Pains are the messengers of death:

از بخار و گرد بود و باد ماست / این همه غمها که اندر سینهاست

دانک کلش بر سرت خواهد ریخت / چون ز جزو مرگ نتوانی گریخت

دانک شیرین می کند کل را خدا / جزو مرگ ار گشت شیرین مر ترا

از رسولش رو مگردان ای فضول / دردها از مرگ می آید رسول

هر که او تن را پرستد جان نبرد / هرک شیرین می زید او تلخ مرد

(I / 2296-2299-2300-2301-2302)

a) All these griefs and worries that we carry in our heart are due to the smoke and dust of our existence and the wind. If you cannot escape from this aspect of death, then be sure they will pour down the whole of it on your head. If this aspect of death is sweet for you, God will make the whole of it sweet for you. Pain comes to you as messengers of death. Do not refuse them, you heedless one! He who lives a sweet life, for him death is bitter. He who adores (is fond of) his body, cannot save his soul.

b) All the worries and troubles that we face are due to our fondness for fame, wealth, and show. If pain comes to you, it comes to you as a reminder of God Who reproaches you because of your negligence, and wants you to be less fond of the body which is your temporary property.

"Between God and His servant are just two veils, all other veils become manifest from these two: health and wealth. He who is healthy says, 'Where is God? I don't know and I don't see'. As soon as he begins to suffer, he says, 'Oh God, Oh God!' and he begins to share his secrets with Him and talking to Him. So you see that health was his veil, and God was hidden under his pain. So long as man has riches, he gathers together the means of achieving his desires. Night and day he busies himself with them. But as soon as he loses his wealth, his ego weakens and he turns round about God" (Discourses, Arberry p. 240) and:

"Someone said, 'I have been negligent'. The master (Rumi) said, 'A thought and reproach comes to a person', so he says, 'What am I doing? Why am I doing it?' This is proof of God's love and favour. Love remains so long as reproach remains. For one reproaches friends, not strangers.

Now reproach is of different kinds. When someone is reproached and feels pain from it and is made aware of it, that is proof that God loves and favours him... For example they beat a carpet with sticks to remove the dust. An intelligent man would not call this "reproach". But if a man beats his own beloved child, this is called "reproach" and in such cases it is a proof of love. So long as you see pain and regret in yourself, that is proof of God's love and favour" (Discourses, Arberry p. 35).

So accept the messengers of God willingly and bravely (T. I/p. 18).

210- Only His friendship can free you from your lower self:

نور خواهی مستعد نور شو   دور خواهی خویش بین و دور شو
ور رهی خواهی از این سجن خرب   سرمکش از دوست و اسجد و اقترب
(I / 3606-3607)

a) If you desire the light, try to deserve it. If you want to be aloof (from the light) then be self-conceited and afar from it (the light). If you want to get rid of this abandoned prison, don't turn your head from Him (the Friend), "Prostrate yourself to Him and be closer to Him".

b) If you want to possess Divine Light, deny your lower self, and sincerely bow down to Him. As the Koran says, "But bow down in adoration and bring yourself closer (to God)" (XCVI/19). Bowing down to God also means remembering God. As Rumi says in his Discourses: "Never be without remembrance of God. For the remembrance of Him is strength and feathers and wings to the bird of spirit. If your goal becomes actualised completely, that is Light upon Light. But in any case through remembrance of God your inward self will be illuminated and you will achieve a degree of detachment from the world... Consider a small box of musk whose opening is narrow; you put your hand into it, but you cannot bring out the musk, yet your hand becomes perfumed and your senses refreshed. So too is the remembrance of God: Even if you do not reach His Essence, yet His remembrance has numerous effects upon you. You actualise tremendous benefits by invoking Him (Discourses, Arberry, p. 183). "In the remembrance of God do hearts find satisfaction" (The Koran, XIII/28). In order to deserve God's love you must strive for His Favour by means of remembrance or by means of bowing down to Him whole-heartedly.

211- Keep your heart clean so that it may be dwelt in by God:

چون ز علت وا رهیدی ای رهین   سر که را بگذار و میخور انگبین
حکم بر دل بعد ازین بی واسطه   حق کند چون یافت دل این رابطه
(I / 3664-3666)

a) Since you have recovered from the sickness into which you had fallen, leave the vinegar and continue to drink honey. Now that your heart has gained connections (with God), He will control your heart directly.

b) Once your heart is cleansed do not dirty it with negative feelings. Try to keep it clean so that God may begin to dwell in it and control it directly.

c) As explained by Mift., "honey" is spiritual attainment, and "vinegar" is worldly worries (see Ibid, 4/221). In other words, once you have purified your heart and purged worldly desires from it, spiritual improvements begin.

212- Separation from God is the biggest pain:

تلختر از فرقت تو هیچ نیست   بی پناهت غیر پیچا پیچ نیست
چون تو ندهی راه جان خود برده گیر   جان که بی تو زنده باشد مرده گیر
(I / 3902-3907)

a) There is nothing more bitter than the separation from God, and without His protection we gain nothing but perplexity (and bewilderment). If you (my Lord) do not give permission to the soul to get closer to You, You regard the souls as dead even if they are able to exist without You.

b) Any achievement in which the assistance of God and His Will is absent, is as transient as this world. The best thing is to win God's favour and to depend on His love, which grants you eternal life in His Presence. Separation from Him is the worst punishment. It is like separating an infant from its mother's breast.

213- Speaking and eating too much is a sign of selfness:

چشم بند آن جهان حلق و دهان	این دهان برند تا بینی عیان
وی جهان تو بر مثال برزخی	ای دهان تو خود دهانه دوزخی
شد فراق صدر جنت طوق نفس	یک قدم زد آدم اندر ذوق نفس
موی در دیده بود کوه عظیم	بود آدم دیده نور قدیم
(II / 11-12-15-18)	a 12 دهانه K + N : زبانه T

a) Close this mouth so that you may see clearly that the gullet and mouth are an eye-bandage to the other world. O mouth, you are yourself the entrance to Hell and O earth, you are like the Intermediate World *(Berzakh)*. Adam took one step towards sensual pleasure, the highest seat of Paradise became a chain of separation around his neck. Adam was an eye of the Eternal Light; a hair in the eye is like a great mountain.

b) The mouth is the external source of eating and speaking (Mift., 2-1/p. 16). The more you control it, the more you learn the secrets of the other world. This world is like the *"Alem-i Berzakh"* (the Intermediate Plane where souls wait until the last day) and you are left here for a time. Adam was an Eye of the Eternal Light, but he was expelled from there because he began to serve his lower self, and a single hair in the eye feels like a mountain.

c) *Berzakh*: literally means "partition". People dwell in this plane after death and before Judgment. As the Koran says, "Before them is a Partition till the day they are raised" (XXIII/100). Adam was dear to God as an eye but when he became involved with his own desires, he became like a mote in the Eye of God.

214- To feel satisfied with your own piety is a sign of pride:

زشت آید پیش آن زیبای ما	رو مکن زشتی که نیکیهای ما
ز آن دعا کردن دلت مغرور شد	چون ترا ذکر و دعا دستور شد
(II / 337-339)	

a) Go, do not commit faults because even our good deeds have no value in the Presence of that Beautiful One. Since you are accustomed to remembrance and regular prayers, due to this habit of praying to God your heart becomes proud of yourself.

b) God is above our praises and prayers. The least we can do is to remember Him and love Him, but while doing this we should not be proud of our piety for only God's help can save us and take us to perfection. We can be a nice person but our being perfect depends on His Will. We should bear in mind that Satan was expelled from Paradise because of his pride. The Punjabi poet of Pakistan (Bulhe Shah) uttered these lines regarding real prayer:

"If God loved those who wash themselves day and night, He would have chosen frogs and fishes;
If God loved those who pray to Him at midnight, He would have chosen bats;
If God loved those who walk (graze) aimlessly in the mountains, He would have chosen cattle;
But Bulhe Shah, God meets (loves) those who have nice feelings and a good heart".

The only thing that counts in the Presence of God is a good intention and a clean heart.

215- Greed hampers piety:

صاف خواهی چشم و عقل و سمع را   بر دران تو پردهای طمع را
هر که دور از دعوت رحمان بود   او گدا چشمست اگر سلطان بود
هیچ کنجی بی دد و بی دام نیست   جز بخلوت گاه حق آرام نیست
(II / 569-588-591)

a) If you want to keep your eyes, hearing and understanding clear (pure), tear the veil of your lower self. He who has fallen aloof from the feast of the Merciful, his eyes are greedy like a beggar's, though he may be a king. No corner (of this world) is without beasts except the place where you are alone with God.

b) It is an aspect of piety to possess a clean heart and that becomes possible by lessening your greed, because greed is the enemy of piety and good intentions. The only safe place on earth is the corner where God can be found.

216- This universe is dust dependent on the wind of Divine Mercy:

وآن جهان هست بس پنهان شده	این جهان نیست چون هستان شده
کژ نمایی پرده سازی میکند	خاک بر بادست بازی میکند
باد را دان علی و عالی نژاد	خاک همچون آلتی در دست باد
بی سواره اسب خود نآید بکار	چشم حس اسب است و نور حق سوار
معنی نور علی نور این بود	نور حس را نور حق تزیین بود
نور حق دریا و حس چون شبنمیست	ز آنک محسوسات دونتر عالمیست
چون خفی نبود ضیایی کآن صفیست	نور حس با این غلیظی مختفیست
عاجزی پیشه گرفت و داد غیب	این جهان چون خس بدست باد غیب
جانها پیدا و پنهان جان جان	تیر پران بین و ناپیدا کمان

(II / 1280-1281-1283-1286-1293-1295-1299-1300-1304)

a) Since this non-existent world has become manifest, that existent world has become hidden (to the eye). It (the whole universe) is dust playing on the wind and it is making tricks and forming veils. The dust is like a tool in the hand of the wind, and know that the wind is high and of high descent. The sensuous eye is like a horse and the light of God is like a rider. Without the rider a horse is useless. The light of sense is decorated by the light of God, this is the meaning of "Light upon Light". The world of vision is the lowest in degree and the Light of God is like the sea and the sense is like a dew drop. Even the light of senses is hidden because of its density. How can you see then the purest Light? This visible world is like the husk in the hand of the unseen wind and has given itself up, helplessly, to the Mercy of God. (You) see the flying arrow while the bow is hidden, the soul is visible while the soul of Souls (Divine Spirit) is concealed.

b) The expression "dust on the wind" describes the celestial clouds (Nebulae) and their helplessness. Nobody knows where those dusty clouds are going to. They are at the mercy of the Divine Wind (Blow). The real (non-existent) world became hidden behind the dense substance of the universe. Since an individual cannot see the electrical energy of the neural system of his own body, how can we expect him to see the pure energy of the soul (spirit)? The Bow is the Command (or Breath) of God which we cannot see, but we see his arrow, the whole universe. "Light upon Light" is a reference to this Koranic verse, "God is the Light of the heavens and the earth. The parable of His Light is as if there were a Niche and within it a Lamp: the Lamp enclosed in glass, the glass as it were a brilliant star; lit from a blessed Tree -an olive, neither of the East nor of the West, whose oil is well-nigh luminous, though fire scarcely touched it; Light upon Light, God doth guide whom He will to His light" (XXIV/35).

217- Telling a lie gives no comfort to the hearts:

دل نیـآرامـد بـگفتـار دروغ   آب و روغن هیچ نفروزد فروغ
در حدیث راست آرام دلست   راستیها دانه دام دلست
خلق مست آرزواند و هوا   ز آن پذیرا اند دستان ترا
(II / 2735-2736-2742)

a) A lie gives no peace to the heart as oil mixed with water kindles no light. In truthful speech there is a comfort of the heart and it is only truth that attracts the heart. People are drunken with cupidity and desire, hence they are easily cheated by you (Satan).

b) It is the truth that consoles a heart, not a lie. People tend to cupidity and, therefore, are liable to be easily deceived by Satan.

218- It is separation from God that is the fuel of Hell:

از فراق این خاکها شوره بود   آب زرد گنده و تیره شود
دوزخ از فرقت چنان سوزان شدست   پیر از فرقت چنان لرزان شدست
هرچ از وی شاد گردی در جهان   از فراق او بیندیش آن زمان
از تو هم بجهد تو دل بروی منه   پیش از آن کو بجهد از وی تو بجه
(III / 3690-3694-3697-3699)

a) Because of separation this soil becomes barren and dry, water goes dirty, yellowish and dark. Hell burns due to separation and the old man trembles so much due to separation. Everything that pleases you in this world will leave you (at the time when you need it). It will escape from you, so escape from it before it intends to leave you.

b) Rumi's concept of Hell and Paradise is that Hell is separation from God and Paradise is the vicinity of God. The farther a man falls away from God, the more he is burnt by the fire of Hell. Although separation from this world is also painful, yet the love of God and His drawing you to Him can neutralise it.

219- Crying over sins repentantly is better than many prayers:

کو نماز و کو فروغ آن نیاز   آن غبین و درد بودی صد نماز

میزدی از درد دل آه و فغان   گر نمازت فوت میشد آن زمان

در گذشتی از دو صد ذکر و نماز   آن تاسف و آن فغان و آن نیاز

(II / 2770-2781-2782)

a) Loss (disappointment) and pain due to missing ritual prayer would have changed into a hundred prayers. What is prayer in comparison with the glow of humble supplication? If you (O Muaviye) had missed your prayers at that time you would have cried and lamented because of heartache. That regret, lamentation, and cries would have been worth more than two hundred litanies and prayers.

b) Rumi refers to Muaviye (died in A.D. 680), son of Ebu Sufyan, whose wife Hind was a bitter enemy of Muhammed. When Muaviye's mother Hind and her husband embraced Islam they were forgiven although they were cruel to Islam (Baki 1-2/601). Emir Muaviye conquered Damascus and Caesarea (in Anatolia) and became the governor of those areas. He is the first individual who built a palace and lived a luxurious life. Upon the death of Khalif Osman he began to fight against Ali, the fourth Khalif and cousin of Muhammed (also see IA, 8/p. 438). These verses belong to Muaviye and his struggle with Satan: "One day Satan woke Muaviye for the morning prayers, at which Muaviye was very surprised and asked Satan why he had done so". Satan replied, "I woke you to make you offer your prayers, otherwise you would be repentant over your missing the prayers and that repentance would be worth more than two hundred prayers". Rumi wants to point out that repentance or crying to God because of sins is more valuable than routine prayers.

220- God sends us hardship to make our inner hidden qualities show themselves:

بر تن ما مینهد ای شیر مرد   حق تعالی گرم و سرد و رنج و درد

جمله بهر نقد جان ظاهر شدن   خوف و جوع و نقص اموال و بدن

با درشتی ساز تا نرمی رسد   گرم باش ای سرد تا گرمی رسد

(II / 2963-2964-3011)

a) O brave man! God most High sends heat and cold, grief and pain to our body; fear and hunger, loss of possessions and body to allow the essence to come to light. O you cold one, be hot so that heat may reach you; be on good terms with hardships so that softness may get you.

b) God brings summer, spring, and autumn to the soil so that it may let its secrets out. Similarly, God sends pain and worries to the body so that it will allow its essence to come out. This is what the Koran says: "Be sure We shall test you with something of fear and hunger, some loss in goods or lives or fruits (of your toil) but give glad tidings to those who patiently persevere" (II/155).

221- Without the kernel a seed is worthless:

ذوق باید تا دهد طاعات بر   مغز باید تا دهد دانه شجر

دانه بی مغز کی گردد نهال   صورت بی جان نباشد جز خیال

(II / 3396-3397)

a) Spiritual delight (taste) is required in order that devotions (prayers) may bear fruit. A kernel is required so that a seed may produce a tree. How can a seed change into a branch without its kernel? A soulless form is nothing but a mere phantasm.

b) The main idea is that prayers must give spiritual pleasure otherwise they are like seeds without their kernel (essence). Perhaps the greatest punishment is that your soul feels no pleasure of spiritual excitement when you pray to God (see also Koner, p. 262).

222- God is the only True Friend:

شاد از وی شو مشو از غیر وی   او بهارست و دگرها ماه دی

هرچ غیر اوست استدراج تست   گرچه تخت و ملک تخت و تاج تست

شاد از غم شو که غم دام لقاست   اندرین ره سوی پستی ارتقاست

گام در صحرای دل باید نهاد   ز آنک در صحرای گل نبود گشاد

ایمن آبادست دل ای دوستان   چشمها و گلستان در گلستان

(III / 507-508-509-514-515)

a) Be happy with God and not with any other. He is like spring while others are like autumn (or winter) or December. Whatever there is, other than Him is dangerous for you even if you possess a throne and a kingdom. Be happy with sorrow for it is the snare of union with God. In this (kind) way the ascent is downwards. Step into the plain of the heart (spirit) because in the plain of the clay (body) there is no opening. The heart is the abode of security, O friends, it is fountain and rose-gardens within rose-gardens.

b) Nothing on earth is eternal but the love of God. Sorrows and pains lead us to God so don't grumble. Due to humility and heedlessness (to worldly charms) you may seem to be going downwards, while in reality they take you upwards to God. Open the windows or doors of your heart which lead to eternal prosperity.

223- Travelling makes you grow like the full moon:

کز سفرها ماه کیخسرو شود   بی سفرها ماه کی خسرو شود

از سفر بیدق شود فرزین راد   وز سفر یا بید یوسف صد مراد

(III / 534-535)

a) It is by travelling that the moon becomes great like Kay Khusrau (the King), how should it become an emperor without travelling? By travelling a pawn (at chess) becomes the queen, and Joseph by travelling gained a hundred objects of his desires.

b) In Sufism much importance is given to travelling. Shams-i Tebrizi travelled a lot and was called "the flying Sun". The moon becomes a full moon by dint of travelling. Thus a Sufi should also travel and try to learn what God has created on the earth and how God punished those who were proud of their fame and wealth. As the Koran says, "Travel through the earth and see what was the end of those who rejected Truth" (VI/II). Anatolia is full of Greek and Roman ruins that tell of those who did a lot in this world but gained nothing. These ruins also moved the heart of Yunus who says:

"Some are possessors of goods and riches,
While others indulge in worldly joys,
Have you ever thought, "Where is the real master?"
These your goods and riches are all in fact fake,
Now it is your turn to pretend to yourself with these mortal toys".
        (Divan of Yunus, Kabaklı, p. 116)

Travelling makes one taste loneliness, which we all suffer here in this world, and reminds us of our real home.

224- Each particle of this world looks dead while it is alive in the other world:

باش تا خورشید حشر آید عیان / تا ببینی جنبش جسم جهان
پاره خاك ترا چون مرد ساخت / خاكها را جملگی شاید شناخت
مرده زین سواند و زآن سوزنده اند / خامش اینجا وآن طرف گوینده اند
ما سمیعیم و بصیریم و خوشیم / با شما نا محرمان ما خامشیم
از جمادی عالم جانها روید / غلغل اجزای عالم بشنوید
فاش تسبیح جمادات آیدت / وسوسه تاویلها نر بایدت

(III / 1009-1011-1012-1019-1021-1022)

a) Wait until the Sun of resurrection becomes manifest, so that you may observe the movement of the world's body (structure). Since a piece of clay has changed you into a man (by the Will of God), you should know that all other pieces of clay and solids will take a form in the same way. They (the solids) are dead on this side (in this world) but are alive on the other side (in the other world); they are silent here but they speak there. They say, "We hear, we see, and we are happy (satisfied), but we are silent to you, the un-initiated, we are mute. In order to hear the noise of the mundane elements go to the living spiritual world from this physical world of solids. There you will hear clearly the rituals of inanimate things and your doubts, vain ideas and false interpretation all will come to an end".

b) As God created us from clay and water and gave life to us so will He make every other inanimate thing alive on the day of resurrection. We will begin to hear what they speak about. Our souls will become so sensitive that they will be able to hear the sound of every atom and will be able to understand the messages and prayers of the mute: "The seven heavens and the earth and all beings therein declare His glory, there is not a thing but it celebrates His praise and yet you do not understand how they declare His glory" (the Koran, XVII/44).

225- The fire of Divine Love burns away worldly forms:

هر که کاملتر بود او در هنر او بمعنی پس بصورت پیشتر
دانشی باید که اصلش زآن سرست زآنک هر فرعی باصلش رهبرست
پس چرا علمی بیاموزی بمرد کش بباید سینه را زآن پاک کرد
پس مجو پیشی ازین سر لنگ باش وقت واگشتن تو پیش آهنگ باش
گر نباشی نامدار اندر بلاد کم نه الله اعلم بالعباد
هست عشقش آتشی اشکال سوز هر خیالی را بروبد نور روز
گوشه بی گوشه دل شه رهیست تاب لا شرقی و لا غرب از مهیست

(III / 1117-1124-1126-1127-1132-1136-1138)

a) He who is more perfect in worldly knowledge (science) is more backward in divine knowledge though he may look physically advanced. In fact the real knowledge is the one that is connected to the far world, because each branch leads to its Reality. Then why do you teach the kind of knowledge that has to be erased from a person's heart? You (the righteous man) don't try to be in front in this world, rather be lame and on the day when you return to that world be the leader. If you have no fame or name in this town or city (or in this world), you are not less known because God knows His servants. Love of God is like the fire that burns away shapes (worldly self-indulgence and difficulties) and the daylight that sweeps away all vain ideas as the cornerless corner (non-dimensional) of the heart is the main road (that leads to God); and is enlightened by the Moon that has neither east nor west.

b) Those who have attained fame and perfection in worldly skills are, usually, weak in divine knowledge because they are proud of their worldly achievements and fail to think of God. Since every branch (of a whole) leads to its reality, worldly knowledge (science) should also lead to its essence (spiritual knowledge). It is this kind of knowledge that Rumi himself learnt through his master Shams-i Tebrizi. Spiritual knowledge raises the dimensional curtains and exposes the Essence.

226- Every cloud has a silver lining:

انبیا گفتند نومیدی بدست فضل و رحمتهای باری بیحدست
بعد نومیدی بسی امیدهاست از پس ظلمت بسی خورشیدهاست
دلبر و مطلوب با ما حاضرست در نثار رحمتش جان شاکرست
در دل ما لاله زار و گلشنیست پیری و پژمردگی را راه نیست
پیش ما صد سال و یکساعت یکیست که دراز و کوته از ما منفکیست

(III /2922-2925-2934-2935-2937)

a) Prophets have said that disappointment is a bad thing and that the Mercy of the Creator is endless. After despair there are many hopes; after many darknesses there are many suns. The Sweet-heart and the Desired One is always ready to help us, in His shower of mercy our soul is thankful. In our hearts there are beds of roses and rose-gardens, old age and sorrows do not dare come that way. For us a hundred years or an hour are all equal because length and shortness (of time) have left us.

b) In the Koran Jacob says to his son, "...Never give up hope of God's Soothing Mercy; truly no one despairs of God's Soothing mercy except those who have no faith" (XII/87). Where you experience worries and troubles or injustices be patient until the Help of God reaches you. Those who have already attained the nearness of God have no fear of time, death, or worldly worries.

227- Where there is a hope there is a will:

تیزی دندان ز سوز معده است	جنبش خلق از قضا و وعده است
ماهی از سر گنده باشد نی ز دم	نفس اول راند بر نفس دوم
چونك بلغ گفت حق شد نا گزیر	لیك هم می دان و خر می ران چو تیر
(III / 3079-3080-3081)	a 3038 نفس N + G : عقل Mift.

a) The action of people depends upon divine destiny and their appointment with it; the sharpness of teeth is caused by the burning of the stomach. The first soul affects the second soul; a fish begins to stink from the head but not from the tail. Despite knowing this fact keep your donkey (body) running forward like an arrow, for God commanded, "Proclaim the message".

b) Again the crucial problem of fate is discussed. Everything is predestined by God. He gave teeth to chew and a demanding, hungry stomach. These are God-given but it is our duty to cook food and offer it to them. Divine Destiny is in the control of God but the minor details are in our hands. "A fish begins to stink in the head" means that everything moves according to predestined fate but it is also our duty to pray and work hard to change the fate that we don't like, because God can change it. If a predestined fate cannot be changed, then what is the use of crying and praying to God? The last verse refers to this Koranic verse: "O Apostle! proclaim the message which hath been sent to thee from thy Lord" (V/70). What would be the use of proclaiming a message if all fates were unchangeable? Hope is the fuel of action (see also III/vr. No. 3093 and item No. 105 of this book).

228- A sufi is not passive, but is ready to face all difficulties:

عـاشـق آنـم کـه هـر آن آن اوست / عقل و جان جاندار یک مرجان اوست

هرکه از خورشید باشد پشت گرم / سخت رو باشد نه بیم او را نه شرم

هر زمان گوید بگوشـم بخت نو / که ترا غـمگین کنم غـمگین مشو

مـن تـرا غـمگین و گریان زآن کنم / تاکت از چشم بدان پنهان کنم

آنکه از شهر و ز خویشان بر خوری / کز غریبی رنج و محنتها بری

(III / 4136-4139-4149-4150-4158)

a) I am the lover of that One Whose Beauty is active every moment (Mift. 2-3/285) and intellect as well as spirit are the slaves of his single pearl (lips= word, see Amdad 3/p. 35). Everyone whose back is warmed by the sun (Light of God) is straightforward (or "fearless"; literally the idiom means "hard faced") and he has neither hesitation nor shyness. Every moment the fresh fate (mercy of God) says in my ears, "I shall make you unhappy and weeping in order to protect you from an evil eye and will give you tribulation so that you may miss your kinsfolk and town in exile".

b) "God is always after a new grandeur" (see item No. 124). So is His lover and the lover cannot remain inactive. Why should a man be afraid if he is supported by God? All troubles that befall a lover of God are to protect him from the jealousy of others and to make him remember his real home (near God) (see also items No. 18 and 117).

229- He who seeks God finds Him:

گر نداری بو ز جان روشناس / رو دماغی دست آور بوشناس

سایه حق بر سر بنده بود / عاقبت جوینده یابنده بود

در شکست پای بخشد حق پری / هم ز قعر چاه بگشاید دری

(III / 4777-4781-4808)

a) If you do not have the scent of the soul that recognises the face, then go and find the brain that can sense the scent. The shadow of God is always upon His slave and finally a seeker is the finder. If one loses his legs God gives him wings (to fly) and even at the bottom of a well He can open a new door.

b) If you haven't been able to open your spiritual eyes, which can differentiate evil from good, then go and find a saint that is able to do so. If you keep on looking for God, you will certainly find Him one day. God is able to help you even at the bottom of the well (at the lower self).

230- Tolerate God's created beings good or bad because of their Creator:

ای مسلمان خود ادب اندر طلب   نیست الا حمل از هر بی ادب

هر کرا بینی شکایت می کند   که فلان کس راست طبع و خوی بد

این شکایت گربدان که بد خوست   که مر آن بد خوی را او بدگوست

زآنک خوش خوآن بود کودر خمول   باشد از بد خو و بد طبعان حمول

لیک در شیخ آن گله ز امر خداست   نه پی خشم و ممارات و هواست

(IV / 771-772-773-774-775)

a) O Muslim (believer) if you are looking for good manners tolerate the ill-mannered (and be patient). If you find someone complaining about others, saying, "That man has a bad nature and poor manners" actually he is being bad natured himself because he is speaking ill of others. Good-mannered is a man who is able to tolerate the ill-mannered calmly and who does not complain or tell of their evil deeds to others. But saints' complaints (reproaches) are due to God's command, otherwise their anger or complaint is not due to their own will or obstinacy (see T. 11-12/ p. 197).

b) It is the sign of good manners not to find faults with others especially in the Mevlevi order. We must avoid belittling others and we should try to tolerate them for the sake of their Creator. With saints it is a different case. They reproach you or criticize you in order to mend your character.

231- The only superiority of man over woman is that he can see the end better:

هر که آخربین تر او مسعود تر   هر که آخربین تر او مطرود تر

فضل مردان بر زنان ای بو شجاع   نیست بهر قوت و کسب و ضیاع

فضل مردان بر زن ای حالی پرست   زآن بود که مرد پایان بین ترست

مرد کاندر عاقبت بینی خمست   او ز اهل عاقبت چون زن کمست

(IV / 1614-1618-1620-1621)

a) The more one is able to see the result, the happier he is; the more one is able to see the stable (this world only) the more one is cast away from God (T. 11-12/ p. 423). The superiority of man over woman, O brave one, is not due to power, richness, or wealth; O servant of time, the superiority of man over woman is because man is more regardful of the end (result). A man who is weak in seeing the result, like a woman, is inferior to those who can see the end clearly.

b) Generally speaking women are more sentimental than men and they do not foresee the result as clearly as men. However, some men are worse than women in foreseeing results. Lucky are those (women or men) who can see what is coming ahead even after death.

232- There is no monastery in Islam:

زآنك شرط این جهاد آمد عدو	بر مکن پر را و دل بر کن ازو
شهوتت نبود نباشد امتثال	چون عدو نبود جهاد آمد محال
خصم چون نبود چه حاجت حبل تو	صبر نبود چون نباشد میل تو
زآنك عفت هست شهوت را گرو	هین مکن خود را خصی رهبان مشو
(V / 574-575-576-577)	

a) Do not tear out your feathers, give up that idea because for this war (against lower self) you need an enemy. Since there is no enemy how can you wage war against them? If you have no feelings of sex, how can you carry out the command of God against it? What use is it to be patient if you have no desire? When there is no enemy then what is the use of an army? Come to yourself, don't make yourself impotent, don't be a monk because piety depends on feelings of lust.

b) Rumi here explains the Tradition of Muhammed that there is no monastic system in Islam. In order to prove your love for God, you have to struggle and fight against your will. For example, wine is there but you do not drink it for the sake of God. Brave is the man who closes his eyes to worldly riches when they surround him. He should not run away from them and go to the mountains for seclusion. When you look at things from God's eyes your desire for them changes. You look at them and see God's Beauty without any greed.

233- God's bounty does not depend on the capacity of man:

داد او را قابلیت شرط نیست	چاره آن دل عطای مبدلیست
هیچ معدومی بهستی نآمدی	قابلی گر شرط فعل حق بدی
تا بداند طالبی جستن مراد	لیک اغلب بر سبب راند نفاد
تا حجب را بر کند از بیخ و بن	دیده باید سبب سوراخ کن
(V / 1537-1542-1549-1552)	

a) The remedy for the heart is the gift of God that changes our heart from state to state. His bounty does not depend on one's capacity. If divine acts depended on capacity, no non-existent thing would come into existence, but things move in accordance with a cause. You need an eye that can tear off the cause and unroot (destroy) the curtains.

b) The heart that has gained mercy and love of God can be softened by Him without any cause, for God's bounty being eternal *(Qadim)* does not depend on any reason (see Mift., p. 301). In fact, if one has a capability (receptivity) for God's emanation, one has it due to His Mercy. Some Islamic theologians believed that to receive God's emanation depends on one's capacity (see Baki, p. 154). Rumi does not agree for he considers God's bounty Eternal. God, in order to provide a goal for a seeker, creates secondary causes but He is not bound to them. Some eyes have the ability to see beyond causes. In Islam there are two kinds of emanations: 1- *Fayz ul-aqdas* = most holy emanation, that can be received by means of the essence (or prototype) of things. 2- *Fayz ul-muqqadas* = the indirect holy emanation, received by phenomenal objects (beings) (for other details see Koner, p. 684 and Mift., p. 302). If God pours His first kind of emanation on a non-believer's heart, he can change into a righteous man at once, as God says in the Koran, "...For God guides whom He wills to a path that is straight" (II/213). But generally, God does not do that unless one struggles for it (the emanation) and fights against secondary causes. This is because God is Just.

234- Those who lack self-discipline are deprived of the divine emanation:

نه ترا از روی ظاهر طاعتی   نه ترا در سر و باطن نیتی
نه ترا شبها مناجات و قیام   نه ترا در روز پرهیز و صیام
نه ترا حفظ زبان ز آزار کس   نه نظر کردن بعبرت پیش و پس
(V / 1826-1827-1828)

a) You have neither outwardly obedience nor inwardly any intention (to be obedient) to God. You offer neither nightly prayers nor vigil; you neither fast nor pray during the day. You did not hold your tongue from hurting a person and you did not look back or ahead to learn a lesson.

b) Rumi here counts the actions that can attract Divine Mercy and Emanation. The first thing is to be obedient to God's orders or at least intend to obey Him. Then one must pray at night and try to refrain from evil deeds during the day. One must also take a look at evil deeds in order to learn a lesson from them and avoid hurting other people's hearts. As Yunus says:

"Once you have broken someone's heart, your prayers are of no use,
This includes all the nations (72 nations), your face and hands are not
yet clean (even if you wash them five times a day)".

(see Divan of Yunus, Baki, p. 176)

235- War and grandeur against infidelity and cruelty is one of the characteristics of Islam:

مصلحت در دین عیسی غار و کوه / مصلحت در دین ما جنگ و شکوه
کی بر آید خانه و انبارها / گر نباشد یاری دیوارها
سقف چون باشد معلق در هوا / هر یکی دیوار اگر باشد جدا
گرنه پیوندد بهم بادش برد / این حصیری که کسی میگسترد
زآنک بی یاران بمانی بی مدد / یار شو تا یار بینی بی عدد

(VI / 494-519-520-522-498)

a) In our religion (Islam) the right thing is war and grandeur (not "terror" as given by Nich. see VI/p. 285) but in Christianity the right thing is to retire to caves and mountains (monasticism). If there existed no ties of friendship between walls, how could there be houses or stores? If every wall was separate, how could the roof hang in the air (without support)? If this rush-mat had no unity (and was not knitted together) it could easily be carried away by the wind. Be a firm friend so that you may find countless other friends because without friends you will be left without help.

b) Rumi disapproves of monasticism, a widespread practice during his time in Konya. He invites people to join in love, unity, and brotherhood; and to unite against infidelity and cruelty (like that of Mongols). No terrorism is allowed in Islam. Some Muslim leaders may have been terrorists but they are exceptions because they act according to egoistic pride, not due to the Will of God, as God says in the Koran, "Shall ye be recompensed with the penalty of humiliation for that ye were arrogant on earth without just cause, and that ye transgressed" (the Koran, XLVI/20). For monasticism the Koran gives these lines: "But the monasticism which they invented for themselves, We did not prescribe them. We (commanded) only seeking for the good pleasure of God; but that they did not foster" (LVII/27). God's kingdom is based on courage, resistance to evil, firmness, law, and discipline so that one upholds truth but in monasticism you miss such activities. God does not like the passive.

236- The reason why God sometimes does not answer a believer's prayers or demands at once:

گر بر آرم حاجتش او وا رود   هم در آن بازیچه مستغرق شود
گرچه می نالد بجان یامستجار   دل شکسته سینه خسته گو بزار
خوش همی آید مرا آواز او   وآن « خدایا » گفتن وآن راز او
طوطیان و بلبلانرا از پسند   از خوش آوازی قفص در می کنند
(VI / 4224-4225-4226-4228)

a) If I answer his prayers, he will run away and will be preoccupied with his play (business). Although he cries to Me wholeheartedly, "O Ye Protector (help me)" yet I let him moan with a broken and tired heart for I am in love with his voice (moaning) and with his revealing his secrets to Me. I like his words, "O my Lord". Don't people put parrots and nightingales in cages because of their sweet voices?

b) A working mother who comes home and finds her baby busy with a toy will try to take that toy away to draw her baby's attention towards her, so that she may hear the lovely words "Mama" that she missed all day in her office. Similarly, God does not let us have what we desire immediately and he wants us to pray and cry to Him. We can address Him in our languages, *Khuda, Tangri, Bhagwan, Deus, God, Lord, Allah*. He likes the lovely feelings that are hidden behind these words but not the words.

237- Be careful, your partial insight is misleading:

صد هزاران اهل تقلید و نشان   افگند در قعر یک آسیبشان
پای استدلالیان چوبین بود   پای چوبین سخت بی تمکین بود
هست هشیاری ز یاد ما مضی   ماضی و مستقبلت پرده خدا
آتش اندر زن بهر دو تا بکی   پر گره باشی ازین هر دو چو نی
تا گره با نی بود همراز نیست   همنشین آن لب و آواز نیست
(I / 2125-2128-2201-2202-2203)   b 2125 is different in MM

a) Thousands of blind followers (Mift., p. 82) and seekers of signs fall into an abyss (of destruction) through a single misleading clue. The feet of the proof-seekers are made of wood and wooden feet are very infirm. Alertness (cleverness) is born of past memories (experiences), the past and the future are actually the curtains that God has drawn on people. Burn them to ashes. How long will you remain captive like the knots of a reed-flute? For as long as the reed-flute is confined in the knots (holes), it tells no secrets but when it finds the lips of a comrade (the divine words of a saint) it begins to produce sound.

b) Those who depend on their intellect (and logic) and try to base their beliefs on proofs, fall into a ditch because (as stated many times by Rumi) the intellect is deceptive and helpless. Come out of the sphere of your mental functions, for that sphere is too narrow to give you accurate knowledge, and follow a man who has Divine Wisdom.

238- Try to diminish your doubts:

هر چه جز عشق خدای احسن است   گر شکرخواریست آن جان کندن است

چیست جان کندن سوی مرگ آمدن   دست در آب حیاتی نا زدن

خلق را دو دیده در خاک و ممات   صد گمان دارند در آب حیات

جهد کن تا صد گمان گردد نود   شب برو ور تو بخسپی شب رود

(I / 3686-3687-3688-3689)

a) Anything that looks nice other than the love of God, even if it is sugar, it is actually agony of spirit. What is the agony of spirit? It is going towards death without obtaining water of life (eternity). People (common folk) have many worries about losing the clay (this body) but they also have doubts about the water of life. Work hard so that a hundred doubts may become ninety (diminish in number), keep on walking even at nights because the nights will pass away if you go to sleep.

b) If you do a lot for this world and do not try to improve your spiritual talents, you have gained nothing. It does not mean that you should give up this world like a *Sadhu* (an Indian Monk) or a Christian monk, but make this world your laboratory for finding God. In this respect, depending on their intentions, a medical doctor, a scientist, or a scholar are all searching for God; and they will find the water of life (eternal happiness).

239- Malice is forbidden in Islam:

کین مدار آنها که از کین گمرهند   گورشان پهلوی کین داران نهند

اصل کینه دوزخست و کین تو   جزو آن کلست و خصم دین تو

(II / 273-274)

a) Don't bear malice (towards anyone). Those who are led astray by malice are buried near the graves of the malicious. The origin of malice is hell, and your malice is a part of that whole and it is an enemy of your religion.

b) Malice or ill will is an aspect of evil (Satanic) deeds. The Koran says: "Satan's plan is (but) to excite enmity and hatred between you" (V/94) and "Say I seek refuge with the Lord of the dawn... from the mischief of the envious one as he practises envy (malignity)" (CXII/5).

240- Anger and hatred are the root of infidelity:

كارگاه خشم گشت و كين وري   كينه دان اصل ضلال و كافري
گفت ازين خشم خدا چه بود امان   گفت ترك خشم خويش اندر زمان
(IV / 112-115)

a) He (a certain man) became the factory (or workshop) of anger and hatred. Hatred, beware, is the root of going astray from God and is infidelity. One man asked Jesus, "What is the way to get rid of divine anger?" Jesus answered, "The remedy of anger is to give up your own anger little by little".

b) God says in the Koran, "Those who spend (their wealth freely) whether in prosperity or in adversity, who restrain anger and pardon all men, for God loves those who do good" (III/134). Pity others so that God may pity you.

241- Don't forget that this world is a temporary abode:

« فى السماء رزقكم » نشنيده   اندرين پستى چه بر چفسيده
هر ندايى كه ترا بالا كشيد   آن ندا ميدان كه از بالا رسيد
هر ندايى كه ترا حرص آورد   بانگ گرگى دان كه او مردم درد
روشنى بخشد نظر اندر علا   گرچه اول خيرگى آرد بلا
عاقبت بينى نشان نور تست   شهوت حالى حقيقت گور تست
(II / 1956-1958-1959-1975-1977)

a) You have heard, "And in heaven is your sustenance" then why have you attached yourself here to this lowness (the world)? Any voice that calls you upwards, think that that voice has come from on high. Any voice that arouses greed in you is the voice of a wolf that tears up a man. Looking upwards gives height to the eyes, though at first it may dazzle your eyes (and mind). Your far-sightedness is a sign of your illumination and your present lust is in reality your grave.

b) It is the duty of a man to discover new worlds in the heavens for God says in the Koran, "...in heaven is your sustenance" (LI/22), which has the double meaning: Seek your food in the sky physically or spiritually and do not fix your eyes on low places. Like a hawk that flies higher and leaves lower places for reptiles.

242- God has His eyes on hearts but not on forms (bodies):

در هوای آنک گویندت زهی   بسته در گردن جانت زهی
رو بها این دم حیلت را بهل   وقف کن دل بر خداوندان دل
ای دلا منظور حق آنگه شوی   که چو جزوی سوی کل خود روی
حق همی گوید نظرمان بر دلست   نیست بر صورت که آن آب وگلست
بحر گوید من ترا در خود کشم   لیک می لافی که من آب خوشم
آب گل خواهد که در دریا رود   گل گرفته پای آب و می کشد
سنگ پر کردی تو دامن از جهان   هم زسنگ سیم و زر چون کودکان

(III / 2240-2241-2243-2244-2252-2254-2277)

a) In order that people may praise you, you have tied your neck with a bowstring. O you, cunning like a fox, give up the tale of hypocrisy and devote heart to the Masters of hearts. God says, "My eyes are fixed on hearts, but not on forms (bodies) that are nothing but mud and water". The Sea wants to call the water back from the mud but you say in vain, "Nay, I am already pure water". The water wants to go back to the Sea from the mud yet the clay holds it by the feet and draws it back. You have filled your skirt with the gold and silver of the world as children fill it with stones.

b) This is a reference to the worldly and false saints who have become prisoners of this world. Worldly wealth and fame have made them blind and they do not want to recognise their Origin.

243- It is a sign of immaturity to take a tight hold of this world like an embryo in the womb:

بسته پایی چون گیا اندر زمین   سر بجنبانی ببادی بی یقین
لیک پایت نیست تا نقلی کنی   یا مگر پا را ازین گل بر کنی
راههای آمدن یادت نماند   لیک رمزی بر تو بر خواهیم خواند
این جهان همچون درختست ای کرام ما برو چون میوهای نیم خام
سخت گیرد خامها مر شاخ را   زآنک درخامی نشاید کاخ را
چون بپخت و گشت شیرین لب گزان سست گیرد شاخها بعد از آن
سخت گیری و تعصب خامیست   تا جنینی کار خون آشامیست

(III / 1280-1281-1290-1293-1294-1295-1297)

a) You are foot-tied to the earth like grass and toss your head to every wind without belief. You have no feet to move to another place or even to take your feet out of this mud (the muddy world). You have forgotten the ways that you had come through, but we shall give you some hints: This world is like a tree and we are like unripe fruits. Unripe fruits hold the branches tight because they do not suit the royal family's table. When they are ripe and deserve lips, they hold the branch loosely. To take a strong hold (of an unchangeable state), to practise prejudice or narrow mindedness, and like an embryo to be happy with its mother's blood are signs of unripeness.

b) A worldly man is so attached to this world that he does not care about anything but its charms like an embryo in the womb of its mother. He does not wish to think of a larger and more peaceful place, while a perfect man like a ripe fruit wants to get free from the branch (this world) in order to decorate the table of his Beloved King. Anything of this world, including kingship and high rank is a chain of slavery (also see vrs. IV/3123-3125).

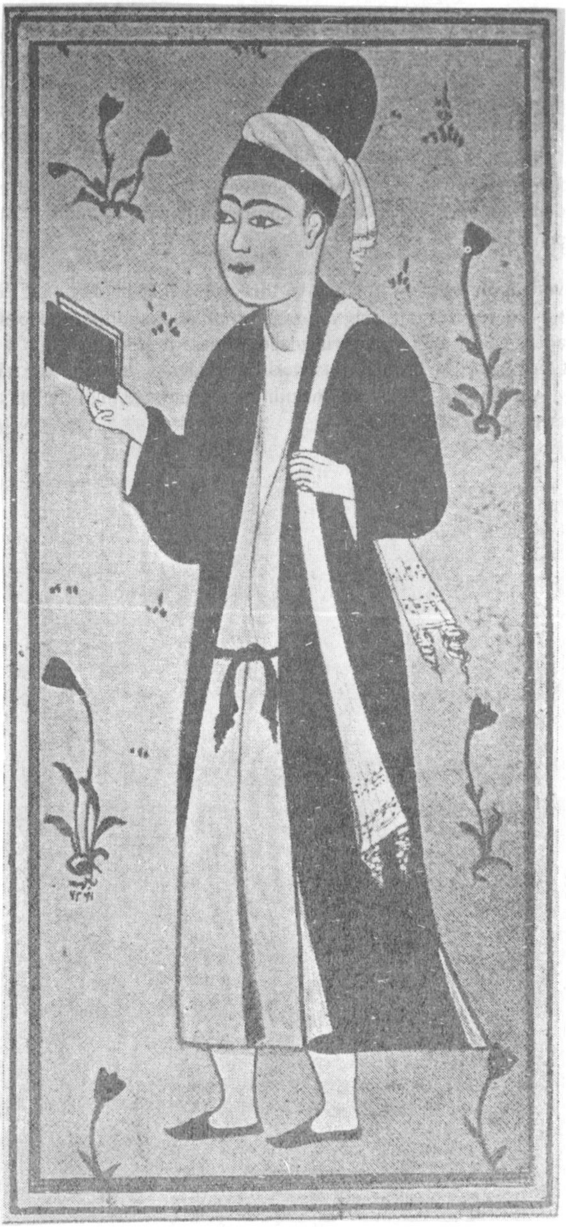

CHAPTER VIII

Step IV: Improvement of soul through indifference to worldly riches (Majnun's sacrifice for Leyli)

This chapter concerns a man who realises that there is another world better than this mortal one, and that he should unload himself of this physical burden to have an easier journey. He needs to clean lust from the mirror of his heart, so that he may see the face of his Beloved more clearly and by the charm of His Beauty he may sacrifice his mortal possessions without feeling sorrow or hesitation. As Rumi says, "If the Beauty of Thy name charms someone, for that one the whole universe has no value. No beauty, no form, no colour, or no smell can attract him any more" (Mejalis, Tur., p. 19). "The rich (worldly men) feel humiliated if they lose their property, but a Sufi *(dervish)* feels ashamed if he begins to collect money or gold" (Rumi's Letters, Tur., XLII, p. 64). "Just as those worms live in that darkness under the earth, so there are men who are content and satisfied to dwell in the darkness of this world, having no need of that world and yearning not for the Vision. Of what use to them would be the eye of clairvoyance and the ear of understanding? Their work in this world prospers with the sensible eye which they possess; since they have no design on the other side, why give them the clairvoyance which would be useless to them?... Now this world goes on by reason of heedlessness; if it were not for heedlessness, this world would not remain in being. Yearning for God, recollection of the world to come, intoxication, ecstasy, these are the architects of the world. If all these displayed themselves, everyone of us would go to that world and not remain here. But God wants us here so that the two worlds may exist. So He has appointed two magistrates, heedlessness and heedfulness, so that both houses may flourish" (Discourses, Arberry, p. 120 and Chittick, p. 59). It is better to follow the advice of the Persian poet Sadi of Shiraz, "Without doubt, there are countless benefits in the sea, yet if you want safety stay on the shore". This world can offer us countless benefits but let us not drown in its sea of charm, because soon the forms on the surface of the sea will be erased by the wind of death. So try to reach the Eternal Sea safely and pay less attention to these worldly forms.

244- **For gnostics the wind of death is soft:**

همچنین باد اجل با عارفان   نرم و خوش همچون نسیم یوسفان
ز آتش شهوت نزورید اهل دین   باقیانرا برده تا قعر زمین

b 860 یوسفان N + G : بستان Mift. : گلستان Kan   (I / 860-862)

a) For the gnostic (or saints) the wind of death is soft and pleasant like the scent of Joseph's wind. The religious are not afflicted by the fire of lust, the rest are taken to the depths of the earth by lust.

b) Death is an appointment for meeting the Beloved. Muhammed said, "The best present for the believer is death" (as narrated by Abu Bekir, see Mift. p. 318). Imam-i Ghazali also says that a gnostic must always remember death, for death is an appointment with the Beloved (ibid, p. 19).

c) The word *"Yusufan"* sounds correct, because it was the scent of Joseph's shirt that opened his father's blind eyes. Nich. translates *"Shehwet"* as "lust" only. However, it has a wider meaning here "sexual desires and love for worldly riches".

245- Malice is diabolic:

در حسد ابلیس را باشد غلو / ور حسد گیرد ترا در ره گلو
با سعادت جنگ دارد از حسد / کو ز آدم ننگ دارد از حسد
ای خنک آنکش حسد همراه نیست / عقبه زین صعب تو در راه نیست

(I / 429-430-431)

a) If on the way jealousy seizes you in the throat, it is the character of Satan to rebel jealously. There is no harder barrier than this. How fortunate is the one who is not a fellow-traveller of jealousy.

b) It is interesting to notice that Satan became the enemy of Adam out of jealousy because Satan, too, loved God, observing His Beauty closely as an angel. But when God created man, he became jealous of him and refused to accept his existence. Satan, like a loyal dog, did not want to see a stranger beside his master.

c) The word *"Hasad"* has no direct English equivalent. It can be translated as "malice"; "grudge"; "jealousy"; or "envy". As a matter of fact *"Hasad"* covers all of them.

246- God does not like the idle:

کسب کن پس تکیه بر جبار کن / گر توکل میکنی در کار کن
بی زبان معلوم شد او را مراد / خواجه چون بیلی بدست بنده داد

(I / 947-932)

a) If you put your trust in God, then set out to work. Sow the seeds, cultivate the crop and then trust the Almighty. If a master hands over a spade to a slave without saying anything his meaning is clear.

b) To trust God does not mean that one should give up working. Many dervishes misunderstand this point. Rumi gives a very good example and says, "If a master (God) gives you two spades (hands) silently, it means that He wants you to work. Don't expect anything from God without hope and labour. Without labouring or acting, faith brings no fruit; water the plant of hope so that it may render fruits.

247- Attain eternal property:

هین بملک نوبتی شادی مکن / ای تو بسته نوبت آزادی مکن
آنك ملکش برتر از نوبت تنند / برتر از هفت انجمش نوبت زنند
برتر از نوبت ملوك باقی اند / دور دائم روحها با ساقی اند
(I / 1369-1370-1371)

a) Beware! Do not be proud of your property (possessions) that you possess by turn. Since you are bound to possessions that are possessed turn by turn, you are also bound to turns. How can you feel then? Those who possess the things of the eternal world that have no turns, for them the drums (of turns) are beaten beyond the seven stars. Beyond these temporary possessions there are eternal properties, and there the spirits are being offered cups of wine by the Cupbearer.

b) Don't be proud of the possessions that have to be handed over to others when you die. The dwellers in the place beyond the seven heavens (Divine Plane) beat drums in your honour (see Mift. p. 175) if you devote yourself to the other world. He who attains the nearness of God is freed from the worries of possessions of this world and to him God (the Beloved) offers cup of spiritual wine.

248- More words on patience:

گر سخن خواهی که گوئی چون شکر / صبر کن از حرص واین حلوا مخور
صبر باشد مشتهای زیرکان / هست حلوا آرزوی کودکان
هرك صبر آورد گردون بر رود / هرك حلوا خورد واپستر شود
(I / 1600-1601-1602)

a) If you want to speak sweetly, like sugar, be patient and refrain from greediness and don't eat that kind of sweet. Patience is the desired food of the intelligent but children ask for sweets (greed). He who endures pain goes higher towards the heavens; he who eats sweets falls behind.

221

b) If you want to speak sweetly like a candy, then learn to be patient and avoid eating worldly food too much (see Mift. 2/p. 246). Patience can be as bitter as medicine but it is better than the delicious food of this world. As Jaferi adds, "Take the tablet of patience, so that you may get rid of worries and troubles" (Ibid, p. 150).

249- Be as soft as clay:

تا دم عیسی ترا زنده کند   در نیاز و فقر خود را مرده ساز

از بهاران کی شود سر سبز سنگ   همچو خویشت خوب وفرخنده کند

خاك شو تا گل برویی رنگ رنگ

(I / 1909 b -1910-1911)

a) Make yourself dead through supplication and spiritual poverty so that the breath of Jesus may revive you and make you fair as well as happy like himself. How can a stone or rock be green in spring and produce flowers with different colours. Be (soft like) clay so that you may produce flowers of various colours.

b) Spiritual poverty means being rich at heart but living a simple life on earth. A life without ostentation and pride. A stone cannot be as productive as soft clay. Surrender your low nature to God so that the divine rain of mercy may render you productive and the speech of a saint (Christ) may turn you into a perfect man.

250-Wakefulness is like a sun and heedlessness is like ice:

استن این عالم ای جان غفلتست   هوشیاری این جهان را آفتست

هوشیاری زآن جهانست و چو آن   غالب آید پست گردد این جهان

هوشیاری آفتاب و حرص یخ   هوشیاری آب وین عالم وسخ

زآن جهان اندك ترشح می رسد   تا نغرد در جهان حرص و حسد

گر ترشح بیشتر گردد ز غیب   نی هنر ماند درین عالم نه عیب

b 2069 نغرد G : خیزد. Mift.   (I / 2066-2067-2068-2069-2070)

a) O beloved friend! The pillar of this world is negligence while (spiritual) wakefulness is troublesome for this world. Wakefulness belongs to that world and when it rules over negligence, this world begins to look mean. Wakefulness is like a sun and worldly greed is like ice; again wakefulness is like water while this world is like dirt. From that world some water leaks (to this side) in order that the greed and jealousy in this world may not increase; and if the leakage increases (continues to leak), there shall remain neither virtue nor evil.

b) It is through negligence that we enjoy the wonders of this world. Once we begin to work on our celestial talents, this world looks simple and mean. As Jaferi explains, "Negligence" here also means ignorance to facts and realities revealed by God (see ibid, 2/ p. 86). Man knows that he is on earth for a short time. Despite this, he keeps on satisfying his ego at the cost of losing his humanity. However, if the Divine realities are exposed and our heedlessness is eliminated, this world becomes valueless and meaningless.

251- He who has divine business cares less for this world:

تا بدانی هرکرا یزدان بخواند   از همه کار جهان بی کار ماند
هر کرا باشد ز یزدان کار و بار   یافت بار آنجا و بیرون شد ز کار
(I / 2120-2121)

a) Be informed that he whom God calls to Himself keeps away from all the worldly affairs, and he who has the business of God's affairs, leaves the jobs of this world.

b) Saints give up worldly business, in order to train God's people, as Rumi did.

252- Seek your essence:

نان دهی از بهر حق نانت دهند   جان دهی از بهر حق جانت دهند
گر بریزد برگهای این چنار   برگ بی برگیش بخشد کردگار
این جهان نفی است در اثبات جو   صورتت صفرست در معنیت جو
(I / 2236-2237-2241)

a) If you give bread (food) in the name of God, they will give you food, too. If you sacrifice life for God, they will give you life in return. If this plane-tree sheds its leaves then God gives it leaves of leaflessness. This world is a negation (of reality), seek the Reality, your form has no value so look for your essence.

b) If someone feeds the poor in the name of God, he will be given spiritual food, and one who sacrifices his life for God will be given a new life in the world hereafter and will be self-sufficient on earth. Rumi says in his Discourses, "When however you have entered the world of spiritual poverty and practised it, God most High bestows upon you kingdoms and worlds that longed for and desired before" (Discourses, Arberry, p. 154).

c) The "plane-tree" stands for a Sufi or a lover of God who sacrifices everything for Him.

253- Seek the company of spiritual friends:

رو بمعنی کوش ای صورت پرست   ز آنک معنی بر تن صورت پرست
همنشین اهل معنی باش تا   هم عطا یابی و هم باشی فتا
(I / 710-711)

a) Go, strive for reality, you the worshipper of forms, because reality is like a wing on forms. Bear the company of spiritual friends so that you may become young and gifted.

b) The company of saints guides you to perfection for saints are, like prophets, the viceroys of God on earth. Seek the people of God for the Koran says: "Enter thou among My servants, enter thou My paradise" (LXXXIX 29-30). "God does not speak to everyone, just as the kings of this world do not speak to every weaver; they have appointed a vizier and a deputy to show the way to the king. God most High has also chosen a certain servant, so that whosoever seeks God, God is in Him. All the prophets have come for this reason, that only they are the way." (Discourses, Arberry, p. 237). Hindus believe in "*Awtar*" = "God's Epiphany in the shape of a man", but can a drop of water be the whole Sea? Similarly, prophets and saints can be representative of God but they cannot be God themselves.

254- Not-being is the mirror of being:

آینه هستی چه باشد نیستی   نیستی بر گر تو ابله نیستی
هستی اندر نیستی بتوان نمود   مال داران بر فقیر آرند جود
چونک جامه چست و دوزیده بود   مظهر فرهنگ درزی چون شود
ز آنک ضد را ضد کند ظاهر یقین   ز آنک با سر که پدیدست انگبین
هرک نقص خویش را دید و شناخت اندر استکمال خود دو اسپه تاخت
3212 b دو اسپه : G ده اسپه .Mift   (I / 3201-3202-3205-3211-3212)

a) What is a mirror of being? (Of course) it is not-being. If you are stupid then choose not-being. Being can be seen by not-being, as the rich take pity (or show generosity) on the poor. If a garment fits and is nicely stitched, then what art can the tailor show? A thing is better known by its opposite as vinegar's taste is better known through honey. Finally he who recognises his own defects (by looking at a perfect man) is able to run two horses (go faster) towards perfection.

b) Things can be known clearly by their opposites. If they were not different from each other, they would be one and the same. We know day by the darkness of night. In the same way we can know our being via our not-being. empty the jar of your selfhood so that God may fill you with the qualities He desires. Don't take your garment to Him but your cloth and let Him show you His art (see T. 5-6/ p. 148). Compare your being with the being of a saint (a perfect man) so that you may discover your deficiencies.

255- The conflict in this world is due to negativity and positivity:

این جهان جنگست کل چون بنگری   ذره با ذره چو دین با کافری

آن یکی ذره همی پرد بچپ   وآن دگر سوی یمین اندر طلب

جنگ فعلی هست از جنگ نهان   زین تخالف آن تخالف را بدان

ذره کآن محو شد در آفتاب   جنگ او بیرون شد از وصف و حساب

این جهان زین جنگ قایم می بود   در عناصر در نگر تا حل شود

پس بنای خلق بر اضداد بود   لاجرم ما جنگییم از ضر و سود

آن جهان جز باقی و آباد نیست   ز آنک آن ترکیب از اضداد نیست

گوهر جان چون ورای فصلهاست   خوی او نیست خوی کبریاست

(VI / 36-37-39-40-47-50-56-63)

a) When you look, you will see that this world is a battlefield. Each atom fights with its opposite as does a believer with a non-believer. One (atom) flies towards the left while the other flies towards the right in search (of their needs). This visible fight is due to the hidden fight. Know that this conflict is born of that conflict. If one atom is naught in the sun, its conflict is beyond calculation and description. This world exists because of the conflict. You can discover this fact when you look at the elements. To sum up, the creation of people (common folk) also depends on opposites. It is because of this that we are also at war with each other for benefit and loss. The other world is nothing but everlasting and flourishing because it is not composed of opposites. The essence or spirit is above such elements too, and has, therefore, the characteristics of God.

b) Partial insight is a captive of the negative and positive elements of this world, while universal wisdom is beyond such limits. The negative elements assist the ascension of the positive elements. Man knows things by their opposites. The existence of opposites makes it possible to differentiate right from wrong. The negative elements are not created for adoption but for recognition. When you leave this sphere of the negative and the positive, and reach near God, the conflict comes to an end.

256- Sleep with Divine Knowledge is better than wakefulness among the ignorant:

خواب بیداریست چون با دانش است   وای بیداری که با نادان نشست

چونک زاغان خیمه بر بهمن زدند   بلبلان پنهان شدند و تن زدند

پس بخسپم باشم از اصحاب کهف   به ز دقیانوس آن محبوس کهف

N لهف Mift. + T کهف b 37   (II / 39-40-37)

a) Sleeping is wakefulness when accompanied by wisdom. But woe to the wakeful man who bore the company of the ignorant. When crows pitch their tents (start living) in gardens the nightingales hide themselves and become silent. Thus I prefer to go to sleep like the men of the caves rather than to be friends with Decanius (the cruel king).

b) As narrated by the son of Abbas, Muhammed said, "To go to sleep after an hour's study (learning) at night is equal to praying to God the whole night" (see Mift. 2-1/p. 38). The first verse refers to this tradition of Muhammed, the sleep of a learned man is better than the prayers of a pious man. It is dangerous for a wise man to sit in the company of the ignorant. When crows (non-believers or the ignorant) increase in number, it is better for the learned and the lovers of God to be silent. Avoid throwing stones in the slush that may splash your clean dress. Be indifferent to the mortal beauty of this world.

257- The spiritual station of a saint is above ordinary worries:

آنکه جان در روی او خندد چوقند   از ترش رویی خلقش چه گزند

آنک جان بوسه دهد بر چشم او   کی خورد غم از فلک وز خشم او

در شب مهتاب مه را در سماك   از سگان و عوعو ایشان چه باك

بانگ سگ هرگز رسد در گوش ماه   خاصه ماهی کو بود خاص اله

کارك خود می گذارد هر کسی   آب نگذارد صفا بهر خسی

(II / 414-415-416-422-418)

a) He in whose face the Beloved smiles sweetly like sugar, is free from the harm of the bitter faces of the people. He whose eyes are kissed by the Beloved how can he be grieved by heaven and its anger. On a moonlit night the moon does not care for the barking of dogs when it passes the (mansion of) *Simak*. The dogs' barking never reaches the ears of the moon, especially the ears of a moon that belongs to God. Everyone is busy with his own tiny business and (pure) water does not lose its purity just because of a piece of husk.

b) He, whose eyes watch the smiling Face of God, does not care what people say or think about him. If a man is under God's direct protection (like the saints) he does not worry about anything. A lover of God is at a high station like a full moon, and is free from rebuking or envy. What can a small husk (the reproaching or backbiting of ordinary people) do to pure flowing water (the perfect man)? "Man has three spiritual states. In the first he pays no heed to God at all, but worships and pays service to everything, woman and men, wealth and children, stones and clods; God he does not worship. When he acquires a little knowledge and awareness, then he serves nothing but God. Again, when he progresses farther in this state he becomes silent; he does not say, 'I do not serve God', neither does he say 'I serve God' for he has transcended these two degrees. No sound from these people issue to the world" (Discourses, Arberry, p. 205).

c) *"Simak"* =the stations of the moon on the 14th day, the full moon.

258- A real Sufi is not a beggar:

دیر یابد صوفی آز از روزگار   زآن سبب صوفی بود بسیار خوار
جز مگر آن صوفئی کز نور حق   سیر خورد او فارغست از ننگ دق
(II / 532-533)

a) A Sufi gets his food late out of luck because of this he might become a glutton. However, the Sufi who is fed with Divine light is free from the shame of beggary.

b) The real Sufi has no greed for worldly food because he is fed by God. In Rumi we encounter two words *"Sufi"* and *"Dervish"*, which he uses as synonyms. *"Sufi"* means a person whose heart is busy with God and nothing else "Dervish" has more or less the same meaning but he also travels from place to place in order to give his heart to none but God, like Shams-i Tebrizi. *"Fakir"*, is used in a more general sense. It may mean a street beggar or a dervish. Since these terms were interchangeable at the time of Rumi, he often tries to explain them: "A Sufi is a person who seeks piety but not a woolen dress, tailoring and walking slowly (majestically for show). To mean people *"Sufism"* has become tailoring (wearing nice dresses) and homosexuality, that is all" (M V/ 363-364). Later in the history of Islam many false Saints, Dervishes, Sufis, and Qalanders brought about degeneration to the term.

259- The light of your spirit is your true friend:

نور جان داری که یار دل شود   روز مرگ این حس تو باطل شود

هست آنچ گور را روشن کند   در لحد کین چشم را خاک آگند

جان باقی بایدت بر جا نشاند   آنزمان کین جان حیوانی نماند

(II / 940-941-943)

a) On the day when you die your carnal senses will disappear; your spiritual light will be the friend of your heart. When dust will fill these eyes in the grave, do you have something that will illuminate it? When your carnal soul is dead, you need the living spirit instead of that.

b) This physical body will perish after death but your spirit will endure. When you need light in the grave, the spiritual light will help you.

260- Demolish the wall of hindrance brick by brick:

فصل او درمان وصلی می بود   پستی دیوار قربی می شود

مانع این سر فرود آوردنست   تا که این دیوار عالی گردنست

تا نیابم زین تن خاکی نجات   سجده نتوان کرد بر آب حیات

(II / 1208-1210-1211)

a) The lowness of the wall enables one to get to the water, each brick falling gives access to the water (see Mift. 2-2/149). As long the wall is high (necked) it is an obstacle to bowing down to the life-water but it is essential to give up this clayey body.

b) "the wall"=the physical body; the water =eternity. If you want to reach the water of Divine Mercy then try to surrender yourself to the Highness of God little by little.

261- The real king:

شاه آن دان کو ز شاهی فارغست / بی مه و خورشید نورش بازغست
مخزن آن دارد که مخزن ذات اوست / هستی او دارد که با هستی عدوست
آنک واقف گشت بر اسرار هو / سر مخلوقات چه بود پیش او
میدهند افیون بمرد زخم مند / تا که پیکان از تنش بیرون کنند
وقت مرگ از رنج او را می درند / او بدآن مشغول شد جان میبرند
پس بدان مشغول شو کآن بهترست / تا ز تو چیزی برد کآن کهترست
(II / 1469-1470-1481-1503-1504-1507)

1469 b بی مه G : برمه. Mift. - Mift. 1470

a) A king is one who is unconcerned with kingship and shines forth without the sun and moon. He whose essence is treasure, is in fact a treasure; and existent is he who is in conflict with his own being. He who becomes aware of God's secret for him it is easy to know the secrets of people. They (doctors) give opium to the injured so that they may take arrows out of his body. Upon death they (the Divine forces) first tear him with pain and when he struggles with it, they take his soul. So be busy with something that is (spiritually) high so that what they (people) take away from you is of minor importance.

b) Spiritually a king is a man who has come close to God. He needs no physical aid to be happy. His inner enlightenment is able to discern all secrets. Keep yourself busy with spirituality in order to forget the valueless charms of this world.

262- Bring the sky under your feet:

آب رحمت بایدت رو پست شو / و آنگهان خور خمر رحمت مست شو
چرخ را در زیر پا آر ای شجاع / بشنو از فوق فلک بانگ سماع
پنبه وسواس بیرون کن ز گوش / تا بگوشت آید از گردون خروش
پاک کن دو چشم را از موی عیب / تا ببینی باغ و سروستان غیب
زاری و گریه قوی سرمایه ایست / رحمت کلی قوی تر دایه ایست
(II / 1940-1942-1943-1944-1951)

a) If you want the water of Divine Mercy then be humble and drink the wine of mercy and become drunk. O brave one! bring the sky under your feet and listen from above the sky to the celestial music. Take the cotton of sceptical ideas out of your ears so that you may also hear the noises from the sky. Clean your eyes and get rid of the hair (obstacle) in your eye so that you may see the garden and cypress-plot (ground) of the unseen world. Lamentation and crying are powerful food. Divine Mercy is the strongest nurse.

b) In order to attract Divine Mercy, be humble. When the wine of Divine Mercy reaches you, you become drunk and forget the worries of this world. If you desire to listen to the Divine Music that has made the whirling universe intoxicated with God, then step beyond this physical sky and leave your cunning ego and scepticism aside. Don't waste your energy on physical attachments, but concentrate it within yourself. The best thing is to ask for God's Mercy by crying over your helplessness, for Rumi adds, "Where there is running water there grows vegetation, and where there are running tears mercy comes into action" (M. I/820).

263- Even the smallest beings (germs) eat:

ذرها دیدم دهانشـان جمله باز   گر بگویم خوردشان گردد دراز
جمله عالم آکل و ماکول دان   باقیـان را مقبل و مقبول دان
این جهان و ساکنانش منتـشر   و آن جهان و سالکانش مستمر
(III / 26-30-31)

a) I have seen tiny beings (germs) with their mouths open. If I enter into details about their food (begin to tell you what they eat), the subject will be prolonged. All the world is eating something and is being eaten by something, see it like that. But the other creatures (the everlasting ones) are preferable and nice. The inhabitants of this world are scattered while the travellers of the other world are persistent and everlasting.

b) Rumi is able to see germs with open mouths that eat other things (in this respect T. calls these verses miraculous see 9-10/ p. 10). Rumi does not want to go into details about what they (the smallest beings) eat, otherwise he would have to write at length. The physical world is based on hunger and greed and on eating each other, but the other world is free of such things. There souls experience life without interruption.

c) *"Zarre"* in Persian means "atom or the smallest being" hence it may mean here "a germ or microbe" in the modern sense; however *"zarre-bin"* means a microscope in the modern Persian.

264- Don't let your bread be unbaked:

گر ز که بستانی و ننهی بجای   اندر آید کوه زآن دادن ز پای
پس بنه برجای هردم را عوض   تا ز واسجد واقترب یابی غرض
در تمامی کارها چندین مکوش   جز بکاری که بود در دین مکوش
عاقبت تو رفت خواهی ناتمام   کارهایت ابتر و نان تو خام
(III / 126-127-128-129)

a) If you keep on taking (stones) from a mountain and do not put anything back, it (the mountain) will come to an end, too. So put something back in place of each wasted breath of yours so that you may obey these words of God, "Bow down in adoration and bring yourself closer to God" (the Koran, XCV/19) and attain your goal. Don't run after completing worldly affairs but run after the pious (religious goals and the Divine Commands), otherwise you will reach that world incomplete, your deeds half done and the bread unbaked.

b) If you waste your breath on physical achievements and ignore your spiritual improvement by failing to pray to God and do righteous things, your old age will be a ruin (Mift. 3-1/p. 38) because worldly affairs are not eternal.

265- The body is the clothing of the soul:

تا بدانی که تن آمد چون لباس   رو بجو لابس لباسی را ملیس
روح را توحید الله خوشترست   غیر ظاهر دست و پای دیگرست
دست و پا در خواب بینی وائتلاف   آب حقیقت دان مدانش از گزاف
آن توی کی بی بدن داری بدن   پس مترس از جسم جان بیرون شدن
عقل جزوی آفتش وهم است وطن   ز آنک در ظلمات شد او را وطن
(III / 1610-1611-1612-1558)

a) Know that the body is the clothing of the spirit, go and seek the weaver of the dress and don't keep on licking (kissing) the dress. To the spirit unity of God is sweeter (than the love of the physical body). There are other hands and feet than these visible ones. In your dream you see many feet and hands and loving friends. Think that all are real and don't regard them as meaningless. In the dream it is you that has a body without having a physical body, so don't be afraid to get out of this living body (death). Partial insight produces opinions, vain ideas, and fancies because its motherland is darkness.

b) Fear of death is with us as long as we are attached to this world. We see many places and people in dreams which should be viewed as real because in some cases they turn out to be true. Similarly the other world may be invisible yet it is also real.

266- Man proposes, God disposes:

هر زمان دلرا دگر رایی بود   آن نه از وی لیك از جایی بود

پس چرا ایمن شوی بر رای دل   عهد بندی تا شوی آخر خجل

این هم از تاثیر حکمست و قدر   چاه می بینی و نتوانی حذر

حاصل اندر خواب نقصان بدن   نیست باك و نی دو صد پاره شدن

(III / 1644-1645-1646-1732)

a) The heart has a different opinion all the time which does not arise from the heart but comes from somewhere else. So why are you sure of the heart's opinion? You promise people and then, in the end, you become ashamed (because you can't fulfill it). It is also because of the Divine Command and Destiny that you see the pit but cannot avoid it. Since this world is a dream, what does it matter if you lose some parts of your body. Don't fear being cut into two hundred (many) pieces.

b) The main idea here is that this world is a dream, do not worry if you experience a bad dream for the real life is Hereafter. Whatever ideas come to you they come from beyond your heart. Then why worry when your will is unable to make them come true? They were not your ideas in any case for you do nothing of your own accord. So always ask God what is good for you and trust Him because only He knows what is right.

267- Do not fear poverty but God:

میکشد شیر قضا در بیشها   جان ما مشغول کار و پیشها

آن چنان کز فقر می ترسند خلق   زیر آب شور رفته تا بحلق

گر بترسندی از آن فقر آفرین   گنجهاشان کشف گشتی در زمین

(III / 2204-2205-2206)

a) The lion of Destiny is dragging us into the jungle while we are busy with worldly business and trades (professions), like the common people who being afraid of poverty sink in briny water up to their throats. If they could fear the Creator of that poverty, treasures would have been revealed to them upon earth.

b) Muhammed said, "Poverty is my pride". This does not mean mendicity but indifference to worldly possessions. Many ordinary people are afraid to be poor although mundane poverty is less dangerous than spiritual poverty.

268-What you sow so shall you reap; death is your mirror:

پیش ترک آیینه را خوش رنگیست   پیش زنگی آیینه هم زنگیست

آنک می ترسی ز مرگ اندر فرار   آن ز خود ترسانی ای جان هوش دار

روی زشت تست نه رخسار مرگ   جان تو همچون درخت و مرگ برگ

(III / 3440-3441-3442)

a) In front of a fair man (a Turk) the mirror is full of colours while in front of a black the mirror is also black. O you who are experiencing death due to fear, you are actually afraid of your own being (see Baki III-IV/ p. 245). It is your own ugly looking face but not the cheek of death. Your spirit is like a tree and the death is like a leaf.

b) "This world is the farm of the other world" is a tradition of Muhammed. Death is your mirror. When you die it will show you your real face. Death is like a leaf: it cannot hurt a tree (the spirit) but gives it a fresh dress.

c) "*Turk*" has many meanings in Persian: a) One with fair face, b) Heedless beauty, c) Drawing ecstasy of God (see Ferheng, p. 243). It does not mean a "Turcoman" as translated by Nich. Turcoman is a tribe of Turks that belongs to the Oghuz family. Let us look at this verse of Rumi:

پارسی گوییم هین تازی بهل   هندوی, آن ترک باش ای آب و گل

"Let us speak Persian (not we are Persian) and give up Arabic; O you who are water and clay be a mole (not "*Hindu*" as Nich. says) of that Turk (Fair One, God)" (M. III/2839).

269- This world is not big enough:

ظاهرش زفت و بمعنی تنگ بر	مردگان را این جهان بنمود فر
سخت تنگ آمد بهنگام مناخ	این زمین و آسمان بس فراخ
بیند او اسرار را بی هیچ بد	غفلت از تن بود چون تن روح شد
نه شب و نه سایه باشد نه ولك	چون زمین بر خاست از جو فلك
چون شهان رفتند اندر لامکان	انبیا را تنگ آمد این جهان
جان ز خفت جمله در پریدنست	هر گرانی و کسل خود از تنست

(III / 3539-3543-3566-3567-3538-3571)   M : N لی ولك : G نه ولك b 3567

a) To the men whose spiritual heart is dead this world appears outwardly bright and great, although it is the narrowest one. This earth and the sky, though they appear wide, become much tighter (narrower) at the time of death (see T. 11-12/p. 928, but Nich. says "sleep"). Negligence is due to the body. When it inevitably changes into Spirit, it begins to observe the Divine Secrets. When the earth becomes non-existent in space (atmosphere) neither night nor shadow nor even the setting of the sun is left. When the prophets (kings) went into the spaceless world, this world became narrower for them. Every state of heaviness and idleness is due to this physical body, otherwise the spirit has a tendency of flying (upwards) because of its lightness.

b) Spirit while in the physical body is confined but when this body dies it is freed and able to move from place to place with a great speed and without any physical hindrance. The other world being beyond these dimensional bounds is commodious.

270- Physically man is a microcosm but spiritually he is a macrocosm:

حق چو خواهد میرسد در یك زمان	هین مشو نومید نور از آسمان
دم بدم خاصیتش آرد عمل	سه هزاران سال و پانصد تا زحل
باطن ما گشته قوام سما	ظاهر آن اختران قوام ما
پس بمعنی عالم اکبر توی	پس بصورت عالم اصغر توی
می رود می آید ایدر کاروان	حاصل اندر یك زمان از آسمان
کی مفازه زفت آید با مفاز	نیست بر این کاروان این ره دراز

(IV / 513-517-520-521-531-532)

a) Come on! don't be disappointed with the Divine light from the heavens, when God wills it comes to you at once. It takes three thousand five hundred years to reach Saturn but the effect (action) of Saturn on the earth takes place every moment. The stars (zodiac powers) appear to control us but our essence is able to control the universe. Consequently, you are physically a microcosm but spiritually a macrocosm. To sum up, every now and then a caravan comes from heaven to earth and goes back to heaven. For the caravan there is no difficulty (the way is not long or distant); for the successful (spiritually developed) people it is not difficult to pass through the desert (the most difficult place on the way to God).

b) In accordance with the Mesopotamian and Greek belief (for example Stoic doctrine) all limbs or parts of the body are under the effect of planets. Rumi says this is true as long as you remain in this body but when you leave it and go closer to God (the Centre), you share the Divine Essence that rules the stars. When you begin to exercise righteousness and pray to God with sincerity, God's caravan (of angels and holy spirits) comes to help you.

271- Divine Art changed nebulae into shining stars:

گرچه شیری چون روی ره بی دلیل / خویش بین و در ضلالی و ذلیل
جسم عارف را دهد وصف جماد / تا برو روید گل و نسرین شاد
ای ببرده عقل هدیه تا اله / عقل آنجا کمترست از خاک راه
سوی حق گر راستانه خم شوی / وا رهی از اختران محرم شوی
کیمیایی که از او یک ماثری / بر دخان افتاد گشت آن اختری
دیده حسی زبون آفتاب / دیده ربانیی جو و بیاب

(IV / 543-548-568-583-591-595)

a) Perhaps you are a lion but if you walk without a guide (a saint) you might become self-conceited and thus mean and full of mistakes. The saint gives the earth's quality of submission to the clayey body of the gnostic (the disciple) so that fresh roses and eglantines may grow (out of that soil). O you who have taken your intellect to God as a present, there it is as worthless as the dust of the road. If you bow down to God sincerely, you will free yourself from the effect of the stars and get closer to God. He is such a Chemist that when his art (effect) falls on the dust smoke (nebula) it changes the nebula into shining stars. Sensual eyes are dazzled by the sun, therefore go and seek Divine eyes and find them.

b) Rumi advises that a saint is like a living prophet and one should follow him leaving his own partial insight aside, especially the intellect of philosophers (see Baki,

IV-V p. 395) who are always in doubt and ask Why? and How? Bear in mind however that a true saint is not like a shop keeper (see M. III/vr. 2390) who expects money or profit from his disciples. To find such a perfect saint is difficult and if you cannot find him then pray to God until His mercy reaches you (as suggested in the previous verses), for His mercy is able to turn a nebula into shining stars.

c) It is interesting to notice that Rumi uses the word *"Dukhan"* which means "smoke" and not "darkness" as translated by Nich. (IV/ p. 364) and it stands for nebula.

272- God concealed the results of worldly business and jobs so that you might risk them:

که بپوشید از تو عیبش کردگار	زآن همی تانی بدادن تن بکار
زو رمیدی جانت بعد المشرقین	بر تو گر پیدا شدی زو عیب و شین
چشم وا شد تا پشیمانی رسید	چون قضا آورد حکم خود پدید
این پشیمانی بهل حق را پرست	این پشیمانی قضای دیگرست
(IV / 1333-1335-1338-1339)	

a) You give yourself to a work because God has hidden its defectiveness from you. If its defectiveness or humiliating nature was made visible to you, your soul would run away from it as far as the east is from the west. When Divine Destiny arrives, your eyes open and you begin to see facts and repent over the result. This feeling of repentance is also an aspect of Divine Destiny. Abandon this repentance and worship only God.

b) If results of your actions go against your will every time, pray to God for His Mercy and stop repenting continuously.

273- Your real homeland is the other world:

که وطن آن سوست جان اینسوی نیست	از دم حب الوطن بگذر مه ایست
این حدیث راست را کم خوان غلط	گر وطن خواهی گذر زآن سوی شط
(IV / 2211-2212)	2211 a مه ایست Y + G : بایست. Mift.

a) Give up the claims of patriotism (nationalism) because, my good friend, your real country is not this world. If you want a country, pass to the other bank of the stream and do not misunderstand this *Hadis* (Tradition of Muhammed).

b) A man's real homeland is the country he experiences after death not this mortal world. Many Muslims misunderstand this Tradition of Muhammed, "The love of country is a part of faith", because it refers to the country Hereafter and not this world which is temporary.

274- Four qualities that one can possess if one has faith (Moses' advice to Pharaoh):

صحتی باشد تنت را پایدار	گفت موسی کاولین آن چهار
که اجل دارد ز عمرت احتراز	ثانیاً باشد ترا عمر دراز
بلک بینی در خراب خانه گنج	مرگ جو باشی ولی نه از عجز رنج
از خرابی خانه مندیش و مه ایست	گنج زیر خانه است و چاره نیست
دو جهانی خالص از خصم و عدو	گفت موسی آن سوم ملک دو تو
موی همچون قیر و رخ چون ارغوان	گفت چارم آنک مانی تو جوان
هست شادی و فریب کودکان	افتخار از رنگ و بو و از مکان

(IV / 2528-2530-2533-2541-2569-2574-2576)

a) Moses said to Pharaoh, "The first quality of the four is health, which keeps your body continually strong. The second quality is long life, from which death will keep away. You seek death not out of pain, but because you find treasure in your ruined house (old body). The treasure is under that (ruined) house, so there is no remedy; don't hesitate to destroy the house, act fast! The third is the twofold empire, you will gain the two worlds (here and Hereafter) without the fear of enemies and their evil actions. The fourth is you will remain young and your hair will always be as black as pitch and your cheeks will be pink like the Arghuwan (flower of the Judas tree, Nich. IV/p. 414). To be proud of perfume, colours, and places (building etc.) is the act of children who are pleased and deceived by such things".

b) Here *"Moses"* means the spirit and *"Pharaoh"* the selfish Flesh. The spirit says to man that if you believe in God you will gain the following qualities: 1- Good health (because you have less worries as you trust in God) 2- Long life and no fear of death (as already explained in the previous verses) 3- You are as happy as a king here and also the Hereafter (because you feel protected by God). 4- Since you have nothing to worry about and to lose in this temporary world you experience endless happiness, which keeps you even physically fresh. You are no more deceived by the transient beauty of this world.

275- To be busier with your inner self, you need Divine Intoxication:

هین کمالی دست آور تا تو هم   از کمال دیگران نفتی بغم
از خدا میخواه دفع این حسد   تا خدایت وا رهاند از جسد
مر ترا مشغولیی بخشد درون   که نپردازی از آن سوی برون
هین بهر مستی دلا غره مشو   هست عیسی مست حق خرمست جو
(IV / 2680-2681-2682-2691)

a) Attain perfection so that you may not grieve because of the perfection of others. Ask God to help you to get rid of the jealousy you have for others so that God may free you from this body. So that He may occupy yourself inwardly and keep you back from being busy with the outer world. Be aware! don't be happy (satisfied) with any kind of intoxication, for Christ (the pure soul) is intoxicated with Divine Love while his donkey (the body of man) is intoxicated with barley (the beer).

b) You, too, try to attain perfection instead of being envious of others' qualities. To do this be busy with your inner self and not with other's perfection or defects. To be completely busy with your inner self, you require the intoxication of Christ, who was able to give up his own ego permanently.

276- Your sustenance is in the hands of God:

این زمین و سختیان پرده ست و بس   اصل روزی از خدا دان هر نفس
رزق از وی جو مجو از زید و عمر   مستی از وی جو مجو از بنگ و خمر
چون بکاری در زمین اصل کار   تا بروید هر یکی را صد هزار
(V / 1490-1496-1491)

a) This land (farm) and leather (Morocco) are all a veil, the real bread comes from God every moment. Therefore, seek bread (food) from God only and not from Tom, Dick and Harry; seek intoxication from Him not from beng and wine. When you want to sow, sow in the real soul so that every single seed may grow a hundred thousand blessings.

b) Worldly sources for earning one's living (be it a field or a piece of leather) are only a medium; the actual provider of food is God as the Koran says, "Truly God is He who bestows the best sustenance" (XXII/58). "The real soil" means the field of the other world. Work for that world.

277- Everything happens according to the will of God:

بهـر آن نبود که تنبل کن در آن   قول بنـده أیـش شآء الله کان
که در آن خدمت فزون شو مستعد   بلك تحریص است بر اخلاص و جد
کار کار تست بر حسـب مراد   گر بگویند آنچ میخواهی تو راد
کآنچ خواهی و آنچ گویی آن شود   آنگهان تنبل کنی جایز بود
حکم حکم اوسـت مطلق جاودان   چون بگویند أیش شآء الله کان
بر نگردی بنـدگانه گرد او   پـس چرا صـد مرده اندر ورد او
(V / 3111-3112-3113-3114-3115-3116)

a) The saying of His (God's) slave, "What God desires takes place" does not mean that one should give up his business and sit idle. It on the contrary, means that one should increase one's labour and should work more. O wise man! If it is said to you that whatever you desire will happen in accordance with your will, you will be truly lucky. Then it will be right if you become lazy for desire will occur anyway. Since it is said, "What God desires takes place" then everything depends on His Command who is Eternal and Absolute. Then why don't you set to working obediently around Him like a slave with the will of a hundred men?

b) The Tradition of Muhammed is, "Everything happens in accordance with God's Will" and many muslims, especially the Jabriye, believed that there is no need for any action since everything is controlled by God. Rumi says if everything is in the control of God then work for Him to win His favour; for that you have to follow His Command.

278- If your heart is with God and His lovers, it does not matter if your body is in the dust or in the dung:

تا دلت زین چاه تن بیرون شود   جهد کن تا این طلب افزون شود
تو بگوئی زنده ام ای غافلان   خلق گوید مرد مسکین آن فلان
هشت جنت در دلم بشگفته است   گر تن من همچو تنها خفته است
چه غمسـت ار تن در آن سرگین بود   جان چو خفته در گل و نسرین بود
(V / 1735-1736-1737-1738)

a) Work so that the desire (of finding God) may increase and your heart may get free of this well (the body). Then people will say, "That poor person has become dead" but you will say to them, "I am still alive, O you heedless ones. Although my body is asleep, like other dead bodies, eight paradises have blossomed in my heart. If the soul is asleep among roses and eglantines, what does it matter if the dead body is buried in the dung".

b) Try to win God's favour: once you do so what does it matter if your body is buried in the dung or in dust, because your soul is happy with God and his lovers.

279- The spiritual body does not die:

هر که گوید شد تو گویش نی نشد	خاک شد صورت ولی معنی نشد
گر ز صورت هارب وگه مستقر	در جهان روح هر سه منتظر
باز هم ز امرش مجرد می شود	امر آید در صور رو در رود
بهر تست این لفظ فکر ای فکرناک	فکر کو آنجا همه نورست پاک
هیچ خانه در نگنجد نجم ما	هر ستاره خانه دارد بر علا
نور نامحدود را حد کی بود	جای سوز اندر مکان کی در رود
(VI / 75-76-77-114-115-116)	a 116 جای سوز G : جان بی سود Koner
	a 115 بر غلا G : بر علا N

a) The form (or appearance) has changed into clay but the essence has not; if someone says so, tell him that the essence has not come to end. In the spiritual world all three actions wait for the command of God, some by escaping forms and some by dwelling in them. When the command of God comes, "Go into forms (bodies)", they do so; and again by the command of God they give up forms and are released. Where there is pure Divine light, there is no idea; O you who give importance to ideas this word "thought" is for you. Each star has a house (a place) in the space but our star has no house. How can the infinite be limited?

b) The essence waits for God's order to enter a body, to get out of it, and to be closer to God in the end: "They will be brought up before us" (the Koran, XXXVI/53). Rumi further says that words belong to the physical world while spiritual knowledge is gained by means of Divine inspiration. Forms are means of smelling the realities behind them (Koner, p. 797). In the world of God, there is no concept of dimension such as time or space.

280- Don't blame your destiny but blame your own faults:

بار خود بر کس منه بر خویش نه   سروری را کم طلب درویش به
این جهان دامست و دانه‌ش آرزو   در گریز از دامها روی آرزو
بر قضا کم نه بهانه ای جوان   جرم خود را چون نهی بر دیگران
گرد خود بر گرد و جرم خود ببین   جنبش از خود بین و از سایه مبین
رنج را باشد سبب بد کردنی   بدز فعل خود شناس از بخت نی
در فسون نفس کم شو غره   کآفتاب حق نپوشد ذره
(VI / 328-378-413-415-428-432)

a) Don't lay your burden on others, lay it on yourself. Don't seek to be a chief, it is better to be a dervish. This world is a trap and its bait is desire; avoid the bait. O young man! don't blame your destiny and why hold others responsible for your own faults? Circle around yourself and try to perceive your own sins. See that the motion of your shadow is because of you and don't blame your shadow for that. If you have pains and sorrows, they can be due to your misdeeds; know that this is the result of your own sins and don't blame your destiny. Don't be deceived by the spell of your carnal desires because the Divine Sun does not conceal a single atom.

b) Rumi advises us not to blame our destiny for unwanted results. We should blame ourselves. The more we want from this world, the more problems we have to face. If you are satisfied with what you have, like a dervish, you lessen your problems.

281- It is possible to change carnal lust into spiritual energy:

چون ببندی شهوتش را از رغیف   سر کند آن شهوت از عقل شریف
همچو شاخی که بری از درخت   سر کند قوت ز شاخ نیکبخت
(VI / 1123-1124)

a) When you don't satisfy lust very much, it changes into noble intellect. It is like cutting a bough off a tree and in its place a fresh and gay bough begins to sprout.

b) We can change our lustful desires into spiritual ones. The more we control our carnal desires, the more our spiritual capacity grows (see also Mift., p. 274).

282- Focus on the result:

گر همی خواهی سلامت از ضرر　　چشم ز اول بند و پایان را نگر
تا عدمها را ببینی جمله هست　　هستها را بنگری محسوس پست
(VI / 1360-1361)

a) If you want to be safe from harm, close your eyes to the beginning and focus your attention on the result so that you may see all the non-existent as existent; and you may see the existent as mean and imprisoned.

b) If we desire to avoid harm, we should look at results. To see the other world more clearly lessen your carnal wishes and let your spiritual eyes see this world as deceptive and meaningless. Thank God for His gifts which are eternal while the gifts of this world are temporary and misleading (see verses 3160-3166).

CHAPTER IX

Step V: Love

The major theme of the six volumes of Rumi's Masnevi is the love of God. The Masnevi is actually a love letter written to the Unseen Beloved. Love is neither touchable nor perceptible by the carnal senses, therefore, love can be explained only by love. In the modern age, many people are so plunged in the materialistic, derivative love that they are like a fish that is dead inside and outside. So it is useless to pour love-water on them for they will never revive. But those who are already in the ocean of true love (love of God) are like a fish that cannot be sated with water, because the more it drinks the thirstier it becomes (as said in verse No. 17). Love is above the boundaries of time, space or even religions. As God is the source of every being so He is the source of love (Chittick, p. 195). He is, in fact, the Centre of love for all His created beings and His signs take us ultimately to Him. God shall give importance to love when we reach Him, "O ye who believe, if any from you turn back from his faith soon will God produce a people whom He will love as they will love Him" (the Koran, V/57). This clearly means that God gives importance to love. In the 12th chapter of the Bhagwad Gita, we come across these lines about God:

"Greater is the toil of those,
Whose thinking clings to the Unmanifest,
For difficult it is for embodied men,
To reach and tread the unmanifest Way.

But those who cast off all their works on Me,
Are solely intent on Me,
And meditate on Me in spiritual exercise (of Yoga),
Leaving no rooms for others (and so really) do Me service.

But if thou art unable in all steadfastness,
To concentrate thy thoughts on Me,
Then seek to win Me,
By effort unremitting.

I love the man who hates not, nor exults,
Who mourns not nor desires,
Who puts away pleasant and unpleasant things,
Who is loyal, devoted, and devout".

(Hindu Scripts, p. 301-302)

In the Koran we find these attributes of Him, "My Lord is indeed full of Mercy and loving-kindness" (XI/90) and "And He is the Oft-forgiving full of loving kindness" (LXXXV/14). "But those of faith are overflowing in their love for God" (II/165). The word *"Wadud"* above, translated as "loving kindness" has a very special meaning. It means "the Beloved one, the One who is very Kind to His created beings and protects them with great love". This is what the Bible says, "Because of his love God had already decided that through Jesus Christ he would make us his sons" (Eph. I/3-6); "I, the Lord... who is not easily angered and who shows great love and faithfulness" (Ex. 34/6); "But I show my love to thousands of generations of those who love me and obey my laws" (Deut. 5/10) and "But for those who honour the Lord, his love lasts for ever" (Ps. 103/17).

After this short review of the scriptures we now turn to what Rumi says about love:

"All the hopes, desires, loves and affections that people have for different things -fathers, mothers, friends, heavens, the earth, gardens, palaces, sciences, work, food, drink-- the saint knows that these are all desires for God and all those things are veils. When men leave this world and see the King without these veils, then they will know that all were veils and coverings, that the object of their desire was in reality that One Thing" (Discourses, 46).

ورنه هم افهام سوزد هم زبان   مجملش گفتم نکردم ز آن بیان
                                              a 1758 نکردم : G + Y   نگفتم N

"I have narrated love in brief, not in detail, for both my perception and tongue would have burnt away" (I/1789) and:

چون بعشق آیم خجل باشم از آن   هرچ گویم عشق را شرح و بیان
چون بعشق آمد قلم برخود شکافت   چون قلم اندر نوشتن می شتافت

"Whatever I begin to tell or explain about love, I feel hesitant about love (for I cannot explain it). When I take a pen and hurry to write about love, it (the pen) begins to tear itself" (I/112-114).

کفر باشد پیش او جز بندگی   هر که اندر عشق یابد زندگی

"He who finds life in love, for him anything other than love is infidelity" (V/1866).

هرچه جز معشوق باقی جمله سوخت   عشق آن شعله ست کو چون بر فروخت

"Love is that flame which, when it blazes up it burns everything except the Beloved" (V/588).

283- If you are not with me, you are with none:

گر با همه‌ای چو بی‌منی بی همه‌ای ور بی همه‌ای چو با منی با همه‌ای
(III / 1614)

a) "If you are with everyone without Me, you are with none;
If you are with Me and with nobody, you are with everyone".

b) This is one of the crowning verses of Rumi. It has therefore been placed within the rubric (see G.). If you are busy with everything other than God, you are actually alone. If you are not busy with anything else but God, you are with everything for the centre of everything is God. You cannot address everyone by means of the radio but if you go to the centre (the broadcasting station), you can address all. Similarly, if you win the favour of God, you can win everyone's favour especially of those who love God.

284- The sea of love:

غرق عشقی‌ام که غرقست اندرین عشـقـهـای اولـیـن و آخـرین
من چو لب گویم لب دریا بود من چو لا گویم مراد الا بود
(I / 1757-1759)

a) I am drowned in (the sea of) love, the sea where the first and last have all drowned. When I utter the word "lip" it changes into the sea and when I say "No" it actually means "none other but Him".

b) This is Rumi's own state. He was submerged in the sea of Divine Love where all other prophets, saints, and lovers of God have drowned and have annihilated in Him.

285- Love is the astrolabe of the Divine Mysteries:

علت عشق ز علتها جداست عشـق اصطرلاب اسرار خداست
عاشقی گر زین سر و گر زآن سرست عاقبت ما را بدآن سر رهبرست
عقل در شرحش چو خر در گل بخفت شرح عشق و عاشقی هم عشق گفت
(I / 110-111-115)

245

a) The ailment of a love is of a different kind, while love is the astrolabe of the mysteries of God. Love, may it be of this world or of that world, finally leads us yonder. Reason is like an ass stuck in the mud, but it is only love that can comment about love and loverhood.

b) Rumi calls love an "ailment" because there is no remedy for it other than getting to the Beloved; and it is like an astrolabe that helps us in finding our way to God (the Beloved). May it be the derivative love of this world or of the other world, both lead us to Reality in the end. If you depend on your intellect and tongue to explain love, you will fail to do so for it is only love itself (your experience of it) that can explain what love is.

c) An astrolabe is used for measuring the altitudes of the heavenly bodies; love is a Divine astrolabe that enables us to scale the attributes of the spiritual heavens.

286- Physical love brings humiliation:

ز آنك عشق مردگان پاینده نیست   ز آنك مرد سوی ما آینده نیست

عشق زنده در روان و در بصر   هر دمی باشد ز غنچه تازه تر

عشق آن بگزین که جمله انبیا   یافتند از عشق او کار و کیا

عشقهائی کز پی رنگی بود   عشق نبود عاقبت ننگی بود

(I / 217-218-220-205)

a) The love of the mortal is also mortal for the dead cannot come back to us. But the love of a Living One in the soul and eyes is always fresher than a bud. Choose that kind of love from which all the prophets gained power and glory. The love that depends on colours (physical charms) is not a true love, it finally ends up in humiliation.

b) If the beloved is strong and everlasting, your love will also be ever-fresh. If it depends on mortal beings, it will soon come to an end leading to humiliation and disappointment. So choose God as your Beloved Who is Immortal.

287- Love is the remedy for all ailments:

او ز حرص و جمله عیبی پاک شد / هر کرا جامه ز عشق چاک شد
ای طبیب جمله علتهای ما / شاد باش ای عشق خوش سودای ما
ای تو افلاطون و جالینوس ما / ای دوای نخوت و ناموس ما
کوه در رقص آمد و چالاک شد / جسم خاک از عشق بر افلاک شد
طور مست و خر موسی صاعقا / عشق جان طور آمد عاشقا
همچو نی من گفتنیها گفتمی / با لب دمساز خود گر جفتمی
بی زبان شد گرچه دارد صد نوا / هرک او از هم زبانی شد جدا
زنده معشوقست و عاشق مرده / جمله معشوقست و عاشق پرده
او چو مرغی ماند بی پروای او / چون نباشد عشق را پروای او

(I / 22-23-24-25-26-27-28-30-31)

a) He whose clothes are torn due to love is freed from all faults and greed. O fruitful love! live long, you have been the remedy for our all ailments. You are the medicine of our sickness, pride and fame. You are thus our Plato and Galen. The earthly body due to love went up to the skies; the mountain *(Sinai)* began to dance and became active. O Beloved! love gave life to Mount Sinai, it was drunken and Moses fell down in a swoon. If I happened to join the lips of a friend myself, I would speak also like the reed-flute. He who has fallen away from his friends that speak the same language, is without tongue even if he knows a hundred sounds (languages). All is the Beloved and the lover is a sheer veil; it is the Beloved that is living while the lover is lifeless. When the Beloved does not care for the love, the lover remains like a bird without wings in a pitiable situation.

b) Here the state of Divine Love has been explained. It has the following qualities:

1) It frees you from worldly worries.
2) It protects you from the fear of death and illness.
3) It is the source of activeness and nimbleness.
4) To explain the state of your own love, you need a friend who can share your feelings (like Shams-i Tebrizi).
5) There is nothing but the Beloved and to reach Him you need the enchanting power of love so that it may free you from the trap of fame and wealth.

c) "The earthly body went up to the sky" here refers to the ascension of the holy Prophet (Muhammed). The Prophet was first transported to the seat of the earlier revelations in Jerusalem and then taken to the seven heavens, even to the Sublime Throne and initiated into the spiritual mysteries of the human soul struggling in Space and Time. The reference to this great mystic story of the *Mi'raj* is a fitting prelude to the journey of the human soul in its spiritual growth in life. The first steps in this growth are through moral conduct -the reciprocal rights of parents and children, kindness to our fellow men, courage and recognising firmness in the hour of danger, a sense of personal responsibility, and a sense of God's Presence through prayers and praise (from the notes of Ali Yusuf, the Holy Quran p. 691). Reference is also made to the story of Moses (see the Koran VII/143) who persistently requested God to show Himself to him: "When Moses came to the place by Us, and his Lord addressed him, he said 'O my Lord show (Thyself) to me, that I may look upon Thee'. God said, 'By no means canst thou see Me (direct); but look upon the mount if it abide in its place then shalt thou see Me'. When his Lord manifested His glory on the Mount, He made it as dust, and Moses fell down in a swoon". This story also shows us that God loves us a great deal but it is not possible to see Him directly while we are in the human consciousness.

288- Without love you earn no Divine Light:

حق فشاند آن نور را بر جانها   مقبلان بر داشته دامانها

هر کرا دامان عشقی نا بده   زآن نثار نور بی بهره شده

جزوها را رویها سوی کلست   بلبلان را عشق بازی با گلست

(I / 760-762-763)

a) God pours the rain of light on souls, the lucky hold up their skirts to receive it. Those who have no skirt of love, they are deprived of the light. The parts have attraction towards their whole, and nightingales have love affairs with roses.

b) Lucky are those who can catch drops of the rain of Divine Mercy. Their love skirts (feelings of love) receive them but those who have no such feelings are deprived of the opportunity. When the light of God falls, one is able to receive a bit of it, and it draws one to its Whole as a nightingale's tiny heart is drawn towards colourful roses. One who is caught up in the darkness of the material world is spiritually lost.

289- God loved Adam's crying in repentance:

زآنك آدم زآن عتاب از اشك رست   اشك تر باشد دم توبه پرست
بهر گریه آمد آدم بر زمین   تا بود گریان و نالان و حزین
ز آتش دل و آب دیده نقل ساز   بوستان از ابر و خورشیدست باز
تو چه دانی ذوق آب دیدگان   عاشق نانی تو چون نادیدگان
(I / 1633-1634-1637-1638)

a) Since Adam escaped God's rage by means of shedding tears, the words of a penitent person should be his tears. Adam came down to earth crying, lamenting and being sorrowful. Make relish (dessert) of your tears and the fire of the heart for the gardens are kept in bloom with clouds and the sun. As you are fond of bread (the food of this world) how will you ever appreciate the pleasure of tears (of a lover)?

b) According to the Koran this is how Adam cried to God, "Get you down, all of you with enmity between yourselves. On earth will be your dwelling place and your means of livelihood for a time" (II/36). "Our Lord! We (Adam and Eve) have wronged our own souls, if you don't forgive us and do not take mercy on us we shall perish" (VII/23). Thus Rumi recommends us to cry and feel repentant like Adam so that we, too, may be forgiven by God.

290- Keep your love of God secret:

تشنگان گر آب جویند از جهان   آب جوید هم بعالم تشنگان
چونك عاشق اوست تو خاموش باش   او چو گوشت می کشد تو گوش باش
بند کن چون سیل سیلابی کند   ورنه رسوایی و ویرانی کند
(I / 1741-1742-1743)

a) If the thirsty look for water, the water also looks for them. Since God is your Lover, be silent. If He is pulling your ears (reproaching you) be all ears to Him. When a flood comes into action make a dam (to control it) otherwise it will bring you notoriety and destruction.

b) Love is not one sided. If you look for God, He also looks for you. When you look for Him, He begins to inspire you, so surrender yourself to Him without complaint. When you do so, be careful for the flood of your ecstasy will carry you beyond the physical limits and people will fail to understand you. So, control yourself otherwise you will be killed, like Mansur or Shams i Tebrizi.

291- In order to win God's Mercy, we must cry and lament:

نالم ایرا نالها خوش آیدش　　از دو عالم ناله و غم بایدش
چون ننالم همچو شب بی روز او　　بی وصل روی روز افروز او
(I / 1774-1775)

a) I lament for He likes lamentation, He wants lamentations and grief from the two worlds (this world and the world Hereafter). Why shouldn't I cry like the night without its day and without (seeing His) illuminating Face?

b) Anyone who starts feeling separate from God will not be happy and will cry day and night. God likes it because He wants to see His lover unhappy without Him in this world. It is for this reason that Rumi says, "I adore my sufferings so that I may please my only King. The tears that people shed for Him are like pearls but many think they are (simple) tears" (I/1778-1780).

292- Love is evergreen:

باغ سبز عشق کو بی منتهاست　　جز غم و شادی درو بس میوهاست
عاشقی زین هر دو حالت برترست　　بی بهار و بی خزان سبز و ترست
(I / 1793-1794)

a) The endless green garden of love has many fruits (tastes) other than sorrow and joy. Love is beyond these two states, it is evergreen and fresh without spring and autumn.

b) The love of God suffers no decline and is beyond any known tastes of this world (like sorrow or joy). Love is not bound by seasons or even religions.

293- The whimsical state of Rumi's love for God:

ده زکوة روی خوب ای خوب رو　　شرح جان شرحه شرحه باز گو
چون گریزانی ز ناله خاکیان　　غم چه ریزی بر دل غمناکیان
چون بهانه دادی این شیدات را　　ای بهانه شکر لبهات را
ای جهان کهنه را تو جان نو　　از تن بی جان و دل افغان شنو
(I / 1795-1798-1800-1801)

a) O Beauteous One! give tithe for your charming face, relate the story of my soul that has been pierced. Since you avoid the laments of those that are dust (mortal), then why do you pour sorrow on the heart of the sorrowful? O you whose sugary lips are priceless (have no equivalent price), why do you try to evade your mad lovers? You are a new soul to the old world. Listen to the cries of this body that has no soul and heart.

b) Here Rumi is intimate with his Beloved and he says to Him, "O my Beloved, please, show Your lovely sweet face as a tithe and tell in detail when my pierced soul will meet its will (see You) (Mift. 1-2/305). My Real Beloved, why do You run away from the laments of men (whose body is made of dust)? Why do You add sorrow to the sorrowful (Baki, I/p.191) by not showing Your Sweet Face? Why do You deprive us of your sweet words and intoxicating proximity (lips)? Being Eternal You are Everlasting and always Fresh while we are only mortal beings, so pity us and bandage the wound of love that You have made".

c) Lips= Proximity of God or His Kindness, sweet words; "body without heart and life"= the mortal body of dust and clay that has fallen away from the Light of God. Here Rumi also prays for those who are unaware of God's love.

294- Our love is sublime:

با خیال وهم نبود هوش ما	از غم و شادی نباشد جوش ما
منزل اندر جور و در احسان مکن	تو قیاس از حالت انسان مکن
حادثان میرند حقشان وارثست	جور و احسان رنج و شادی حادثست
(I / 1803-1805-1806)	

a) Our emotion is not because of sorrow or happiness, our consciousness does not depend on imagination or thought. Do not compare our state (of lovers) with that of normal human being's states and do not let your assumptions depend on mercy and cruelty, for mercy or cruelty, sorrow or happiness are all temporary feelings. They pass away and Reality (God) rules them.

b) A lover of God's perception (knowledge) or excitements (states) does not depend on carnal senses. They depend on inner feelings. So, don't judge him by looking at his outer happiness or sorrow (Mift., 2/308). A worldly lover is happy when he can see his beloved and unhappy when he cannot see. The lover of God is beyond such temporary pleasures for his love is true and eternal.

295- The partial intellect is the enemy of the Divine Love:

عاشق از خود چون غذا یابد رحیق عقل آنجا گم بماند بی رفیق
عقل جزوی عشق را منکر بود گرچه بنماید که صاحب سر بود
زیرك و داناست اما نیست نیست تا فرشته لا نشد آهریمنیست

b 1981 گم بماند بی G + N : گر شود ای Mift. (I / 1981-1982-1983)

a) When the lover of God is fed with pure wine within himself, at that stage partial insight denies love, although it seems to know many facts (realities). It is clever and knowledgeable, yet it is not naughted. Unless the angel is naught (in Divinity), it is a devil.

b) Partial insight is connected with the ego, while Universal Wisdom comes out of the Sea of Divine Wisdom. If we bring our sensual lower self under the control of our spirit, we attain real and everlasting pleasure the source of which is the Love of God. How can partial insight realise love, because when the love comes it goes. An angel is an angel when it is beyond the partial insight but if it is still a captive of the carnal desires, it is not an angel.

296- Mercy of God is many times more than the mercy of parents:

صد پدر صد مادر اندر حلم ما هر نفس زاید در افتد در فنا
حلم ایشان کف بحر حلم ماست کف رود آید ولی دریا بجاست
خود چه گویم پیش آن در این صدف نیست الا کف کف کف کف
(I / 2675-2676-2677)

a) Within My Mercy a hundred fathers and mothers are born every moment and then vanish. Their (parents') mercy is like the sea of My Mercy; foam disappears but the sea remains. What can I say about the pearl (of Divine Mercy)? In the presence of that pearl, this oyster-shell is but the foam of the foam of the foam.

b) No love can be compared with the love and kindness of God for love of parents is transient. It comes to an end with their death while God's love is eternal (like the foam that appears and disappears yet the sea is always there). God's kindness is like the pearl while parents' love is like an oyster-shell and like the foam of foam of foam (that is very weak). But the eternal Sea is always hidden under that foam.

297- A lover of the part is not a lover of the Whole:

عاشـقـان كل نى عـاشـق جزو   ماند از كل آنك شد مشتاق جزو
چونك جزوى عاشق جزوى شود   زود معـشـوقـش بـكل خود رود
ور تو گـويى جزو پيـوسـتـه كلست   خار ميخور خار پيـوسـتـه گلست
چون رسولان از پى پيـوستـن اند   پس چه پيوندندشان چون يك تن اند
                                                                (I / 2801-2802-2811-2813)

a) The lovers of the Whole are not the lovers of the part and he who is fond of the part is deprived of the Whole. When a part falls in love with a part, it (the beloved) soon goes back to its Whole and if you say that a part is attached to its Whole then eat thorns. They are the part of the whole. If the prophets' duty is to connect the part with its Whole then what shall they bring together if they are all one and a whole?

b) When one falls in love with the Whole (God), he should not fall in love with its parts (the riches of this world) because the parts are like the sun light on the wall. When the sun goes, the sunlight also goes with it from the wall. So concentrate your love on the sun.

298- Lovers of God never die for His love cannot be buried:

آفتابا ترك اين گلشـن كنى   تا كه تحت الارض را روشن كنى
آفتـاب معرفت را نقل نيـست   مشرق او غير جان و عقل نيست
خاصه خورشيد كمالى كآن سريست   روز و شب كردار او روشن گريست
حس خفاشـت سوى مغرب دوان   حس در پاشت سوى مشرق روان
42 a + b كنى G + N كند MM   (II / 42-43-44-47)

a) O sun, you leave this rose garden so that you may illuminate the other sides of the earth (by going to its other side). But the sun of Divine Knowledge has no motion, its east is not other than Soul and wisdom. Especially, the Sun of Perfection that has the quality of illuminating everything in the universe day and night. Your bat-like senses run towards the west while your pearl-shedding senses run towards the east.

b) Rumi says that the physical sun illuminates visible objects and in order to illuminate the other sides of the earth, it has to rotate. But the Spiritual Sun (God) illuminates every soul and intellect without motion and It shines on us day and night. Your carnal senses draw you towards darkness, as a bat is drawn, yet your spiritual feelings lead you towards sunrise. Rumi continues, "The essence (the food of which is Divine Light) is only concerned with knowledge and wisdom, it has nothing to do with a Turk or an Arab (racial discrimination)" (MI, 56). According to these verses, piety includes learning and enlightenment through wisdom. In other words the piety (taqwa) of an ignorant person is useless.

299- Love the Essence not the forms:

عشق او پیدا و معشوقش نهان   یار بیرون فتنه او در جهان
این رها کن عشقهای صورتی   نیست بر صورت نه بر روی ستی
آنچ معشوقست صورت نیست آن   خواه عشق این جهان خواه آن جهان
آنچ بر صورت تو عاشق گشته   چون برون شد جان چرا پس هشته
پرتو خورشید بر دیوار تافت   تابش عاریتی دیوار یافت
(II / 701-702-703-704-708)

a) His (real) love is manifest but his Beloved is hidden, his outer friend is a great trial (by means of temptation) in this world. Leave these beloveds that have forms because true love has neither forms nor is it in the form of a lady. That which is a beloved has no forms, be it the beloved of this world or of that world. O you who have fallen in love with forms, why do you quit a beloved when it dies and its soul flees? The rays of the sun have fallen on the wall and the wall has borrowed that light.

b) Unless one attains Universal Wisdom, one cannot see that it (God's love) is behind each object or being. It is His love behind every form. If a form attracts you be it the form of your beautiful beloved of this world, it is in fact the reflection of that Real Beloved like the sun's rays on a wall. Some mystics at the time of Rumi would fall in love with the forms of beautiful women or young boys (with generally no sex involved). Rumi warns them, "Why don't you keep on loving them when they are dead?". The thing they loved was only the form and not the essence. Make haste and find the Real Love behind all these veils of Beauty.

300- Everything is mortal except love:

رو نـعـمـره نـنـکـسـه بـخوان   دل طلب کن دل منـه بر استخوان
کآن جمـال دل جمـال بـاقـیـسـت   دو لبش از آب حیـوان ساقیست
خود همه آبست و هم ساقی و مست   هرسه یک شـد چون طلسم تو شکست
(II / 715-716-717)

a) Go and recite this Koranic text, "If we grant long life to any, we cause him to be bent over (make him humbler by bending)" (XXXVI/68). Seek a heart (full of love) and don't set your heart on the bones because the beauty of the heart is the everlasting one; and His two lips are a cupbearer of the life-giving water. He Himself is water, cupbearer and drunken; all three become one when the spell of your being is undone.

b) Don't put your trust in the physical structure of a man, because he will first change into an old man, weak and helpless like a child and then he will die and turn into bones. God's loving heart (spirit) however will exist for ever. His (God's) lips (the source of love and intoxication) offer you eternal life. God appears in all forms--the life water (love), a cupbearer (a saint) and the drunken (the disciple). Niyazi Misri (a great Ottoman mystic poet of the 17th century) illuminates this pantheistic view in the following lines:

"Örttü bu bazarı kesret gözlerin kalkın veli,
Arif olan cümle yüzden seni seyran eyledi".

(Divan-ı Niyazi Misri, p. 74)

"God covered the eyes of the people with the veil of the bazaar of multitudinousness yet the knower (gnostic) can see Thy Beauty through all these faces (forms)".

301- Love revives the dead:

از محبت دردها صافی شود   از محبت، دردها شـافی شـود
از محبت مرده زنده می کنند   از محبت شـاه بنده می کنند
این محبت هم نتیجه دانش است   کی گزافه بر چنین تختی نشست
(II / 1530-1531-1532)

a) Because of love dregs become clear, because of love pains come to an end. Due to love the dead is made living, due to love a king becomes a slave. But this love is the result of wisdom, by stupidity who could ever sit on a throne of love?

b) Rumi explains that love is so sublime that a stupid man cannot understand or appreciate it, although God's love has the power of healing pain and giving new life to the dead. It is possible to understand Divine Love and His messages of love by means of wisdom and knowledge, especially through the infinite knowledge. A scientist or a researcher experiences the Divine Beauty more than an ordinary man.

c) At least nine verses to be found in the Indian group beginning with "*Az muhabbet*" ="due to love" (see for instance MM. 2/p. 148) do not belong to Rumi as the language and the style also tell. They are not found in the "G" or "N".

302- Love is beyond religions or nationalities:

آتشی از عشق در جان بر فروز   سر بسر فکر و عبارت را بسوز
عاشقانرا هر نفس سوزید نیست   برده ویران خراج و عشر نیست
در درون کعبه رسم قبله نیست   چه غم ار غواص را پا چیله نیست
تو ز سرمستان قلوزی مجو   جامه چاکان را چه فرمایی رفو
ملت عشق از همه دینها جداست   عاشقان را ملت و مذهب خداست
(II / 1763-1765-1768-1769-1770)

a) Light up a fire of love in your soul, burn away thoughts and words totally. Lovers have to burn every moment for taxes and tithes are not imposed on a ruined village. There exist no formalities of *Ka'abe* within *Ka'abe* and what does it matter if a diver has no snow-shoes? Do not seek guidance from intoxicated lovers, why do you ask about repairing your clothes from those whose own garments are torn. Religion of love is different from all religions, lovers' religion or belief is God.

b) When the love of God rules your thoughts and intellect, it burns away everything but the presence of God. As a ruined village is exempt from taxes, similarly a ruined heart which loves God is not confined to the formal prayers. In the presence of God Himself what does a Qible mean? If you are not a lover of God yourself then don't go after the lovers, because they are intoxicated with the love-wine and no prayers are imposed on the intoxicated ones (as the Koran says, "Approach not prayers with an intoxicated mind..." IV/43) and they cannot be your guide if you are an orthodox.

303- Satan became jealous of mankind because of his love of God:

ترک سجده از حسد گیرم که بود   آن حسد از عشق خیزد نه از جحود
در بلا هم می چشم لذات او   مات اویم مات اویم مات او
(II / 2642-2647)

a) "Grant that my refusing to prostrate myself to Adam was because of jealousy, jealousy is born of love not of rebellion. Even in woe I am tasting His delights: I am confounded by Him, confounded by Him, confounded by Him". (words of Satan).

b) In Islam the belief is that Satan refused to prostrate himself to Adam when God ordered him to do so as the Koran says: "And behold, We said to the angels, 'Bow down to Adam, and they bowed down except *Iblis* (Satan), he refused and was haughty. He was of those who reject faith" (II/34). Rumi says that Satan was jealous of man because he did not want God to create man who would be his rival in love. Even jealousy or malice towards His creatures because of love is not acceptable since it is a sign of ego and haughtiness.

304- Love increases reality and thus senses receive pleasure of Divine Intimacy:

باغ و بستان را کجا آنجا برند	سوی شهر از باغ شاخی آورند
بلک آن مغزست وین دیگر چو پوست	خاصه باغی کین فلک یک برگ اوست
بوی افزون جوی و کن دفع زکام	بر نمی داری سوی آن باغ گام
تا که آن بو نور چشمانت شود	تا که آن بو جاذب جانت شود
عشق در دیده فزاید صدق را	دیدن دیده فزاید عشق را
حسها را ذوق مونس می شود	صدق بیداری هر حس می شود
(II / 3230-3231-3232-3233-3238-3239)	a 3233 عشق G : نطق Nich.

a) The branches of trees are brought from gardens to the town but the gardens and orchards are not taken to the towns; especially the garden (trees) of which the whole universe is a leaf, in other words that world is the essence and this world is the skin only. If you don't take a step towards that garden then (at least) seek more scent and get rid of your influenza. That smell will attract your life (soul) and will be the light of your eyes. Seeing with the eyes increases love, and love in the eye increases Reality. Reality awakens every sense and in this way carnal senses receive pleasure (consolation) of spiritual intimacy.

b) Whatever we see here in this world is a tiny (worth a leaf) reflection of the other world. If you want to enjoy more, then tend to the world unseen (Mift. 2-4/ p. 114) or at least try to receive a scent of the other world that can freshen you with the spiritual smell. Once you begin to feel God and observe Him with your spiritual eyes no doubt is left and you begin to love Him more.

305- Love is for the Enduring Beloved:

هست معشوق آنک او یک تو بود   مبتدا و منتهاات او بود
چون بیابی اش همانی منتظر   هم هویدا او بود هم نیز سر
صوفی ابن الوقت باشد در مثال   لیک صافی فارغست از وقت و حال
عاشق حالی نه عاشق بر منی   بر امید حال بر من می تنی
تو بهر حالی که باشی می طلب   آب می جو دایماً ای خشک لب
هر کرا بینی طلبگار ای پسر   یار او شو پیش او انداز سر

(III / 1418-1419-1426-1428-1439-1446)

a) The real beloved should be single and he should be the beginning and the end. When you find such a beloved, don't wait for any other for he is both manifest as well as mystery. Verbally, the Sufi is "a son of time" but a real Sufi has nothing to do with time or state. You are in love with the spiritual states, but not Me, you are attached to Me from the hope of the state. Keep on searching for God in whatever state you may be; you have dry lips keep on looking for water. O my son, whomsoever you see busy with the search, become his friend and devote yourself to him.

b) The first lines refer to God for only God is One and Everlasting, so look for His love. Many say that a Sufi is "a son of time", that is, he lives only for the moment he is in and he does not think of the future or the past. Rumi says actually a true Sufi is without any concept of time and the spiritual states he undergoes, because his aim is God not the states. Don't be attached at any state but keep searching for God because it is a long journey towards Him. If you find others who are searching for God also make friends with them and pray to God for His Mercy, "Reveal your wonderful love and save me" (the Bible, Pss. 17/7).

306- All praises go to God directly or indirectly:

مدحها شد جملگی آمیخته   کوزها در یک لگن در ریخته
زآنک خود ممدوح جز یک بیش نیست   کیشها زین روی جز یک کیش نیست
دانک هر مدحی بنور حق رود   بر صور و اشخاص عاریت بود
معنی تکبیر اینست ای امام   کای خدا پیش تو ما قربان شدیم

(III / 2123-2124-2125-2143)

a) All praises become joined like the jars poured out into one basin because the Praised One is not more than one and, therefore, all religions are one. Know that all praises go to God by His light and they (the praises) are lent to forms and persons (temporarily). O *Imam* (the priest) the meaning of "*Allah-u Akbar*" is "O my Lord we sacrifice ourselves to Thee".

b) All praises go to God directly or indirectly for they are like the water-drops that meet ultimately at the Sea. As long as all religions (or orders as given by T.) worship the same One God, their religions are the same for they praise the same God. It is the greedy lower self that divides people into different groups. Praises of God depending on His attributes are unchanging (as we see in all religions) and were there long before man came to earth so they are borrowed by people and things. They are nobody's invention. In the last verses, Rumi reminds the Muslim priest (Imam) what he says everyday when calling people to prayers, "*Allah-u Akbar* = Allah is the greatest", actually means "sacrifice everything for Him".

307- When loves arrives all kinds of religious disputes come to an end:

جز خیال وصل او دیار نیست	اندرو جز عشق یزدان کار نیست
خانه‌ام پرست از عشق احد	خانه را من روفتم از نیك و بد
دو جهان یك دانه پیش نول عشق	هرچه جز عشقست شد ماكول عشق
عاشق آزادی نخواهد تا ابد	بنده آزادی طمع دارد ز جد
ورنه كی وسواس را بستست كس	پوزبند وسوسه عشقست و بس
كه بدان تدبیر اسباب سماست	غیر این عقل تو حق را عقلهاست
كو ز گفت وگو شود فریاد رس	عشق برد بحث را ای جان و بس

(V / 2803-2804-2726-2729-3230-3234-3240)

a) There is no idea of any other work than love of God in the heart of the saint. Nothing else dwells in his heart but the idea of meeting Him. I have swept the house clean of good and evil and it is full of Divine Love. Whatever exists there except love is devoured by love and the two worlds are like a tiny grain in the presence of love's beak. Can a grain eat up a bird? Can the manger ever feed on the horse? A slave wants whole heartedly to be set free (Baki, p. 245) while a lover wants to be a slave forever. It is only love that can close one's mouth and eradicate temptations, otherwise who can close the door of temptations? God has other intelligences than yours with which He rules (solves) the celestial affairs. My dear friend, it is love that has won religious conflict (has overcome all discussions) and can help you when you are fed up with (sarcastic) religious conflicts and speeches.

b) It is by means of love that you can get rid of worldly worries, and its greatness brings all disputes to an end. Love is above the religious conflicts and it looks meaningless when you attain God's proximity, but to reach that stage you need religious discipline.

308- Love is beyond the limits of belief or disbelief:

زآنك چشم وهم شد محجوب فقد وهم را مژده ست و پیش عقل نقد
لاجرم از کفر و ایمان برترست زآنك عاشق در دم نقدست مست
کوست مغز و کفر دین او را دو پوست کفر و ایمان هر دو خود دربان اوست
قشر پیوسته بـمغز جان خوش است قشرهای خشك را جا آتش است
بر قراضه مهر سکه چون نهم زر عقلت ریزه است ای متهم
تا شوی خوش چون سمرقند و دمشق جمع باید کرد اجزا را بعشق

(IV / 3278-3280-3281-3283-3287-3289)

a) For opinion (thought) some incidents can be good news while for intellect they are ready cash (reality) because the eye of an opinion is veiled by misunderstanding. A true lover is intoxicated by the present love (ready cash) and is, therefore, beyond belief or disbelief. Both belief and disbelief are his door keepers for he is like a kernel (the stone of a fruit) and for him faith and infidelity are like the peel (of a fruit). The dry peel (of a fruit) is fuel for fire while peel attached to the kernel is happy. The gold of your intellect has fallen into pieces, O you doubter! How can I put a stamp on the scattered pieces of gold? You should unite them all by means of love so that you may become prosperous and happy like Samarqand and Damascus.

b) A lover's ideas are above belief or disbelief while a sceptical man is happy to be busy with some tiny signs of God. Love, by making the lover think only of God takes him up to a stage where infidelity or belief, scepticism or blind faith change into one reality: the Beauty of God.

"A lover is a marvellous thing, for he receives strength, grows, and gains vitality from the Image of his Beloved. Why is this surprising? The image of Leyla gave constant strength to Majnun and became his food (spiritual source). When the image of a derivative beloved possesses the potency and effective power to strengthen the lover, why do you wonder that the True Beloved's Image should bestow strength upon the lover, both in his outward form and in the Unseen World?..." (Discourses, p. 119-120).

Those who stop at the peel of a fruit (discussion of belief or disbelief) and go dry with it, deserve the loveless existence. The lover being closer to the Essence is more confident. A sceptical man's ideas are scattered and unsettled and it is love that can bring them together.

309- Be a moth not a candle for the sake of love:

صید بودن خوشتر از صیادیست	عشق می‌گوید بگوشم پست پست
آفتابی را رها کن ذره شو	گول می کن خویش را و غره شو
دعوی شمعی مکن پروانه باش	بر درم ساکن شو و بی خانه باش
سلطنت بینی نهان در بندگی	تا ببینی چاشنی زندگی
(V / 411- 412-413-414)	

a) Love whispers into my ears, "It is better to be a prey than a hunter". Cheat yourself and be deluded. Give up being a sun, be an atom. Be without a house and live at My gate. Don't claim to be a candle and be a moth; so that you may taste (the real) life and observe the kingdom hidden by slavery.

b) Nothing can be claimed in the Presence of the Beloved. The way that leads to Him is the way of selflessness:

"True thought is that which opens a way, the true way upon which a king advances,
The true king is he who is a king within himself, not because of treasures and armies..." (M II/3207-3208).

310- A true lover is above need and greed:

بند هستی نیست هر کو صادق است	عشق نان بی نان غذای عاشق است
عاشقانرا هست بی سرمایه سود	عاشقانرا کار نبود با وجود
چون عدم یك رنگ و نفس واحدند	عاشقان اندر عدم خیمه زدند
جوع ازین رویست قوت جانها	عشق باشد لوت و پوت جانها
(III / 3020-3021-3024-3034)	

a) The food of a lover is the love of the bread that has no existence, he who is a true lover is not a captive of existence. Lovers have nothing to do with existence, they have a prophet without a capital. Lovers have pitched their tents in non-existence and they are one-coloured and one-souled like the world of non-existence. Love is the meat and drink of souls, hunger from this point of view is the energy of souls.

b) It is the intoxication of love for God that renders one needless and indifferent to worldly demands. In other words, someone who is still fond of delicious foods and rich living cannot be a true lover of God for a true lover of God does not live for himself. The lovers of God are made selfless in the Sea of Unity.

311- Every atom of the universe shares in the Essence of Love:

هیچ عاشق خود نباشد وصل جو   که نه معشوقش بود جویای او

در دل تو مهر حق چون شد دوتو   هست حق را بی گمانی مهر تو

جذب آبست این عطش در جان ما   ما از آن او و او هم آن ما

جمله اجزای جهان زآن حکم پیش   جفت جفت و عاشقان جفت خویش

هست هر جزوی ز عالم جفت خواه   راست همچون کهربا و برگ کاه

(III / 4393-4396-4499-4401-4403)

a) No lover seeks union by himself unless the beloved looks for him. When the love of God is doubled in your heart, surely God also has love for you. Attraction to water causes thirst in us because we are a part of it and it is a part of us. All the particles (atoms) of the universe are paired as mates (and they are in love with each other). Every atom of the universe is in search of its mate (attracted by poles) like an amber and the blade of a straw.

b) All things take part in God's Love. Since we contain water and other elements in our body, it is attracted to the earth and due to this attraction it falls sick and wants to go back to its physical origin (Koner, p. 409). Similarly, being a particle of God, our spirit is attracted to Him. Those whose spirit is unaware of the Origin will remain between the devil and the deep sea which brings about a sense of great oppression. Rumi further explains the point:

"The body's attraction is to plants and running waters because its origin belongs to them; the tendency of spirit is towards wisdom and knowledge (that leads to Him) while, again, attraction of body is to orchards and meadows and vines" (III/4436-4437). It is a duty of the lover to find his Beloved who is hidden behind the curtains of material things.

312- Why does God sometimes not fulfill your resolutions?:

عزمها و قصدها در ماجرا گاه گاهی راست می آید ترا
تا بطمع آن دل نیت کند بار دیگر نیت را بشکنند
ور بکلی بی مرادت داشتی دل شدی نومید امل کی کاشتی
عاشقان از بی مرادیهای خویش با خبر گشتند از مولای خویش

a 4665 عاشقان G + N : عاقلان T + Mift (III / 4462-4463-4464-4466)

a) In some cases your decisions and resolutions are fulfilled. This is because your heart may form an intention but again He destroys your decisions. If He kept you completely disappointed your heart wouldn't sow new hopes. Lovers, however, by means of their disappointments become fully aware of their Beloved.

b) Many times things move according to our will, but God sometimes frustrates them to remind us of His Existence. In order to keep our hopes fresh, He does not completely disappoint us. Lovers of God are exceptions for by practising disappointments, they train themselves to depend on the will of God and wait patiently for the results that God wants them to experience.

313- Love is beyond all ties:

با دو عالم عشق را بیگانگی اندرو هفتاد و دو دیوانگی
غیر هفتاد و دو ملت کیش او تخت شاهان تخته بندی پیش او
مطرب عشق این زند وقت سماع بندگی بند و خداوندی صداع
پس چه باشد عشق دریای عدم در شکسته عقل را آنجا قدم
بندگی و سلطنت معلوم شد زین دو پرده عاشقی مکتوم شد
کاشکی هستی زبانی داشتی تا زهستان پرده ها بر داشتی
هرچ گویی ای دم هستی از آن پرده دیگر برو بستی بدان

(III / 4719-4721-4722-4723-4724-4725-4726)

a 4719 بیگانگی G : بیگانگی‌است Mift. - b دیوانگی G : دیوانگی‌است Mift.

a) Love is a stranger in the two worlds (here and hereafter). It has seventy two kinds of (many) madness. His (lover of God's) religion is beyond that of seventy two nations' religions, and kings' thrones are like tied up pieces of wood. At the time of

Sema (Dervish Dance) the singer says, "Slavery is a tie and lordship is a headache". So what is love? It is the sea of non-existence where the legs of intellect are broken. Slavery and kingship are known (manifest) while love is concealed behind these two curtains. Would that our being had a tongue, it would have removed the veils (revealed secrets) of the existent beings. O you breath of this existence whatever you utter about Him you add more curtains to His secrets.

b) Here Rumi makes clear that love for God is above all formalities of religions, feelings, and languages. Rumi says, "Alas were there a spiritual tongue, too, that would reveal the secrets of the eternal world. With this mortal tongue no matter how hard you may try, you fail to define love; and the more we try to explain it, the more complicated it becomes".

314- Only by the Grace of God can love increase:

چون بجویی تو بتوفیق حسن   باده آب جان بود ابریق تن
چون بیفزاید می توفیق را   قوت می بشکند ابریق را
بی تفکر پیش هر داننده هست   آنک با شوریده شوراننده هست
(III / 4743-4744-4748)

a) When you desire (or seek) love, by the grace of God your spirit turns into wine and your body into a jar (of Divine Wine). When He increases the wine of His grace the jar falls into pieces. Every knowledgeable man knows without thinking that where there is a disturbance, there is a disturber.

b) To attain the love of God, you have to desire first and when God pours the wine of His love in your body, it breaks, and when you feel such a disturbance, know that God is there.

315- Love discovers the real Beauty:

عشق در هنگام استیلا و خشم   زشت گرداند لطیفانرا بچشم
هر زمرد را نماید گندنا   غیرت عشق این بود معنی لا
لا اله الا هو اینست ای پناه   که نماید مه ترا دیگ سیاه
(IV / 866-867-868)

a) Love at the time of domination and anger (motivation) makes beautiful things look hideous to the eyes. Jealousy of love shows each diamond (emerald) as a leek; and this is the real meaning of "there is no God but Him" (for everything except His face looks ugly to you).

b) When the love of God dominates one's heart nothing looks more beautiful than His face. The moon will look like a black (burnt) pan (see vr. No. 868). The actual meaning of the Koranic verse, "There is no God but Him" is that there is nothing as beautiful as God.

316- God loves mankind as a mother loves her child:

گفت چون طفلی بپیش والده | وقت قهرش دست هم در وی زده
خود نداند که جز او دیار هست | هم از و مخمور هم از اوست مست
مادرش گر سیلیی بر وی زند | هم بمادر آید و بر وی تند
از کسی یاری نخواهد غیر او | اوست جمله شر او و خیر او

(IV / 2923-2924-2925-2926)

a) He (God) said to Moses, "Your state is that of a child who sticks to its mother even if she is angry. The baby is unaware of other people of the house, it is intoxicated with its mother's love. Even if its mother smites the baby, it goes back to her and stays around her. The baby asks for no one's help except its mother's and she is its good and its evil (everything)".

b) God only punishes a man for his own good. There are various reasons for punishing him. Try to understand your sin and pray to God sincerely for His forgiveness. Go back to Him like a child for it is only His love that can protect you from every trouble.

317- A draught of the Real Beauty:

جرعه بر ریختی زآن خفید جام | بر زمین خاک من کاس الکرام
هست بر زلف و رخ از جرعه ش نشان | خاک را شاهان همی لیسند از آن
جرعه خاک آمیز چون مجنون کند | مر ترا تا صاف او خود چون کند
جان چو بی این جیفه بنماید جمال | من نتانم گفت لطف آن وصال

(V / 372-373-375-385)

a) You (my Lord) have poured a draught upon the dusty earth out of that secret cup (of love-wine) from which your prophets and saints (select people) drink. There is a sign of that draught on the locks and face (cheeks) of the fair; it is because of this that kings lick that earth (physical beauty). If His draught mixed with dusty clay makes people so mad, then how effective His pure wine (of love) will be! When the Spirit exposes His comeliness without the carcass, I cannot explain the pleasure of that particular moment of meeting.

b) It is the Beauty of God in everything that attracts people. Ever since God created this world by pouring a draught of His love wine onto the earth, all beauties carry the signs of that draught on their cheeks and locks; and it is due to this draught that great kings and people with high rank lick and kiss that clay (physical bodies). This is actually the spiritual Beauty of God hidden behind physical curtains. If the hidden beauty can make people go mad, then what will happen if God exposes His Beauty?

"I hide thy secrets even from my being (body), for a stranger is not fit to be a fellow-holder of a secret".

(From Divan-i Khusrau, p. 32)

318- God Himself is the reward of love:

عاشقانرا شادمانی و غم اوست   دست مزد و اجرت خدمت هم اوست

غیر معشوق ار تماشایی بود   عشق نبود هرزه سودایی بود

عشق آن شعله ست کو چون بر فروخت   هرچه جز معشوق باقی جمله سوخت

این کسی داند که روزی زنده بود   از کف این جان جان جامی ربود

وآنک چشم او ندیدست آن رخان   پیش او جانست این تف دخان

عمر و مرگ این هر دو با حق خوش بود   بی خدا آب حیات آتش بود

از خدا غیر خدا را خواستن   ظن افزونیست و کلی کاستن

(V / 586-587-588-594-595-771-773)

a) For lovers of God happiness and sorrow are God Himself; He is their wages for service. If they have a view other than their Beloved's, it is not love but only vain passion (for them). Love is that flame which, when it blazes up, burns everything except the Beloved. This is known by him who was alive for a day (a short time) and received a cup from the Soul of Souls; and he whose eyes failed to see those faces, to him this heat of smoke (the dust and clay) is the life. Both life and death are sweet with God; without Him water of life (eternity) is fire. To ask from God anything other than God Himself is to have the feeling that things desired increase in number although they decrease (or perish).

b) A lover's heart contains nothing but the sight of God. God Himself is the price for his deeds and he is not concerned with paradise or hell, as the famous woman saint Rabia Adeviyye (d. A.D. 801) used to pray to God, "O my Lord if I pray Thee for the fear of Hell put me in Hell; and if I pray Thee for the sake of Paradise, forbid Paradise to me; I pray to Thee for I love only Thee". Those who do not see God's epiphany in things, for them all forms of dust and clay are realities and their eyes remain veiled.

319- Those who are true lovers of God do not fear death:

تلخ نبود پیش ایشان مرگ تن   چون روند از چاه و زندان در چمن

وا رهیدند از جهان پیچ پیچ   کس نگرید بر فوات هیچ هیچ

گوید ای یزدان مرا در تن مبر   تا درین گلشن کنم من کر و فر

(V / 1713-1714-1723)

a) For lovers of God physical death is not bitter because they pass from a prison and a well to a large garden. They get free from the painful world and no one cries over the death of nothing. The lover of God prays to God, "O my Lord don't put me back in the physical body again so that I may live a happy life in the garden of roses (joys)".

b) Lovers of God are already physically dead for they have no other desire than God. Rumi himself called his death "The meeting with the Beloved". A lover of God is happy to be close to God and he does not want to come back to this world.

320- Due to love nothing is left in me but the Beloved:

گر نبودی عشق هستی کی بدی   کی زدی نان بر تو و کی تو شدی

نان تو شد از چه ز عشق و اشتها   ورنه نان را کی بدی تا جان رهی

بر من از هستی من جز نام نیست   در وجودم جز تو ای خوش کام نیست

همچو سنگی کو شود کل لعل ناب   پر شود او از صفات آفتاب

(V / 2012-2013-2023-2025)

a) If there were no love, there would be no existence. How should bread attach itself to you and become a part of you? Bread became you because of your love (desire) and appetite, otherwise how could bread have access to your soul? In my being there is left nothing but my name; in my being there exists nothing but Thee who is my only desire (see Baki, p. 190), like the stone that turns entirely into a pure ruby and is filled with the qualities of the sun.

b) Food is accepted and digested by our body because of desire and want (love). If there were no love, bread would not dissolve in the body and change into a part of it. Similarly, it is the love of God that annihilates us in Him.

321- A difference between an ascetic and a mystic:

عقل حارس خیره سر گشت و تباه   تا در آمد حکم و تقدیر اله
سیر زاهد هر مهی یك روزه راه   سیر عارف هر دمی تا تخت شاه
وصف بنده مبتلای فرج و جوف   عشق وصف ایزدست اما که خوف
(V / 2166-2180-2185)

a) When the decree of God arrives, the protective reason becomes giddy-headed and dies. A mystic's progress is every moment towards the throne of the King while the progress of a pious man (ascetic) is one day's journey every month. Love is the attribute of God but fear is the characteristic of a man who is addicted to sex and stomach.

b) In these verses Rumi makes a distinction between an ascetic who prays and fasts out of the fear of God and His Hell (wrath), and a mystic (or lover of God) who does everything for God alone. A mystic is not afraid of God but afraid of himself and of losing God. A worldly man is afraid to lose this world which is his only property, but a lover of God is happy to lose this world for the sake of God.

322- God does not need sleep or food neither do His lovers:

روحها را می کند بی خورد و خواب   او ندارد خواب و خور چون آفتاب
تا ببینی در تجلی روی من   که بیآ من باش یا هم خوی من
همچو باران می رسم از آسمان   بانگ آبم من بگوش تشنگان
بانگ آب و تشنه و آنگاه خواب   بر جه ای عاشق بر آور اضطراب
(VI / 578-579-591-592)

a) He (the Beloved) needs no sleep or food, like the sun and therefore He makes the spirits also to be without food and sleep. He (God) says, "Come be Me or be in My Nature so that you may see My Face when I unveil it. I am the sound of water in the ears of the thirsty, I come down like rain from the sky (to water your dry land). Move on, you lover, free yourself of agitation (see Baki, p. 427). Look, there is the sound of water and you are thirsty, how can you sleep?" (Mift. p. 158).

b) Since God, the Beloved, does not sleep (as the Koran says, "No slumber can seize Him, nor sleep" II/254), His love makes the soul like Him. His rain of Divine Love falls continuously and if He finds you asleep (negligent to His love) He can deprive you of that rain. So be alert all the time.

323- In love humiliation and reputation are all the same:

بر در ناموس ای عاشق مه ایست	عشق و ناموس ای برادر راست نیست
نقل و قوت قوت مست آن بود	مطرب جان مونس مستان بود
وین شراب تن ازاین مطرب چرد	آن شراب حق بدآن مطرب برد
تا که در هر کوزه چه بود آن نگر	جسمها چون کوزه های بسته سر
کوزه این تن پر از زهر ممات	کوزه آن تن پر از آب حیات
(VI / 612-644-646-650-651)	

612 a عشق و ناموس ای Y + G : ای برادر عشق ناموس Mift.

a) O brother, love and reputation (pride) are not agreeable things, therefore, do not stand at the gate of reputation. A musician is a good friend of the intoxicated; he is like the appetizer, food, and source of energy. Spiritual wine is offered by that musician but carnal wine is offered by the worldly musician. Bodies are like tied up jars, so you can see what they contain. The jar of that (spiritual) body is full of life-water, but the jar of this body is full of life-poison.

b) In love no personal humiliation or reputation is of any value. The lover of God (or a saint) who is a musician of that world leads you to eternity and Reality while the musician of this world leads you along with wine to carnal pleasures. Music is of two kinds: 1- that which invites you to the love of God 2- that which leads you to worldly pleasures. Rumi himself preferred the former type of music. Man's body is like different jars, some are filled with the life-water while others are filled with poisonous water.

324- Everything is in action due to love:

بر قضای عشق دل بنهاده اند	عاشقان در سیل تند افتاده اند
روز و شب گردان و نالان بی قرار	همچو سنگ آسیا اندر مدار
تا نگوید کس که آن جو راکدست	گردشش بر جوی جویان شاهدست
گردش دولاب گردونی ببین	گر نمی بینی تو جو را در کمین
ای دل اختروار آرامی مجو	چون قراری نیست گردون را ازو
در عناصر جوشش و گردش نگر	گر نمی بینی تو تدویر قدر
(VI / 910-911-912-913-914-916)	

269

a) Lovers (of God) have fallen in a strong flood and have set their hearts on the Command of Love. They are like a millstone turning day and night restlessly moaning. Its turning is a proof for those who look for a river and thus nobody can say that the river is motionless. If you fail to see the hidden river, then do see the moving (or turning) water-wheel of heaven. Since the heavens are restless because of Him (or because of His love) you, too, my heart like a star give up rest. If you don't see the revolution or action of Fate then see the action and movement in the elements.

b) The restlessness of lovers is due to the action of Divine Love that has put all atoms, stars and galaxies into action. How can the tiny heart of a lover stay still. If you cannot see the motion of the river of the Divine Love, then at least see the motion of the spiritual currents that are the waves of that Sea. Without God's love nothing would be in action. Nothing would grow and there would be no life on the earth (see also V/3854). Stars and planets would all come to an end.

325- If repentance is a worm, then love is a dragon:

توبه وصف خلق و آن وصف خدا	توبه کرم و عشق همچون اژدها
عاشقی بر غیر او باشد مجاز	عشق ز اوصاف خدای بی نیاز
ظاهرش نور اندرون دود آمدست	زآنک آن حسن زراندود آمدست
جسم ماند گنده و رسوا و بد	وا رود آن حسن سوی اصل خود
(VI / 970-971-972-974)	

a) Repentance is like a worm while love is like a dragon; repentance is the attribute of people (Baki, p. 495 not "man" Nich.) and love is the attribute of God. Love is the attribute of God who needs nothing; love for anything other than God is unreal. Because other (the worldly) beauty is like a gilded object, the outside of it is bright while the inside of it is dark like smoke. The (real) beauty goes back to its Source and the body remains dirty (rotten), mean and bad.

b) The beauty of this world is the reflection of that Real Beauty. Since love is the attribute of God, it is eternal and goes back to its Source even if the physical body comes to an end.

326- Reason seeks profitable things while love is reckless:

عشق باشد کآن طرف بر سر دود   عقل راه نا امیدی کی رود

عقل آن جوید کز آن سودی برد   لا ابالی عشق باشد نی خرد

عقل از سودای او کورست و کر   نیست از عاشق کسی دیوانه تر

دفتر طب را فرو شوید بخون   گر طبیبی را رسد زین گون جنون

(VI / 1966-1967-1979-1981)

a) Reason never treads the path to desperation. It is love that runs headlong towards that. Reason seeks beneficial things while love is reckless. There is no one more insane than the lover for his reason is blind and deaf because of love. If a doctor is caught by such madness, he will wash his medical book with (the tears of) blood.

b) Carnal reason is egoistic. Since love for God is beyond the boundaries of lower self, it may appear to be madness to others. If a doctor who bases his diagnoses on logic falls in love with God, he will leave knowledge aside and will surrender to God's will. Rumi advises further:

"O you who have entered the religion of love, turn your face to yourself, because it is the Inner One of you that is in love with you".

327- Lovers pray twenty four hours a day:

عاشقانرا فی صلاة دائمون   پنج وقت آمد نماز و رهنمون

زآنک بی دریا ندارند انس جان   نیست زرغبا وظیفه ماهیان

در پی هم این و آن چون روز و شب   عشق مستسقیست مستسقی طلب

در میانشان فارق و فاروق نیست   در دل عاشق بجز معشوق نیست

(VI / 2669-2672-2675-2680)

a) The ritual prayer that is a guide is five times a day, but lovers are involved in prayers twenty four hours'. "Visit me once a week" is not the ration of fishes for they have no spiritual joy (or love) without the sea. The lover is thirsty and seeks a thirsty one, like night that looks for day. In the heart of lover there is nothing (no other idea) but the idea of the Beloved and there is nothing to separate them or divide them.

b) There are five times prayers in Islam to be offered but for lovers of God those are not enough for they are with God twenty four hours a day as God says, "Those who remain steadfast to their prayer" (the Koran, LXX/23). In other words a lover has the realisation of God's Presence in every moment and when it settles in the depth of his heart, every breath becomes his prayer (see also Jafer, p.188). A true lover is like a fish he cannot live without the water of the sea of Love.

328- Love is a great power:

جملـه رنجـوران دوا دارنـد امیـد   نالـد ایـن رنجـور کم افزون کنیـد

خوشتـر از ایـن سم ندیدم شربتی   زیـن مرض خوشتـر نباشد صحتی

زیـن گنـه بهتـر نباشـد طاعتـی   سالها نسبـت بدیـن دم ساعتـی

(VI / 4598-4599-4600)

a) All the sick hope to recover but not this sick one: (the lover) cries and says, "Increase my sickness" and he continues to say, "I have not seen any sweeter drink than this poison and there is not any better health than this sickness from love. No act of piety can be better than this sin (of love), years compared with this moment are like an hour".

b) Lovers' only cure is the sight of their Beloved and all transient things such as time, disease, pains, fatal poison are valueless things. Love power is greater than all these and takes the lover to a high stage where God's Beauty gives him endless pleasure, which is worth the price.

CHAPTER X

Step VI: Devotion and Submission

A Sufi or a lover of God is ready to die physically before his natural death and lives more and more spiritually. This means that he transfers his being, including his moral attainments, from the physical body to the spiritual one. To do this Divine Wisdom is required. In Islamic mysticism there are three stage of knowledge: 1- The knowledge of certainty *(Ilm'ul Yakin)* 2- The eye of certainty *(Ayn'ul Yakin)* 3- The truth of certainty (Hak'ul Yakin). At the first stage one tries to find God by means of intellectual proof. At the second stage, one being more unaware of lower self observes the Divine Secrets. At the third stage, one reaches the Reality and sees It with one's spiritual eyes (see Mehdi Tevhidi, p. 106). In addition to these stages there are four paths towards God: I- The Orthodox path (according to the tradition of Muhammed), *"Shariyat"* which is essential for the discipline of an individual. II- Choosing a path *"Tarikat"*. This path can be any Sufi order such as Mavleviya, Kadriya, Nakshbandiya and so on under the guidance of a Sheykh of that tarikat. One must surrender one's egoistic intellect to him, sincerely. III- *Ma'rifet* = "Gnosticism". It is attained when the mind of a Sufi is cleansed of all worldly worries. IV- *Hakikat* = "Reality" is the last goal which all religions aim at. For the true lovers of God, as explained in the previous chapter, *Shariyat* and *Tarikat* are of less importance. As Yunus says:

"Şeriat, tarikat yoldur varana,
Hakikat, ma'rifet andan içeru".

"The *Shariyat* and the *Tarikat* are ways for those who want to reach there (somewhere); but the *Hakikat* and the *Ma'rifet* are the innermost things (the essence)".

"Turn to God in humble petition" (Discourses, p. 17). Wherever you are and in whatever circumstances you find yourself, strive always to be a lover, and a passionate lover at that. Once love has become your property you will be a lover always, in the grave, at the resurrection, and in Paradise forever and ever. When you have sown wheat, wheat will assuredly grow, wheat will be in the stock, wheat will be in the oven.

Majnun desired to write to Laila. He took a pen in his hand and wrote these verses:

"Your name is upon my tongue,
Your image is in my sight,
Your memory is in my heart,
Whither then shall I write" (Discourses, p. 55).

"Your image dwells in my sight, your name is never off my tongue, your memory occupies the depths of my soul, so whither am I to write a letter, seeing that you go about in all these places? The pen broke and the page was torn" (Discourses, p. 178); "It is not feasible for you to say of the person who has found the way of God, 'He was more God's kin, more His familiar, more connected with Him than I'. So nearness to God is not to be attained save through servanthood. He is the Giver Absolute, He filled the skirt of sea with pearls, He clothed the raiment of the rose, He bestowed life and spirit on a handful of dust, all out of pure disinterest and without any precedent. All the parts of the world have their share from Him. When a person hears that in a certain city there lives a generous man who bestows mighty gifts and favours, he will naturally go there in the hope of enjoying his share of that man's bounty. Since therefore God's bountifulness is so renowned and all the world is aware of His graciousness, why do you not beg of Him and hope to receive from him a robe of honour and a rich gift?" (Discourses, p. 179-180) and "Man has three spiritual states. In the first he pays no heed to God at all, but worships and pays service to everything, woman and man, wealth and children, stones and clods; God he does not worship. When he acquires a little knowledge and awareness, then he serves nothing but God. Again, when he progresses farther in this state he becomes silent; he does not say, 'I do not serve God', neither does he say, 'I serve God', for he has transcended these two degrees" (Discourses, p. 205).

Love without devotion and sacrifice is not love. A person can love but when you say to him "Do me a favour", he says, "I love you whole heartedly but don't ask me to do you a favour". This is not love. Similarly, God has created us for the sake of love and when He asks us to save time, money, and wealth. for Him we feel reluctant to do so yet we claim to love Him. This is absurd. Love requires sacrifice, the kind of sacrifice that Majnun made for Leyli *(Laila)*. "How heavy seems to you waking up in the morning (for prayers), truly you don't love Me but the sleep" (M. Iqbal).

329- Be non-existent here so that you are reborn there:

محو می باید نه نحو اینجا بدان گر تو محوی بی خطر در آب ران

آب دریا مرده را بر سر نهد ور بود زنده ز دریا کی رهد

چون بمردی تو ز اوصاف بشر بحر اسرارت نهد بر فرق سر

(I / 2841-2842-2843)

a) You need self-effacement in this world not grammar. If you are self-effaced then you can enter the water (sea) without fear for the sea-water carries a dead body (on its surface) but if you are still alive, you cannot escape the sea. If you kill your human characteristics, the sea will carry you on to the top of its head.

b) In this world you need to study the art of denying your lower self more than you need to make scientific studies of words, philosophy, logic and so on. In case you want to be helped by God (here the Sea) then depend on Him completely just as a dead body leaves itself to the sea. In other words sacrifice your lower self to the path of God.

330- Ask for the help of God only:

نصرت از وی خواه کو خوش ناصراست   عیسی روح تو با تو حاضر است

عیش کم نآید تو بر درگاه باش   بر دل خود کم نه اندیشه معاش

خاصه چون باشد عزیز درگهی   ترک چون باشد بیابد خرگهی

(II / 450-454-456)

a) The Jesus of your spirit is always with you. Ask for his help because he is a good helper. Don't burden your heart with worries about earning your living, your food will not lessen if you stay at the threshold of God. If there is a Turk he will certainly find a tent, especially when he is favoured by the Court (of God).

b) Your Jesus, like enlivening spirit, is with you twenty four hours a day so ask its help, "He is with you wheresoever you may be" (the Koran, LVII/4) and "Truly God is He who bestows the best provision" (XXII/58). When a brave soldier *(Turk)* comes to the battlefield he is provided with all the requirements by the commander (see Mift. 2-1/p. 172) especially when he is favoured by the ruling King. This verse does not invite a person to mendicity or laziness. On the contrary, it invites one to serve God (like a fighting Turkish soldier) and to ask only from God.

c) Jesus: Signifies the holy spirit; the pure essence of a man.

331- God's assistance is like the sea water:

جمله نالان پیش آن دیان فرد   صد هزاران عاقل اندر وقت درد

استعینوا منه صبراً او صلات   هر نبیی زو بر آورده برات

آب در یم جو مجو در خشک جو   هین ازو خواهید نه از غیر او

(IV / 1171-1181-1182)

a) At the time of worries many (hundreds and thousands of) wise men cry (for help) to the Unique Judge. Every prophet has received from Him the guarantee and "Seek help of Him with patience and prayers" (is the command of the Koran). Beware, ask of Him and not of anyone else, seek water in the Sea not in the dried up river-bed.

b) All wise men (including scientists and doctors), when they find themselves helpless they ask for God's help because he is a Unique Judge. Every prophet has obtained a guarantee of God's help for his people as the Koran says, "O you who believe! seek help with patience, perseverance, and prayers: for God is with those who patiently persevere" (II/153). Restraining from fear, anger and carnal desires is part of patience. Ask only from God for whatever you need not from the people of rank (for they are like a dry river-bed).

332- A perfect man's body is House of God:

کعبه هر چندی که خانه بر اوست   خلقت من نیز خانه سّر اوست
تا بکرد آن کعبه را درویی نرفت   واندرین خانه بجز آن حی نرفت
چشم نیکو باز کن در من نگر   تا ببینی نور حق اندر بشر
(II / 2245-2246-2249)

a) Without doubt if the *Ka'abe* is a place for worshipping Him, yet my body is also a house of His secrets. Ever since He made the *Ka'abe* He did not go into it, but this house (of my body) none other but He (Who is Everlasting) entered. Open your eyes wide so that you may see the light of God in human kind and me.

b) For the Muslims the *Ka'abe* is the centre for prayers and thus the house of God but a heart of a lover is a place where God visits continuously. If your spiritual eyes are open, you can see His part in man.

333- Death is a natural thing:

زندگانی آشتی ضدهاست   مرگ آن کاندر میانشان جنگ خاست
این عجب نبود که میش از گرگ جست   این عجب کین میش دل در گرگ بست
(I / 1293-1292)

a) Life depends on peace (reconcilement) of the contrary elements. Death occurs when wars take place among them. It is not strange that a sheep runs away from a wolf, on the contrary it is strange that the sheep falls in love with the wolf.

b) It is due to God's command that opposite elements like heat and water stay together in the human body and when they revolt (lose their balance) death takes place. The surprising thing is not the death itself, but how these different elements in the body, like a wolf (lower self) and a sheep (soul), can stay together? Their separation is natural (Mift 2/p. 147 and T. 3/682).

334- He who has more awareness, has more of life:

خاك و آب و باد و نار با شرر   بی خبر با ما و با حق با خبر

ما بعكس آن ز غير حق خبير   بی خبر از حق وز چندين نذير

جان نباشد جز خبر در آزمون   هر كرا افزون خبر جانش فزون

جان ما از جان حيوان بيشتر   از چه ز آن رو كه فزون دارد خبر

a 2370 خاك و آب : N + G   T آب و باد   (II / 2370-2371-3326-3327)

a) Clay, water, air, and burning fire are unaware of us but they are aware of God. We, on the contrary, are aware of everything other than God and unaware of His messages. At the time of trial, life is nothing but consciousness; and he who has more of that has more of life. If our life is above that of animals, it is due to the fact that man has more conscience.

b) Inanimate things are submissive to the Divine Will without objection. Even the cells of our body obey the command of God but many of us because of our partial insight (trivial consciousness) deny God's presence. We are in the middle. We should either be like the angels to understand fully what God is or be inanimate (elements) to obey Him without thinking. A semi-learned person is always dangerous. Man being half animal and half spirit, is in between except the saints who have ascended to the angelic stage.

335- To be able to see one's own faults is greatness:

ای خنك جانی كه عيب خويش ديد   هر كه عيبی گفت آن بر خود خريد

ز آنك نيم او و ز عيبستان بدست   و آن دگر نيمش ز غيبستان بدست

گر همان عيبت نبود ايمن مباش   بوك آن عيب از تو گردد نيز فاش

(II / 3034-3035-3038)

a) How fortunate is the man who is able to see his own faults. Anyone who finds fault with others, actually buys them for himself because half the body of a man belongs to this world (full of faults) and half of his body belongs to the other (faultless) world. If you don't have the fault you found with others; don't be sure, maybe the same fault can appear in you.

b) An ordinary man is half animal and half spirit, he can either be ruled by animality or by spirituality. It depends on his efforts. As long as we are bound to this world we are liable to make mistakes. So don't find faults with others but help them to get free of their materialistic fetters that hinder their devotion to God.

336- The real intoxication:

مستی کآید ز بوی شاه فرد / صد خم می در سر و مغز آن نکرد
باده حق راست باشد نی دروغ / دوغ خوردی دوغ خوردی دوغ دوغ
ور نگویی عیب خود باری خمش / از نمایش وز دغل خود را مکش
گر تو نقدی یافتی مگشا دهان / هست در ره سنگهای امتحان
راستی پیش آر یا خاموش کن / وآنگهان رحمت بین و نوش کن
تو دعا را سخت گیر و می شخول / عاقبت برهاندت از دست غول

(III / 673-689-742-743-752-757)

a) The intoxication caused by the smell of the smell of the Only King is greater than the intoxication caused by many (hundred) jars of wine in the head and brain. The wine of God is true not false, you have drunk buttermilk and buttermilk. If you don't want to say your faults, then at least be silent and don't kill your Self with show and trickery. If you have any (spiritual) money, do not open your mouth for there are touchstones on this path, beware! Be honest or be quiet, then see the mercy of God and drink it silently. If you want to get rid of the Devil, stick to prayers and cry to God.

b) These verses address those who hypocritically claim to be lovers of God. They understand a few spiritual facts (for instance dreams) and begin to boast of them. Here silence is better for pride is the characteristic of the Devil.

337- The intoxication of this world is temporary:

ای سگ گرگین زشت از حرص و جوش / پوستین شیر را بر خود مپوش
غره شیرت بخواهد امتحان / نقش شیر و آنگه اخلاق سگان
همچو من از مستی شهوت ببر / مستی شهوت ببین اندر شتر
باز این مستی، شهوت در جهان / پیش مستی، ملک دان مستهان
قطره از بادهای آسمان / بر کند جان را ز می وز ساقیان
که ببویی دل در آن می بسته اند / خم باده این جهان بشکسته اند
آب شیرین تا نخوردی آب شور / خوش بود خوش چون درون دیده نور

(III / 788-789-819-820-823-825-822)

b 822 خوش بود : G خوش نماید MM.

a) O ugly mangy dog, don't put on the skin of a lion because of your greedy lust and excitement. Soon the roar of a (real) lion will test you and then your resemblance to a lion will disappear and your canine character will show up again. Like me get rid of the intoxication of lust and (to learn a lesson) look at the intoxication of a camel. The intoxication of lust in this world is valueless when compared with the intoxication of the angels. A single drop of celestial wine makes one give up the worldly intoxication and the cup bearer (the beauty). Since they (the pure souls) have set their hearts on the smell of that wine, they have broken the wine jars of this world into pieces... As long as you have not tasted the pure water, to you this briny water will taste nice, like a lovely light in the eyes.

b) Rumi addresses false Sheykhs who try to hide themselves under the skin of lions although they are like greedy dogs. Don't be temporarily drunk like a camel for spiritual intoxication is everlasting; if you have not tasted spiritual joy, in your eyes this worldly intoxication has meaning. It is the spiritual drunkenness that will keep your eyes closed to the charms of this world. "Now this revolving (of the universe) takes place within a narrow space, for such are the circumstances of this material world. Cry unto God, saying, 'O God, grant to me, instead of my present journey and revolving, another revolving which shall be spiritual; seeing that all needs are fulfilled by Thee, and Thy bounty and compassion are universal over all creatures'. So represent your needs constantly, and never be without the remembrance of Him. For the remembrance of Him is strength and feathers and wings to the bird of the spirit" (Discourses, p. 183).

338- To a true lover of God no religious duties look heavy:

مست باشد در ره طاعات مست	هر که خوابی دید از روز ألست
بی فتور و بی گمان و بی ملال	می کشد چون اشتر مست این جوال
اندرین دنیا نشد بنده و مرید	در ألست آنکو چنین خوابی ندید
می نهد با صد تردد بی یقین	پای پیش و پای پس در راه دین
(III / 2348-2349-2353-2355)	

a) He who has dreamed of the Day of "*Alest*" is intoxicated with (the wine of) devotion. He, like a drunken camel, carries this load without infirmity, suspicion, and fatigue. He who failed to dream of the day of "*Alest*" cannot be an obedient person or a disciple. He is now backward and now forward in the way of belief, and takes steps with much hesitation and distrust.

b) For a person who has recalled the Divine words, "*Alestu bi Rabukum?*" and has begun to feel God's love, for him no Divine duties are heavy. He is happy to carry them out. But for him who cannot remember the day, all religious rituals seem to be heavy and boring.

c) In the Koran we find these lines, "When thy Lord drew forth from the children of Adam from their loins, their descendants and made them testify concerning themselves (saying): "Am I not your Lord?=*Alestu bi Rabukum?*" (who cherishes and sustains you?) they said: "Yea (or you are)" (VIII/171). In this verse God's love for mankind is implicit and *"Alest"* is a reference to these words in Islamic mysticism.

339- A lover of God can always see the positive side of his affliction:

ای خروسان از وی آموزید بانگ   بانگ بهر حق کند نه بهر دانگ

گر نداری از نفاق و بد امان   از چه داری بر برادر ظن همان

بدگمان باشد همیشه زشت کار   نامه خود خواند اندر حق یار

مبتلی چون دید تأویلات رنج   برد بیند کی شود او مات رنج

(V / 1974-1980-1981-1993)

a) O cocks, learn crowing from the cock because he crows for God and not for money. If you do not possess hypocrisy and wickedness then why do you think evil of your brothers (other people)? The evil thinker always thinks evil of others and reads his own book (passes his own remarks) about his friends. When an afflicted person is able to see different remedies to his pains, he feels victorious and not a victim.

b) Rumi addresses the preachers or the Muazzins of the mosque who are paid to call people to prayers five times a day. He tells them to take a lesson from the cock who wakes people up every morning only for God and asks for no money (see Koner, p. 703). Many religious people cherish ill feelings, which is forbidden in Islam as the Koran says, "O you who believe in God, avoid suspicion (evil feelings) as much as possible for suspicion in some cases is sin and spy not on each other, nor speak ill of each other behind their backs..." (XLI/12). A man with evil feelings sees others as he himself is. A lover of God faces an affliction bravely until God's Mercy reaches him.

340- Let your pains attack your body but not the spirit:

یک سبد پر نان ترا بر فرق سر   تو همی خواهی لب نان در بدر

هوش را توزیع کردی بر جهات   می نیرزد تره آن ترهات

آب هش را می کشد هر بیخ خار   آب هوشت چون رسد سوی ثمار

نعمت حق را بجان و عقل ده   نه بطبع پر زحیر پر گره

بار کن پیگار غم را بر تنت   بر دل و جان کم نه آن جان کندنت

بر سر عیسی نهاده تنگ بار   خر سکیزه می زند در مرغزار

(V / 1073-1084-1085-1092-1093-1094)

280

a) One basket full of bread is on your own head, yet you go from door to door pleading for a piece of bread. You have scattered your attention in every direction while your vanities are not worth a straw (a green herb). Every root of a thorn (physical desire) is drawing the water of your senses, so how can it reach the roots of your fruit (the spiritual understanding)? Grant the bounty of God to your soul and intelligence, but not to your nature which is full of knots and twists. Let your body receive arrows and sorrows, but do not lay your anxiety upon the heart and spirit. Don't place the pack or load on the head of Jesus (your spirit), while your donkey (body) is grazing happily in the meadow.

b) God has armed you with His help and Mercy, yet you ask for other's help. You water your thorns (vain ideas) and ignore your orchard (your divine goal). Give your full attention and energy to your intelligence and soul but not to your greedy ego. Why don't you place your burden of sorrows and worries on this physical body and protect your spirit?

341- God is manifest from every direction:

هر کرا باشد ز سینه فتح باب	او ز هر شهری ببیند آفتاب
چون محمد پاك شد زین نار و دود	هر کجا رو کرد وجه الله بود
چون رفیقی وسوسه بد خواه را	کی بدانی ثم وجه الله را
حق پدیدست از میان دیگران	همچو ماه اندر میان اختران
b 1399 شهری N ذره T	(I / 1399-1397-1398-1400)
b 1398 بدانی N + G : بینی Mift	

a) He who has a gate open in his heart, can see a sun in every city. When Muhammed cleaned himself of this fire and smoke (lower self), wherever he turned his face, he saw God's face. But if you are friends with evil ideas and inner notions, you will not know the real meaning of "There is the face of God". God is manifest among other (objects) like the moon is among the stars.

b) He who is able to discover a door that leads to God, the spiritual light within himself, is able to see God's manifestation in every being (city). If you, too, like Muhammed want to see God's face everywhere then clean your mind of sceptical ideas and evil feelings for others. This the verse of the Koran that is referred to here:

"To God belong the east and west, whithersoever ye turn there is the Presence (Face) of God, for God is All-Pervading" (II/115).

342- God is Jealous out of love:

جمله عالم زآن غیور آمد که حق   برد در غیرت برین عالم سبق

او چو جانست و جهان چون کالبد   کالبد از جان پذیرد نیک و بد

(I / 1763-1764)

    a) The reason why there exists jealousy throughout the world is that God has surpassed the world in jealousy. God is like a Soul and the universe is like His body. The Body receives good or bad from the Soul (Essence).

    b) God is jealous so is the world. A man's body takes its physical characteristics from his spirit. Similarly, the whole universe takes its characteristics from God for He is the Light of heaven and earth. When God loves a man, He is jealous towards anything that hinders His love. "For the Lord's name is the Jealous God and a jealous God he is" (the Bible, Exodus 34/14). This jealousy of God is not of the negative kind but it is from excess of love.

    c) The Arabic word "*Ghayur* =Jealous" needs some explanation. Its noun is "*Ghayret* or *Ghayre*". In mysticism "*Ghayret*" means "anything other than God that draws one's attention" Baba Tahir uses it in this sense (see Ferheng-i Seyyid Jafer, p. 353). For God it means His great love that comes into action when his lover (man) forgets him being busy with something else. "*Ghayur*" in Persian also has the same meaning: "Jealous" (see Steingass, p. 901). In Turkish the word "*Ghayret*" has an entirely different meaning "A great labour, endeavour and protection (perhaps due to jealousy). In Urdu "*Ghayret*" means "shame, embarrassment". It is customary in Islam to include the word "*Ghayur*" among the Divine Attributes while no such attribute is found in the Koran.

343- Every kind of intoxication depends on our existence:

باده از ما مست شد نی ما ازو   عالم از ما هست شد نی ما ازو

ما چو زنبوریم و قالبها چو موم   خانه خانه کرده قالب را چو موم

(I / 1812-1813)

    a) The intoxication (fermentation) of wine depends on our being intoxicated, the universe came into being for us and not we for the universe. We are like bees while our bodies are like the wax (honeycomb). Our souls have made cells after cells like those in a honeycomb.

b) God created everything for the sake of love, therefore, the fermentation (or the chemical reaction) and intoxication of the wine of this world is nothing compared to our intoxication with love. These cells of our bodies are for our souls and when they grow spiritually they leave their cells. Here honeycomb does not refer to different bodies for the same soul (see Mift. 2/310) but different bodies for different souls. These verses also make it clear that God created the world for our souls, not souls for the world. Thus the goal of man should be the spiritual world and not this mortal world.

344- Belief or disbelief are all His creation:

کفر و ایمان عاشق آن کبریا   مس و نقره بنده آن کیمیا
(I / 2446)

a) All non-believers as well as believers are the creation of God, copper and silver are bound by His chemical powers.

b) When we see through the eyes of God, believers and non-believers are both slaves of God. It is up to God to punish a non-believer or forgive him. This is why Rumi did not belittle even the Mongols who had their own way of believing in God.

345- Not every bird eats figs:

بر سماع راست هر کس چیر نیست   لقمه هر مرغکی انجیر نیست
خاصه مرغی مرده پوسیده   پر خیالی اعمیی بی دیده
نقش اگر غمگین نگاری بر ورق   او ندارد از غم و شادی سبق
نقش ماهی را چه دریا و چه خاک   رنگ هندو را چه صابون و چه زاک
وین غم و شادی که اندر دل خطیست   پیش آن شادی و غم جز نقش نیست
(I / 2763-2764-2766-2765-2768)

a) Not everybody is ready to listen to (spiritual) facts and the fig is not the food of every bird; especially a bird that is dead, putrid, and blind due to his fancies. If you draw a sorrowful portrait on paper, it has no experience of sadness or happiness. For a picture of fish it does not matter whether it is in the sea or on land; for the colour of a Hindu it makes no difference if you use soap or black vitriol. The sorrow and happiness that we possess hidden in our hearts are like pictures when compared to the happiness and sorrow of the other world.

b) If a man has no spiritual inspiration, he is like a picture and all of his feelings are artificial. In other words his body is like an extinct seed that has no impulse to grow. His pleasures and sorrows are temporary and without depth. A picture of fish needs no water (the Divine Water); the soul of an atheist is similar. He has no hunger for love of God. If your body has not discovered what your soul is, you are like a garment that has no knowledge about its wearer whom it serves day and night. Take off the worldly clothes in order to discover your essence (see verses 2770-2772).

346- About the saints:

زآنك دل با اوست یا خود اوست دل	عقل اینجا ساکت آمد یا مضل
رایت عین الیقین افراشتند	نقش و قشر و علم را بگذاشتند
می‌کنند این قوم بروی ریش خند	مرگ کین جمله از و در وحشت‌اند
بر صدف آید ضرر نی بر گهر	کس نیابد بر دل ایشان ظفر

(I / 3489-3493-3495-3496)

a) Here (at the stage of saints) wisdom either stops or goes out of control. (It is unknown) whether the heart is with God or God is the heart Himself. They (the saints) quit forms, covers and knowledge; and raise the banner of vision of certitude. Death that others fear is a matter of fun for them. (Because they know) No one can ever be victorious over their hearts (feelings) and the damage falls on the oyster-shell and not on the pearl.

b) When a lover of God is at the stage between "*Ayn ul-Yaqin*" (the vision of certitude) and "*Haqq ul-Yaqin*" (real certitude) he is not sure whether God is in his heart or God is his heart (see Mift., 4/173). For them neither forms nor books that contain knowledge are of any use for discerning the vision of certitude. For them the body is only a shell because their soul (the pearl) is safe and untouched by worldly worries.

347- The curtain on the gate of soul:

این زبان پرده است بر درگاه جان	آدمی مخفیست در زیر زبان
ذره ذره حق و باطل را جدا	نور فرقان فرق کردی بهر ما
هم سوال و هم جواب از ما بدی	نور گوهر نور چشم ما شدی
پختگی جو در یقین منزل مکن	ز آتش ار علمت یقین شد از سخن
این یقین خواهی در آتش در نشین	تا نسوزی نیست آن عین الیقین

(II / 845-852-853-860-861)

a) (The quality of) a man is hidden under his tongue, this tongue is a curtain on the gate of soul. It is for us that the Koran shows differences between the good and the bad and has separated atom by atom right from wrong. If the light of essence were the light of our eyes, we would ask questions and would get answers to them by ourselves. If by speaking about fire you have learnt (believed) what fire is, then go further and do not stop there. Unless you burn in fire it cannot be called "the Vision of Certitude" and if you want real belief then sit in the fire.

b) It is not easy to discover the real character of a man unless he speaks. In this case, tongue is like a curtain on the chamber of your personality. In other words, one should speak carefully. The Koran and other religious books show us the differences between good and bad, but if we have the Divine Light within us, we can be guided by that. The Vision of Certitude is the stage of "seeing is believing" but that is not all. If you want to see fire truly (real certitude) then you have to go into it and allow your lower self to burn.

c) The word "*furkan*" used in verse no. 852 does not refer only to the Koran but any "criterion": it can be any scripture.

348- God does not look at your outer appearances:

تو برای وصل کردن آمدی   یا برای فصل کردن آمدی

ما زبان را ننگریم و قال را   ما درون را بنگریم و حال را

ناظر قلبیم اگر خاشع بود   گرچه گفت لفظ نا خاضع رود

چند ازین الفاظ و اضمار و مجاز   سوز خواهم سوز با آن سوز ساز

b 1751 یا برای فصل کردن G : نی برای فصل کردن Mift (II/1751-1759-1760-1762)

b 1759 روان G + T : درون Mift + N

a) "Have you (O Moses) come upon the earth to unite or to separate people from each other? We don't look at people's language or speeches, we look at their spirits and (inner) states. If a heart is humble, We look at it, even if the words uttered are indecent". How long will you use metaphors and secret expressions? I want burning, be a comrade with the burning and burn.

b) These famous verses (1751-60) are the words of God to Moses who had reproached a simple shepherd who had expressed love for God in indecent language. If you have a humble and clean heart then words have no meaning, for God knows our hearts. The tongue has no value. Find a friend whose heart is burning with the love of God (like that of Shams-i Tebrizi or Sallah al-Din).

c) The Arabic word "*Khashiya*" means "to humble oneself, a devastated place where no dwelling is left"; naturally here it means "a humble heart busy only with God".

349- It is spiritual worth that counts:

عاشقی کآلوده شد در خیر و شر   خیر و شر منگر تو در همت نگر

باز اگر باشد سپید و بی نظیر   چونك صیدش موش باشد شد حقیر

جان چه باشد با خبر از خیر و شر   شاد با احسان و گریان از ضرر

روح را تاثیر آگاهی بود   هر کرا این بیش اللهی بود

(VI / 135-136-148-150)

a) A lover (of God) may be soiled by good and evil, don't look at his good and evil, but look at his courage (and toil). If a falcon is white and unique, it may be worthless if it hunts only mice. What is soul? It is that by which you discriminate between good and evil. It is happy with kindness and unhappy with bad results. But (spiritual) wakefulness is the effect of the spirit, he who has it in abundance is the man of God.

b) "Soul" (distinguished from spirit) here means the physical vitality that is bound to the carnal senses and the carnal senses convince a man that "A bird in the hand is worth than two in the bushes". However, the bird in the hand is artificial. It will soon disappear. It is the spiritual wisdom that can realise what God is.

350- Ask so that you may be given:

در طلب زن دایما تو هر دو دست   کی طلب در راه نیکو رهبر است

لنگ و لوك و خفته شکل و بی ادب   سوی او می غیژ و او را می طلب

گه بگفت و گه بخاموشی و گه   بوی کردن گیر هر سو بوی شه

(III / 979-980-981)

a) Hold your hands up for a request (to God), for request is a good guide in the right path. Be lame and limping or bent in body or drawn face or even imprudent, creep towards Him and desire Him, sometimes by speaking, sometimes in silence and sometimes by sensing His smell, seek Him everywhere.

b) Whatever your spiritual state may be don't be disappointed about the mercy of God, as the Koran says, "O my servants who have transgressed against their souls, despair not of the Mercy of God" (XXXIX/53). Try your best to reach Him, follow His lovely scent that may lead you to Him.

351- Those who do not worship God, are forced to worship kings or rulers:

آنچنانك حق ز گوشت و استخوان   از شهان باب صغیری ساخت هان
اهل دنیا سجده ایشان کنند   چونك سجده کبریا را دشمنند
آن سگان را این خسان خاضع شوند   شیر را عارست کو را بگروند
(III / 2998-2999-3002)

a) God has built a small gate of bones and the flesh of kings, just think! Since worldly people do not worship God (or prostrate themselves to Him), they prostrate themselves before kings. To those dogs (kings) these people show respect. The lion (a lover of God) is ashamed to be obedient to them (or that man).

b) Those who don't want to prostrate themselves to God, are made to bow to the kings, rulers, and officers who are the *"Bab-i Saghir"* (a small gate made by Moses in the wall of Jerusalem in order that the insolent and the wicked bow when they enter it). But those who love God bow to Him only and thus enjoy the freedom of Soul. Rumi further says, "They are afraid of God's dogs (the rulers) and not of the Sun of Reality" (vr. 3004).

352- Man is a captive of secondary causes and reasons:

تو ز طفلی چون سببها دیده   در سبب از جهل بر چفسیده
با سببها از مسبب غافلی   سوی این روپوشها زآن مایلی
لیك من زآن ننگرم رحمت کنم   رحمتم پرست بر رحمت تنم
(III / 3153-3154-3159)

a) Since your childhood you have seen (secondary) causes and have, therefore, become attached to them out of ignorance. You are busy with the secondary causes but are unaware of the Causer and incline to these veils (of secondary causes). But I (always) forgive you disregarding your act of ignorance for My Mercy rules My Body (Being).

b) Our partial insight is focused on causes and does not like to seek the realities behind them. Scientists and philosophers are stuck when they face a strange event without a secondary cause and they subconsciously say, "O Lord", it is only then that they remember the Causer Who can do anything without causes. God is so kind that He forgives them although they do not recognise Him without a reason. The non-existent world has no causes and is, therefore, beyond our comprehension. For example, it is not easy for a person to believe that Mary gave birth to Jesus without a father or that Jesus could heal the sick.

353- Anything we lose in life may save a greater mishap:

هرچ از تو یاوه گردد از قضا   تو یقین دان که خریدست از بلا

ما التصوف قال وجدان الفرح   فی الفواد عند اتیان الترح

گفت لا تاسوا علی ما فاتکم   إن أتی السرحان واردی شاتکم

کآن بلا دفع بلاهای بزرگ   وآن زیان منع زیانهای سترگ

این ریاضتهای درویشان چراست   کآن بلا بر تن بقای جانهاست

(III / 3260-3261-3264-3265-3349)

a) Whatever you lose because of your destiny, believe that it has bought (taken) some portion of your adversity. (Someone asked) "What is Sufism?" the answer was, "To possess joy and ease in the heart at the time of affliction". God has said (in the Koran), "Do not feel sorry for what you lose" if the wolf comes and destroys your sheep. Because that mishap is to protect you from a greater mishap and that loss is to save you from bigger losses. Do you know why the Dervishes suffer (practise) afflictions on earth? Because these corporeal sufferings give an everlasting life to the spirit.

b) All troubles and worries that we face here in this world are to save other bigger catastrophes. This is how a true believer (a Dervish or a Sufi) should think and he should not blame God. However, if the trouble is unbearable, he can pray to God humbly, the sign of devotion. Actually pains and worries make death easier and they are part of the preparation for the eternal journey and training before going to the other world. "In order that you may not despair over matters that pass you by, nor exult over favours bestowed upon you, for God does not love any vain-glorious boaster" (LVII/23) and "Verily with every difficulty there is a relief" (XCIV/6).

354- A wise man is farsighted:

عاقل از انگور می بیند همی   عاشق از معدوم شی بیند همی

غم چو آینه ست پیش مجتهد   کاندرین ضد می نماید روی ضد

این دو وصف از پنجه دست ببین   بعد قبض مشت بسط آید یقین

(III / 3754-3762-3764)

a) A wise man can see wine in grapes, a lover can see things in the non-existent. Sorrow is a mirror in front of a struggler in which he can see an opposite face to his problem. Observe these two qualities in the fingers of your hands; when you close your fist, naturally, the opening comes.

b) A wise man is able to foresee a result but a saint (lover of God) is able to go farther into the non-existent world. Similarly you can see the happy end of worries that you have today. It is by means of sorrows that you can see the opposite face of the matter and try to discern the cause of sorrows. If you are in conflict today, you will be comforted tomorrow. Your prayers and fasting may seem to be torture today but they will bring real happiness later (T. 11-12/983).

355- The difference between the mercy of man and the Mercy of God:

رحمتش نه رحمت آدم بود که مزاج رحم آدم غم بود
رحمت مخلوق باشد غصه ناک رحمت حق از غم و غصه ست پاک
رحمت بی چون چنین دان ای پدر نآید اندر وهم از وی جز اثر
ظاهرست آثار و میوه رحمتش لیک کی داند جز او ماهیتش
(III / 3632-3633-3634-3635)

a) His Mercy is unlike the mercy of a man because in man's mercy sorrow is mixed. The mercy of the created being is mixed with anxiety and worries but the mercy of God is free from anxiety and worries. His Mercy is unconditioned, know that, and, therefore, it cannot be conceived; though its sign can be felt. The fruits and traces of His Mercy are manifest while only He knows the essence (the real quality) of His mercy.

b) God's mercy is pure while a man's mercy is tinged with sorrows and pity. Man pities a helpless man and gives him food and money because of sorrow while God is freely merciful (see T. 11-12/950). In some cases His Mercy may look adverse for He gives diseases and worries to train a man for a better end and in these cases only God knows the goodwill that is behind them. So don't be disappointed if you have to wait for His mercy.

356- Prostrate yourself and come closer:

گفت واسجد واقترب یزدان ما قرب جان شد سجده ابدان ما
حج زیارت کردن خانه بود حج رب البیت مردانه بود
(IV / 11-15)

a) Our God has said, "Prostrate yourself and come closer". Thus our physical prostration means going closer to Spirit (Essence of God). The pilgrimage is to visit God's house but visiting the Master of the house is the real act.

b) In the Koran God says, "Don't obey him (the infidel), make prostration (to Me) and come closer" (XCVI/19). This refers to the physical prostration that a Muslim practises everyday and to the spiritual submission of a lover of God. Similarly, the physical pilgrimage is to go to Mecca, but the spiritual pilgrimage is to meet God.

357- Hearts find satisfaction in the remembrance of God:

نور حس و جان بابایان ما   نیست کلی فانی و لا چون گیا

لیك مانند ستاره و ماهتاب   جمله محوند از شعاع آفتاب

آب ذكر حق و زنبور این زمان   هست یاد آن فلانه و آن فلان

دم بخور در آب ذكر و صبر كن   تا رهی از فكر و وسواس كهن

پس كسانی كز جهان بگذشته اند   لا نیند و در صفات آغشته اند

در صفات حق صفات جمله شان   همچو اختر پیش آن خور بی نشان

432 a بابایان N + G : بی پایان MM. (IV / 432-433-437-438-442-443)

a) The light of the senses and the spirits of our ancestors are not entirely destroyed like grass (a worthless thing). But like the stars and the moon, they become submerged in sunbeams. Water is the remembrance *(Zikr)* of God and time is the wasp -the memories of this and that person. Hold your breath †in the water, remember God, and be patient so that you may get rid of old ideas and fears. Nevertheless, those who have passed away are not destroyed but are submerged in the attributes of God. Their attributes are unnoticeable stars in the presence of the sun of Divine Attributes.

b) During the day the stars and moon are invisible due to the sunlight, so are our ancestors who have passed away; they are absorbed in the Divine Light according to their capacities for the attributes of God. *Zikr* (remembering) God is like pouring water on our bitter memories of the past or of the dead yet time buzzes in our ears (like wasps) and brings memories back. By this Rumi simply means that if you want to get rid of the painful memories of the dead then remember God (recite His names).

358- God's Light protects His lovers:

چون نباشد حارس آن نور مجید   كه هزاران آفتاب آرد پدید

تو بنور او همی رو در آمان   در میان اژدها و كژدمان

پیش پشت می رود آن نور پاك   می كند هر ره زنی را چاك چاك

(IV / 608-609-610)

a) Why shouldn't that glorious light protect you while it creates thousands of suns (solar systems)? You can walk in safety with His light through dragons and scorpions (evil beings and events). The holy Light goes in front of you and tears the waylayers into pieces.

b) God says in the Koran, "The day when God will not permit to be humiliated the Prophet and those who believe with him. Their light will run forward before them and by their right hands, while they say: Our Lord! perfect our light for us, and grant us forgiveness for Thou hast power over all things" (LXVI/8) and "One day shalt thou see the believing men and the believing women how their light runs forward before them" (LVII/12). The question is what is this light? It is the Light of God that is recollected by a soul (spirit) by means of prayers and piety. Once you are protected by the Light of God, your surrender to Him becomes easy. Diabolic hindrances (scorpions and dragons) on the way to God are eradicated by Him by means of His Light.

359- Lovers of God love God only:

قبله عارف بود نور وصال	قبله عقل مفلسف شد خیال
قبله باطن نشینان ذوالمنن	قبله ظاهر پرستان روی زن
خوی آن را عاشق نان کرده ایم	خوی این را مست جانان کرده ایم
قبله معنی وران صبر و درنگ	قبله صورت پرستان نقش سنگ

(VI / 1897-1900-1904-1899)

a) The *qibla* (a direction of worshipping, Mecca) of a gnostic is the Light of meeting God. The *qibla* of a philosopher's intellect is only a dream (vain ideas). The *qibla* of those who live on the esoteric food (dwelling) is the Bounteous God while the *qibla* of those who worship outer forms is a woman's face. We (God) have created his (worldly man's) instinct as bread-lover and other's (God loving man's) instinct as intoxicated with the Beloved. The *qibla* of the spiritual people is patience and long suffering and the *qibla* of the form-worshippers is an image of stone.

b) All people worship something. A philosopher worships his ideas while a worldly individual worships the worldly beauty but a lover of God worships God although he has to persevere.

360- Look for God within yourself:

آنچ حقست اقرب از حبل الورید   تو فگنده تیر فکرت را بعید
ای کمان و تیرها بر ساخته   صید نزدیك و تو دور انداخته
فلسفی خود را از اندیشه بکشت   گو بدو کوراست سوی گنج پشت
خویش را عریان کن از فضل و فضول   تا کند رحمت بتو هر دم نزول
(VI / 2353-2354-2356-2371)

a) God (Reality) is closer to you than your jugular vein, yet you have cast your arrow of ideas far off. O you who have provided yourself with the bow and arrows the prey is near and you have shot the arrow far away. A philosopher killed himself from thinking and scepticism. Go and tell him that he has his back turned toward the treasure (see Mift. p. 150 and Koner p. 867). If you want Divine Mercy to reach you continuously then do free yourself from vain talk (or claims).

b) Since the Koran says that God is closer to you than your jugular vein, then why do you seek Him elsewhere? A philosopher (or a sceptical thinker) is lost in thinking until the last day while a sincere believer surrenders to the Will of God without objection because it is not possible for the limited partial insight to perceive God truly.

361- Silence is the sea while speech is the river:

خامشی بحرست و گفتن همچو جو   بحر می جوید ترا جورا مجو
هرك او اندر نظر موصول شد   این خبرها پیش او معزول شد
چونك با معشوق گشتی هم نشین   دفع کن دلالگان را بعد ازین
(IV / 2062-2067-2068)

a) Silence is like the sea while speech is like a river. The sea is looking for you, so don't seek a river. He who has reached the stage of observing God for him this information is useless. When you are already sitting beside your Beloved then send away the matchmaker.

b) The sea despite being vast is silent but a river (a stream) makes more noise. When you come closer to God you become silent like the sea but when you are still on the path to God (like a stream) you are noisy and full of excitement. Once you are with God, you need no intermediary.

362- Divine help comes silently:

حق اگرچه سر نجنباند برون پاس آن ذوقی دهد در اندرون
عقل را خدمت کنی در اجتهاد پاس عقل آنست کافزاید رشاد
حق نجنباند بظاهر سر ترا لیک سازد بر سران سرور ترا
آنچنانک داد سنگی را هنر تا عزیز خلق شد یعنی که زر
جسم خاکست و چو حق تابیش داد در جهان گیری چو مه شد اوستاد
(IV / 3484-3486-3487-3489-3491)

a) God does not shake His Head outwardly (shows no action), yet thinking about Him (or feeling His protection) gives inner satisfaction. You serve your insight by working, and regard of insight increases your righteousness. Although, God does not nod His Head outwardly, yet He makes you the chief of chiefs, as He gave such an art to a stone (gold) that it became dear to all people. Your body is made of earth yet when God gave it (a spark of) His light, it became as adept as a moon in conquering the world.

b) God may not seem to answer to your petitions by nodding His Head outwardly yet He gives you the feeling of His presence by means of His inner spiritual contact. Your spiritual insight develops righteousness, but it is only by means of God's Mercy that a piece of stone changes into gold. Similarly, your body may be made of clay, yet it may change into a perfect being by means of God's favour.

363- The faithfulness of a believer puts out the fire of hell:

بگذر ای مومن که نورت می کشد آتشم را چونک دامن می کشد
دوزخ از مومن گریزد آنچنان که گریزد مومن از دوزخ بجان
(IV / 2710-2712)

a) "Pass by quickly O you believer! for your skirt (of piety) puts out my fire" (says Hell). Hell runs away from a believer *(Mu'min)* just as the believer runs from it whole heartedly.

b) Hell does not want to come face to face with a true believer, for the protective Divine Light in front of him extinguishes its fire.

364- Be a hawk not a crow:

پیش تبدیل خدا جان باز باش	هین بده ای زاغ این جان باز باش
که هر امسالت فزونست از سه پار	تازه می گیر و کهن را می سپار
مرغ روحت بسته با جنسی دگر	زین بدن اندر عذابی ای بشر
دارد از زاغان و جغدان داغها	روح بازست و طبایع زاغها
(V / 808-809-842-843)	b 843 جغدان G : تن بسی Mift.

a) O crow give up this life and be a falcon, play with your life (sacrifice yourself) in the Presence of God's changing from shape to shape (from state to state). Take the new and give away the old because every new year is more valuable than the past three years. O human being you are in trouble because of this body, for the bird of your soul is attached to another kind of bird (the spiritual bird).

b) The spirit of a true believer is like a falcon that wants to fly back to its master. The body of a man is like a crow. It wants to stick to the dirt and filth of the earth. When the spirit is thus caged with earthly birds such as crows, owls or vultures, it has no peace for it belongs to the other kind of birds.

As the Koran says, "Everyday in new splendour does He shine" (LV/29) so if a man wants to follow God, he must fly from state to state, too.

365- It is your clean heart that God wants:

نی بنقش سجده و ایثار زر	من ز صاحب دل کنم در تو نظر
حق بگوید دل بیآر ای منحنی	صد جوال زر بیآری ای غنی
ور ز تو معرض بود اعراضیم	گر ز تو راضیست دل من راضیم
تحفه او را آر ای جان بر درم	ننگرم در تو در آن دل بنگرم
(V / 870-881-882-883)	

a) I look at you through My lovers (saints) but not through the prints of your prostrations (in prayers) and alms (gold that you give as alms). O rich man, bent in prayers, if you take a hundred sacks of gold to God, He will still ask you to bring a nice heart instead. If your own heart is pleased with you, I am also pleased; and if it is against you, I am against you also. We don't look at you but at your heart which is the gift you can bring Me, O My beloved.

b) "The owner of a heart" means the saint who is with God twenty four hours a day and it is through him that God looks at us. As God says in the Koran "But only he (will prosper) who brings to God a sound heart" (XXVI/89). A sound heart is the one that loves God and His created beings with positive feelings, as M. Iqbal adds:

"He who has no secret pains (of love), has a body but no soul".

366- The currency of the other world is love and two crying eyes:

جان بسی کندی و اندر پرده   زآنک مردن اصل بد نآورده

تا نمیری نیست جان کندن تمام   بی کمال نردبان نآیی ببام

گرز بر خود زن منی درهم شکن   زآنک پنبه گوش آمد چشم تن

نه چنان مرگی که در گوری روی   مرگ تبدیلی که در نوری روی

مور بر دانه بدآن لرزان شود   که زخرمنها، خوش اعمی بود

مایه در بازار این دنیا زرست   مایه آنجا عشق و دو چشم ترست

(VI / 723-724-732-739-806-839)

a) You have suffered much pain, yet you are veiled (covered in the body) because dying (to self) was the real goal and you have not fulfilled it. Unless you die (before your death), your pains cannot come to an end, for if you don't climb up ladders how can you come to the roof? Strike the mace on your selfhood and smash it into pieces because your physical eyes are like cottoned ears. Don't choose the kind of death that takes you to a grave, but a kind of death that transforms you into Light. An ant trembles for a grain because it is blind to other wonderful heaps of grains. The capital required for this world is gold while the capital required for the other world is love and two crying eyes.

b) Rumi suggests that lover should die to the physical self in accordance with Muhammed's tradition "Die before you die" (see the heading Nich. Vol. VI). Unless you kill your worldly greed completely, you cannot attain spirituality. The capital you need for the other world is not the wealth of this world but your repentance (two crying eyes) and your love of God.

367- Keep silent in the company of good friends:

چونک در یاران رسی خامش نشین   اندر آن حلقه مکن خود را نگین

رختها را سوی خاموشی کشان   چون نشان جویی مکن خود را نشان

زآنک ما ینطق رسول بالهوی   کی هوا زاید ز معصوم خدا

(VI / 1592-1594-1602)

a) When you come into a company of friends, sit silently. Don't make yourself a diamond of the ring. Direct your course towards silence, since you are looking for signs (of God) don't make yourself a sign (a target of attention). For a prophet does not speak from self-will and he does not speak out of desire because an innocent person of God never speaks for the sake of show.

b) Out of reverence don't speak and try to show all your knowledge to others when you join friends' company. Rumi himself did not speak in the company where Shams or other friends were present. It had become a custom among the Mevlevis that they would not speak or try to draw the attention of people by speaking in company. They always preferred to listen to others.

368- Veil the faults of others because God is the "Veiler" (Sittar):

ستر کن تا بر تو ستاری کنند   تا نبینی ایمنی بر کس مخند

آنچ بر تو خواه آن باشد پسند   بر دگر کس آن کن از رنج و گزند

تو مراقب باش بر احوال خویش   نوش بین در داد و بعد از ظلم نیش

(VI / 4526-4528-4532)

a) Hide the faults of others so that God may hide your sins. Do not laugh at anyone unless you yourself are safe. Whatever amount of pain or injury you approve for yourself give to others. Keep a close watch on your own behaviour. See peace and comfort in justice, and poison in injustice and cruelty (see Koner p. 921).

b) Since God is the "Veiler" of people's faults, it is also your duty to veil others' sins, because God wants His lovers to do as He Himself does. Be more concerned with yourself and your character than with others'.

CHAPTER XI

Step VII: Bewilderment (unveiling of some secrets) and need of a spiritual guide

We have already explained what a *Sufi*, a *Dervish*, and a *Qalander* is. They are all lovers of God who have set out on a journey towards Him. But saints (or Sheykhs) are those who have already attained the Proximity of God. "They *(Avliya)* come after the prophets. They are those who have become aware of (some) Divine Secrets that ordinary people fail to have access to" (Ferheng-i Seyyid Jaferi p. 72). In this respect they are representatives of the prophets (especially of Muhammed) on earth. This is what Rumi says about them in his Discourses:

"Seek the People of God. Enter thou among my servants. Enter thou My Paradise (the Koran, LXXXIX/29-30). God does not speak to everyone, just as the kings of this world do not speak to every weaver. They appoint ministers and representatives so that through them people may find the way to them. In the same way God has singled out some certain servants, so that everyone who seeks Him may find Him within them. All the prophets have come for this reason. Only they are the Way" (Ibid, p. 237).

"Whoever possesses a partial insight is in need of instruction, but the Universal Wisdom is the originator of all things. Those who have joined the partial insight to the Universal Intellect so that the two have become one are the prophets and saints" (Ibid, p. 152).

"Although the words of the great saints appear in a hundred different forms, yet, since God is One and the Way is one, how should their forms be two? They appear different in form, but they are one in meaning. In form there is diversity, in meaning all is concord.

For example, a prince orders a tent to be sewn. One person makes the rope, another prepares the stakes, another weaves the cloth, another stitches, another rends, another employs a needle. These forms are different and diverse; but, united in meaning, they perform a single task" (Ibid, p. 57-58).

God has created man to be His vicegerent on earth (as the Koran says see II/30), but can all men be God's vicegerent on earth? No, only those who follow God's commands sent to him by means of His messengers (prophets) for God cannot address every vicegerent in their own physical language. It is for this reason that God says in the Koran, "Say: Obey God His Messenger" (III/31). Saints (*"Valiullah"* =friends of God, Pirs or Sheykhs) are those who represent the prophets on earth in all forms whether physical or spiritual. The saints are in no sense God or even prophets. There is no better friend than God Himself. "And besides Him you have no patron *(Vali)* or helper" (the Koran, II/107) and "God is the Protector *(Vali)* of those who believe" (III/68).

"*Vali*" and its plural form "*Avliya*", an Arabic word, is used for saints. But it is also one of the attributes of God (as given in the above verses from the Koran). "*Vali*" means "a favourite friend of God, a sincere friend, a servant, a holy man". Since they represent the prophets on earth, they should live simply without greed as Christ or Muhammed did. In order to recognise a true saint, we must know the lives of prophets very well. Prophets' lives are our criteria for judging saints. We have to be very careful about the false saints who have certain supernatural powers with the help of Satan. "A disciple who is trained by a man of God will have a pure and purified spirit. But he who is trained by an impostor and hypocrite and who learns theory from him will be just like him: despicable, weak, incapable, morose, without any exit from uncertainties, and deficient in all senses: "As for the unbelievers--their protectors are idols, that bring them forth from the light into shadows" (the Koran, II/257)" (Discourses, p. 44).

In this chapter Rumi throws light on the true saints and a *Salik* (a traveller to God) who after curbing his lower self, may be able to see Divine Secrets and become bewildered. It is probably at this stage that he needs more help of a living saint than at any other stage. Water is water, be it in the sea, a lake, a stream, a jar, a glass, or even a drop. God, likewise, is God in all forms be it the heart of a sinner, a lover, a Sufi, a prophet, or even a false saint. It is the quantity that counts. How can a dirty drop of water be the Pure Sea?

"*Avliya*" is also called "*Murshid-i Kamil*" (the perfect spiritual guide or one who instructs a traveller *(Salik)*. "By the command of God, there is found a *Vali* at every age to instruct people. He is a real viceroy of Muhammed. A chief saint is also called "*Kutub*" (pole, axis) or "*Ghaus*" (a highest saint)". (Mift. II-I/p. 292). Whatever their names they are all lovers of God with different degrees. Now, we turn to the verses of Rumi on saints.

369- A saint is beyond the limits of this world:

صاحب دل را ندارد آن زیان   گر خورد او زهر قاتل را عیان

زآنک صحت یافت و از پرهیز رست   طالب مسکین میان تب درست

او ز قعر بحر گوهر آورد   از زیانها سود بر سر آورد

چون قبول حق بود آن مرد راست   دست او در کارها دست خداست

جهل آید پیش او و دانش شود   جهل شد علمی که در ناقص رود

(I / 1603-1604-1608-1610-1612)

a) A lover of God is not harmed by the fatal poison even if he drinks it apparently. Because he has attained spiritual health and become free of physical abstinence. The wretched seeker of God has still a fever (therefore he must continue abstinence). The saint brings pearls from the depth of the sea, and from losses he is able to gain profits. When the righteous man (the saint) is accepted by God, his hands at work are like the hands of God. When ignorance comes to him it changes into knowledge; but if knowledge goes to an ignorant person, it changes into ignorance.

b) In the above verses the sick man is he who is still looking for God and the healthy one is the saint. A saint, therefore, no longer needs to practise abstinence. It does not mean that he is free to commit sins freely but he is decorated with the attributes of God which forbid him to do anything wrong. Even if he seems to be doing something wrong outwardly, God changes it into right. This recalls Eflaki's story about Rumi: Rumi one day asked the great doctor of his time Akmeluddin to prepare an anti-constipation solution for his friends (about 17 in number) of which Rumi drank almost all the dose. The doctor went mad when he saw that nothing happened to his Master. Rumi uttered these lines, "If a saint drinks poison, it changes into a (tasty) drink; but if a searcher (of God) drinks it, he loses his senses (head)" (see Eflaki, 3/40).

370- Saints are the owners of hearts:

چون بتذکیر و بنسیان قادرند / بر همه دلهای خلقان قاهرند
صاحب ده پادشاه جسمهاست / صاحب دل شاه دلهای شماست
(I / 1675-1678)

a) Since saints are able to make you remember and forget things, they have power over all creatures' hearts. The king of a town (village) is the master of bodies, but the saints are the kings of your hearts.

b) In the feudal system the owner of a village is the owner of the farmers. Rumi says that they can control only bodies but the saints are the owners of hearts. They can win your heart spiritually.

371- The characteristics of a saint:

بهر عارف فتحت ابوابهاست	آن دلی کو مطلع مهتابهاست
با تو سنگ و با عزیزان گوهرست	با تو دیوارست با ایشان درست
پیر اندر خشت بیند بیش از آن	آنچ تو در آینه بینی عیان
جان ایشان بود در دریای جود	پیر ایشان‌اند کین عالم نبود
پیشتر از کشت بر بر داشتند	پیش ازین تن عمرها بگذاشتند
بی سپاه و جنگ بر نصرت زدند	بی دماغ و دل پر از فکرت بدند
ورنه خود نسبت بدوران رویتست	آن عیان نسبت بایشان فکرتست
هم یکی باشند و هم ششصد هزار	چون از ایشان مجتمع بینی دو یار
در عدد آورده باشد بادشان	بر مثال موجها اعدادشان
نفس واحد روح انسانی بود	تفرقه در روح حیوانی بود

(II / 165-166-167-168-169-175-176-184-185-188)

a) The heart where moon's beams rise is the opening of the doors (of reality) for a gnostic. It may be a wall for you, but it is a door for them (the gnostics). It may be a stone for you but for the dear friends, it is a pearl. Whatever you see clearly in a mirror, the saint sees more than that in a brick. Saints are those whose spirit lived before the existence of this universe in the Divine Sea of Bounty. Before this body they lived other lives. They obtained harvest (the fruit) before sowing it. Without brain and mind they were full of thought; without army and war they gained victory. That open (pure) observation for them (the saints) was like the stage of thinking (of past and future) which for ordinary people (those who are away from the Divine Light) is only a vision. When you see two friends of them, they are actually one and at the same time they are six hundred thousand (many). Their number is like the waves of the sea caused by the wind. It is the animal soul that is separate, the human spirits are all one.

b) A gnostic can discover what is in the hearts of people, but the same hearts can be a wall for ordinary people who cannot see what is behind that wall (Mift. 1-2/p. 88). A saint is able to see atoms inside a solid. Saints existed with God in the non-existent world before the creation of the worlds of mind and matter. They saw God's Light openly and were drowned in the Sea of Beauty. They are the part of the Divine Essence that has no physical restriction, and physically they may look separate but in reality they are one, because God is One. To them the Reality is unveiled in its truest form. In the Koran we come across these verses about the equality of the prophets, "The Apostle believed in what has been revealed to him from his Lord, as do the men of faith. Each one (of them) believes in God, His angels, His books, and His apostles: We make no distinction (they say) between one another of His apostles" (the Koran, II/285). Rumi continues, "Since God sprinkled His light upon them (mankind), they are one. His light never becomes separated" (verse No. 189). It refers to the following Tradition of Muhammed: "Without doubt, God the Almighty, created everything (everybody) in the darkness and then poured His light upon them" (Jami-Sighir, I/p. 58).

372- The importance of the men of God (the prophets and saints):

طالبان را زآن حیوة بی بهاست   انبیا را در درون هم نغمهاست
کز ستمها گوش حس باشد نجس   نشنود آن نغمها را گوش حس
هر دو در زندان این نادانیند   که پری و آدمی زندانیند
اولا گوید که ای اجزای لا   نغمههای اندرون اولیا
زین خیال و وهم سر بیرون کنید   هین ز لای نفی سرها بر زنید
جانها سر بر زنند از دخمها   گر بگویم شمه زآن نغمها
گرچه از حلقوم عبدالله بود   مطلق آن آواز خود از شه بود

(I / 1919-1920-1923-1925-1926-1928-1936)

1919 a انبیا N : اولیا Mift. - 1920 b ستمها N : سخنها Mift.

a) The prophets, too, have inner (secret) musical notes that give valuable life to seekers. Sensory ears are unable to hear them (the notes) for they are filled with dirt (injustice and cruelty). Jinn *(Peri)* and human kind are all captive of the imprisonment of ignorance. The inner notes of a saint first say, O you particle of non-existence take your head out of the negation born of selfhood *"la"* (there is no God) and throw away your ideas and imaginations. If I sing for you some of those saintly notes, your souls will lift up their heads from the tombs (the physical bodies). Surely, that song comes from God, although it comes through the throat of a slave of God (a saint).

b) Revelation to a prophet is a precious source for those who look for God. But one needs a clean heart and a negated lower self to be able to make use out of that source. The reviving melodies of inspirations continuously guide a saint and warn him against his lower self either directly or indirectly (via another guide).

373- Saints make us drunk inwardly:

اندرونی کاندرونها مست ازوست
نیستی کین هستهامان هست ازوست
کهربای فکر و هر آواز او
لذت الهام و وحی و راز او
(I / 2080-2081)

a) The saint's inner world (hearts) makes our inner hearts drunk. His non-existence is of such a kind that our existence is born out of that. The attraction of his ideas and every sound produced by him has the taste of revelation, inspiration and Divine mystery.

b) Here Rumi says that saints' words reveal Divine secrets which make the inner self of man intoxicated as the words of Shams-i Tebrizi did Rumi's.

374- Don't rebel against the servants of God:

سرکشی از بندگان ذوالجلال
دانک دارند از وجود تو ملال
کهربا دارند چون پیدا کنند
کاه هستی ترا شیدا کنند
کهربای خویش چون پنهان کنند
زود تسلیم ترا طغیان کنند
2492 a : G پیدا   N پنهان
(I / 2491-2492-2493)

a) If you rebel against the servants of the Almighty, they, too, begin to hate your being. The saints have amber. When they show it, they make your being go mad and when they hide their ambers (spiritual qualities) your submission changes into rebellion (against God).

b) Saints have a magnetic power like that of an amber which can draw your being like a piece of straw. But if they hide their spiritual powers from you, you may rebel against God.

375- The spirit of a Saint cannot be hurt:

روح صالح قابل آزار نیست
نور یزدان سغبه کفار نیست
روح صالح قابل آفات نیست
زخم بر ناقه بود بر ذات نیست
بی خبر کآزار این آزار اوست
آب این خم متصل با آب جوست
زآن تعلق کرد با جسمی اله
تا که گردد جمله عالم را پناه
(I / 2518-2516-2520-2521)

a) The spirit of a pious man is not capable of being hurt, the light of God cannot be subdued by the infidel. The spirit of a pious man is not liable to troubles because pains befall him only on his body (the female camel) while his spirit is safe. (Many) do not know that to torture this water (the saint) means to torture God, for the water of this jar is joined to the water of that River. Since the body of a saint is attached to the body of God, he is the refuge of the whole universe.

b) The infidel cannot injure the spirit of a saint but they may injure his body. They are spiritually attached to God. So if you injure them, you actually injure God Himself and who can fight God? As God says repeatedly in the Koran, "Behold verily on the friends of God there is no fear, nor shall they grieve".

c) The word "*Salih*" used here instead of "*Vali*" has a double meaning. It is the name of a prophet whose sacred she-camel was killed by the people of Thamud, and literally it means "a pious person". It is a rank above the ascetic (see Ferheng-i Seyyid Jaferi). Thamud are mentioned by name in an inscription of the Assyrian King Sargon, dated 715 B.C., as a people of Eastern and central Arabia (for other details see Yusuf Ali, The Holy Quran, p. 360).

376- "*Pir*" does not mean "a white haired man":

ای بسا ریش سیاه و مرد پیر   ای بسا ریش سپید و دل چو قیر
پیر پیر عقل باشد ای پسر   نه سپیدی موی اندر ریش و سر
آن سپیدی مو دلیل پختگیست   پیش چشم بسته کش کوته تگیست
آن مقلد چون ندارد جز دلیل   در علامت جوید او دایم سبیل
آنک او از پرده تقلید جست   او بنور حق ببیند آنچ هست

(IV / 2161-2163-2166-2167-2169)

a) There are many who have black beards but they are wise; and there are many who have white beards but their hearts are pitch-black. O son, old is the man who is old in intelligence and wisdom not in the whiteness of the hair or the beard. That whiteness of hair is proof of maturity for those whose eyes are closed (bandaged) and have weak sight. Since the blind imitator recognises nothing but external proofs, he searches through the path by means of outer signs. He who has jumped out of the veil of imitation beholds everything with the Light of God.

b) There is a Turkish proverb, "Intelligence is in the head and not in the age". Many religious guides have white beard and hair in order to attract their followers, but actually the beard means nothing. It is no sign of sagacity. Those who have no Divine Light within them can easily be cheated by such people. So be careful. You can also become a saint through striving as Rumi says, "Toil so that you may become a sage of religion and intelligence and as the universal wisdom you may become the seer of your innerself" (IV/2178). "Toil" here means "try to be righteous and pious by following God's orders". To see the realities of God first one has to organise and discipline oneself:

377- Choose a guide:

پیر را بگزین که بی پیر این سفر   هست بس پر آفت و خوف و خطر
پس رهی را که ندیدستی تو هیچ   هین مرو تنها ز رهبر سر مپیچ
پیر تابستان و خلقان تیر ماه   خلق مانند شب اند و پیر ماه
(I / 2943-2945-2939)

a) Choose a saint for without him this journey is full of misfortune, danger and fear. So, do not set out on a path that you haven't travelled before. Beware, do not go alone without a guide. The saint is like summer and people are like autumn. The saint is like a moon while people are like night.

b) If you are lucky to find a true saint then ask for his help because he knows the path to God. A saint is like summer for the spiritual field while the people around us are like autumn for that field. "Whoever enters the Way without a guide will take a hundred years to travel a two-day journey... Whoever undertakes a profession without a master becomes the laughing stock of a city or a town" (III/588-590).

378- Don't be proud of your saintliness:

ای برادر بر تو حکمت جاریه ست   آن زابدال است و بر تو عاریه ست
شکر کن غره مشو بینی مکن   گوش دار و هیچ خودبینی مکن
بس رباطی که بباید ترک کرد   تا بمسکن در رسد یک روز مرد
گر شود پر نور روزن یا سرا   تو مدان روشن مگر خورشید را
(I / 3255-3257-3260-3262)

a) O brother, the wisdom that flows in on you is via a saint *(Abdal)* and for you it is only a borrowed thing. Thank God and don't be proud and vain, be all ears to it (my advice). There are many inns (states) on your way to your house! Consequently, leave them behind so that you may reach your own house. If you see your windows or your house illuminated, think it because of the sun (the saint).

b) If you happen to receive Divine Inspiration don't be proud of it for it comes to you by permission of God. When you have access to a certain spiritual stage never say that it is sufficient because there are countless other stages still to cover. As Muhiddin al-Arabi says, "Any end is only a stage towards Unity" (see Mift. 4-1/113). "The house without a window is hell: the foundation of religion, o servant of God, is to make windows" (III/2404) and "As the soul has its power in the body so is the power of the saint *(Abdal)* in my souls" (I/3273).

c) *"Abdal"* in Masnevi does not mean a penniless vagabond or a Dervish, but "A man who has purged his evil self and has changed his being into an angelic being" (see Baki, I/p. 62-63). *"Abdal"* is the plural of *"Bedel"* ="substitution" (see also Lugat-i Masnevi, fol. 58b). "The secret saints of God are seven in number" (Ferheng-i Seyyid Jaferi, p. 9) and "The seven saints on earth that can change themselves into other shapes (bodies)" (MM. I/25 the preface). The Turkish common word *"aptal"* = "a stupid person" is probably derived from the same root but has lost its original meaning as "a saint".

379- Saints are there to be envied by the infidel:

انبیا را واسطه زآن کرد حق	تا پدید آید حسدها در قلق
زآنک کس را از خدا عاری نبود	حاسد حق هیچ دیاری نبود
آن کسی کش مثل خود پنداشتی	زآن سبب با او حسد برداشتی
چون مقرر شد بزرگی رسول	پس حسد نآید کسی را از قبول
پس بهر دوری ولی قایمست	تا قیامت آزمایش دایمست
مهدی و هادی ویست ای راه جو	هم نهان و هم نشسته پیش رو

(II / 811-812-813-814-815-818)

a) God sent prophets to earth by means of them so that He may let the feelings of the malignantly envious come forth because nobody can be envious of God on earth as you can't find Him anywhere on earth. A prophet is in the likeness of a man himself and can, therefore, be envied. Since Muhammed's greatness has become established no one can envy him. Therefore, a saint comes continuously to perform the same duty and this trial (of making people envious) will continue until the last day. O seeker of the right way, a saint is a guide and leader who has sat in front of Him secretly as well as openly.

b) In order to provoke men's jealousy God sends the perfect prototype of men to the earth who, by making them envious, charms them into piety and righteousness. Satan also provokes his followers against the models (the prototype individuals).

380- The secret saints of God:

صد هزاران پادشاهان نهان   سر فرازانند زآن سوی جهان
نامشان از رشک حق پنهان بماند   هر گدایی نامشان را نخواند
(II / 931-932)

a) Hundreds and thousands of hidden spiritual kings have been exalted in the other world. Their names have remained undisclosed due to the jealousy of God and no Dervish can announce their names.

b) Some lovers of God, like Juneyd-i Baghdadi, Muhiddin al-Arabi, Beyazid-i Bastami and Rumi have been known to the public because of their duties but many saints (lovers of God) pass through this world silently. Their names are kept secret because of God's love and jealousy. They have high rank in the other world.

381- Seek a perfect man when you visit a town:

گفت حق اندر سفر هر جا روی   باید اول طالب مردی شوی
که بکاری بر نیآید گندمی   مردمی جو مردمی جو مردمی
(II / 2221-2224)

a) God said "Wherever you go when travelling look for a perfect man (of the town)". He who sows grass does not get wheat. So, seek a man, a (real) man.

b) It was a custom among the Seljuk and Ottoman Turks to visit a saint before they set out on a journey. No Koranic verse refers directly to this custom. There are two verses given by Taki and Mift.: "Do not they travel through the land, so that their hearts (and minds) may thus learn wisdom" (XXII/46) and "It is He who has made the earth manageable for you, so travel its road and enjoy of the sustenance" (LXVII/15).

382- It is better to be rebuked by the saint than to be honoured by the mean:

مر ترا دشنام و سیلی شهان   بهتر آید از ثنای گمرهان
صفع شاهان خور مخور شهد خسان   تا کسی گردی ز اقبال کسان
زآنک ازیشان دولت و خلعت رسد   در پناه روح جان گردد جسد
(II / 2585-2586-2587)

306

a) The swearing and striking of the spiritual masters is better than the praises of the infidel. Receive the slaps of the kings (spiritual masters) and don't eat the honey of the mean so that you may also become an honourable man like them. It is because of them that you obtain contentment (or spiritual richness) and the robe of honour. Your carnal body changes into a holy spirit.

b) The reproaching of God's men is better than the praises of the infidel for they reproach you to mend your character. The *"shah"* here means the men of God or Sheykhs but not the rulers of this world as Mift. expresses.

383- A saint's heart is always wide awake even if he sleeps:

آنك دل بيدار دارد چشم سر   گر بخسپد بر گشايد صد بصر
گر تو اهل دل نه بيدار باش   طالب دل باش و در پيكار باش
ور دلت بيدار شد می خسپ خوش   نيست غايت ناظرت از هفت و شش
شاه بيدارست حارس خفته گير   جان فدای خفتگان دل بصير
                                  (III / 1223-1224-1225-1227)

a) He whose heart is awake though his physical eyes may be asleep, he has many (spiritual) eyes open. If you are not a lover of God then remain wide awake and ask for that kind of heart and work hard. If your heart has become awake, go to sleep peacefully for eyes are not closed (absent) upon the seven heavens and all directions. Suppose that the guard is asleep, but the King is awake. Let my soul be sacrificed for those sleepers whose hearts are able to see.

b) God never goes to sleep, "...no slumber can seize Him. Nor sleep..." (II/255). The lover of God's heart is also awake although outwardly he may be asleep, and God watches over him.

384- Saints are like your mirrors:

نقش او فانی و او شد آينه   غير نقش روی غير آنجای نه
گر كنی تف سوی روی خود كنی   ور زنی بر آينه بر خود زنی
ور ببينی روی زشت آن هم توی   ور ببينی عيسی و مريم توی
                                  (IV / 2140-2141-2142)

a) His own form has come to an end, he has become a mirror for others in which only the shapes of others can be seen. If you spit at the mirror you actually spit on your own face and if you strike at the mirror, you strike at yourself. If you see an ugly face, it is your face or if you see Christ or Mary (in the mirror) it is again you yourself.

b) A lover of God is so clean that in him there is left no lower self and whatever we see in him is our own face.

385- Saints should be able to keep secrets:

سر غیب آنرا سزد آموختن که ز گفتن لب تواند دوختن
در خور دریا نشد جز مرغ آب فهم کن والله اعلم بالصواب
(III / 3387-3388)

a) Learning Divine Secrets suits a man who can seal his lips and does not reveal them to others. It is only the water-fowl that can go under the sea; try to understand this although God knows better.

b) Not all people on earth can be saints just as all birds cannot swim or go under the sea and if they try to go under water they may drown. Whatever Divine Secrets you begin to receive don't tell others for telling them to others is a sign of ego.

386- If you want to talk to God, talk to a saint:

هر که خواهد همنشینی خدا تا نشیند در حضور اولیا
از حضور اولیا گر بسکلی تو هلاکی زآنک جزو بی کلی
(II / 2163-2164)

a) He who wants to sit with God, let him sit in the presence of saints and if you quit their presence on purpose, you will die for then you are a part without its whole.

b) Once you enter the protection of the saints, they will give you spiritual food and you will begin to live on that, but if you quit them you may die for your food will be cut off.

387- A perfect man:

هفت دریا اندرو یک قطره جمله هستی ز موجش چکره
جمله پاکیها از آن دریا برند قطرهایش یک بیک میناگرند
(V / 1880-1881)

a) In him the seven seas are like a single drop. All existence is like a tiny atom of those waves. All purities are obtained from the sea and each drop of that sea is reviving (is able to work a spiritual regeneration).

b) "The seven seas"="all the seas known in the old days" (Baki gives their names see II/p. 520). Here they refer to the spiritual greatness of a saint. There is no limit to perfection in God's attributes (see Jaferi, p. 562) and the universal Wisdom is endless. In this sense a saint has limitless knowledge and greatness.

388- Consult the living:

مشورت را زنده باید نکو که ترا زنده کند وآن زنده کو
سوی دریا عزم کن زین آبگیر بحر جو و ترک این گرداب گیر
پند گفتن با جهول خوابناك تخم افگندن بود در شوره خاك
(IV / 2209-2234-2264)

a) It is better to consult a man who is spiritually alive, and he who makes you feel alive where is he? Set out from this lake towards that sea, seek the sea and leave this eddy. To give advice to a sleeping ignorant person is like casting seeds in nitrous soil.

b) If you need advice, consult a spiritual master, but you will not find him easily. In order to get rid of this eddy (your body) seek the lake (a saint) who by reviving you can lead you to the Sea of eternity. However, it is useless to give advice to an ignorant person who knows nothing of the spiritual world. "It is better to bid him farewell".

389- Seek the interpretation of the Koran from those who have no lower self left:

معنی قرآن ز قرآن پرس و بس وز کسی کآتش زدست اندر هوس
پیش قرآن گشت قربانی و پست تا که عین روح او قرآن شدست
(V / 3128-3129)

a) Ask the (real) meaning of the Koran from it alone or from a person who has burnt away his sensual desires. That person has humbled and sacrificed himself in front of the Koran and thus has become like the Koran.

b) If you want to learn the essence of the Koran discover its secrets in the following ways: 1- Find the meaning of a verse by looking at other verses of the Koran that relate to it. 2- By asking a saint who is perfect in physical piety as well as in spiritual virtue.

390- Seek spiritual nurse:

دایه کو طفل شیر آموز را   تا بنعمت خوش کند بدفوز را
گر ببندد راه آن پستان برو   بر گشاید راه صد بستان برو
پس حیات ماست موقوف فطام   اندک اندک جهد کن تم الکلام
چون جنین بود آدمی بد خون غذا   از نجس پاکی برد مومن کذی
از فطام خون غذااش شیر شد   وز فطام شیر لقمه گیر شد
وز فطام لقمه لقمانی شود   طالب اشکار پنهانی شود
(III / 46-47-49-50-51-52)

a) Where is that nurse who can sweeten the mouth of a baby with other kinds of food because the baby's mouth is smelling (due to sucking milk). If she closes baby's way to her teat, she may open other blocked ways (for the baby) to a hundred gardens (of delight). To cut a long story short, our life depends on weaning, so try little by little to do so. When man was an embryo in the womb, his food was blood. Similarly, a (true) believer draws purity from filth. Through his being weaned from blood, milk becomes his food; and by weaning from milk he changes into a taker of (delicious) solid foods. Through his being weaned from solid foods, he becomes Luqman and a seeker of hidden games.

b) We need a nurse (saint) who can gradually wean us from worldly food to the spiritual food. Our mouths are smelling like those of babies because of mundane foods. We need a saint that can introduce new tastes of the spiritual world to us so that our carnal desires may lessen. Luqman was a wise man who had medical knowledge. Here it means that you rise to the stage where you know exactly what food is good for you and what is not. "O you who are thirsty and heedless, come! We are drinking the water of Khizr (life giving water) from the stream: the speech of the saint". (III/4302).

391- A saint is able to see the inner being of a person:

گرچه دانی دقت علم ای امین   ز آنت نگشاید دو دیده غیب بین
او نبیند غیر دستاری و ریش   از معرف پرسد از بیش و کمیش
عارفا تو از معرف فارغی   خود همی بینی که نور بازغی
کار تقوی دارد و دین وصلاح   که ازو باشد بدو عالم فلاح
(VI / 261-262-263-264)

a) O trustworthy scholar! You may know the minutiae of knowledge (science) yet by that your spiritual eyes do not open. He (the scholar) does not see anything else but a turban and beard and if he wants to know about the perfection or non-perfection of a man, he asks a knower (the announcer). O gnostic! You are above a knower for you can see (all things) by yourself, because you are a rising light. The whole thing is to be God-fearing, pious, and righteous which makes you happier in both worlds.

b) Again Rumi says that a scholar can learn all details of a science but if his spiritual eyes are not open, he cannot see other facts. If he wants to know divine facts, he asks a saint who is able to discern the inner state of a man with a single glance (see Mift. p. 79).

c) *"Ma'arif"* in the above lines means a man who announces the presence of visitors (see Baki, p. 403).

392- Saints' graves are ennobled:

تا نهد بر گور او دل روی و کف	خاك گور از مرد هم یابد شرف
چون مشرف آمد و اقبال ناك	خاك از همسایگی، جسم پاك
به ز صد احیا بنفع و انتشار	ای بسا در گور خفته خاك وار

(VI / 3008-3009-3012)

a) The earth of a grave is ennobled by a saint's dead body, so that a person of the heart (a true believer) lays his face and hands on his grave. The earth becomes honoured and exalted because of being the neighbour of a clean body (of a saint). Many who are sleeping in graves like dust are better than living ones in providing benefits and spiritual grace.

b) Rumi says that even the dead body of a saint is sanctified. Lovers of God come to visit his grave, as many visit Rumi's tomb today, to have spiritual contact with the saint. The Koran says, "For the Hereafter they are already in despair, just as the unbelievers are in despair about those (buried) in graves" (LX/13).

393- Physical and spiritual doctors:

بر سقام تو ز تو واقف ترند	این طبیبان بدن دانش ورند
که بدین آیاتشان حاجت بود	این طبیبان نو آموزند خود
تا بقعر باد و بودت در دوند	كاملان از دور نامت بشنوند
دیده باشندت ترا با حالها	بلك پیش از زادن تو سالها

(IV / 1794-1799-1800-1801)

a) These physical doctors are knowledgeable and they know more about your sickness than you do. These physical doctors are new learners and they need symptoms. The perfect men know your name (identity) from a distance, and they can penetrate into the depths of your being. They can even go back (in time) and see your states before your birth.

b) Physical doctors are dependent on outer symptoms while spiritual doctors (the saints) can probe into your being with divine sight. They can even go back into the pre-birth states and see the causes of the sicknesses.

394- The fatal system of the saints are beyond these skies:

هر کرا با اختری پیوستگیست   مر ورا با اختر خود هم تگیست

اخترانند از ورای اختران   که اختراق و نحس نبود اندر آن

سایران در آسمانهای دگر   غیر این هفت آسمان مشتهر

راسخان در تاب انوار خدا   نی بهم پیوسته نی از هم جدا

(I / 751-754-755-756)

a) He who has an attachment to a star, keeps pace with that star. There are stars beyond these (physical) stars that are free from combustion or a bad omen. They rotate in other heavens beyond these seven heavens (the physical skies) known to us. They depend on the shining Light of God and they are neither tied to each other nor are they separate.

b) Saints belong to other heavens. Materialistic people's destinies depend on the zodiac signs while a saint's destiny is beyond these in the Proximity of God, and he is illuminated by His Light. Saints are not influenced by the celestial stars.

395- Don't trust everyone:

آدمی خوارند اغلب مردمان   از سلامعلیک شان کم جو امان

سر نهد بر پای تو قصاب وار   دم دهد تا خونت ریزد زار زار

همچو شیری صید خود را خویش کن   ترک عشوه اجنبی و خویش کن

کیست بیگانه تن خاکی تو   کز برای اوست غمناکی تو

(II / 251-260-261-264)

a) Most people are men eaters. Don't trust their *"Salaams"* (their greetings). Like a butcher, he lays his head at your feet and blows in the wind to shed your blood (as a butcher does to separate the skin of a goat). Hunt your own prey like a lion and quit the flatteries of your relatives or strangers. Do not make your home in others' land, do your own work, don't do a stranger's work. Who is the stranger? It is your body and it is due to it that you suffer.

b) Rumi, himself being a kind-hearted man, warns us to be careful of some people who are as cruel as a butcher. If a butcher kisses the goat's legs, he does it to take the skin of the goat out, not out of love. If you can't find a saint then go on struggling until you are helped by God (see T. 5-6/p. 93). Don't trust your body much, it is a stranger and it will leave you to serve another's land. You can rely on your own land, in other words your spirit.

396- Be careful of a false saint:

پیشوای بد بود آن بز شتاب　　　　می برد اصحاب را پیش قصاب

ریش شانه کرده که من سابقم　　　سابقی لیکن بسوی مرگ و غم

هین روش بگزین و ترک ریش کن　　ترک این ما و من و تشویش کن

(V / 3346-3347-3348)

a) That goat is a bad leader because he takes his followers quickly towards the butcher. He (the male-goat) has combed his beard saying, "I am the foremost". Yes, you are the foremost but towards death and sorrow. Come to yourself! Choose a right path and give up the beard and leave your ego and troubled thoughts.

b) A false saint may have a nice beard and a good looking face, but he is dangerous to his followers like a he-goat that also has a beard and leads the goats to a slaughter house. "You are the disciple and guest of someone who in his vileness will steal away all your attainments. He is not victorious himself, how can he make you victorious? He does not give you light but gives you darkness. Since he has no light himself how can others receive light by associating with him? Like a blind man who cures eyes; with what shall he anoint your eyes other than wool? He has no scent or trace of God, but his claims are greater than those of Seth or Adam" (I/2266-68-2272).

397- Saints are the insight of insights:

عقل تو همچون شتربان تو شتر / می کشاند هر طرف در حکم مر
عقل عقلند اولیا و عقلها / بر مثال اشتران تا انتها
چه قلاوز و چه اشتربان بیاب / دیده کان دیده بیند آفتاب
اینت دریای نهان در زیر کاه / پا برین که هین منه در اشتباه
عالم کبری بقدرت سحر کرد / کرد خود را در کهین نقشی نورد
(I / 2497-2498-2500-2503-2506)

a) Your sensual insight is like a camel-driver and you are the camel, and it drives you to every direction by uttering some bitter words (orders). The saints are the insight of insights and up to the end all insights are in their control like a camel. What is the guide and what is the camel driver? Find an eye that beholds the Sun (God). They are like an ocean hidden under straw, beware don't step on it by mistake (carelessly). The macrocosm showed strong magic and in a small microcosm it contained itself.

b) If you are not a perfect man (or a saint who has control over his sensual gratification), then this worldly intellect will control your physical body and its desires as a camel driver will control a camel. If you are unable to vanquish your selfhood, seek a saint who is like an ocean hidden under straws. Don't step hastily on it as you may drown in it. A saint's body is outwardly a microcosm but in fact it is a macrocosm (see also vr. IV/521).

398- The prophets:

چون خدا اندر نیاید در عیان / نایب حق اند این پیغمبران
نه غلط گفتم که نایب با منوب / گر دو پنداری قبیح آید نه خوب
نه دو باشد تا توی صورت پرست / پیش او یک گشت کز صورت برست
در معانی قسمت و اعداد نیست / در معانی تجزیه و افراد نیست
(I / 673-674-675-681)

a) Since God is not manifest on earth, the prophets are His viceroys. Actually I made a mistake by calling the prophets "viceroy" because if we regard them as two, they and their God Whom they represent, we are mistaken and it is bad to think so. As long as you worship forms, they look like two, for those who have got rid of the concept of forms, they are one. In the spiritual world there is no concept of number and division; and there are no partitions and individuals.

b) Here again Rumi says very clearly that God and His elect (prophets and saints) are not two different things for in the other world no partition exists. However, it does not mean that we should worship prophets or saints because they are like receivers and speak what God speaks. They are not God themselves.

399- A dark grave is better than a heart that has no Divine Light:

از برون پیرست و در باطن صبی   خود چه چیزست آن ولی و آن نبی

دوزخ و جنت همه اجزای اوست   هرچ اندیشی تو او بالای اوست

ابلهان تعظیم مسجد می کنند   در خرابی اهل دل جد می کنند

مسجدی کآن اندرون اولیاست   سجده گاه جمله است آنجا خداست

خانه آن دل که ماند بی ضیا   از شعاع آفتاب کبریا

تنگ و تاریکست چون جان جهود   بی نوا از ذوق سلطان ودود

گور خوشتر از چنین دل مر ترا   آخر از گور دل خود برتر آ

(II / 3101-3106-3109-3111-3129-3130-3132)

a) Outwardly he may be old but inside he is young, do you know what a saint or a prophet is? (Mift. 9-4/p. 78). Hell and paradise are all parts of his body and whatever you think of him, he is beyond that thought. The mosque that is inside the saint is the place of prostration for all. Fools venerate the mosque and torture the possessors of the heart. The heart that remains without the illumination of the Magnificent Sun rays is dark and narrow like the soul of Jews (Chit. gives "like miser's soul", p. 37 but Nich. is correct) and are deprived of the Loving King's sweet taste. A grave is better than such a (dark) heart, so come on and get out of this grave.

b) A saint can outwardly be old as they name him *"Pir"* ="an old man" in Persian, Urdu and Turkish but inwardly he is young because his soul is full of life. Paradise (the Mercy of God) and Hell (the Wrath of God) are part of a saint's being. He has control over them since he is with God. If he is angry with you, God is angry with you, and if he is happy with you, God is happy with you (Mift. and MM). A saint's heart is like a mosque and you can pray to God in his presence. A heart without Divine Light is as dark as a grave. "Jew" here means "a timid person" and not the Jewish race.

400- Don't shout and raise your voice at a beggar:

جود می جوید گدایان و ضعاف   همچو خوبان کآینه جویند صاف

روی خوبان ز آینه زیبا شود   روی احسان از گدا پیدا شود

پس ازین فرمود حق در والضحی   بانگ کم زن ای محمد بر گدا

(I / 2745-2746-2747)

a) Beggars and the helpless seek generosity like the beautiful that look for a mirror. The face of the beautiful becomes charming because of the mirror; the face of kindness and generosity is brought to light by the beggars. Consequently, they are the mirrors of Divine Kindness, and those who are with God have absolute generosity.

b) In the above lines *"Fakir"* has a different meaning. There is a well known Tradition of Muhammed, "My poverty is my pride". This means that my exoteric poverty enabled me to remember God everytime, and there is left nothing in me other than God. There are *"fakirs"* in this sense. They give up everything and live from hand to mouth on alms. Among such people true lovers of God can also be found. As God says in the Koran, "Therefore treat not the orphan with harshness, nor repulse the petitioner" (XCIII/9-10). As in the case of saints, there are false beggars who live on others' money and take alcohol. As the Koran says above, even to such people we should behave politely for only God knows who is closer to Him. Besides, God loves generosity. If you expect mercy of God, then take pity on his poor and needy creatures. Rumi now continues with the condition of a false dervish (or *Fakir*).

401- The false dervish:

نقش سگ را تو میندار استخوان   نقش درویشست او نی اهل نان
پیش نقش مرده کم نه طبق   فقر لقمه دارد او نی فقر حق
ذات نبود وهم اسما و صفات   گر توهم می کند او عشق ذات
حق نزاییدست او لم یولد است   وهم زاییده ز اوصاف و حدث
(I / 2752-2753-2757-2758)

a) He is the picture (a copy) of the dervish and he does not deserve bread. Don't put bones in front of a picture of a dog. He (the false dervish) is in need of a morsel of food not of Reality and don't put a plate (of food) in front of a dead picture. If he thinks that he is in love with the Essence of God, perception only of Divine Attributes is not God's Being. Ideas are created things and are born of thought. God is born of none and "He gives birth to none".

b) Rumi here wants to make a distinction between a real and a false dervish. Dervishes and fakirs are the lower class of Sufis. A hypocritical dervish worships morsels of food while a true dervish worships only God. A false dervish is attached to the attributes of God and cannot see yonder for even those names are shapes and forms, while God has no shape. A real dervish's target is even beyond those names.

402- Upon the Unseen World:

غیب را ابری و آبی دیگرست   آسمان و آفتابی دیگرست

هست باران از پی پروردگی   هست باران از پی پژمردگی

همچنین سرما و باد و آفتاب   بر تفاوت دان و سر رشته بیان

همچنین در غیب انواعست این   در زیان و سود و در ربع و غبین

این دم ابدال باشد زآن بهار   در دل و جان روید از وی سبزه زار

گر درخت خشک باشد در مکان   عیب آن از باد جان افزا مدان

(I / 2035-2037-2040-2041-2042-2044)

a) The unseen world has different clouds, water, sky and sun. There is rain for nourishing and for decaying. Similarly, winter, wind and the sun are all different; and thus find the end of the rope (the hint). In the same way, in the unseen world loss and gain, sorrow and fraud are of a different type. The breath of a saint comes from the spring of the other world which makes the green garden flourish in heart and soul. If you see any dry tree in a place (this world), don't think that the defect of the tree is because of the life-giving wind (breath).

b) The universe of the other world is not like ours; and if one is able to open one's eyes to that unseen world, one has an entirely new source of knowledge and pleasures (Taki 2/p. 76). The breath of a saint brings news of the other world, but if some fail to receive it don't blame the saint.

403- There are seven hundred curtains of light to be covered before you reach God:

زآنک هفصد پرده دارد نور حق   پرده های نور دان چندین طبق

از پس هر پرده قومی را مقام   صف صف اند این پردهاشان تا امام

اهل صف آخرین از ضعف خویش   چشمشان طاقت ندارد نور پیش

وآن صف پیش از ضعیفی بصر   تاب نآرد روشنایی بیشتر

روشنی کو حیات اولست   رنج جان و فتنه این احولست

احولیها اندک اندک کم شود   چون ز منصد بگذرد او یم شود

(II / 821-822-823-824-825-826)

a) Because the Light of God has seven hundred (many) veils these veils of light can each be considered as a layer Behind each layer of light, there is a station of people and thus these layers are like rows that reach up to the front line. Those in the last line (in the rear) have no power and their eyes cannot tolerate the Light as much as those in the front line. Those in the front line, however, cannot bear the strong rays of the front light because of the weakness of their sight. The light that is life-giving for the front line is dangerous and painful for the line at the back (who have squint eyes). When they (the squinters) pass the layers of the light one by one, they, too, begin to lose their squint and become part of the Sea (of Light).

b) The Central Light is the Divine Light and circling around it are the lines of the spirits according to their purity. Saints (especially Kutubs) are closer to the Central Light. Others also try to get closer and immerse themselves in the Sea of Light. The main idea here is that the closer you get to God the happier you are. The more you get away from the Centre, the more lost and abandoned you feel. A Koranic verse says, "God is the protector of those who have faith, from the depths of the darkness He will lead them forth into light. Those who reject faith their patrons (Satanic guides) are evil ones, from light they will lead them forth into the depths of darkness" (II/257).

404- About narrow-minded people:

عاشق تصویر و وهم خویشتن کی بود از عاشقان ذوالمنن
عاشق آن وهم اگر صادق بود آن مجازش تا حقیقت می کشد
شرح میخواهد بیان این سخن لیک می ترسم ز افهام کهن
(I / 2759-2760-2761)

a) A person who is in love with his own pictures of reality and ideas how can he be one of those who love God (the Most Generous)? Nevertheless, if that lover of false conception is sincere, it can lead him to Reality. This point needs further explanation, but I am afraid of the old-fashioned (fanatic) people.

b) The person who loves God without thinking of his egoistic demands is the true lover. God does not deprive even the lovers who have ego, if they are sincere in loving God, as He says, "And those who strive in Our (cause), We will certainly guide them to our paths for verily God is with those who do right" (the Koran, XXIX/69). Rumi further says about short-sighted people: "Old minded and short sighted people create hundreds of evil ideas" (I/2762).

405- Every atom has a door that opens to God:

هر هوا و ذره خود منظریست   ناگشاده کی گرد آنجا دریست
تا بنگشاید دری را دیدبان   در درون هرگز نجنبد این گمان
چون گشاده شد دری حیران شود   پر بروید بر گمان پران شود
(I / 3766-3767-3768)

a) Every atom (and air) is a window that opens to God. Where there is a door how can it remain closed (forever)? (see T. 5-6/1734 and Mift. 1-4/246). Unless the man or the guard opens the door, this idea never stirs, the door opens and the bird of hope begins to fly.

b) Each atom is like a door of knowledge that opens to God but you have to open it (work on it). You discover atomic power, and the great energy it conceals and the air that carries gases of different kinds. "The guard" here may mean the spiritual guardian of God.

406- The source of life:

این صدفهای قوالب در جهان   گرچه جمله زنده اند از بحر جان
لیک اندر هر صدف نبود گهر   چشم بگشا در دل هریک نگر
گر بصورت بنگری کوهی بشکل   در بزرگی هست صد چندانک لعل
لیک پوشیده نباشد بر تو این   کز همه اعضا دو چشم آمد گزین
هم زمین و بحر و هم مهر و فلک   زنده از وی همچو از دریا سمک
(II / 1023-1024-1026-1028-1036)

a) These bodies, like shells, are all in life due to the Sea of soul, but not every shell has a pearl. Open your eyes and see into each heart. If you look at the shape of a mountain, it is a hundred times larger than a diamond. It is not concealed from you that two eyes are above all other parts of the body. The earth and ocean, as well as the sun and the sky are all living like the fish that is able to exist because of the sea.

b) The source of life is God Himself. He is like a sea and all other created things or beings are like a fish. Don't be deceived by the size of things: they may be as big as a mountain, but not as valuable as a small diamond. Similarly, a man may be strong and healthy looking yet if he has no good heart he is worthless, too.

407- Show us things as they are:

ای مسیر کرده ما را در جهان   سخره و بیگار ما را وا رهان
طعمه بنموده بما وآن بودن شست   آنچنان بنما بما آنرا که هست
(II / 466-467)

a) O God who has made difficult things easy for us, free us from vain obligations and unpaid duties. This world showed us a morsel, although it was a bait, so "Show us the things as they are".

b) There are many things that attract us and we keep on doing them not knowing what the result will be. We need the help of God for only He knows what the result will be. We are often tricked by the deceptive charms of this world. We can pray to God as Muhammed did, "God show me things as they are".

408- God is with us through our spirit:

جان کل با جان جزو آسیب کرد   جان ازو دری ستد در جیب کرد
همچو مریم جان از آن آسیب جیب   حامله شد از مسیح دلفریب
آن مسیحی نه که بر خشک و ترست   آن مسیحی کز مساحت برترست
پس ز جان جان چو حامل گشت جان   از چنین جانی شود حامل جهان
پس جهان زاید جهان دیگری   این حشر را وا نماید محشری
(II / 1183-1184-1185-1186-1187)

a) The Universal Soul came in contact with the individual soul. The soul took a pearl from it and put the pearl in its chest (heart). The individual soul thus became pregnant like Mary, who was pregnant with the charming baby (Jesus). It was not the kind of Jesus to be found on the earth or on the water but the Jesus that is from far beyond (non-dimensional world). So when the soul has been impregnated by the Soul of souls, by the same Soul the whole universe is impregnated.

b) The individual soul received a drop of the Sea of Unity (called Spirit), and will keep it until it is set free by death. "Jesus" in the above lines means Christ's holy spirit but not his body (see T. 7-8/392). This world, in the manner of our body, is also pregnant with the Divine Command and will give birth to a new world. It, too, has pangs and pains. Therefore, real happiness and relief exist after death. "He has written faith in their hearts, and strengthened them with a spirit from Himself" (the Koran, LVIII/22). It was this Spirit that impregnated the Virgin Mary; and it is the same Spirit that impregnated His lovers with spiritual potential (Mift. 2-2/143).

409- Don't reveal Divine Secrets to everyone:

این زبان چون سنگ و فم آهن وشست وآنچ بجهد از زبان چون آتشست
سنگ و آهن را مزن برهم گزاف گه ز روی نقل و گاه از روی لاف
زآنك تاریکست و هر سو پنبه زار در میان پنبه چون باشد شرار
جانها در اصل خود عیسی دمست یك دمش زخمست و دیگر مرهمست
گر حجاب از جانها بر خاستی گفت هر جانی مسیح آساستی

a 1592 فم آهن G : هم آتش N   (I / 1593-1594-1595-1598-1599)

a) This tongue is like a (flint) stone and the mouth is like iron. Whatever comes out of the tongue is fire. Do not strike the stone and the iron in vain, sometimes for telling a story or sometimes for just a chat. Because it is dark and there is a cotton field all around, how then can a spark be (harmless) among cotton? Spirits in their original forms (nature) have the life-giving effect of Jesus' breath, one breath of which is a wound, the other of which is an ointment. If you raised the bodily veils from the spirits, the speech of each spirit would be like the breath of Messiah.

b) This is a wonderful comparison between the tongue and mouth. The tongue is like a flint stone and the mouth is like steel. One has to be very careful with this implement. In the darkness of this world we don't know who is good and who is bad. The fire of the words uttered may burn the cotton fields (labours) around us. Those who have become free of the lower self like Jesus, their speeches have a great effect on people.

410- Every happy moment is deceptive:

هر زمانی که شدی تو کامران آن دم خوش را کنار بام دان
بر زمان خوش هراسان باش تو همچو گنجش خفیه کن نه فاش تو
تا نیاید بر ولا ناگه بلا ترس ترسان رو در آن مکمن هلا

(IV / 2147-2148-2149)

a) Whenever you are successful; Beware! that is the moment when you are at the edge of a roof. At the time of happiness take care of it (that moment) like a treasure so that the pleasure may not change into a mishap. Go into that ambush carefully and cautiously.

b) Many who receive spiritual aid become intoxicated and begin to reveal their secrets, like Hallaj-i Mansur (838-921 A.D.) who said "I am Reality (God)" and was killed at Baghdad. Beyazid-i Bastami (d. 874) endangered his life by saying "Inside my robe there is left nothing but God" (see vol. IV/vrs. 2101). In the same way if you have Divine secrets don't reveal them or you will fall from the edge of a roof. To reveal your secrets and be proud of them, is a sign of your self-conceit which God does not like (see also III/vrs. 18-19-20 for similar advice).

411- Rumi is not allowed to reveal other secrets of God:

گر گشاید دل سر انبان راز   جان بسوی عرش آرد ترک تاز
من تمام این نیآرم گفت از آن   منع می آید ز صاحب مرکزان
(I / 1479-1680)

a) If a heart tries to open the bag of secrets the soul will rush madly towards the highest heavens. I cannot tell you all about it, because the ones in the Centre don't allow me to disclose (the secrets) further.

b) Rumi says that he cannot reveal Divine secrets any further, because the angelic powers of the Centre don't let him do so; and if anyone tries to reveal Divine secrets his soul will fly towards the Centre, quickly (he will be withdrawn to the Centre).

412- Secrets can be disclosed only to lovers of God:

راز جز با رازدان انباز نیست   راز اندر گوش منکر راز نیست
گفت از بانگ و علالای سگان   هیچ وا گردد ز راهی کاروان
مه فشاند نور و سگ عوعو کند   هر کسی بر خلقت خود می تند
b 14 خلقت G : طینت Taki   (VI / 8-12-14)

a) The secret is only a partner with a knower of secrets and is not a secret in the ears of an infidel. He (Noah) said, "Does a caravan return from a journey because of barking and noise of dogs?" The moon keeps on shedding light while the dogs keep on barking. Everyone acts according to his nature. If dirt is bad for our eyes, it is like sugar for dogs and pigs.

b) Spiritual secrets are revealed only to those who know what God is. If you reveal them to a non-believer he may make fun of you. It is better to mind your own business and continue to love God. Nobody can harm you if you are sincere. There is a Turkish proverb relevant here: "*İt ürür, kervan yürür* =Although dogs keep on barking, the caravan keeps on going".

413- The table of lovers is like the hermitage of Christ:

صومعه عیسیست خوان اهل دل	هان و هان ای مبتلا این در مهل
جمع گشتندی ز هر اطراف خلق	از ضریر و لنگ و شل و اهل دلق
بر در آن صومعه عیسی صباح	تا بدم اوشان رهاند از جناح
او چو فارغ گشتی از اوراد خویش	چاشتگه بیرون شدی آن خوب کیش
جوق جوقی مبتلا دیدی نزار	شسته بر در در امید و انتظار
جملگان چون اشتران بسته پای	که گشایی زانوی ایشان برای
خوش دوان و شادمانه سوی خان	از دعای او شدندی پا دوان

(III / 298-299-300-301-302-305-306)

a) The table of lovers of God is like the hermitage of Jesus. O you who have got used to them (the lovers), don't leave their gate. All sorts of people, the blind, the lame, the palsied, the robe wearers (Sufis) would gather together from all parts of the world, and they would wait till morning at the door of Jesus' hermitage so that they might obtain his breath to become free of their sins. When that man of good religion finished his routine orations (prayers), he would come out of his cell in the morning and would say, "O you afflicted ones! All your demands have been met by God". At this all the people, like camels whose knees have been untied, would run towards their houses, happy and gay. Their feet would become untied due to Jesus' prayers.

b) The living saints are like Christ. Their spiritual description as "The table of the lovers of God" is as reviving as that of Christ. So, don't abandon their gate. "*Ehl-i Dil* =the lovers who have given hearts to the Same Beloved".

414- Be persistent in your belief:

وقت درد مرگ از آن سو می نمی	چونک دردت رقت چونی اعجمی
این از آن آمد که حق را بی گمان	هرکه بشناسد بود دایم بر آن
عقل جزوی گاه چیره گه نگون	عقل کلی ایمن از ریب المنون
عقل بفروش و هنر حیرت بخر	رو بخواری نی بخارا ای پسر

(III / 1141-1143-1145-1146)

a) When you experience pains or death you incline towards God and when they (the pains) pass away you become ignorant (indifferent to God). This is because only he who knows God without doubt will be busy with Him. The partial insight is now ruling and now overthrown, while the universal insight is safe from all kinds of events (pains, worries, death and so on). Therefore, sell the (partial) insight and buy the state of Divine Bewilderment. Go to lowliness and not to Bukhara (the centre of learning).

b) As long as you are veiled by the partial insight, you are still struggling between belief and non-belief as the Koran says, "Now, when the trouble touches a man, he cries to Us; but when We bestow a favour upon him as from Ourselves", he says: "This has been given to me because of a certain knowledge I had. Nay but this is a trial, but most of them don't understand" (XXXIX/49). A lover of God who has attained the stage of Divine Bewilderment is free from his ego and is unaware of the worldly events. This stage is mentioned as "The Valley of Astonishment" by Feriduddin Attar (see The Conference of the Birds, C. S. Nott, Arkana 1954, p. 119). It is the love of God that frees you from the sadness caused by bewilderment. "The station of Bewilderment comes after "*Tawhid* =Unity of God". It is a state where all other forms and knowledges disappear and only the existence of God, as it was before physical creation, is in view" (see Kusheyri's Treatise, p. 475). Rumi was content to stay in Konya after he found his spiritual master Shams and he did not go to Bukhara for further studies.

415- When you are already with God, what value can religious books have?:

پیش سلطان خوش نشسته در قبول   زشت باشد جستن نامه و رسول
من بپیشت حاضر و تو نامه خوان   نیست این باری نشان عاشقان
(III / 1405-1409)

a) For a man who is seated happily beside the Sultan, it is disgraceful to look for a letter or a messenger to send to him. "I am present in your presence, but you are reading my letter; it is not a sign of a (True) lover".

b) If you are already in the presence of your beloved, what value do letters have? It would be awkward to read a beloved's letter if the beloved is there. Similarly, it is bad manners to read the Bible or the Koran when you are in the presence of your Beloved (God). This is a very high stage, a stage where you observe

"Thou ask my heart's situation, but I am dumbfounded by thy face,
I want to say some words, but my words do not come to my mouth".
(see Mift. 3/I p. 251)

416- Your heart is the mosque itself:

باغـها و میوه‌ها اندر دلـست / عکس لطف آن برین آب و گلست

جمله مغروران برین عکس آمده / بر گمـانی کـین بـود جنت کده

می گریزند از اصـول باغها / بر خیـالی می کنند آن لاغها

ای خنک آنرا که پیش از مرگ مرد / یعنی او از اصل این زر بوی برد

مسجدست آن دل که جسمش ساجدست / یـار بد خروب هرجا مسجدست

بر کن از بیخش که گر سر بر زند / مر ترا و مسجدت را بر کند

نیست آن سوً رنج فکرت بر دماغ / که دماغ و عقل روید دشت و باغ

(IV / 1365-1368-1369-1372-1383-1385-1427)

a) Orchards and fruits are in the heart (soul) and the reflection of their beauty is falling on the external world. All those who come to this reflection in the hope that it may become paradise for them are deceived. They are actually running away from the real orchards and are making merry over empty dreams. Lucky is the man who managed to die (to this world) and got a scent of that real vineyard. This heart is a mosque if the body worships (prostrates itself before) it but the bad friend (your lower self) is like a carob tree in that mosque. So uproot that tree, which otherwise will demolish your mosque. In the other world, the brain is not burdened with these worries (of this world). Thus even the desert and gardens produce the brain and intellect.

b) The original gardens and orchards (sources of happiness) are in the other world. Whatever is here in this world is nothing but a dream. For example, when we are happy nature looks lovely to us, but when we are unhappy everything looks gloomy and sad. This means that real unchangeable happiness is spiritual as God says in the Koran, "The life of this world is but goods and chattels of deception" (III/185). Those who think this world has everything that they need, and are satisfied with what their deceptive intellect shows, are mistaken. If your body bows to your heart (surrenders to it), you can find the Essence and your real mosque inside you reveals itself. But if your heart bows to the body (serves your own ego), you are in the temporary mosque. In the other world trees, deserts, and seas have intellect. What privilege then will you have in the Presence of God other than His love?

417- The earth and the sky are like an apple of the Divine Tree:

آسمانها و زمین یك سیب دان   کز درخت قدرت حق شد عیان
تو چو کرمی در میان سیب در   وز درخت و باغبانی بسی خبر
آن یکی کرمی دگر در سیب هم   لیك جانش از برون صاحب علم
(IV / 1869-1870-1871)

a) Suppose that this earth and sky (all the universe) are an apple and they appeared on the tree of the Divine Power. You are like a worm in it and you don't know either the tree or the gardener. There is another worm that is in the apple, too, but its soul has hoisted the banner of (the Divine Power) from outside.

b) All the visible universe is like an apple while God's Power is like a tree on which it has grown and ripened. The poor worm in it has no knowledge of the tree or of the apple itself like the fishes in an aquarium who are not aware of the water or the feeder or like the cells of our body who know nothing of us. But the Saint is like a worm that has discovered more about the tree, the apple, and the Gardener.

418- Holy spirits are always ready to help us:

ساحره دنیا قوی دانا زنیست   حل سحر او بپای عامه نیست
ور گشادی عقد او را عقل ها   انبیا را کی فرستادی خدا
پس وصال این فراق آن بود   صحت این تن سقام جان بود
ای که صبرت نیست از دنیای دون   چونت صبرست از خدا ای دوست چون
گر ببینی یك نفس حسن ودود   اندر آتش افگنی جان و وجود
خفته باشی بر لب جو خشك لب   می دوی سوی سراب اندر طلب
تا بود که سالکی بر تو زند   از خیالات نعاست بر کند
موج بر وی می زند بی احتراز   خفته پویان در بیابان دراز
(IV / 3196-3197-3209-3212-3215-3228-3237-3240)

a) This world, the witch, is a powerful cunning woman; it is not in the hands of common people to undo her witch-craft and if they could undo it, God wouldn't send prophets to the earth. Union with this world is separation from the other world, and health of this physical body is the sickness of the spiritual body. O you who have no patience to do without this mean world, then how can you have patience without God, O my friend? If you happen to see God's Beauty for a moment, you will cast your soul and body in fire (destroy it). (It is strange that) You are sleeping with your lips dry on the bank of a river and are running towards a mirage in search of water. You may meet a saint on the path (of your life) and he may free you from the vain idea of sleeping. The waves come and beat at him (the saint) without hesitation, although he is asleep he can run in the long endless wildernesses.

b) This world is cunning like a witch and a simple man cannot resist her spell; only the Mercy of God can reverse her charm. "With My Punishment I visit whom I will; but My mercy extendeth to all things. That (Mercy) I shall ordain for those who do right and practise regular charity, and those who believe in Our Signs" (the Koran, VII/156) and "Ask and you will receive; seek and you will find; knock and the door will be opened" (the Bible, Math/7). Once you have a glimpse of the Divine Epiphany, nothing of this world will truly attract you any more. On the contrary, if your spiritual eyes are not open, you will sense the Breath of God even if it is closer to you than your jugular vein because you are enchanted by this witch (the world).

419- On the spiritual path all egoistic ideas are idols:

پیش بینی این خرد تا گور بود   وآن صاحب‌دل بنفخ صور بود
همچو موسی نور کی یابد زجیب   سخره استاد و شاگرد کتاب
منصب تعلیم نوع شهوتست   هر خیال شهوتی در ره بتست
زآن کله مر چشم بازان را سدست   که همه میلش سوی جنس خودست
چون برید از جنس با شه گشت یار   بر گشاید چشم او را باز دار
گر نخواهی هر دمی این خفت خیز   کن ز خاك پای مردی چشم تیز

(IV / 3311-3314-3317-3337-3338-3372)

a 3337 را سدست G : شداست Mift.

a) The foresight of this intellect reaches only to the grave (its earth) but that of a spiritual man to the blast of the trumpet (of resurrection). The one who is blindly obedient to a teacher and follows books, how can he find light in his own heart like Moses? The job of teaching and being taught is also a part of the carnal desires. On the path of the spiritual progress all egoistic ideas are idols. (And notice that) A hood is placed on the eyes of falcons to blind them because they have a bias for their own kind. When the falcon is cut off from its own kind, it becomes a friend of the King (its owner), and the falconer unveils its eyes. If you don't like this going to sleep and getting up again, then go and find the dust of a saint's feet (enter his service).

b) This insight guides you to the grave but the universal wisdom guides you until the last day of resurrection (see Mift., p. 260). If you really want to find God, He is not confined in books: seek Him in the heart of a saint. Close your carnal eyes to these worldly charms so that like a falcon you give up this world and get used to the arm of your Real Master. If you don't want up and downs in your spiritual progress and want to go straight to God then enter the service of a saint.

420- God is with you as your intellect is:

کآن شهی که می ندیدندیش فاش   بود با ایشان نهان اندر معاش
چون خرد با تست مشرف برتنت   گرچه زو قاصر بود این دیدنت
چه عجب گر خالق آن عقل نیز   با تو باشد چون نه تو مستجیز
بی تعلق نیست مخلوقی بدو   آن تعلق هست بی چون ای عمو
                                    (IV / 3677-3678-3680-3695)

a) The King whom they failed to see clearly with them was secretly with them through out their lives, like the intelligence that rules your body, which you don't see. It is a matter of no surprise if the Creator of the intellect is also with you while you are not aware of it (or think it is not proper see Lugat-i Masnevi, No. 2042, fl.17a). No living beings are disconnected from Him but that connection is without "Why and How".

b) We don't see our own intellect and we don't know what it is. Similarly, God is hidden within us, and our ego may refuse to recognise it. "Every thought and idea that you conceive, thereto God is closely attached, for it is He who gives being to that idea and thought and presents them to you. Only He is so exceeding near that you cannot see Him" (Discourses, Arberry, p. 180).

421- If you want to increase your spiritual attainment, speak less:

چون بیآمد در زبان شد خرج مغز   خرج کم کن تا بماند مغز نغز
مرد کم گوینده را فکرست زفت   قشر گفتن چون فزون شد مغز رفت
پوست افزون بود لاغر بود مغز   پوست لاغر شد چو کامل گشت و نغز
                                    (V / 1176-1177-1178)

a) When your words come to the tongue, the essence is wasted, so use fewer words so that your precious essence may not waste away. The man who speaks less has sound ideas, but when speech increases (like the skin of a fruit) the essence becomes less. If the skin is thick, the essence (kernel) is less and if the essence is increased the skin becomes thinner.

b) Our spiritual improvement is like the skin of a fruit. Think of a walnut. If the skin is thick the kernel is thin, and if the kernel is thick the skin is thin. In the same way if one speaks too much one's spiritual improvement is less, and vice versa.

422- All forms are like bowls and they are known by what God pours into them:

عشق را بر حی جان افزای دار عشق بر مرده نباشد پایدار
سنگ اندر چشمه متواری شود چون ز سنگی چشمه جاری شود
آنچ حق ریزد بدآن گیرد علو کاسها دان این صور را و اندرو
(V / 3272-3283-3285)

a) Love for the dead is not eternal, keep your own love on the Living One who increases spiritual life. When a fountain runs out of a rock, the rock disappears behind the fountain. Know that these forms are like bowls, and they acquire value through whatever God pours into them.

b) If you love a mortal being your love will also be mortal, but if you love an Immortal Being, your love will also be immortal. When a spring gushes out of a rock, the rock is hidden behind it. Similarly, when God's light comes forth, our physical body is hidden behind it. Regard these forms as bowls and evaluate them by the amount of Divine Light poured into them by God, in other words try to see the Divine Epiphany in them.

423- Keep by the Sea of Mercy of God:

آید از دریا مبارک ساعتی رحمتی بی علتی بی خدمتی
گرچه باشند اهل دریابار زرد الله الله گرد دریابار گرد
(V / 3624-3625)

a) Auspicious is the hour when God's Mercy comes without labour and service. For God's sake, keep by the Sea although the faces of the sea people may look pale and colourless (fatigued).

b) To some people Divine Mercy comes without labour, but that auspicious event occurs especially when you keep close to the lovers of God, despite the fact that they may have pale faces and torn off clothes (see Mift., p. 2314).

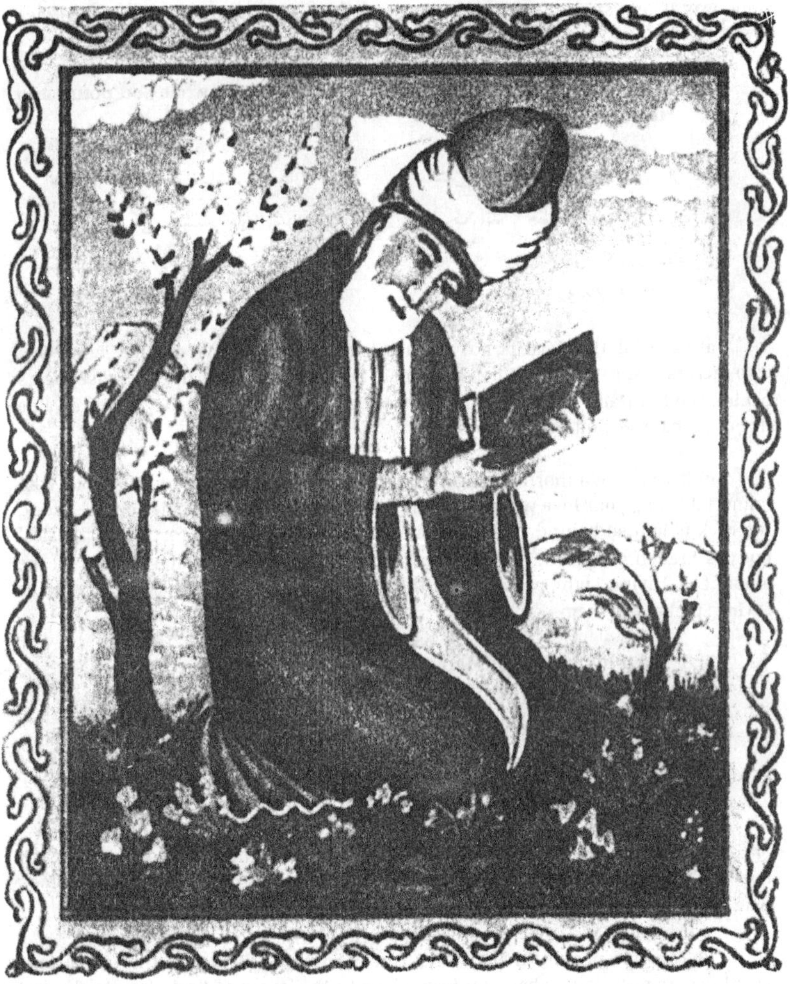

CHAPTER XII

Step VIII: Observation of God in every phenomenon

Spiritual essence is the inner aspect of form which has no dimension or colour.

"Everyone has turned his face toward some direction, but the saints have turned toward the direction without directions" (M. V/350).

"Colourlessness is the root of all colours, peace is the root of all wars".
(M. V/59)

"Form comes into existence from the Formless, just as smoke is born from fire" (M. VI/3712).

It is the spiritual essence which when discovered within ourself or in other things leads us to Unity where neither form nor existence is left. The last two chapters of this book (XII and XIII) will deal with these key stages of the spiritual life. As we go towards Unity (Chapter XIII), we notice that the details become shorter, too, for we climb up the peak of the spiritual mountain.

It is the wind in the Ney that gives life to it, otherwise it is the dry piece of reed. In the same manner, it is the Light of God that gives life to man's body. By means of this inner light we can find a path to God.

"Know that the outward form passes away, but the world of essence remains forever" (M. II/1020).

"After all, how does this inanimate cloud know that it must send down rain in season? You see the earth how it nurtures plants and makes one into ten. Well, Someone does this. See Him by means of this world, and take replenishment from Him. Just as you take replenishment from the essence of the world through the world's form" (Discourses, p. 51).

"When we say God is not in the heavens, we do not mean that He is not in the heavens. What we mean is that the heavens do not encompass Him, but He encompasses them. He has a connection to the heavens, but it is ineffable and inscrutable, just as He has established an ineffable and inscrutable connection with you. Everything is in the hand of His Power. Everything is the locus of His Self manifestation and under His control. So He is not outside the heavens and the created worlds, nor is He completely inside them. In other words, these do not encompass Him, but He encompasses them" (Discourses, p. 219).

"Seize upon the outward, even if it flies crookedly! In the end, the outward leads to the inward" (M. III/526).

The essence of man possesses the heart, the spirit and the intellect which after compression *(Kabz)* extend *(bast)* and join with the Universal Source. The centre of creation on earth is man. All other created things should bow to him. This universe is a part of man, even if man appears to be a part of it.

We should not bow to the forms and shapes of this world because the more Divine Attributes we collect within ourselves, the more things around us bow to us:

"He whose intellect dominates his sensuality is higher than the angels, and he whose sensuality dominates his intellect is lower than the beasts" (Discourses, p. 90).

"Know that (the world of) created beings is like pure and limpid water in which the attributes of the Almighty are shining" (M. VI/3172).

"The whole sum of pictured forms (phenomena) is a (mere) reflection in the water of the river: when you rub your eye, (you will notice that) all of them are really He" (M. VI/3183).

424- Unicolority of Oneness:

نیست یکرنگی کزو خیزد ملال   بل مثال ماهی و آب زلال
گرچ در خشکی هزاران رنگهاست   ماهیان را با یبوست جنگهاست
(I / 502-503)

a) It is not the kind of unicolority that one is bored with but rather like that of fishes and clear water. Doubtlessly, there are thousands of colours on earth, yet fishes are at war with dryness.

b) "Unicolority" here means the formlessness and colourlessness in the world of Oneness. A question can be asked "Can't a world of colourlessness be boring?" Rumi says that souls are like fish, they will never be fed up with colourlessness just as fishes are never fed up with the water they live in.

425- The real eye is the one that observes only God:

آدمی دیدست و باقی پوستست   دید آنست آن که دید دوستست
چونک دید دوست نبود کور به   دوست کو باقی نباشد دور به
(I / 1406-1407)

a) Man is an eye, and the rest is skin. But the real eye is the one that sees only the Friend. If one fails to see the Friend, it is better to be blind, and if the friend is mortal it is better to keep away from him.

b) If a man cannot perceive Reality then there is little use for the sensory eyes and the intellect (see Mift. I-2/ p. 188) and it is this faculty of perceiving reality that holds a man above animality.

426- Don't stay at the gate:

هر که محراب نمازش گشت عین   سوی ایمان رفتنش می دان تو شین

هر که با سلطان شود او همنشین   بر درش بودن بود عیب و غبین

(I / 1765-1767)

a) It is humiliation for a person whose arch *(Mihrab)* in prayers is the Presence of God and yet he goes back to (the tradition) belief; and he who has become an intimate friend of the sultan it is awkward and foolish for him to stay at the door (of the palace).

b) A person who has attained the Presence and the View of God, should not turn back to religious details. It will be like staying at the door of a Beloved who wants you to come inside.

c) *"Mihrab"* is the arch of the mosque where the muslim priest (the imam) stands in front of the other lines of worshippers.

427- Every being is related to the essence:

جزو کل نی جزوها نیست بکل   نی چو بوی گل که باشد جزو گل

لطف سبزه جزو لطف گل بود   بانگ قمری جزو آن بلبل بود

(I / 2905-2906)

a) The parts of the whole are not parts in relation to the Whole not even like the scent of a rose which is regarded as a part of the rose. The beauty of the green plant is the part of the Rose's beauty, the coo of the turtle-dove is a part of that Nightingale.

b) Here Rumi explains what he means by "the part of the Whole" throughout the Masnevi. Every creature is related to the Whole (God) in essence not in the physical sense. The turtle-dove and nightingale are two different birds, apparently, but as far as the Essence is concerned they are one. The hand of an individual is a part of him, but it is not him. Similarly, everything is a part of God but is not God Himself. Besides, the whole is dependent on its parts while God is not.

428- The light of the heart is concealed in a drop of blood:

هرك باشد شاه دردش را دوا   گر چو نی نالد نباشد بی نوا
من نیم جنس شهنشه دور ازو   لیك دارم در تجلی نور ازو
جنس ما چون نیست جنس شاه ما   مای ما شد بهر مای او فنا
چون فنا شد مای ما او ماند فرد   پیش پای اسب او گردم چو گرد
آخر این جان با بدن پیوسته است   هیچ این جان با بدن ماننـد هست
تاب نور چشم با پیه است جفت   نور دل در قطره خونی نهفت

(II / 1167-1170-1173-1174-1179-1180)

a) He whose remedy is the king's help, he may seem to wail like the Ney, yet he is not helpless. I don't claim to be of the kind of the king of kings (God), far be this idea from Him! but I have of the light of Him in my manifestation. Since my kind is not of the kind of the king, our being has become non-existent in order to enliven His Being. When our being becomes non-existent and He remains alone, I circle around the feet of his horse, like dust. After all, soul is connected with the body, but does soul have any likeness to the body? The brightness of the light of an eye is connected with the fat (aqueous humor) and the light of the heart is hidden by a drop of blood.

b) If God helps those who lament like the Ney (as Rumi did) they are not truly unhappy for God replies to their wailing. He may seem to be helpless outwardly, but the Divine Help is always with him (see MM 2/114). These are the words of a Hawk (metaphorically a lover of God) "I am not congener of God, but His light (spirit) is with me. When I become non-existence (physically), only God remains and my dust (spirit) will whirl around His Being for God's traces do not disappear". The light of vision has nothing to do with the fat or the fluid of a body, yet they are interrelated, so is the light of the heart related to its blood-cells. They live for themselves but indirectly they live for us. In the same manner, spirit has no likeness with the flesh, yet it is the source of our life.

429- Two opposite wings for balance:

زآن همی گرداندت حالی بحال   ضد بضد پیدا کنان در انتقال
تا دو پر باشی که مرغ یك پره   عاجز آمد از پریدن ای سره

(II / 1552-1554)

a) God makes you to pass from state to state, manifesting an opposite by means of the opposite in the change. So that you may have two wings (negative and positive) for a single winged bird fails to fly, o you excellent reader.

b) In order to reach God from this physical world, the judgment has to learn difference between good and bad which are like two wings, left and right. The left wing is the bad (negative) one, and the right wing is the good (positive) one. There is a reference to the Koranic verse, "Peace be upon thee from the companions of the right hand" (LVI/91 and 27, 38). God, however, is above opposites and when you reach Him neither good nor bad is left. Nich. and Mift. add that hope and fear *(khawf and rija)* are also two opposite elements that take a man to God. If a man has only fear, he loses hope of reaching God; if he has only the hope of being forgiven, he becomes spoilt and proud.

430- Be friends with everyone and visit the sick:

در عیادت رفتن تو فایده ست   فایده آن باز با تو عایده ست

فایده اول که آن شخص علیل   بوک قطبی باشد و شاه جلیل

ور نباشد قطب یار ره بود   شه نباشد فارس اسپه بود

حاصل این آمد که یار جمع باش   همچو بتگر از حجر یاری تراش

چون ترا آن چشم باطن بین نبود   گنج می پندار اندر هر وجود

(II / 2143-2144-2145-2150-2155)

a) To visit a sick person is fruitful for you. One benefit is that he will visit you in return (when you are sick). The first (other) benefit is that the sick man may be a saint and a glorious friend, and if not he can (at least) be your fellow-traveller. He may not be a king (a saint), he may be an ordinary cavalier *(dervish)*. Nevertheless, be friendly with everyone and like an idol-maker carve a friend out of stone. If you don't possess the spiritual eye, then think that each person has some kind of treasure in him.

b) If you visit a sick person you have the following benefits: 1- The sick person will visit you when you fall sick 2- If he is a saint (a lover of God) he will pray for you 3- He may be a simple man but a dervish. "Carve a friend out of stone" does not mean worship idols (Mift. 2-3/118), but create a good friend like Pygmalion out of weak characters. If you cannot discover by your spiritual senses a good man, then, at least, think that everyone has some hidden quality.

431- Peace dwells in reality:

جامه پوشان را نظر بر گاز رست / جان عریان را تجلی زیورست
یا ز عریانان بیکسو باز رو / یا چو ایشان فارغ از تن جامه شو
ور نمی تانی که کل عریان شوی / جامه کم کن تا ره اوسط روی
جمله خلقان سخره اندیشه اند / زآن سبب خسته دل و غم پیشه اند
در گذر از نام و بنگر در صفات / تا صفاتت ره نماید سوی ذات
اختلاف خلق از نام اوفتاد / چون بمعنی رفت آرام اوفتاد
(II / 3523-3524-3525-3559-3679-3680)

    a) Those who wear clothes look for a launderer but for naked souls manifestation of the Divine Light is adornment. Either turn away from the naked (give them up) or like them you, too, give up (the fondness) garments and if you cannot live fully naked in that case lessen your garments so that you may walk in the middle. All creatures are a captive of thought and because of this they are sad and tired. Turn away from your names (or fame) and look (aim) at Divine Attributes that may lead you to God. Name is the apple of discord among people, and when you reach the meaning (essence) only then you can find real peace.

    b) "To be naked" here means to feel no particular desire towards worldly needs and to thank God for what you already have. In other words, don't choose expensive clothes. If it is impossible for you to live without wearing expensive clothes, then at least choose the middle way for it is greed that misleads you. As is said in the Koran, "We made you an ummat (group of believers), just balanced (way of intermediacy), that you may be witnesses over the nations" (II/143). Once you come to know the Unity of God, you are satisfied with what God has given you and you can sacrifice your clothes and other possessions for the needy.

432- Raise the curtain of physical forms to see Reality:

گر ز صورت بگذرید ای دوستان / جنتست و گلستان در گلستان
صورت خود چون شکستی سوختی / صورت کل را شکست آموختی
بعد از آن هر صورتی را بشکنی / همچو حیدر باب خیبر بر کنی
(III / 578-579-580)

    a) If you, my friends, pass beyond shapes and forms, there are paradises and rose gardens within rose gardens. When you have destroyed and broken your own form, you learn to break all other forms, too. After that you may break all other forms like Ali (the Caliph of Islam) who uprooted the gate of Khaybar.

b) Those who lack spiritual eyesight look at the shape and forms of worldly things, and are prisoners of them. When their spiritual eyes are open they can discover new worlds behind these forms. Similarly, science has made discoveries and has gone beyond the forms of the phenomenal objects. Ali uprooted the gate of Khaybar with Divine help and you can also overcome your ego which is the thickest veil between you and God.

433- There is no time and space in the other world:

لامکانی که درو نور خداست   ماضی و مستقبل و حل از کجاست
ماضی و مستقبلش نسبت بتوست   هر دو یک چیزند پنداری که دوست
یک تنی او را پدر ما را پسر   بام زیر زید و بر عمر و آن زیر
نسبت زیر و زبر شد ز آن دو کس   سقف سوی خویش یک چیزست و بس
نیست مثل آن مثالست این سخن   قاصر از معنی نو حرف کهن
(III / 1151-1152-1153-1154-1155)

a) The placelessness that possesses the light of God has no past, future or present. Past and future are only for you, but actually they are one although you regard them as two separate things. One person is to him father but to us son: the (concept) roof is below Zeyd and above Omer. It is because of the two persons that there is "below" and "above" otherwise the roof itself is one thing. These words have only similarity but not the true example because old words fail to express new ideas.

b) Dimensional concepts such as length, width, above and below and so on belong to this world. In the world Hereafter there is no such concept. It is because of this that our mind cannot conceive of the Divine Systems.

434- The sensual eye is like the palm of our hand:

از نظر گاهست ای مغز وجود   اختلاف مومن و گبر و جهود
چشم حس همچون کف دستست و بس   نیست کف را بر همه او دست رس
چشم دریا دیگرست و کف دگر   کف بهل وز دیده دریا نگر
ما چو کشتیها بهم بر می زنیم   تیره چشمیم و در آب روشنیم
ای تو در کشتی تن رفته بخواب   آب را دیدی نگر در آب آب
(III / 1258-1269-1270-1272-1273)

a) O essence of existence, the difference between the true believer, the infidel, and the Jew arises from the object of view. The sensual eye is like the palm of the hand which cannot reach (control) the whole body. The eye of a sea (a spiritual eye) is different from the sea-foam (physical phenomena). Get rid of the foam, try to see through the eyes of the Sea (God). We are dashing against each other like boats. Our eyes are darkened, though we are in bright water. O you who have gone to sleep in your boat of the body, you have seen the water; then see the water of water (the Essence).

b) If we have no spiritual breadth of vision, we see what the physical eyes show, and we try to judge an object (or an event) according to how our carnal senses feel or see it (see the story of the blind men who described the elephant as they felt it) (M.III/1259). However, a true lover's horizons are infinite. As M. Iqbal says (see page No. 94).

We fight for water although our boats are in the sea of the pure water. In another story, people with different nationalities fought for the same thing (see M. II/ vr 3681-3690). A certain person gave a dirhem to four men who wanted to buy something to eat for themselves. The Turk said, "I want the *"üzüm"* and the Persian said, "I want the *"angur"* while the Arab said, "I want the *"inab"* and the Greek asked for *"stafili"* (staphyle). They were all asking for the same thing and when some wise man who knew the four languages showed them grapes, they all joined him. In like manner, we look for God saying, "*Bhagwan, Ram, Devta, Khuda, Tanrı, Deus, Allah* and so on." and when our lower self veils Reality, we fight out of our egos and not out of God Who is so close to us.

c) The metaphors used in the above lines are: 1- "water of water =the Essence, God". 2- "bright water =Spiritual Unity". 3- "foam of the sea =the physical phenomena" 4- "palm of the hand =carnal senses".

435- The snow-made toys of this world:

تا تو طفلی پس بدانت حاجتست	این تصور وین تخیل لعبتست
فارغ از حس است و تصویر و خیال	چون ز طفلی رست جان شد در وصال
حق خریدارش که الله اشتری	مال و تن برفند ریزان فنا
می زند اندر تزاید بال و پر	هر گمان تشنه یقین است ای پسر
علم کمتر از یقین و فوق ظن	ز آنک هست اندر طریق مفتتن
و آن یقین جویای دیدست و عیان	علم جویای یقین باشد بدان
آنچنانک از ظن می زاید خیال	دید زاید از یقین بی امتهال
که شد علم الیقین عین الیقین	اندر الهیکم بیان این ببین

(III / 4112-4113-4115-4118-4120-4124-4125)

a) These fanciful ideas and thoughts are like dolls, as long as you are a baby you need them. When your spirit is freed from your childhood and meets God, it is liberated from sensual perception, fanciful notions and vain ideas. The goods and bodies of this world are melting away to nothing like ice and God purchases them for (the Koran says) "God hath purchased". Every suspicion is thirsty for certainty and as the suspicion grows, it begins to struggle more and more (by opening its wings like a bird) in order to reach certainty. For on the path of test, knowledge is inferior to certainty and superior to suspicion (opinions). Know that knowledge seeks certainty and certainty looks for vision and manifestation. Doubtlessly, vision is born of certainty just as an idea is born of a suspicion. See the meaning of this statement in the Koran where the verse begins as "*Ilhakum* =(the good things of this world) divert you (from the more serious things)" (CII/1) and continues as "Knowledge of certainty is changed into vision of certainty" (CII/5-4).

b) Again in the Koran it is said, "God hath purchased of the believers their persons (beings) and their goods for in return theirs is the garden of Paradise" (IX/111). On earth man expects return for what he pays in money or in sacrifice. God buys the mortal things that we sacrifice for Him, in other words our goods and wealth that we give to the poor, our kith and kin in return God gives us ever-lasting Felicity -the Paradise of His love. The more you sacrifice of yourself, the more God grants you spiritual certainty as in the story of Abraham, who was ready to sacrifice his own beloved son, but God sent a ram instead.

436- Good and evil in this world are relative things:

پس بد مطلق نباشد در جهان   بد بنسبت باشد این را هم بدان
مر یکی را پا دگر را پای بند   مر یکی را زهر و بر دیگر چو قند
خلق آبی را بود دریا چو باغ   خلق خاکی را بود آن مرگ و داغ
منگر از چشم خودت آن خوب را   بین بچشم طالبان مطلوب را
بلک ازو کن عاریت چشم و نظر   پس ز چشم او بروی او نگر
(IV / 65-67-69-75-77)

a) In this world there is no (absolute) definite evil. Know this, that it is relative. Something that serves as a foot to one person can be a fetter for another. For water-creatures the sea is a garden while for earthly creatures it is death. Don't look at that good person through your own eyes, look at him (the desired one) through his seekers. It is even better to borrow eye and sight from Him and look at his face by means of them.

b) A thing good for one situation can be bad for another. Evil and good are relative conceptions. When you see through God's eyes nothing is good or bad.

437- God's attributes are infinite:

از پی آن گفت حق خود را بصیر   که بود دید ویت هر دم نذیر
از پی آن گفت حق خود را علیم   تا نیندیشی فسادی تو ز بیم
نیست اینها بر خدا اسم علم   که سیه کافور دارد نام هم
(IV / 215-217-218)

a) God called Himself "Observer" *(Basir)* so that He may restrain you from sin by keeping an eye on you and He called Himself "Hearing" *(Sami')* so that He may close your lips to a vain speech. These Divine Names are not like our proper names, because we can call a black person *Kafur* (Camphor).

b) The Names of God, generally accepted 99 in number in Islam, are also relative. But man cannot call God with the names of which he cannot conceive, "To God belong the most fair names, call ye then on Him thereby" (the Koran, VII/179). God allows us to call Him with the names that we can understand. God has countless other names for He cannot be confined within the frame of these names.

438- The souls of animals are separate while those of man are united:

مومنان معدود لیک ایمان یکی   جسمشان معدود لیکن جان یکی
غیر فهم و جان که در گاو و خرست   آدمی را عقل و جانی دیگرست
باز غیر جان و عقل آدمی   هست جانی در ولی آن دمی
جان حیوانی ندارد اتحاد   تو مجو این اتحاد از روح باد
جان گرگان و سگان هر یک جداست   متحد جانهای شیران خداست
(IV / 408-409-410-411-414)

a) The faithful are many, but Faith is one. Their bodies are many but their souls are one. Man has a different kind of soul and intelligence than that of cows and donkeys. Similarly, a saint also has a kind of soul and intelligence that others don't have. Animal souls have no unity, therefore do not seek this unity in the souls of those who act according to carnal desires. The souls of wolves and dogs are all separate, but the souls of God's lions (prophets, saints and lovers of God) are all one.

b) In the Koran it is said of believers, "The believers are but a single brotherhood" (XLIX/10) and the Tradition of Muhammed says, "the learned are one soul" (see the heading of the Masnevi, IV/294). So those who are believers of God are like one body. They are above animal souls but saints are even higher, beyond the angelic level. In short, all have levels according to their spiritual capacities.

439- God has created man in His likeness:

خلق ما بر صورت خود کرد حق   وصف ما از وصف او گیرد سبق
چونک آن خلاق شکر و حمد جوست   آدمی را مدح جویی نیز خوست
(IV / 1194-1195)

a) God has created our character in accordance with His. Our attributes take lessons (are affected) from His Attributes. Since that Creator wants us to praise Him and thank Him, a man, too, likes to be praised.

b) Not all attributes of God can be possessed for example God is "Creator" *(Khaliq)* and man cannot create a living being. But there are attributes that can be possessed by man such as: "*Alim* =Knowledgeable"; "*Sami* =Listener and so on.

c) The word above is not "*Khalq*" but "*Khulq*". *Khalq* =creation, but *Khulq* =character, disposition. It is "*Khulq*" as noted in the "G" which was corrected in the presence of Sultan Veled (see also Baki, IV/p. 453).

440- The real world appears to be non-existent:

نیست را بنمود هست و محتشم   هست را بنمود بر شکل عدم
بحر را پوشید و کف کرد آشکار   باد را پوشید و بنمودت غبار
چون مناره خاک پیچان در هوا   خاک از خود چون بر آید بر علا
کف همی بینی روانه هر طرف   کف بی دریا ندارد منصرف
نفی را اثبات می پنداشتیم   دیده معدوم بینی داشتیم
(V / 1026-1027-1028-1030-1032)

a) God has shown us the non-existent as existent and great; He has shown the existent in the form of non-existent. He has hidden the sea and made the foam visible, He has made the wind invisible while the dust is visible. When the dust whirls in the air as high as a minaret, it is due to the wind, otherwise how can the dust rise up? You see the foam floating and moving over the sea water, it cannot move without the existence of water. We have seen the negative as positive for we have eyes that see the negative only.

b) The other world is the positive of this world. Since our eyes see only the negative, the positive is concealed from us. However, we can sense the other world as we see dust lifted by the wind if we wish and work for some spiritual achievement. This world is only a shadow of the other world as Ibn ul-Arabi says:

كل مافى الكون وهم او خيال   او عكوس فى الرايا او ظلال

(Everything that exists in the world is either an idea or a mere image or a reflection and a shadow in the mirror). This is however an ancient idea which existed in Platonism and Hinduism long before Islam. "*Brahman Satiyam Jaganmithiya* =God is the Reality and the Truth while the world is a dream".

441- Satan is like a dog at God's gate:

ملك ملك اوست فرمان آن او   كمترين سگ بر در آن شيطان او
تركمان را گر سگى باشد بدر   بر درش بنهاده باشد رو و سر
كودكان خانه دمش مى كشند   باشد اندر دست طفلان خوارمند
باز اگر بيگانه معبر كند   حمله بر وى همچو شير نر كند
(V / 2939-2940-2941-2942)

a) The kingdom is His and the command is also His; and His Devil is the meanest dog at His gate. If a Turcoman has a dog at his door, it keeps its head and face at that door (due to loyalty). His (Turcoman's) children pull the dog's tail and it remains humble and obedient. However if a stranger passes by, it attacks him like a tiger.

b) Satan or Iblis is an enemy of man and God and the tempter of Eve in the Bible. He can masquerade as an angel, "Well no wonder! Even Satan can disguise himself to look like an angel of light. So it is no great thing if his servants disguise themselves to look like servants of righteousness. In the end they will get exactly what their actions deserve" (the Bible, 2. Cor. 11/14). Islam throws further light upon his disobedience: "And behold we said to the angels 'Bow down to Adam' and they bowed down. Not the Iblis, he refused and was haughty. He was of those who reject faith" (the Koran, II/34) and "God said, O Iblis what is your reason for not being among those who prostrated themselves? He said, 'I am not one to prostrate myself to men, whom Thou didst create from sounding clay, from mud moulded into form!' God said "Then get thee out from here for thou art rejected and accursed" (the Koran, XV/32-34) and "Satan's plan is to execute enmity and hatred between you, with intoxicants and gambling, and hinder you from remembrance of God; and from prayer will ye not then abstain" (V/94). Rumi says that Satan is like a loyal dog at the gate of God and he cannot hurt the lovers of God as a dog is loyal to a Turcoman family.

442- This body is like a guest-house and ideas are like the guests:

هست مهمان‌خانه این تن ای جوان   هر صباحی ضیف نو آید دوان
هین مگو کین ماند اندر گردنم   که هم اکنون باز پرد در عدم
هرچه آید از جهان غیب وش   در دلت ضیفست او را دار خوش
(V / 3644-3645-3646)

a) O young man, this body is like a guest-house, every morning a new guest comes running (to this place). Beware, don't say that he (the guest) has become a burden on you because he, too, will soon fly back to the non-existent world. Whatsoever comes to you from the invisible world to your heart is your heart guest, take care of him (it).

b) Ideas, worries, and happiness visit our heart but they all come temporarily. Whatever ideas visit us whether sad or happy, should not trouble us because they are guests and come from the yonder world. They all come from God to test us.

443- Whatever God does, does well:

فکر غم گر راه شادی می زند   کارسازیهای شادی می کند
خانه می روبد بتندی او ز غیر   تا در آید شادی نو ز اصل خیر
می فشاند برگ زرد از شاخ دل   تا بروید برگ سبز متصل
غم ز دل هرچه بریزد یا برد   در عوض حقا که بهتر آورد
(V / 3678-3679-3680-3683)

a) If sorrow hides happiness, it is making preparations for another joy. It is cleaning the house of everything else so that real happiness may come to dwell here from a positive source. It (sorrow) is scattering the yellow leaves from the bough of the heart in order that evergreen leaves may grow here again. Whatever sorrow takes away from the heart in return it brings something better.

b) Many chide God when they meet a problem although they don't know what will come next. Rumi says sorrows come to train our heart to clean it for the visit of a more permanent happiness. Ibrahim Haqqi of Erzurum (1703-1772) has a nice poem on the same subject:

"Only God changes evilness into goodness,
Don't think that others can do it for you,
A gnostic prefers to watch it all from afar,
Let's see what God will do;
Whatever He will do, will do all right,
All your deeds will end up right,
Worries and sorrows are then all in vain,
He (Mighty God) only performs His art for you,
Let's see what God will do;
Whatever He will do, will do all right".

Happiness and sorrows are in the service of a believer for he knows why they come and go. For him they are all the same (Koner, p. 764).

444- This is a topsyturvy world:

وآن مماتی خفیه در قشر حیات   این حیاتی خفیه در نقش ممات
ورنه دنیا کی بدی دار الغرور   می نماید نور نار و نار نور
آن انا مکشوف شد بعد از فنا   کی شود کشف از تفکر این انا
(V / 4135-4136-4146)

a) This life is concealed in the picture of death, that abode is death concealed in the husk of life. Here light looks fire, and fire light; otherwise how could this world be the abode of deceptive pride? How could this "I" be revealed by mere thought. This "I" can only be revealed (discovered) after passing from lower self.

b) The life of this world is deceptive for everything seems upside down. Real life is hidden behind the door of death, and this abode which you adore is hidden in the husk of (this mortal) life. In this world the divine light (good deeds see Mift. 5/299) looks like the source of troubles and pains while evil deeds look like real life. To discover your real being (the essence) you must destroy your lower self.

445- The order of this world is based on fear and anxiety:

حق ستون این جهان از ترس ساخت / هر یکی از ترس جان در کار باخت
حمد ایزد را که ترسی را چنین / کرد او معمار و اصلاح زمین
این همه ترسنده اند از نیک و بد / هیچ ترسنده نترسد خود ز خود
آن حسی که حق بر آن حس مظهرست / نیست حس این جهان آن دیگرست
آن حکیمک وهم خواند ترس را / فهم کژ کردست او این درس را
هیچ وهمی بی حقیقت کی بود / هیچ قلبی بی صحیحی کی رود

(VI / 2201-2202-2203-2206-2218-2219)

a) God has created of fear the column of this world, and because of fear everyone has devoted himself to work. Praise be to God who made fear the architect and reformer of this world. All these people are afraid of losing good and (suffering) evil, but none is afraid of himself! (Koner, p. 873). The sense by which God can be discovered is not the sense of this world. That poor philosopher calls fear "imagination". He has misunderstood the lesson. How can there be imagination without reality? Does the heart incline to a place that has no reality (or to a place that is not a right place to go to?) (see Koner, p. 874 and Baki, p. 562 but Nich. says: How should any false coin pass into circulation without a genuine one?).

b) People are forced to work or labour under some kind of fear and anxiety created by God. The fear is not caused by false ideas, as philosophers may think, but by God who wants to keep a balance on earth. It is by means of counterfeit money that man can recognise what real money is. Similarly, we know truth by comparing it with evil. So whatever God has created is not meaningless. Try to discover the real facts behind each event.

نقی علی نوری

CHAPTER XIII

Step IX: Unification

In this last chapter the traveller reaches the stage of "annihilation" *(fana)* and achieves "subsistence" *(baka)* with God. All vestiges of man's lower self must be completely destroyed before he arrives at this stage where he observes that he is a part of God, and that everything he derives comes from Him only.

"The people of God have become wholly God's and their faces are turned on God; they are preoccupied with and absorbed in God" (Discourses, p. 102).

"There is a world of bodies, a world of ideas, a world of fantasies and a world of suppositions. God most High is beyond all worlds, neither within them nor without them". (Ibid, p. 110).

"God most High is not contained within this world of ideas, nor in any world whatsoever. For if He were contained within the world of ideas, it would necessarily follow that he who formed the ideas would comprehend God, so that God would then not be the Creator of the ideas" (Ibid, p. 111).

"The nature of absorption is that the one absorbed is no longer there; he can make no more effort; he ceases to act and to move; he is immersed in the water. Any action that proceeds from him is not an action, it is the action of the water. But now if he strikes out in the water with his hands and feet, he is not said to be submerged; if he utters a cry, 'Ah, I am drowning', this too is not called absorption". (Ibid, p. 55).

"When the soul has been united with God, to speak of that Soul (God) is to speak of this soul, and to speak of this soul means to speak of that Soul". (M. VI/4040).

"When God chooses a servant for His closest station, He offers him the eternal Bounty. God purges his exoteric show and esoteric hypocrisy; and does not let any other love enter his heart except His Own. He bestows upon him His Bounty. He (God's servant) begins to observe the realities of this existent world with the eyes that learn a lesson (from each phenomenon). He is able to see the Real Artist behind His art (of this world). He passes from the stage of destiny to the stage of the Maker of destiny and has no interest in created things for he loves the Creator. There remains no danger in this world for him, and he never thinks of the world Hereafter. His food is the remembrance of his Beloved. His body melts away from anxiety for seeing his Beloved and his heart dissolves for love of his Beloved..." (Mejalis, Per. p. 80, Tur. p. 69).

Rumi, referring to himself and his dervishes, writes this sentence:

"Because the Dervishes are in control of the Divine Sea, they have no control of their own" (Mektubat, Tur. p. 137).

What is the best way to attain Unity after destroying one's lower self? The best way as suggested by Rumi is to try to adopt some possible attributes of God, although many are inaccessible. For the interest of our readers we give here some of God's attributes that can be possessed by men or at least can be tried:

1- *Rabb:*

a) The Lord, the Cherisher and Sustainer.
b) Man can receive his guests or the poor cordially and offer them things to eat.

2- *el-Sittar:*

a) the Veiler, God veils sins of His slaves.
b) Similarly, man can also veil others' faults and sins.

3- I- *er-Rahman* II- *er-Rahim* III- *el-Ghaffar* IV- *al-Hakim* V- *el-Ghafur* VI- *el-Wadud:*

a) I- the Benefactor (the Merciful), II- the Compassionate, III- the Indulgent, the Pre-eminent Pardoner, IV- Slow to punish, V- the Very Indulgent, VI- the Very Loving.
b) Man can love all creatures, forgive others, and can take pity on the helpless.

4- *el-Mu'min:*

a) the Believer, He who has full faith in Himself.
b) Man can be self confident, and trusting in God can accomplish good deeds.

5- *el-Karim:*

a) the Generous.
b) Man can be generous to others (especially to the needy).

6- *el-Musawwar:*

a) the Organiser, the Composer of forms.
b) Man can organise things, can devote himself to art.

7- *el-Wahhab:*

a) the Constant Giver.
b) Man can help the poor or other needy people by giving them what they need.

8- *el-Razzak:*

a) the Dispenser of all goods or needs.
b) Man can provide food and help the poor.

9- *el-'Alim and el-Hakim:*

a) I- the Knower of everything II- the Wise.
b) Man can improve his knowledge by learning and research.

10- *el-Adl:*

a) the Just.
b) Man should try to be just.

11- *el-Wali:*

a) the Protector, the Friend also el-Hafiz.
b) Man can protect the needy and the helpless.

12- *el-'Afu:*

a) the Forgiver of sins.
b) Man should learn to forgive others.

13- *el-Hadi:*

a) the Guide.
b) Man can help others by guiding them to the right path.

14- *al-Badi or even al-Mubdi:*

a) the Inventor and the Creator.
b) Man can invent things and can make things.

15- *el-Sabur:*

a) the Patient, Slow to punish.
b) Man can learn to be patient in every respect.

16- *el-Semi' and el-Basir:*

a) I- the Hearer II- the Seer.
b) Man should try to be alert to finding God's signs, His secrets and wisdom.

17- *el-Wakil:*

a) the Trustee.
b) Man should also try his best to win the trust of others.

18- *el-Khabir:*

a) the Sagacious, the Knower of secrets.
b) Man must try to see the Divine Secrets in every phenomenon.

446- Only His face shall endure:

كلّ شى هالك جز وجه او
هرك اندر وجه ما باشد فنا
زآنك در الاست او از لا گذشت

چون نه در وجه او هستى مجو
كلّ شى هالك نبود جزا
هرك در الاست او فانى نگشت
(I / 3052-3053-3054)

a) Everything is perishing except His face, unless you are in His face don't look for existence. Anyone who has become non-existent in Our Face (God's Face), "everything is perishing" does not apply to him. He who is still in a stage other than God, is not yet annihilated in Him; and he who has passed the stage of "other than God" is with (in) God.

b) It is said in the Koran, "Everything that exists will perish except His Face, to Him belongs the command and to Him you will be brought back". (XXVIII/88). As already explained "His Face" means "His Identity or His Whole Essence"; the epithets given above are only a small part of that Whole. If man is still busy worshipping things or persons other than God, he is still away from His Beautiful Face. M. Iqbal refers to the idea in his following verses:

ایك سجده جسے تو گراں سمجهتا هے   هزار سجدے سے دیتا هے آدمى كو نجات

"The act of prostrating yourself once (to God) seems to be heavy for you, actually it saves you from prostrating yourself a thousand times (to others)".

"Anything that shall keep existing out of this being is the faces of friends" (Makalat-i Shams, I/p. 279).

447- Finally the cups sink:

می دود چون کاسه‌ها بر روی آب   صورت ما اندرین بحر عذاب
چونك پر شد طشت دروی غرق گشت   تا نشد پر بر سر دریا چو طشت
(I / 1110-1111)

a) Our forms in this sweet sea are running like cups on the surface of water; unless they are filled up, they stay on the surface of water like a dish (they don't sink).

b) These verses are left unexplained by Baki and many other commentators but Mift. gives the following explanation:

"Here sea means the edgeless spirit and cups the physical body". When bodies are filled up with the light of the universal wisdom they lose their forms and drown in the Sea of Unity. Bahr. gives similar meanings but changes "intellect" to love.

448- I love even Thy torturing me:

وانتقام تو ز جان محبوبتر   ای جفای تو ز دولت خوبتر
ماتم این تاخود که سورت چون بود   نار تو اینست نورت چون بود
بوالعجب من عاشق این هر دو ضد   عاشقم بر قهر و بر لطفش بجد
عاشق خویشست و عشق خویش جو   عاشق کلست و خود کلست او
(I / 1566-1567-1570-1574)

a) O You whose torturing is better than the wealth of this world, and whose revenge is worthier than this life, if His fire (of life) is so, than how (great) shall His Light be? If mourning for You is this, then how will the festival be? He is in love with the Whole, (actually) He is the whole Himself. He loves Himself and seeks His own Love.

b) God's torturing which leads us to righteousness is better than the deceptive wealth of this world. There is a pleasure even in yearning for God because of separation from Him; think then about the happiness of meeting *(vuslat)* with that Beloved! Attributes of God are manifest in the created and non-created things and God loves them all for they are His parts.

449- Don't think of anything else but God:

چون زنم دم کآتش دل تیز شد / شیر هجر آشفته و خون ریز شد
قافیه اندیشم و دلدار من / گویدم مندیش جز دیدار من
خوش نشین ای قافیه اندیش من / قافیه دولت تویی در پیش من
ما چه باشد در لغت اثبات و نفی / من نه اثباتم منم بی ذات و نفی
من کسی در ناکسی در یافتم / پس کسی در ناکسی در بافتم
(I / 1724-1727-1728-1734-1735)

a) As the fire of my heart has grown fierce, how can I say anything? The lion of separation has become raging and blood-shedding; and my Sweetheart says to me, "Don't think of anything else but My Vision". Sit at ease O you the rhyme-composer, you are a treasure of rhymes in My Presence. What is meant by the word "Ma" ("we" in Persian), it is positive and negative. I am not positive (in this sense) I am negative and nothing. I found real personality in non-existence, therefore, my being is annihilated in the Non-Existent.

b) Here Rumi narrates his experience as a lover of God. He can no longer bear separation from God. Rumi has attained God's nearness, yet his journey of love with Him has not come to an end. "Ma" in Arabic has double meaning: it means "negation" and "affirmation" and in Persian it means "we". Rumi has generally used "Ma" (we) for "I" and he says that it actually means "nothing" (as in Arabic). In the presence of a beloved it is impossible to think of other things even of rhymes.

450- Why should I worry about dying?:

من چه غم دارم که ویرانی بود / زیر ویران گنج سلطانی بود
غرق حق خواهد که باشد غرق تر / همچو موج بحر جان زیر و زبر
ای حیوة عاشقان در مردگی / دل نیابی جز که در دل بردگی
(I / 1744-1745-1751)

a) Why should I worry that I will be ruined, for the treasures of royal persons are found under ruins. He who is drowned (annihilated) in God wants to be drowned further. His soul is like waves that come up and go down. O you, the life of lovers is death, and you will not get a heart unless you sacrifice yours.

b) If you want to win God's heart, you have to surrender yours. Once you are drowned in the sea of Divine Love, you want to drown further due to the pleasure it gives.

451- After union with God there remains no "I" or "We":

راســتی کن ای تو فخر راستان   ای تو صــدر و من درت را آســتان
آســتـان و صدر در مـعـنـی کجاست   ما و من کو آن طرف کآن یار ماست
مرد و زن چون یك شـود آن یك توی   چونك یكها محـو شـد آنـك توی
این من و ما بهر آن بر ساختی   تا تو با خود نرد خدمت باختی
تا من و توها همه یك جان شوند   عـاقبت مسـتـغـرق جـانـان شـونَد
(I / 1783-1784-1786-1787-1788)

a) O You the pride of righteous people, put me right. You are at the Throne and I am at the threshold (of that palace). (As a matter of fact) there exists no throne or threshold in the spiritual world. In the place where our Beloved is there is no "I" and "We". When man and woman become one that "One" is you. When the units become non-existent your unity prevails. You have created this "I" and "We" so that you may set up a game of service (you yourself become a servant and the Master (see Mift. p. 302). When the "I" and "you" merge they ultimately submerge in the Beloved.

b) Here Rumi is very sincere and straightforward with God. A beloved generally tests a lover with tricks. Rumi says to God, "Since I have become dust at your doorway then, please, give up testing me". When God becomes manifest no duality (men and women, "I" and "We") remains. They are all absorbed in the sea of Unity like rain drops.

452- Unity with God:

ای برادر صبر کن بر درد نیش   تا رهی از نیش نفس گبر خویش
کآن گروهی که رهیدند از وجود   چرخ مهر و ماهشان آرد سجود
چون دلش آموخت شمع افروختن   آفتاب او را نیـآرد سوختن
چیست توحید خدا آموختن   خویشـتن را پیش واحد سوختن
(I / 3002-3003-3005-3009)

a) O brother bear the pains of the sting (of this world) so that you may free yourself from the sting of your infidel (cruel) lower self, because the group that has escaped from the lower self, is worshipped by the sky, the sun, and the moon. As he has learnt to light the candle of his own heart, the sun fails to burn him. How to learn the Unity of God? Well, it is to burn yourself in the Presence of that One.

b) Many do not like to bear worldly pain for the sake of God, although they will save you from the continuous pain that the lower self creates for you. Once one's heart is illuminated by God's Light, physical tortures do not bother him much. In fact to achieve unity one has to destroy one's self-existence (greed of lower self).

453- Show me the state where no speech exists:

ای خدا جانرا تو بنما آن مقام   که درو بی حرف می روید کلام

تنگتر آمد خیالات از عدم   زآن سبب باشد خیال اسباب غم

زآن سوی حس عالم توحید دان   گر یکی خواهی بدآن جانب بران

(I / 3092- 3095-3099)

a) O Lord, show my soul the state where speech without words is born. This world of example is very small as compared to the world of non-existence. This world of example is therefore full of worries (and stresses). The world of Unity is beyond these senses; if you desire Unity go in that direction.

b) The reason for the relative contraction of the worlds of mind and matter is that this world is confined within the frame of time, space, and language, so come out of the carnal senses that confine you.

454- God takes the jars of our briny water and gives us the fresh drinking water instead:

چیست آن کوزه تن محصور ما   اندرو آب حواس شور ما

ای خداوند این خم و کوزه مرا   در پذیر از فضل الله اشتری

کوزه با پنج لوله پنج حس   پاک دار این آب را از هر نجس

تا شود زین کوزه منفذ سوی بحر   تا بگیرد کوزه من خوی بحر

لولها بر بند و پر دارش ز خم   گفت غُضّوا عن هواً أبصارکم

(I / 2708-2709-2710-2711-2714)

a) Our confined body is like a jar in which there is the briny water of our senses. O my God, please, accept this jar and jug of mine and purchase it through Your Mercy. The jar has five spouts of five senses, please keep its water from all kinds of dirt, so that there may open a passage towards the Sea and this (my jar) may adopt the characteristics of that Sea. Close its spout and keep the jar filled with spiritual wine. God said, "Close your eyes to vain desires".

b) "Water in the jar" is the soul of man in his body. Rumi says to God, "Please take it and put in Thy Sea of Pure water so that my soul too become pure. Enable me to keep that pure water of your Clean Light in my jar (part of Thy Spirit)", as you say in the Koran, "Say to the believing men that they should lower their gaze and guard their modesty" (XXIV).

455- Where is the Batsman?:

گوی چوگانیم چوگانی کجاست	ما شکاریم این چنین دامی کراست
ساعتی زاهد کند زندیق را	ساعتی کافر کند صدیق را
تا ز خود خالص نگردد او تمام	زآنک مخلص در خطر باشد ز دام
آن رهد کو در امان ایزد است	ز آنک در راهست و ره زن بی حدست
(II / 1310-1312-1313-1314)	

a) We are the prey, to whom does this kind of trap belong? We are the ball of a polo-bat but where is the Batsman? In a moment he makes the true believer change into an infidel and changes an infidel into a strong believer because an obedient believer always has the danger of a trap ahead, unless he is totally lost in God, because he is still on the way and there are countless brigands (on the path), yet he who is under God's protection is safe.

b) We are totally in the hands of God who can do with us what He wants. So look for Him (the Source) so that He may protect you from worldly dangers.

456- In fire a piece of iron is like fire:

رنگ آتش دارد الا آهنست	آن منم خم خود "انا الحق" گفتنست
ز آتشی می لافد و خامش وش است	رنگ آهن محو رنگ آتش است
هست مسجود ملایک ز اجتبا	آدمی چون نور گیرد از خدا
پاک کی گردد برون حوض مرد	ای تن آلوده بگرد حوض گرد
سوی دریا راه پنهان دارد این	زآنک دل حوض است لیکن در کمین
(II / 1347-1348-1353-1361-1364)	

a) To say that I am the jar is like saying "I am God". A piece of iron takes the colour of fire yet is iron, because the piece of iron has become non-existent in the colour of fire, it is silent yet it boasts of being fire. When man receives the Light of God, he is worshipped even by the angels because he is a selected one. O you who having a filthy body take a turn around the pool, how can you be clean unless you enter it (the pool)? Heart is a water pool but a secret way through it leads to the Sea.

b) "Jar" here means a glass jar in which a liquid takes the colour of that jar when seen from outside, and metaphorically it means "totality" which is characteristic of God. It is like claiming "I am God" (the words of Hallaj-i Mansur). Don't think that you have become God like a piece of iron that looks like fire and sees itself as fire. "Pool" is the Unity of God in which you should jump in order to clean yourself fully, and from there you should try to reach the Sea of Unity.

c) Huseyin b. Mansur al-Hallaj (857-922 A.D.):

A great Sufi who wrote books on Sufism. He was educated at Basra. He played an outstanding role in converting Turks to Islam. He travelled to Mecca, Khorasan, Isfahan, Kum, Kashmir, and to the Turkish lands -Hotan and Turfan- to spread Islam. On his third journey to Mecca he asked people to kill him because of his selfhood. Finally, he said *"Ana'l Hak"* = "I am God" or literally "I am the Truth". At this fanatic Muslims crucified him like Christ. Some learned men took his side and some opposed him on the ground that he did not follow the sayings of Muhammed (his Traditions). This conflict still continues among the Muslim scholars. Rumi gives the example of heated iron in the above lines. The Mevlevis have a Ney named after him *"Ney-i Mansur"* (for other details see İA, 5-1/p. 168-169). Mansur believed that God could enter the human body, all religions are right (see Javid Sunar, p. 49). He also said, "To leave this world is the piety of selfhood, to leave worrying about the other world is the piety of the heart, and to leave oneself is the piety of soul" (Tezkiret ul-Avliya, p. 119).

457- **He whose aim is the depth of the sea disregards the superficial beauty of the sea:**

در صفات آنست کوگم کرد ذات   صنع بیند مرد محجوب از صفات

کی کنند اندر صفات او نظر   واصلان چون غرق ذاتند ای پسر

وصلت عامه حجاب خاص دان   طاعت عامه گناه خاصگان

کی برنگ آب افتد منظرت   چونک اندر قعر جو باشد سرت

(II / 2812-2813-2816-2814)

a) The man who lacks Divine Attributes sees only the created things. He who loses his own being can possess the Divine Attributes. Since those who have reached the Divine Being are lost in it, O my son, they can no more look at His Attributes. Piety and prayers of the common people are a sin for the elect ones and common people's reaching God is a curtain for the selected people (saints and prophets). If one's head is in the depth of the sea, one cannot cast one's eyes on the surface of the water.

b) T. and MM. give the following explanation:

"It is said that the follower (traveller) has four stages to pass through: 1- At this stage he remembers God by watching His created things (called *"Mahjub"*). 2- He watches created things through the Divine Attributes (called *"Ma'rifet"* =Gnosticism and one who practices it is called *"Arif"*). 3- A stage where the traveller watches only God and His attributes are left behind (the people at this stage are called *"Mustaghraqin"* =those who are lost in God, the name of this sage is *"Fana fi-Allah"*). 4- At this stage the traveller observes God along with His Attributes. In other words, he sees abundance in Unity and Unity in abundance, and those who manage to reach this stage their piety is not equal to the piety of the laymen". T. gives an example: *"Khaliq"* (the Creator) is one of the attributes of God. Now, if someone sees His created beings, he feels God through them. But he is able to see only one of the Attributes of God. Actually God has countless attributes. However, those who see with God and through His Attributes are free to see beyond the creatures (or forms).

458- A lover of God is only relatively non-existent:

گفت این مغلوب معدومیست کو   جز بنسبت نیست معدوم ایقنوا
این چنین معدوم کو از خویش رفت   بهترین هستها افتاد و زفت
او بنسبت با صفات حق فناست   در حقیقت در فنا او را بقاست
جمله ارواح در تدبیر اوست   جمله اشباح هم در تیر اوست
آنک او مغلوب اندر لطف ماست   نیست مضطر بلک مختار ولاست
(IV / 397-398-399-400-401)

a) God said (to David) "The kind of man who is overwhelmed by Me is only relatively non-existent, be sure of it. This kind of non-existent who passes out of himself is the best of all beings and the greatest". He is non-existent only in relation to God's Attributes, and he has attained eternal life with God due to annihilation in Him. All spirits are at his beck and call and all bodies are under his control. He who is overwhelmed in our Grace, is not forced to be so, on the contrary he has chosen devotion to Us willingly.

b) It is essential to see in what sense Rumi has used the words *"Fena"* and *"Baqa"*. The best explanation is found in the treatises of Rumi's predecessors -Abdulkerim Kusheyri (986-1072 A.D.) and Kalabazi of Bukhara (d. A.D. 994).

Fena: After *Fena* comes *Baqa. Fena* means to destroy all the worldly desires and to be controlled fully by God's Will (Kalabazi, p. 188). The man who is at this stage is controlled in all respects by God including in religious rituals. When ignorance goes knowledge comes; when lusty desires for this world are destroyed, the Divine Will rules a man (Kusheyri, p. 198). For a man at this stage, generally speaking, there is no difference between a wall or a woman (Kalabazi, p. 183) in other words he is lost in God from top to toe. He is like "the people of the cave". After this stage comes "*Baqa*" where man is submerged in the Will of God and attains eternity with God. However, it should be borne in mind that he is not God, but he is directly connected to God. Many religious people misunderstood this critical point and began to worship such men (the perfect men) (this is the warning of Ali Hejveri, see Kashf al-Mahjub, p. 265). As we already said above, "a drop is not the whole sea".

459- A Dervish is destroyed in God's attributes:

نیست گشته وصف او در وصف هو   هست از روی بقای ذات او

نیست باشد هست باشد در حساب   چون زبانه شمع پیش آفتاب

هستی‌اش در هست او روپوش شد   پیش شیری آهوی بی هوش شد

خویش را در کفه شه می نهد   نبض عاشق بی ادب بر می جهد

با ادب تر نیست کس زو در نهان   بی ادب تر نیست کس زو در جهان

(III / 3670-3671-3676-3678-3679)

a) His being is present due to his existence (otherwise) his attributes are lost in God's Attributes like the flame of a candle in the presence (light) of the sun. He (the Dervish) is actually non-existent, but so to say he exists. In the presence of lion a deer is senseless, the deer's being is veiled in the existence of the lion. A lover's pulse beats fast regardless of reverence and equates itself with the King. No one is irreverent on earth like him, yet secretly no one is as reverent as he.

b) A lover of God *(Dervish)* is lost in the light of God as the candle is in the presence of the sun. A lover of God when intoxicated with Divine Wine may become drunk and irreverent like Hallaj-i Mansur by saying "I am God" but such words are not out of disrespect of God, they are the sign of ecstasy born of love and when he comes to himself he is humbler before God than others.

460- When you arrive at the river of Eternity get lost in it:

جوی دیدی کوزه اندر جوی ریز   آب را از جوی کی باشد گریز
آب کوزه چون در آب جو شود   محو گردد در وی و جو او شود
وصف او فانی شد و ذاتش بقا   زین سپس نه کم شود نه بدلقا
(III / 3912-3913-3914)

a) When you see the river pour the water of your jug into it. Why should water (your spirit) be afraid of the river? When the water of the jug is poured into the river, the water gets lost in it, and becomes a part of that river. His own attributes come to an end while his essence (spirit) attains eternity in that Being. After this (unification), he neither becomes less nor is he destroyed.

b) When you come close to the water of Eternity, let your essence join it. It is after this that your attributes cease to exist and you submerge in Divine Attributes, and the journey with God begins.

461- Music reminds you of God's words, "Am I not your God?" :

پس حکیمان گفته اند این لحنها   از دوار چرخ بگرفتیم ما
بانگ گردشهای چرخست این که خلق   می سرایندش بطنبور و بحلق
ما همه اجزای آدم بوده ایم   در بهشت آن لحنها بشنوده ایم
گرچه بر ما ریخت آب و گل شکی   یادمان آمد از آنها چیزکی
پس غذای عاشقان آمد سماع   که درو باشد خیال اجتماع
قوتی گیرد خیالات ضمیر   بلک صورت گردد از بانگ و صفیر
(IV / 733-734-736-737-742-743)

a) Hence the philosophers said, "These musical sounds we have taken from the rotating of the universe" and whatever the public plays on the pandore and sings with it, are the sounds of the universal revolution. We all have been a part of Adam (genetically) and therefore, we heard those sounds in Paradise. Although, now, the water and clay of our body has covered us with doubt yet we remember something of that (the sounds heard in Paradise). Since there is the idea of gathering (unification and meeting) in the *Sema* (dervish dance), it is the food of lovers of God. The ideas of our mind (heart) are empowered and, in some cases, changed into forms through the musical sounds and beautiful singing.

b) Music is a reminder of the sweet words of God, "Am I not your God?" (see the Koran, VII/171) which come to us by means of the genetic link with Adam who had an opportunity to hear God's melodious voice. Since music is above language in expressing feelings, it is closer to the Voice of God. This is how the sound of the Ney spoke to Rumi. *Sema* is a reminder of the Unity.

c) By "the philosophers" the Pythagorean School is referred to which Rumi had certainly studied at Balkh.

462- God neither increases nor decreases:

ذات را افزونی و آفات نی   در اثر افزون شد و در ذات نی

آنچ اول آن نبود اکنون نشد   حق ز ایجاد جهان افزون نشد

در میان این دو افزونیست فرق   لیک افزون گشت اثر زایجاد خلق

تا پدید آید صفات و کار او   هست افزونی اثر اظهار او

کو بود حادث بعلتها علیل   هست افزونی هر ذاتی دلیل

(IV / 1665-1666-1667-1668-1669)

a) The increment is in the effect and is not in the Essence. God did not increase by the creation (invention) of this universe. He did not change at all (He did not become what He wasn't before). But the phenomenal being has increased because of the creation of things by God. There is a great difference between these two kinds of increments. The increase of the effect is His manifestation, so that His Attributes and actions may be made visible. The increment in any being is the proof that it is originated and subject to causes.

b) The increasing and decreasing of being belongs to creation and not to the Creator (Koner, p. 518). Many spirits come out of the non-existent world to the phenomenal world and this does not result in any diminution of that world. Whatever is manifest in this world is the shadow of the fixed prototypes *(Ayan-i Sabita)*. How can God decrease or increase? Whatever is visible in this world is the shadowy form of His attributes.

463- **When your physical body, weak like a drop, joins the Sea of Unity it has no more worldly worries:**

زآنك این هوی ضعیف بی قرار   هست شد زآن هوی رب پایدار
هوی فانی چونك خود فا او سپرد   گشت باقی دایم و هرگز نمود
همچو قطره خایف از باد و ز خاك   که فنا گردد بدین هر دو هلاك
چون باصل خود که دریا بود جست   از تف خورشید و باد و خاك رست

(IV / 2614-2615-2616-2617)

a) This weak and unstable being has come into being through the eternal Being of God, therefore, if this mortal being (the being of man) surrenders itself to Him, it becomes eternal also and never dies. Like a drop of water that (the body) is afraid of wind and the earth, yet it does not perish because of these two elements. When it joins its Origin, the Sea, it is freed from the fear of the sun, wind, and the earth.

b) Since the drop of our spirit has come from the sea of Divine Unity let it join that Unity where there is no fear of earthly death and where you are under the protection of God. One should hurry up when the Sea is inviting you:

هین بده قطره خود را بی ندم   تا بیابی در بهای قطره یم

(IV / 2619)

(Be aware! O you who are like a drop, sacrifice yourself without hesitation so that you may buy a sea in return for a drop).

464- **One who is near God is above religious and worldly worries:**

خود طواف آنك او شه بین بود   فوق قهر و لطف و کفر و دین بود
زآن نیآمد یك عبارت در جهان   که نهانست و نهانست و نهان
گرچه از یك وجه منطق كاشف است   لیك از ده وجه پرده و مكنف است
پس بلا و رنج بایست و وقوف   تا رهد آن روح صافی از حروف
هر دل ار سامع بدی وحی نهان   حرف و صوتی کی بدی اندر جهان
آنچ عین لطف باشد بر عوام   قهر شد بر عشق كیشان كرام

(IV / 2967-2968-2973-2985-2979-2982)

b 2973 پرده و مكنف : G ترك مزلفعت K دیگر مكنف MM
a 2968 عبارت : G عبادت. Mift.
b 2982 ناز نینان : G عشق كیشان MM
b 2985 تا رهد : G تا دمد MM

a) The circulation (around God) of a man who is observant of the King (God) is above wrath and grace, above belief and infidelity. Not a single line (or word) can explain his situation because his state is hidden, hidden, hidden. Words may explain certain spiritual states but they may also hide ten others (states). Thus in order to free the pure soul (essence) of words, one needs pains, sorrows and patience. If all hearts were able to receive the secret inspirations there would be no need of a voice and words on earth. Moreover, whatever is a grace for the common public is a torture for His elect ones (respectworthy lovers of God).

b) For those who have achieved the proximity of God, His wrath or mercy, religious belief or even disbelief have no importance, because they are already with God. Their state cannot be explained by means of language. The more you try to explain it, the more complicated it becomes.

465- Man can be submerged in Divine Light:

این أنا هو بود در سر ای فضول   ز اتحاد نور نه از رای حلول

جهد کن تا سنگیت کمتر شود   تا بلعلی سنگ تو انور شود

صبر کن اندر جهاد و در عنا   دم بدم می بین بقا اندر فنا

(V / 2038-2039-2040)

a) This saying "I am Him" (of Mansur) was subconsciously due to the oneness of the Light, O you vain speaker, not because of the doctrine of incarnation. Work so that your stony nature (heart) may soften and your stone may also change into a ruby. Fight against your ego and face difficulties so that each moment you may see annihilation after every non-existence.

b) Hallaj-i Mansur did not utter the famous words "I am God" because he thought that he was God, but because he became the part of His Light (see here the example of fire and the piece of iron item No. 457). Every moment you can observe sustenance *(Baqa)* after a non-existence *(Fena)* (see also item No. 459).

466- Man is the closest creature to God:

أحسن التقویم از عرش او فزون   أحسن التقویم از فکرت برون

گر بگویم قیمت این ممتنع   من بسوزم هم بسوزد مستمع

استخوان و باد رو پوشست و بس   در دو عالم غیر یزدان نیست کس

(VI / 1006-1007-1023)

a) Man is created in the best proportion and is above God's heaven and his perfection is beyond comprehension. If I try to say the inaccessible man, I will burn and so shall the listener. Actually, there is nobody other than God in this world and in the world Hereafter, (a man is) a veil of bones and wind, and that's all.

b) A prototype man (a prophet or saint) is above God's throne *(Arsh)*, as the Koran says, "We indeed created man in the best form (nature and mould)" (XCV/4). Because a perfect man is a vicegerent of God on earth like Moses, Christ, and Muhammed. It is the duty of a man to preserve the pattern in which God created him. If a man rebels against God, he rebels against his true nature, which is above heavens and the Divine Throne and is inexplicable. Man is created above all other creatures in these two respects: 1- Physically: Man is an admirable being because of his anatomy and because of his mental functions (eye-sight, hearing, memory and so on.) (see also Jaferi, V. 13/p. 400). 2- Spiritual side of a man: It is above verbal explanation. As Yunus says, *"Ete kemiğe büründüm, Yunus diye göründüm"* ="I put on bones and the flesh and showed Myself as Yunus".

467- In the salt-mine of Unity all become unicoloured:

همچنان ای خواجه تشنیع زن	از بلا و فقر و از رنج و محن
لا شك این ترک هوا تلخی دهست	لیك از تلخی، بعد حق بهست
گر جهاد و صوم سختست و خشن	لیك این بهتر ز بعد ممتحن
چون شدی نومید در جهد از کلال	از جناب حق شنیدی که تعال
خافض است و رافعست این کردگار	بی ازین دو بر نیآید هیچ کار
خاک را بی بین خلق رنگارنگ را	می کند یك رنگ اندر گورها
کآن جهان همچون نمکسار آمدست	هرچه آنجا رفت بی تلوین شدست
از جهود و مشرك و ترسا و مغ	جملگی یك رنگ شد زآن الپ الغ
صد هزاران سایه کوتاه و دراز	شد یکی در نور آن خورشید راز
روز نحر رستخیز سهمناك	مومنانرا عید و گاوانرا هلاك

(VI / 1767-1768-1769-1846-1847-1857-1856-1862-1863-1876)

a) Similarly, O honourable man, you complain against affliction and poverty, against distress and labouring. Without doubt, giving up of sensuality is painful but it is better than the pain caused by falling away from God. Although war (for God) and fasting are harsh, they are still better than being away from God. Just when you are disappointed due to weariness and labouring, then you hear God saying, "Come". He is "*Hafiz*" and "*Rafi*", without these two Epithets (the Exalter and the Abaser) no work is accomplished. Look at earth, it changes the bodies of the dead into unicolour. For that world is like a salt-mine; whatever goes there becomes colourless. That Hero (God) renders all-be it a Jew, polytheist, Christian, or Magian, into a single colour. These are hundreds of shadows, long and short; they change into one size in the Light of that Secret Sun. On that terrible day of slaughter, the resurrection is a festival for true believers and a day of slaughtering for the cattle (non-believers).

b) This world is the world of colours (dimensions) and the other world has no such thing. We face troubles and sorrows in this world due to the different colours and forms while the other world has no such problem. Therefore, one should not be sorry to lose this world but one should worry about losing the Divine Favour. God alone can exalt or bring one low. As the Koran says, "Thou enduest with honour whom Thou pleasest and Thou bringest low whom Thou pleasest. In Thy hand is all good. Verily, over all things Thou hast power" (III/26). But God exalts only true believers.

468- The stage where God is close to us:

ما چو واقف گشته ایم ز چون و چند   مهر بر لبهاء ما بنهاده اند
تا نگردد رازهاء غیب فاش   تا نگردد منهدم عیش و معاش
ما همه گوشیم گر شد نقش گوش   ما همه نطقیم لیکن لب خموش
آهن و سنگ از برونش مظلمی   اندرون نوری و شمع عالمی
(VI / 3526-3527-3529-3579)

a) Now that we have become aware of stations and deeds of the spiritual world, they have sealed our lips so that the mysteries of the secret world which might destroy the life and livelihood of this world may not be revealed (MM. p. 337). We are all ears though the form of the (physical) ears have gone; we are able to talk although we don't utter a word. Steel or stone are outwardly dark, but inwardly they are the lamp (candle) and light of the universe.

b) When the Divine Secrets are revealed to saints, they must not reveal them in order to keep the balance of this world. They (the saints) are to talk even after death just as steel or iron looks dark outwardly but within them is concealed the atomic light (power).

469- My Lord I wish only Thee:

از قدح گر در عطش آبی خورید   در درون آب حق را ناظرید

آنك عاشق نیست او در آب در   صورت خود بیند ای صاحب بصر

صورت عاشق چو فانی شد درو   پس در آب اکنون کرا بیند بگو

حسن حق بینند اندر روی حور   همچو مه در آب از صنع غیور

(VI / 3643-3644-3645-3646)

a) If in thirst you drink water from a cup, you see God in it. He who is not in love with God, will see only his own face in it. O man of insight, since a lover's image has disappeared in Him (the Beloved), whom shall he see in the water? He (the lover) sees the comeliness of God in the faces of Houris because of His jealousy, like the moon reflected in the water.

b) Once a lover's will becomes God's will, he sees God everywhere. The true lover of God will find God's reflection in the faces of Houris in Paradise.

470- The sun is hidden in an atom:

آفتابی در یکی ذره نهان   ناگهان آن ذره بگشاید دهان

ذره ذره گردد افلاك و زمین   پیش آن خورشید چون جست از کمین

(VI / 4580-4581)

a) A sun is concealed in an atom and suddenly that atom opens its mouth. The ... nd the universe fall into pieces when that sun darts out from its ambush.

b) A saint has the whole Sun compacted in him like atomic energy in an atom. When It is exposed the whole universe becomes non-existent.

After all this admonition, if an immature man fails to understand the state of a mature man, then there is no other remedy but to bid him farewell.

SELECT BIBLIOGRAPHY AND ABBREVIATIONS

Abdulbaki: (see Baki, Rumi).

Amir Khusrau Dihlevi, "*Divan-ı Kamil*", Said Nefisi, Intisharat-i Javidan, Tehran.

Ankaravi: İsmail Ankaravi, "*Fatih ul-abiyat*", Matbaa-yi Amire, 1872 (Ottoman Commentary on the Masnevi).

Atesh, Ahmed, "*İstanbul Kütüphanelerinde Farsça Manzum Eserler*", I, Milli Eğitim Basımevi, İstanbul, 1968.

Bahr: Mevlana Abdul'ali Muhammed Bahr'ul-Ulum, Munshi Nowolkishor, India, 1876.

Baki, (Rumi): Abdulbaki Gölpınarlı, "*Mevlana Celaleddin*", İnkılap Kitabevi, İstanbul, 1951.

Baki: Abdülbaki Gölpınarlı, "*Mesnevi Tercemesi ve Şerhi*", İnkilap ve Aka Kitabevleri, İstanbul, 1981.

Baldwin, Marshal W., "*History of the Crusades*", University of the Pennysylvania Press.

Bhagwat Gita: Indian Council for Cultural Relations New Delhi, 1959.

Boyle, J. A., "*The Cambridge History of Iran*", vol.5, Cambridge at the University Press, 1960.

Browne: Edward Granville Browne, Literary History of Persia, Cambridge, 1969.

Büyük İslam Tarihi: Çağ yayınları, İstanbul, 1986.

Chittick: William C., "*The Sufi Path of Love*", State University of New York Press, Albany, 1983.

Discourses of Rumi: Arberry, A.J., Redwood Burn Ltd., London, 1975.

Divan: "*Kulliyat-i Divan-ı Shams-i Tebrizi*", Muessese-yi Emir Kebir, Tehran, Iran.

Eflaki: Eflaki, Ahmed Dede, "*Ariflerin Menkıbeleri*", Tahsin Yazıcı, Hürriyet Yayınları, İstanbul, 1973 and "*Manakib al-Arifin*", Türk Tarih Kurumu, Ankara, 1959, (Persian text).

Encyclopaedia of Islam: "*The Encyclopaedia of Islam*", Luzac and Co., London, 1986.

Ferheng-i Nurbakhsh, Dr. Javad Nurbakhsh, Intisharat-i Khangah, Tehran, 1366 Shemsi.

Ferheng-i Seyyid Jafer: see Seyyid Jafer's Dictionary.

Ferheng-i Zeban-i Farsi: Persian Dictionary, Mahshid Moshiri, Soroush Press, Tehran, 1990.

Feruzanfer, "*Mevlana Celaleddin*", Milli Eğitim Bakanlığı, İstanbul, 1990.

Fihi ma fih: (Discourses of Rumi): Turkish Trans. by Abdulbaki, Remzi Kitabevi İstanbul (Persian text), "*Kitab-i Fihi ma fih*", Bedi'uzzaman Feruzanfer, Tehran University, Amir Kebir, 1969.

Fuad Köprülü: "*Türk Edebiyatında İlk Mutasavvuflar*", Diyanet İşleri Başkanlığı Yayınları, Ankara, 1976.

Gibb: E. J. W. Gibb, "*A History of Ottoman Poetry*", Luzac and Company Ltd, London, 1958.

Hasan Özönder, "*Konya Mevlana Dergahı*", Kültür Bakanlığı Yayınları 1107, Ankara, 1989.

Hindu Script: R. C. Zaehner, "*Hindu Scriptures*", Everman's Library, New York, 1968.

İ.A.: "*İslâm Ansiklopedisi, İslâm âlemi tarih coğrafya etnoğrafya ve biyografya lûgati*", M.E.B., İstanbul, 1970.

İbrahim, Kafesoğlu, "*Harezmşahlar Devleti Tarihi*", Türk Tarih Kurumu Basımevi, Ankara, 1956.

Ibtidanama, Sultan Veled, Abdulbaki Gölpınarlı, Güven Matbaası, Ankara, 1976.

Jaferi = Taki.

Jami Sighir: Imam Suyuti, Jami us-saghir (a book of Muhammed's Traditions), Yılmaz Ofset, İstanbul.

Jan Rypka, "*History of Iranian Literature*", D. Reidel Publishing Co., Holland, 1968.

Javid Sunar, "*İslam Tasavvufu Tarihi*", Ankara Üniversitesi Basımevi, Ankara, 1978.

Javri, İbrahim Chelebi, Takvim Khane-yi Amire, 1260 (versifed commentary on forty verses from the Masnevi).

Kabaklı: Ahmed Kabaklı, "*Yunus Emre*", Toker Yayınları, İstanbul.

Kalabazi: Süleyman Uludağ, "*Doğuş Devrinde Tasavvuf*", Kalabazi, Dergah Yayınları, İstanbul, 1979.

Kan = "*Masnevi-yi Mevlevi-yi Manevi*", Muhammed Rahmetullah, Kanpur, India, 1916, (Persian commentary based on several saintly scholars).

Kashf al-Mahjub: Sheykh Ali Hijveri, Islamic Publications Lahore (Urdu translation Miyan Tufel), 1967.

Kaymaz, Nejat, "*Pervane Mu'in ud-Din Süleyman*", Ankara Üniversitesi, Dil ve Tarih Coğrafya Fakültesi, 1970.

Koner: Muhlis Koner, "*Mesnevi'nin Özü*", Yeni Kitap Basımevi, Konya, 1961.

Kusheyri: Abdulkerim Kusheyri, "*Kuşeyri Risalesi*", Süleyman Uludağ, Dergah Yayınları, İstanbul, 1981.

Lugat-i Masnevi, Muhammed Yahya b. Mu'min, (A.D. 1527), MS No. 204, Mevlana Museum Konya.

M = Masnevi

Maarif: Bahaeddin Veled, "*Maarif*", Kutupkhane-yi Tuhuri, Tehran.

Maarif of Tirmizi: Burhaneddin Muhaqqaq-i Tirmizi, Seyyid, "*Maarif*", Chapkhane-yi Danishgah, Tehran; and "*Maarif*", Abdulbaki, Türkiye İş Bankası Kültür Yayınları, Ankara.

Makalat: Shams-i Tebrizi, "*Şems-i Tebrizi Konuşmaları*", Turkish text by Nuri Gencosman, Hurriyet Yayınları, İstanbul; "*Makalat-ı Shams-i Tebrizi*", Ahmed Khushnevis, Muessese-yi Matbuat-i Atayi, Tehran, 1349.

Masnevi: (M) Nicholson, R. A., "*The Mathnawi of Jalallu'ddin Rumi*", Luzac and Co. London, 1943 etc. for Persian text: "*Masnevi-yi Manevi*", Nasrullahpur Javadi, Amir kebir, Tehran.

Mehdi Tevhidi: see Preface of "*Nefahat ul-Uns*".

Mejalis-i Saba: Mevlana Jelal al-Din, Trans. by Abdulbaki, Konya Turizm Derneği, Konya, 1965.

Mektuplar (*Mektubat* = Rumi's Letters): Abdulbaki Gölpınarlı, İnkılap ve Aka Kitabevleri, İstanbul, 1963; Muhammed Riyaz, "*Mektubat-u Khutbat-i Rumi*", Iqbal Acedemy, Lahore 1988; "*Mektubat-i Mevlana Jelal al-Din*", Chapkhane-yi İstanbul, 1937.

Merçil, Erdoğan, "*Müslüman-Türk Devletleri Tarihi*", İstanbul Üniversitesi, İstanbul, 1985.

Meyerovitch: Eva de Vitray Meyerovitch, "*Rumi and Sufism*", The Post Apollo Press, California.

Mift: "*Miftah ul-Ulum*", Muhammed Nezir Sahab, Sheykh Ghulam Ali and Sons, Lahore.

M. Iqbal = Muhammed Iqbal

MM: Kazi Seyyid Sejad Hüseyin, "*Masnevi-yi Mavlevi-yi Ma'nevi*", Al-feysal Neshiran vu Tajiran-i Kutub, Lahore.

Nefahat ul-Uns: Abdurrahman Jami, Kitab Ferushi-yi Mahmudi, Tehran.

Nich: see Masnevi.

Niyazi Divanı: Niyazi Mısri, İstanbul Marif Kitaphanesi, İstanbul.

Ramazan: Şeşen, Ramazan, "*Selahaddin Eyubi ve Devlet*", Çağ Yayınları, İstanbul, 1987.

Refat Yinanç, "*Mevlana'nın Şahitlik Ettiği Selçuklu Sultanı II. Gıyaseddin Keyhusrev Vakfıyesi*", Mevlana Bildiriler, Konya.

Risalet-ul Nushiye: (see Yunus Emre, Abdulbaki).

Rumi's Letters: (see *Mektuplar*).

Satoğlu, Abdullah, "*Seyyid Burhaneddin*", İKB Yayınları, Kayseri.

Schimmel, Annemarie, "*The Triumphal Sun*", Fine Books London, 1978.

Selçuklu Tarihi, İ. Kafesoğlu, Milli Eğitim Basımevi, İstanbul, 1972.

Seyyid Jafer's Dictionary: Dr. Seyyid Jafer, Ferheng *(Lugat-i İstilahat u Tabirat-i İrfani)*, Kutupkhane-yi Tuhuri, Tehran.

Sipehsalar: Feriduddin Ahmed-i Sipahsalar, "*Mevlana ve Etrafındakiler*", 1001 Temel Eser, Tercüman, İstanbul, 1977; "*Risale-yi Sipahsalar*", Mahmud Ali Seyyid, Kanpur 1319 H.

Steingass: "*Persian-English Dictionary*", Librairie Du Liban, Beirut, 1970.

Şerafeddin: Gölcük, Şerafeddin, "*Kelam*", Selçuk Üniversitesi, Konya, 1988.

T: Tahir ul-Mevlevi, "*Mesnevî*", Ahmed Said Matbaası, İstanbul, 1971.

Taki: Muhammed Taki Jaferi, "*Tefsir u Naqd u Tahlil-i Masnevi-yi Jelal al- Din Muhammed Mevlevî*", Intisharat-i İslam, Iran.

Tezkiret ul-Avliya: Feriduddin Attar, (Muhammed Khan Kaznevi), Intisharat-i Merkez, Iran.

The Bible: "*Good News Bible*", The Bible Societies, Collins, Fortona; "*The New Bible*", Oxford University Press, 1972.

The Koran: Abdullah Yusuf Ali, "*The Holy Quran*", Dar'ul Arabia, Beirut.

Timurtaş: Faruk K. Timurtaş, "*Yunus Emre*", Kültür Bakanlığı Yayınları 380, Ankara, 1980.

Turan, Osman, "*The Cambridge History of Islam*", vol.I, Cambridge at the University Press, 1970.

Turan, Osman, "*Selçuklu Tarihi ve Türk İslam Medeniyeti*", Dergah Yayınları, İstanbul, 1980.

Türkiye Selçuklular Hakkında Resmi Vesikalar, Türk Tarih Kurumu Basımevi, Ankara, 1988.

Türk Lügatı: Hüseyin Kazim Kadri, Maarif Vekaleti, Devlet Matbaası, İstanbul, 1927.

Türkiye Tarihi: Ali Sevim and Yaşar Yücel, Türk Tarih Kurumu Basımevi, Ankara, 1989.

Velednama: Sultan Veled, Kutupkhane-yi İkbal, Tehran.

Yaşar Ocak: "*Babailer İsyanı*", Dergah Yayınları, İstanbul.

Yunus Emre: Abdulbaki, Eskişehir Turizm Derneği, 1965.

Yurtaydın, G. Hüseyin, "*İslam Tarihi Dersleri*", Ankara Üniversitesi İlahiyat Fakültesi Yayınları, 1988.

INDEX

Abbasids, 10
Abdullah b. Hammuya, Tajeddin, 10
Abdulkadir Geylani, 9
Abdulkerim Kusheyri, 357
Abdulmelik Ata, 35
Abdurrahman Jami, 66
Abraham (the Prophet), 103, 107, 113, 133, 339
Abu Bekir Tebrizi, 220
Abu Jehil, 83, 127
Abu'l Hakam Amr b. Hisham b. al-Mugira, 83
Adham, İbrahim, 4
Afghanistan, 58
Ahmad, Akhi, 34, 35
Ahmed, Fakih, 38
Ahmed Khatibi, 13
Ahmed Khojendi, 3
Ahmed Yesevi, 35, 36
Akmeluddin, 299
Ala al-Din Kayqubad I, 1, 2, 13, 19, 20
Ala al-Din Kayqubad II, 1, 22, 28
Ala al-Din Muhammed Khwarazmshah, 1 - 4, 7
Ala al-Din Tekish (see Tekish)
Ala al-Din Tepe, 4
Alameddin Kayseri, 29, 57
Alanya, 19
Allahabadi, Akbar, 74
Alexander the Great, 4
Ali (the Caliph of Islam), 35, 202, 336, 337
Ali Hejveri, 358
Altunpa, 12
Amasya, 21
Anatolia(n), 1, 2, 7, 9, 10, 11, 19 - 21, 23, 29, 30, 33, 35 - 37, 41, 137, 204
Anatolian Seljuks, 29
Andkhui, 2
Antalya, 11, 19, 23
Anushtekin, 2
Alp Arslan, 19
Arberry, Arthur John, 64
Arslan Baba, 35
Arslan, Qilich, (see Qilich)
Arslan II, Qilich (see Qilich)
Arslan IV, Qilich (see Qilich)

Atabek, Mejededdin, 27
Atesh, Ahmed, 68, 71
Atsiz, 2
Avicenna, 48
Awhadeddin-i Kirmani, 10, 21, 33
Ayyaz, 1
Azerbayjan, 3, 61

Baba Ilyas, 21
Baba Ishak, 21, 36
Baba Tahir, 282
Badreddin Tebrizi, 57
Baghdad, 3, 4, 6, 7, 9, 10, 23, 33, 36, 177, 322
Bahaeddin Razi, 3
Baha al-Din Zekeria, 32
Bahaeddin Veled, Sultan ul-Ulama Muhammed, 1 - 4, 6 - 14, 41, 42
Balchik, Ahmed, 3
Balkh, 2 - 9, 13, 42, 360
Basra, 356
Baybars, 23
Bayju Noyan 21, 23
Behramshah, Fahreddin, 11
Bektashi Vali, 21, 35, 36
Berke Khan, 23
Beyazid-i Bastami, 32, 46, 47, 306, 322
Beyshehir Lake, 23
Bukhara, 2, 4, 35, 324
Bulhe Shah, 199
Burhaneddin Muhaqqaq-i Tirmizi, Seyyid, 41 - 44, 52, 139
Byzantines, 19, 22

Cairo, 61
Central Asia, 19, 35, 58
Chengiz Khan, 3, 8
China, 3
Christ (Jesus), 20, 35, 52, 57, 109, 113, 114, 136 - 138, 161, 188, 190, 222, 238, 244, 275, 287, 298, 307, 320, 321, 323, 356, 363
Crimea, 23
Cyprus, 12

Damascus, 10, 11, 41, 42, 46, 48, 49, 51, 202, 260
Davud al-Kayseri, 32
Diyarbakir, 61

Ebu Bekir, Tebrizi, 46
Ebu'l Hasan Ali b. Ismail al- Eshari al-Basri, 7
Ebu Mansur al-Maturidi, 6
Ebu Sufyan, 202
Eflaki (Ahmed), 7, 9, 24, 27, 29, 31, 34 - 36, 44, 47, 48, 51 - 53, 55 - 57, 59, 299
Egypt, 23, 111
Emir Huseyinoğlu, 3
Emir Musa, 12
Emir Nureddin, 36
Ephesus, 194
Erzinjan, 11, 20
Erzurum, 21 - 23
Evren, Akhi, 10, 33, 34, 48
Eyyubids, 10

Fahreddin Ali, 23
Fahreddin Behramshah, 11
Fahreddin Ebubekir, 22
Fahreddin Razi, 7, 8, 34
Fahreddin-i Iraqi, 31, 32
Feriduddin Attar, 9, 54, 133, 324
Feruzanfer, Bedi uz-zaman, 63, 64, 66, 68
Firgani, Sheykh Seyyid, 32

Genja, 33
Gevher Khatun, 58
Ghazna, 1 - 3
Ghaznavids, 1, 2
Ghiyas al-Din Kaykhusrev II, 1, 19, 21, 24, 28
Ghiyas al-Din Kaykhusrev III, 1, 24
Ghurids, 2
Ghuz (Oghuz Turks), 1, 2, 19, 233
Gölpınarlı, Abdulbaki, 61, 64, 65
Gulsheni, Ibrahim, 61
Gumach Khatun, 28
Gurgench, 2 - 4
Gümüş Tekin Melik Ahmed Ghazi, 20
Gürkhan, 2

Halagu Khan, 23
Hallaj-i Mansur, 249, 322, 356, 358, 362
Hafız-ı Shirazi, 68, 70
Hasan al-Basri, 5
Hasan Gulsheni, Seyyid, 61
Herat, 4

Hotan, 356
Husammeddin Chelebi, 34, 41, 52, 53 - 56, 59 - 61, 63, 65, 73
Huseyin Khatibi, 13

Ibn Jabeyr, 10
Ibn Sheddad, 10
Ibn ul-Arabi, 31, 32, 34, 305, 306, 341
Ibn ul-Ethir, 4
Ibrahim Haqqi, 343
Ilyas b. Ahmed al-Kayseri, 20
Imam-i Ghazali, 220
Inaljik, 3
India, 1, 2, 29, 41, 58, 59, 61
Iplikçi Jami, 12
Iqbal, Afzal, 63
Iqbal, Muhammed (M. Iqbal), 94, 109, 126, 157, 173, 194, 274, 295, 338, 350
Iran, 1, 3, 19, 21, 29, 58
Isfahan, 356
Ismail Rusukhi Dede Ankaravi, 65, 68
Ismeti Khatun, 11
Istanbul, 23, 34, 61
Izzeddin Kaykavus I, 11, 24
Izzeddin Kaykavus II, 1, 22, 24

Jacob (the Prophet), 111, 149, 152
Jaferi, 222, 223
Jehm b. Safvan, 6
Jelal al-Din Karatay, 22, 26
Jelal al-Din Khwarazmshah, 19, 20
Jemal al-Din Savi, 10
Jend, 2
Jerusalem, 37, 248, 287
Jonah (the Prophet), 164
Joseph (the Prophet), 111, 149, 204, 219, 220
Juneyd-i Baghdadi, 32, 306

Kadi Sejjad Huseyin, 66
Kalabazi (Kalabazi of Bukhara), 357
Karakhatais, 2, 4
Karaman (Larende), 11, 12, 37, 42, 58, 60
Karatay (medrese), 22, 26
Kashmir, 356
Kayseri (Caesarea), 19, 21, 23, 28, 33, 34, 44, 52, 202
Kazaks, 35
Kazim Kadri, 53

Kemal al-Din Ebu al-Kasım Omar, 41
Khizr, 47, 310
Khorasan, 2, 6, 21, 34, 36, 356
Khusrau Dehlevi, Emir, 68, 266, 324
Khuzistan, 3
Khwarazm(s), 1 - 5, 12, 13, 20
Kira Khatun, 58
Kirshehir, 34, 36
Konya, 4, 7, 9, 10 - 13, 19 - 23, 30 - 34, 37, 42, 46, 48, 49, 52, 56, 58, 59, 212, 324
Köpek, Sadeddin, 21
Kubadabad Palace, 23
Kum, 356
Kushans, 4

Larende (see Karaman)
Laskaris, Theoderos, 23
Luqman, 310

Mahmud of Gazna, 1
Malatya (Melitene), 20, 21, 31, 33
Mansur Ata, 35
Mecca, 9, 10, 36, 37, 290, 291, 356
Mejdeddin, Sheykh, 33
Melike Khatun, 58
Meram, 37
Mersin, 11
Merv, 2, 4
Meyerovitch, Eva de Vitray, 64
Mongke Khan (Mengu), 22
Mongol(s), 3, 4, 19, 20 - 24, 30, 212, 283
Moses, 47, 57, 63, 115, 248, 285, 287, 327, 363
Muaviye, 202
Muhammed (the Prophet, the Messenger), 13, 14, 21, 27, 31 - 33, 35, 41, 43, 46, 49, 61, 65, 78, 83, 88, 90, 100, 127, 154, 156, 171, 172, 181, 183, 188, 202, 210, 220, 226, 233, 236, 237, 239, 248, 273, 281, 295, 297, 298, 301, 305, 316, 320, 356, 363
Muhammed Akhi, 53
Muhammed Ala al-Din, 51, 58
Muhammed b. Abdullah al-Konevi al-Veledi, 59
Muhammed b. al-Huseyin b. Ahmed al-Balkhi, 13
Muhammed Iqbal (see Iqbal)
Muhammed Nazir Mavlavi, 66
Muhammed Rahmatullah, 66
Muhammed Riyaz, 64
Muhammed Taki Jafer, 66, 68, 86

Muhiddin al-Arabi (see Ibn ul-Arabi)
Muin al-Din Suleyman Pervane, 23, 24, 26 - 29, 57
Muizzib al-Din Ali, 24
Mumine Khatun, 41
Muzafferuddin Amil Chelebi, Emir, 58

Nasir al-Din Konevi, 32
Nasir al-Din Mahmud al-Khoyi, Sheykh, 33, 34
Nasir li-dinillah, Caliph, 9
Nejmeddin Daya Razi, 33
Nejmeddin Kubra, 13, 33
Nejmeddin, Sultan Seyyid, 38
Nicholson, Reynold A., 61, 66, 73, 81, 162, 220, 335
Nimrud, 103, 104
Nishapur, 2, 9, 36
Niyazi Misri, 255
Nizameddin Ali, 23
Nizami of Ganja, 11
Noah (the Prophet), 16, 98, 322

Oghuz (see Ghuz)
Oktay, 20
Omar (the Caliph of Islam), 336, 337
Omar Khayyam, 46
Omar Rushan, 61
Osman (the Caliph of Islam), 202
Osman Khan, 2, 3
Oxus, 2
Özbeks, 35

Pakistan, 41, 58
Paleologos, Mihail, 23
Peking, 3
Pervane (see Muin al-Din Pervane)

Qarakhanids, 1, 4
Qarluks, 4
Qilich Arslan, 19, 23
Qilich Arslan II, 2, 19
Qilich Arslan IV, Rukneddin, 1, 22 - 24, 28
Qutb al-Din Muhammed (Seljuk Sultan), 2

Rabia Adeviyye, 266
Rukneddin Sejasi, 33

Sadi Shirazi, 73, 219
Sadrettin Konevi, 21, 27, 30 - 33, 56
Sahra, 2
Samanids, 1, 4
Samarqand, 2 - 4, 6, 7, 260
Sanai, 44, 54
Sanjar, 2
Sasanian(s), 4, 21
Selah al-Din Zerkub, 42, 47, 51 - 53, 61, 63
Selaheddin Eyyubi, 10
Selimoğlu, Abdulvahid, 57
Seljuk Khatun, 11
Seljuk(s), 1, 2, 4, 7, 10, 19, 20 - 22, 306
Seyyid Sultan Ibrahim Sani, 36
Shah Ismail, 61
Shahidi, 66
Shams al-Din Hasoğuz, 22
Shams al-Din of Isphahan, 22
Shams al-Din Yahya, Emir, 58
Shams-i Tebrizi (Shams al-Din Muhammed Tebrizi), 11, 14, 33, 34, 41, 44 - 49, 51, 52, 62, 63, 69, 139, 204, 206, 227, 247, 249, 285, 296, 302, 324
Sharaf al-Din Samarqandi, Khuaja, 58
Sheref al-Din Mosli, 32
Sherafeddin, Seyyid, 34
Shibli Nu'mani, 64
Shihab al-Din Ghuri, 2
Sinachak, Yusuf, 66
Sipahsalar, 7, 9, 46, 51
Siraj al-Din, 32
Sivas, 19, 21, 23, 33
Soğdak, 23
Solomon (the Prophet), 144
Solhad, 23
Suhreverdi, 9
Suleyman Shah, 19
Sultan Suleyman, 61
Sultan Veled, 7, 8, 42, 44, 47 - 49, 51, 58, 59, 61

Tahir'ul Mevlevi, 65, 81
Tarsus (Ephesus), 194
Tatars, 4, 5
Tebriz, 33
Tekish, Ala al-Din, 2
Terjuman, Bahaeddin, 22
Terken Khatun, 2, 3

Tirmiz, 2
Tokat, 20, 21, 32
Turcoman(s),12, 19 - 21, 23, 24, 30, 34, 35, 51, 233, 342
Turfan, 356
Turkistan, 21, 35
Tus, 2

Urtar, 3

Vasil b. Ata, 5

Wakhsh, 7 - 9, 41

Yahya Efendi, 60
Yassıchimen, 20
Yunus Emre, 35, 37 - 39, 44, 70, 87, 124, 204, 211, 273, 363
Yusuf-i Hemedani, 35

Ziya al-Din, 34